Epic and Exile

FLASHPOINTS

The FlashPoints series is devoted to books that consider literature beyond strictly national and disciplinary frameworks, and that are distinguished both by their historical grounding and by their theoretical and conceptual strength. Our books engage theory without losing touch with history and work historically without falling into uncritical positivism. FlashPoints aims for a broad audience within the humanities and the social sciences concerned with moments of cultural emergence and transformation. In a Benjaminian mode, FlashPoints is interested in how literature contributes to forming new constellations of culture and history and in how such formations function critically and politically in the present. Series titles are available online at http://escholarship.org/uc/flashpoints.

A complete list of titles begins on page 289.

Epic and Exile

Novels of the German Popular Front, 1933–1945

Hunter Bivens

NORTHWESTERN UNIVERSITY PRESS | EVANSTON, ILLINOIS

THIS BOOK IS MADE POSSIBLE BY A COLLABORATIVE GRANT FROM THE ANDREW W. MELLON FOUNDATION.

Northwestern University Press
www.nupress.northwestern.edu

Digital Printing

Library of Congress Cataloging-in-Publication Data

Bivens, Hunter, author.
Epic and exile : novels of the German Popular Front, 1933-1945 / Hunter Bivens.
pages cm. — (FlashPoints)
Includes bibliographical references.
ISBN 978-0-8101-3148-4 (pbk. : alk. paper)
ISBN 978-0-8101-3149-1 (ebook)
1. Exiles' writings, German—History and criticism. 2. Anti-fascist movements in literature. 3. German fiction—20th century—History and criticism. 4. Marchwitza, Hans—Criticism and interpretation. 5. Seghers, Anna, 1900–1983—Criticism and interpretation. 6. Claudius, Eduard—Criticism and interpretation. 7. Brecht, Bertolt, 1898–1956—Criticism and interpretation. I. Title. II. Series: FlashPoints (Evanston, Ill.)
PT749.A56B58 2015
833.912099206914—dc23

2015011480

∞ The paper used in this publication meets the minimum requirements of the American National Standard for Information Sciences—Permanence of Paper for Printed Library Materials, ANSI Z39.4811992.

Contents

Acknowledgments

Research for this book was made possible by the financial support of the Deutscher Akademischer Austauschdienst (DAAD), the Humanities Division of the University of Chicago, and the Institute for Humanities Research at the University of California, Santa Cruz (UCSC). I would also like to thank the German Academy of the Arts Literature Archives and the Bertolt Brecht Archive in Berlin for their valuable assistance.

I have presented portions of this project at conferences of the German Studies Association and the American Comparative Literature Association as well as at UCSC. I am grateful for the productive comments that I have received from colleagues in these venues. I am also very honored to have had the chance to discuss this project in its early stages with Simone Barck and Ursula Heukenkamp, two of the most important literary critics of the former German Democratic Republic.

I am also indebted to readers of drafts of chapters and interlocutors over the years that I have been working on this project, especially Katie Trumpener and Loren Kruger for their guidance in my formation at the University of Chicago, as well as Robert von Hallberg, Eric Santner, David Levin, and Andreas Gailus. In addition, I am grateful to Leslie Morris for encouraging me in my studies early on. I owe a significant debt to the intellectual generosity of the UCSC Literature Department, particularly Loisa Nygaard, Tyrus Miller, Susan Gillman, Christopher Connery, Bali Sahota, and Gopal Balakrishnan in the History of Conscious Department for conversations and suggestions that have shaped this work, as well as current and former graduate students in the Literature and History of Consciousness departments at UCSC, particularly Johanna Isaacson, Evan Calder Williams, Erik Bachmann, Erica Smeltzer, Maya Gonzales, Madeline Lane McKinley, and Jeb Perucker. I would also like to thank John Urang for many years of intellectual camaraderie, as well as Benjamin Robinson, Helen Fehervary, Jamie Trnka, and many others. I am grateful to Edward Dimendberg for his careful reading of this manuscript. Finally, of course, thanks to my friends and family for their patience and support.

Abbreviations

AP Walter Benjamin, "The Author as Producer." In *Selected Writings*. Vol. 2, Part 2, 1931–1934. Ed. Michael W. Jennings, Howard Eiland, and Gary Smith, 768–82. Cambridge, MA: Belknap Press, 1999.

AR Peter Weiss, *The Aesthetics of Resistance*. Vol. 1. Trans. Joachim Neurgoschel. Durham, NC: Duke University Press, 2005.

BB Alfred Döblin, "Der Bau des epischen Werks." In *Aufsätze zur Literatur*, 109–32. Olten: Walter Verlag, 1963.

GE Oskar Negt and Alexander Kluge, *Geschichte und Eigensinn*. Frankfurt: Zweitausendeins, 1981.

GO Eduard Claudius, *Grüne Oliven und nackte Berge*. Halle: Mitteldeutscher-Verlag, 1976.

HN Georg Lukács, *The Historical Novel*. Trans. Hannah Mitchell and Stanley Mitchell. Lincoln: University of Nebraska Press, 1983.

HT Ernst Bloch, *Heritage of Our Times*. Trans. Neville Plaice and Stephen Plaice. Cambridge: Polity Press, 1991.

IN Alexander Abusch, *Der Irrweg einer Nation: Ein Beitrag zum Verständnis der deutschen Geschichte*. Berlin: Aufbau-Verlag, 1946.

K Hans Marchwitza, *Die Kumiaks*. Berlin: Aufbau-Verlag, 1955.

MC Bertolt Brecht, *Mother Courage and Her Children: A Chronicle of the Thirty Years' War*. Trans. Eric Bentley. New York: Grove, 1966.

ML Helga Gallas, *Marxistische Literaturtheorie: Kontroversen im Bund proletarisch-revolutionärer Schriftsteller*. Neuwied: Hermann Luchterhand Verlag, 1971.

MT Raymond Williams, *Modern Tragedy*. Peterborough, Ontario: Broadview Press, 2001.

NOD Ernst Bloch, "Nonsynchronism and the Obligation to Its Dialectics." Trans. Mark Ritter. *New German Critique* no. 11 (Spring 1977): 22–38.

PR Bertolt Brecht, "Popularity and Realism." In *Aesthetics and Politics*, by Theodor W. Adorno et al., 79–85. New York: Verso, 1977.

RB Georg Lukács, "Realism in the Balance." In *Aesthetics and Politics*, by Theodor W. Adorno et al., 28–59. New York: Verso, 1977.

SC Anna Seghers, *The Seventh Cross*. Trans. James A. Galston. Boston: David R. Godine, 2004.

ST Walter Benjamin, "The Storyteller: Observations on the Works of Nicolai Leskov." In *Selected Writings*. Vol. 3, 1935–1938. Ed. Howard Eiland and Michael W. Jennings. Cambridge, MA: Belknap Press, 2002.

TN Georg Lukács, *The Theory of the Novel: A Historico-Philosophical Essay on the Forms of Great Epic Literature*. Trans. Anna Bostock. Cambridge, MA: MIT Press, 1971.

Epic and Exile

Introduction: "A Feeling for History"

The Popular Front Novel

Alain Badiou frames the 1930s as the pivotal moment in the short twentieth century, the Soviet century shaped by the energies unleashed by the Great War and the October Revolution and the attempts to contain and turn back this revolutionary wave.[1] In this short century, the 1930s is the switching between the epic and the tragic, the moment where the Soviet century becomes indistinguishable from the totalitarian century as the emancipatory claims of the revolution find themselves at an impasse. "In the century, 1937 is a year of no little importance," Badiou writes:

> It is the metonymical year in which something essential unfolds; an absolute distillate of the essence—of an excess in the essence—of the Stalinist terror, the year of what is called the "Great Terror." Things begin to take a wrong turn in the Spanish Civil War, which is like an internal miniature of the entire century, since all of the century's major political actors are present within it (Communists, fascists, international workers, farmers in revolt, mercenaries, colonial armies, fascist states, "democracies," etc.). It is the year in which Nazi Germany enters irreversibly into the preparations for total war. It also represents the major turning point in China. In France, it becomes evident that the Popular Front has failed.[2]

In many ways, this passage provides an itinerary for the present book. In Anna Seghers's antifascist classic, *The Seventh Cross* [*Das siebte Kreuz: Ein Roman aus Hitlerdeutschland* 1942], the refugee Georg Heisler reads about the battle of Teruel and the Japanese invasion of Shanghai as he makes his way through the web of Nazi repression in October 1937 (SC 219), whereas Eduard Claudius's protagonist in his Spanish Civil War novel *Grüne Oliven und nackte Berge* [Green Olives and Bare Mountains 1944] is wounded at the battle of Teruel and sent back to Paris to witness the collapse of the French Popular Front. It was also in 1937 that Georg Lukács published his study in Popular Front aesthetics, *The Historical Novel*, in Moscow during the reign of the Great Terror. Neither a survey of German exile literature nor a comprehensive summation of the extensive critical work on this period, *Epic and Exile* instead casts key narrative, historical, and affective dilemmas into relief through close readings of a few important works produced at this moment of crisis. The German antifascist émigrés at the center of this project, primarily Bertolt Brecht, Anna Seghers, Hans Marchwitza, and Eduard Claudius, were simultaneously in the middle of these events and exiled to their margins. All of these figures had taken part in and were shaped by the political and culture struggles of the Weimar Republic, and each was aligned with the Communist Party of Germany (KPD), members of what Claudius would later describe as "the guild of the specter" that had famously been haunting Europe since the 1840s. Each was in his or her own way involved in the key moments of the European Popular Front movement of the 1930s. Seghers and Brecht were active in the organizations, publications, and conferences that gave voice to the fragile antifascist populist classicism of these years, bringing together figures as diverse as Robert Musil, Maxim Gorky, André Breton, and Mike Gold. Marchwitza and Claudius, writers who had been recruited out of the working class by the Communist press in the Weimar Republic, both fought for the Spanish Republic in the International Brigades. All of these figures managed to stay ahead of the advancing armies of National Socialist Germany, "changing countries oftener than our shoes," to quote Brecht.[3] Brecht and Marchwitza found their way to the United States, Brecht ending up in Hollywood. Marchwitza arrived in New York City and worked in construction and painted houses. Anna Seghers found herself in Mexico City, outside of Moscow, the largest community of KPD exiles in the 1940s, where she was a founding member of the antifascist Committee for a Free Germany, while Claudius spent most of World War II in a Swiss internment camp until making his way to Italy to fight the Germans in the Garibaldi partisan brigades. All returned to Germany after the war to play key roles in the building of a postfascist socialist culture in the German Democratic Republic.

This book looks closely at four works that I argue point toward the particular narrative and representational dilemmas and limits of German Popular Front literature. They are not meant to be exemplary, however, nor is this book to be taken as a literary history of the period. What links the writers and texts that I analyze, aside from their political convictions and the shared fact of exile, is a preoccupation, which each text handles differently, with these aporias of the Popular Front. These texts take up a precarious space of inbetweenness, thematically and formally, that emerges most clearly in their generic and spatial dimensions. My project thus returns to the cultural debates of midcentury Marxism, the so-called Brecht-Lukács debate, around literature and social class, art and labor, but now at the fault line between space and topos for writers whose claim to speak for popular liberation is belied by their expulsion from the everyday life of the people whose voice they claim to be. In the German case, the central topos for this process is *Heimat*, or homeland, deployed no less by the Communist Party of the Popular Front era than it was by the Nazis, which in Germany since the nineteenth century has denoted a spatialized sense of social inclusion.[4] In the works of the authors analyzed in this volume, we find a complicated narrative reconstruction of the proletarian experience of classical modernity, a "daily combat at close quarters,"[5] shaped by figures of claustrophobia, blockage, and confinement. This proletarian modernity, evoked in Alfred Döblin's descriptions of Berlin east of the Alexanderplatz or in the crowded industrial suburbs where Franz Kafka locates his court in *The Trial*, is the contested space of naturalism and realism within midcentury modernism, an indeterminate zone of subalternity and resistance, a zone between the creaturely plebeian and the revolutionary proletarian. In other words, the ambiguity and contested character of space in these novels overdetermines the portrayal of class as well.

The horizon of a popular front epic literature, I argue in the following chapters, is the reworking of classical, or received, narrative forms in order to render them adequate to this experience of proletarian modernity. For the writers and critics discussed in this book, this project acquired particular urgency in the context of the class struggles of the Weimar Republic and the epochal defeat of the German workers' movement in 1933. The works examined in the following chapters offer not only cognitive maps, to borrow a term from Fredric Jameson, of German fascism and itineraries for the struggle against it; they represent genealogical accounts of how the period's structures of feeling, both fascist and antifascist, came into being. At the same time, these affective genealogies are spatially situated ones, and this dimension of place acts as an "imaginary," an alternative, counterfactual dimension, through which the actual social and physical dispensation of space is contested.[6] This complex dialectic of place and temporality comes to the fore in the almost geological layering of historical struggles in many German exile novels, not only in the return to the historical novel in this period but in novels that treat the present as history. The awareness of what Ernst Bloch theorized as "non-contemporaneity," the uneven layering of temporalities, lends many German exile novels that chronicle-like aspect that Walter Benjamin noticed in Anna Seghers's work,[7] and this opens onto the decentered spatiality of the narrated present and onto the condition of exile itself, even as the authors discussed increasingly turn to the more traditional form of the historical novel. These novels, then, hover in different ways between the promises of working-class emancipation and the catastrophic defeats of the 1930s, between a commitment to everyday life and perspective of exile, between utopia and tragedy, and between realism and modernism. The epic dimension to these works, then, lies in their grappling with the problem of narrative adequacy, which is to say in the development of novelistic forms that register the catastrophes of proletarian modernity without for all that turning away from the legacies of plebeian and working-class struggle and resistance.

The works considered in this book span the immediate aftermath of the National Socialist seizure of power in 1933 to the collapse of the German Popular Front movement on the eve of World War II in 1939.[8] This decade was a pivotal moment in what Arno Mayer has called the "Thirty Years War of the general crisis of the twentieth century."[9] These were years of unrelenting and crushing defeats for the forces of the left, both in Europe and around the globe. At the same time, they were the years of the fragile yet deep-reaching formation of that second global culture with "its social roots in the huge migration from the rural Third World to the trench towns of the planet" but with "its aesthetic roots" in the "worldwide movement of plebeian authors and writers to create a proletarian culture, a socialist realism."[10] Michael Denning uses this formulation to describe the coming into being of a second, broadly working-class culture that continued to shadow the global penetration of commodity aesthetics, from high modernism to Hollywood cinema, in the twentieth century. This second culture encompasses Soviet socialist realism but also the Popular Front projects of figures like Richard Wright and Orson Welles in the United States and the postcolonial cinema of figures like Sembene Ousmane and Julio Garcia Espinosa. The Popular Front years of the 1930s fused a partisan internationalism with the aspirations of a national popular culture in Europe, the Soviet Union, the United States, Latin America, and the European colonies. This Popular Front culture was essentially defensive in the face of what seemed to be the inevitable triumphs of fascism and reaction, particularly in Europe, where writers on the left found themselves maneuvering in the precarious zones between antifascist solidarity and revolution, between bourgeois tradition and proletarian culture, between mass democratic aspirations and the necessity of party discipline, and between the threat of fascism and a solidarity with the Soviet Union that became increasingly necessary as it became more and more difficult to justify in the light of the Great Terror and the nonaggression pact between the USSR and Germany. As Peter Weiss declares in the notebooks for his monumental three-volume novel of the Popular Front period, *The Aesthetics of Resistance* [*Die Ästhetik des Widerstands* 1975–81], "anyone who survived the 1930s up to the war could only have climbed over the dead" (AR 9).[11]

The metaphor of climbing over the dead can be interpreted in a number of different senses, from the betrayal and treachery that was often necessary for surviving these dark times to a more complicated negotiation of the legacy of domination and resistance that informed a Popular Front cultural politics appearing, in the words of Walter Benjamin, as "the avenger that completes the task of liberation in the name of generations of the downtrodden."[12] This was the redemptive aspiration that underlay the renewed engagement with tradition and popular history. Writing on Benjamin's twelfth thesis on the philosophy of history, Michael Löwy illuminates the fundamental attitude of Popular Front culture to *die Erbe*, or popular heritage, a key term in the debates on the literary left in the 1930s, along with realism, popularity, and partisanship. Benjamin, Löwy argues, "contrasts the historical continuum, which is the creation of the oppressors, with tradition, which is that of the oppressed."[13] The traditions of the oppressed are discontinuous, broken, disarticulated, and driven underground and must gain continuity, their own claim to social reality, through the urgency of the present insofar as the present is a moment of danger, of the catastrophe of historical continuity itself, now revealed in the hypermodern barbarism of the Nazis: "We must weave into the 'warp' of the present the threads of a tradition that has been lost for centuries."[14] Indeed, this weaving of the promises and horrors of the past into the warp of the present is an attempt to redeem history as tragedy through the genre of the epic. Raymond Williams writes, "The successful revolution . . . becomes not tragedy but epic; it is the origin of a people or its valued way of life."[15] Epic, in the more prosaic usage of narrative prose and also in the sense of a redemptive recovery of the unity between popular history and everyday life as a source of plebeian resistance and a resource for antifascist struggle, haunts the literature of the Popular Front, especially its German manifestations. The epic in this doubled sense informs the renewed urgency of the novel in exile as a genre uniquely suited to the weaving of the past into the present, and the weaving of the present itself into the fractured and precarious traditions of the oppressed, a "plebeian tradition," to borrow the title of Hans Mayer's famous essay on Brecht.

The term "plebeian" has an ambiguous status in Marxist thinking about class. Marx sometimes used the term in an almost interchangeable way with "the proletariat," and Engels figured the propertyless and landless plebeian masses of Europe's decaying feudalism in early modernity as the historical progenitors of the revolutionary workers of the nineteenth century.[16] The plebeian in this sense is at once a historical category, encompassing of course the plebs of the Roman Republic as well as the propertyless urban masses of the modern. In both cases, the plebeian is a figure for the socially excluded, "those who have no part," as Jacques Rancière has it.[17] Beyond this, however, "plebeian" describes a certain attitude in Marxist thinking. Indeed, Lenin fondly quoted Marx to this effect in his pamphlet *Two Tactics of Social Democracy*. "The terror in France," Marx had written of the revolution, "was nothing else than a plebeian method of settling accounts with the enemies of the bourgeoisie: with absolutism, feudalism, and philistinism." Claiming the Jacobin lineage for his own Bolshevik faction, Lenin writes that the Russian proletariat, too, must deal with tsarism "in the plebeian manner." "Plebeian" here denotes a stance of militant decision.[18] There is, however, another common usage of this term in Marxist theory that is reflected in the very passage of Marx's 1848 article in the *Neue rheinische Zeitung* that Lenin quotes here, and that is precisely that in this plebeian method is a struggle for the aims of another, here of the bourgeoisie.[19] It is not the struggle for an organized class for social power, which is to say that it is not a sovereign struggle. What separates the proletariat in the Marxist imaginary from the plebeian masses is the question of historical agency and power. The proletariat is "the particular class whose economic conditions of existence prepare it for this task and provide it with the possibility and the power to perform it."[20] The question that haunts these antifascist novels is one of how to maintain this Leninist optimism in the face of the crushing defeat of the workers' movement in 1933.

The plebeian, as the term is used in this book, is less of a substantial figuration of a social group than it is a stance or an attitude in the Brechtian sense, that is to say a way of acting and thinking or, to put it another way, a structure of feeling.[21] Mayer draws attention to this plebeian structure of feeling in Brecht's work, particularly in the ironic reversal of values exemplified in *Mother Courage*. This plebeian structure of feeling strips away the language of ideological veiling through appeal to higher values of heroism, duty, and sacrifice, and speaks of bare interest. This is the unadorned view from below, the voice of the subaltern.[22] Yet one must avoid the temptation to identify this stance with a character or class. Thus Brecht would insist in the 1950s, "plebeian was a thoroughly washed out concept if it is not applied in a concrete historical manner."[23] I will argue in this book that the plebeian is a way of framing a crisis of representation in relationship to the notion of the proletariat itself as the subject of history. This ambiguity is a question of the relationship of the proletariat to the oppressed classes of the ancien régime and the feudal past, with its inherited "inner habits of obedience and subservience, submissiveness to traditional authority."[24]

The proletariat, in the English industrial novel or French naturalism, was often portrayed as subaltern to the point of creatureliness, reduced to bare suffering and survival. This depiction of the proletariat as a creaturely collective is what Engels had already criticized in 1889 in his famous letter to Margaret Harkness, in whose novel *City Girl* "the working class figures as a passive mass, unable to help itself and not even showing any attempt at striving to help itself." Echoing later Marxist critiques of naturalism, Engels asserts, "the rebellious reaction of the working class against the oppressive medium that surrounds them, their attempts—convulsive, half conscious, or conscious—at recovering their status as human beings, belong to history and must therefore lay claim to a place in the domain of realism."[25] The plebeian then follows the "revolutionary proletariat" as its bad conscience, for as the travails of socialist realism in the twentieth century have demonstrated, the "active side of working class life," as Engels put it, has proved far more difficult to portray. Thus much literature of the working class remains stranded between the extremes of the steely-eyed positive hero on the one hand and the broken, ragged vagabond on the other. In the figure of the plebeian, the working class threatens to devolve back into the *Pöbel* or rabble of the suffering and creaturely poor from which the proletariat putatively emerged as a class for itself, with organizational forms potentially capable of remaking the world in its own image.[26] The figure of the plebeian arises in many of these novels then as a kind of uncanny historical remainder within the proletariat, as the bearer of *Eigensinn* or obstinacy, a kind of stubborn refusal of social responsibility, or what Hegel referred to as "a freedom . . . enmeshed in servitude."[27] And yet, as we shall see, it is precisely this discontinuous tradition of popular suffering and obstinacy that a Popular Front aesthetics seeks to redeem.

Viewed in this way, as the ambiguation of proletarian agency, the plebeian is thus a central figure in a novelistic view of history, which, I argue in this book, ghosts the explicit commitment of the authors under discussion to an ultimately optimistic Marxist-Leninist view of history as a process leading to the victory of the proletariat. The defeat of the German workers' movement can be read out of both the preoccupation with plebeian structures of feeling and the reinvestment of the traditional novel form widespread among German antifascist authors in the exile period. As Lukács famously pointed out in his own period of "permanent despair over the state of the world," the novel is itself essentially an epic form of the very impossibility of epic, or as the "epic of a world abandoned by God" (TN 29). To some degree tragic in its very form, the genre itself is founded on the fundamental dissonance of the relationship between life and form, between the empirical and the transcendent, "a form in which," as Terry Eagleton writes, "essence and existence can never coincide, in which meaning and value are always elsewhere."[28] The novel differs from the tragedy, as Lukács points out, in its focus on the extensive totality of the world, the great web of things, relationships, and everyday processes that make up social being, as opposed to the sudden confrontations that mark the tragic form, not the "spiritual essences" of the tragedy but the "degraded empirical world."[29] The novel is the genre that "portrays the great transformations of history as transformations of popular life"

(HN 48–49). Whereas the drama reflects, for Lukács, the punctual crises of the historical experience, "the great convulsions, the tragic breakdowns of the world," the novel centers on the disintegration of the worlds of everyday life (144). This is what Lukács calls "the epic collision," in other words, "the complexity, multiplicity, intricacy and 'cunning'... of those trends which produce, solve, or abate such conflicts in social life" (142). It is no coincidence that Lukács, writing on the historical novel in the mid-1930s, at the height of the Popular Front period, thus aligns the vocation of this epic form with populist history from below. "The most important thing," he writes, "is to show how the *direction* of a social tendency becomes visible in the small, imperceptible capillary movements of individual life" (145). Focusing on the level of everyday life as a historical formation, the novel becomes a genre of the impossibility of the everyday in its conflictual inertia and contradictory unsustainability, of what Lukács considers the regressive factors that make up the extensive totality of social life, "that great series of natural circumstances, human institutions, manners, customs, etc." Here another aspect of the tragic character of the novel emerges, since "the regressive motif is only an expression of those general objective forces which are necessarily stronger than the will and resolve of the individual" (146).

The novel is thus, as has often been noted, a genre of defeat, both personal and collective, but also one that, as Fredric Jameson puts it, has the vocation of "making history appear" as a structured ensemble of constraints and possibilities.[30] In this account, the novel draws close to what Loren Kruger describes as "the tragedy of the commoner," a mode of tragedy that has passed from the elevated sphere of destiny and the world historical individual into the no less harrowing prose of plebeian everyday life.[31] The Popular Front novels discussed in this book complicate the distinctions between tragedy and novel, haunted by the vanishing horizon of an absent epic that would redeem the catastrophe of the century. In the final chapter of the book, a sustained reading of Bertolt Brecht's *Mother Courage and Her Children* will demonstrate that Brecht's "epic" operation on the classical form of the tragedy is in many ways an attempt to discover modes of figuration for the same historical impasses that provoke Lukács's speculations on the resurgence of the historical novel in the literature of the Popular Front period. Both the tragedy of the commoner and the Popular Front novel, I will argue, are animated by a fundamentally tragic category of pathos. For Jameson, in his rewriting of the basic categories of narrative in terms of Aristotle's theory of poetics, pathos becomes the fundamental category of narrative itself, the vocation of which "is to make visible to us the way in which people fall under the power of fate, in which they fail, in which they know the experience of defeat and of submission."[32] Pathos, for Jameson, is where the objectivity of history, which is perhaps a more apt term than fate, shapes representation through the very possibility of a plot, whether novelistic or tragic. The German novels of the Popular Front, at least the ones discussed here, share the aspiration to shift the question of emplotment away from the individual and to reinscribe the individual into a collective emplotment, the story of a "we" under erasure, a precarious plural agent that these novels can only figure against the background of historical impasse.[33] Such an epic "we" evokes Jameson's observation in another context that "all plot may be seen as a movement toward utopia" in the formal sense that it is concerned with "the development of the various elements through the time for form."[34]

Peter Weiss would decades later attempt to solve this narrative and actantial contradiction between the isolated individual caught up in history as its victim and the collective protagonist who would make history in his own rewriting of the historical novel in *The Aesthetics of Resistance*. In the famous ekphrastic scene with which it begins, three young Berlin workers contemplate, on September 22, 1937, the Pergamon Frieze and its depiction of the Gigantomachy, the battle between the Olympians and the giants, which the novel takes as its own centerpiece, the interpenetration of history and myth as a primal scene of class struggle, in which the sons and daughters of the demoness of earth are initially and forever subjugated by the forces of privilege. "We looked back at our prehistoric past," Weiss's narrator explains, "and for a moment the prospect of the future likewise filled up with a massacre impenetrable to the thought of liberation." The figure that would redeem such an impenetrable massacre, Heracles, "the earthly helper whose courage and unremitting labor would bring an end to the period of menace," is present in the frieze only in the figuration of his absence, "a sign bearing his name, and the paw of a lion's skin that had cloaked him." It will be the vocation of the Popular Front, and indeed of an aesthetics of resistance itself, to give material form to this prophecy of a collective protagonist who might liberate the subjugated monsters of the earth. Thus the protagonist's friend, Hans Coppi, "called it an omen that Heracles, who was our equal, was missing, and that we now had to create our own image of this advocate of action" (AR 7).

But defeat itself is never simple. Again and again, we see the attempt in these novels to maintain fidelity, to evoke the language of Alain Badiou, to the traumatic event of the revolution and the tremendous appeal and promise of human liberation that was embodied by industrial modernity and the workers' movement. The revolutionary wave that followed World War I was the "last pan-European uprising of peoples."[35] Yet in distinction to the October Revolution in Russia, the German revolution never happened. By the mid-1920s, the revolutionary wave had crested, leading in Germany to more than a decade of strife, revolutionary and counterrevolutionary violence, and economic upheaval culminating in the rise of fascism and World War II. As Pierre Broué argues in his magisterial history of the period, "the defeat of the KPD in 1923 ultimately did not represent the defeat of Bolshevism, Spartacism, or, still less Communism. It was the defeat of the whole German socialist movement."[36] This is not epic but tragedy in the proper sense that Williams discusses in his book as the poetics of failed revolution, which Loren Kruger then describes as a "tragically incomplete or downright failed assault on the longstanding 'violence and disorder' of the 'institutions' that maintain power."[37] Broué elaborates the global significance of the German tragedy of 1923:

> The fiasco of Germany's "failed October" in 1923 was to mark a decisive point in postwar history. At this pivotal point for Europe, the initiative passed back into the hands of the bourgeoisie, who were not to lose it again. Within the Communist International, beginning with the Russian Communist Party itself, the defeat of 1923 represented, if not the starting point, at least the decisive acceleration in a process of degeneration, the most negative aspects of which can often be directly linked to the greatest hopes of this inhuman year.[38]

To give a sense of the expectations set on the German October within the Communist movement, recall Grigory Zinoviev's comments in 1923 as head of the Third International: "We shall soon see that the autumn of 1923 marks a turning point, not only for Germany, but for the whole of humanity."[39] This defeat of the German and European workers' movement in 1933 can be traced to the failure of the post–World War I German revolution, a point that emerges explicitly in the novels of the proletarian writers Hans Marchwitza and Eduard Claudius. As Sebastian Haffner argued in *Failure of a Revolution*, "the collective hero of the revolution, the German working class, never recovered from the blow" of 1918, and "the same workers who in 1918 . . . fought so courageously and lucklessly, found their fighting spirit broken when fifteen years later they would have needed it again—against Hitler."[40]

The question of the "collective hero of the revolution" is belabored explicitly in the texts analyzed in this book, and it is also a question that is central to thinking about the literary forms, primarily the novel, through which Popular Front writers attempted to represent the historical course of the twentieth century. These writers, as committed revolutionaries, remain programmatically loyal to the very narrative of martyrdom and redemption that Rosa Luxemburg set as a cornerstone of the KPD political imaginary. Even before her murder at the hands of the Social Democratic Party–supported *soldateska*, mercenaries, and irregulars, she articulated this position in her final article of 1919.[41] Under no illusions about the outcome of the Sparticist uprising, Luxemburg proclaims, "revolution is the only form of 'war' . . . in which the final victory can be prepared only by a series of 'defeats'!"[42] Luxemburg then goes on to discuss the great defeats of the nineteenth-century European proletariat, from the revolt of the Lyon silk weavers in 1831 to the Paris Commune, drawing the balance between those that point to future struggles and those that foreclose revolutionary futurity, which result from "the revolutionary action itself being paralyzed by incompleteness, vacillation, and inner frailties." Luxemburg characterizes the Spartacus uprising as falling between these two poles but ends on a note of optimism with her famous prophesy addressed to the forces of order who have carried the day: "the revolution will 'raise itself up again clashing,' and to your horror it will proclaim to the sound of trumpets: *I was, I am, I shall be*."[43] While this rhetoric of what might be called optimistic tragedy informs the novels of many revolutionary émigrés, these works are no less shaped by the suspicion and disavowal of the notion that what is at hand might be a defeat beyond redemption, not just a bloody setback but irrevocable loss and dissolution of the revolutionary horizon.[44] Anna Seghers voices this fear in *The Seventh Cross*:

> a whole generation had to be annihilated. These were our thoughts on that terrible morning: then for the first time we voiced our conviction that if we were to be destroyed on that scale, all would perish because there would be no one to come after us. Almost unprecedented in history, the most terrible

> thing that could happen to a people, was now to be our fate: a no-man's land between the generations, which old experiences would not be able to traverse. If we fight and fall, and another takes up the flag and falls too, and the next one grasps it and he too falls—that is natural, for nothing can be gained without sacrifice. But what if there is no longer anyone to take up the flag, simply because he does not know its meaning? . . . The best that grew in the land was being torn out by the roots because the children had been taught to regard it as weeds. (SC 164–65)

In these speculations, Seghers is no longer speaking of a productive defeat, or indeed even of the kind of defeat that Luxemburg dismissed as paralyzing for the movement like that of the German bourgeois revolutions of 1848, but rather of the radical undermining of the very conditions of the possibility of victory or defeat itself, which is to say the annihilation of that very collective protagonist of the historical promise of the revolution. This is a question not of defeats or victories but of the legibility of the German revolutionary tradition itself, of the very recognizability of its flag.

In many ways, it is exile that differentiates the German Popular Front from its French, Spanish, or U.S. contemporaries, even as changing discourses, practices, and orientations of KPD-aligned writers paralleled developments in these countries. In his work on Lukács's postwar writings, Tyrus Miller describes this general Popular Front consensus as a constellation of four major emphases:

> the necessity of alliances of a wide range of progressive forces against fascism and reaction; the importance of the progressive, popular cultural heritage of eighteenth and nineteenth century European culture in articulating these alliances on the basis of common understanding; the participation of Communists in coalitions and organizations that pursued progressive, but not necessarily socialistic ends; and the importance of linking intellectual life with the social activity of the popular masses.[45]

This turn toward the popular and a broad antifascist consensus has often been cast in the research on German exile literature as a turn away from the formal innovations of the modernist 1920s toward a moralistic recuperation of the conventions of nineteenth-century realism. A similar resurgence of the concern with what might be called a social realism, if not a socialist realism, was a common aspect of Popular Front aesthetics but one that recent books on the period by Ehrhard Bahr and Bettina Engelmann argue in different ways is not a break with modernism but was itself a continuation of modernist innovation, or at least partook in the crises of representation that undergird modernist aesthetics.[46]

Popular Front aesthetics can be realist and modernist and focus on the opacities and contradictions of everyday life. The antifascist exile of 1933 to the late 1940s led to a cooling among the émigrés of the artistic and literary modernist experiments of the Weimar Republic and to a return to realism and the traditional novel form, even as the politics of the Popular Front led authors to engage more deeply with questions of national history and everyday life, aspects of social experience often less evident in the avant-garde culture of the 1920s. Whereas on the eve of Hitler's seizure of power there was a de facto consensus across the German literary scene that the novel—besieged by modernist experimentation, mass culture, and social upheaval—was a genre in crisis, by 1935 the novel had become the most favored and esteemed literary form of the German antifascist emigration. The recent objections of so many writers and critics that the novel was unsuitable in its very form as a means of representing the life world of industrial modernity seemed to fade into the background, as German literature became shaped by a newfound interest in seemingly traditional, perhaps even archaic, forms. Yet the return to the novel in the German exile was one that tended toward the epic, as Lukács famously put it. In these novels the individual protagonist is increasingly estranged in the Brechtian sense, either portrayed as an allegory of historical and popular forces, as in Heinrich Mann's monumental historical novels on the French king Henry IV, or placed firmly in the ensemble of social relationships as both an aftereffect and an actor in definite historical situations. These are, in this sense, attempts at a collective novel. As Lukács points out, this tendency toward the epic can remain a tendency only as long as the contradictions of domination and resistance that structure class society remain unresolved.[47]

If the Popular Front era seems marked by a return to realism, it is now a realism that has already passed through the modernist avant-gardes, a realism that has lost its innocence, if realism ever possessed any in the first place.[48] Rather than take sides in this continuing debate between modernism and realism, I seek to historicize the terms of this debate, showing that what characterizes the novels of Germany's antifascist literary exile is precisely the negotiation of realist and classically modernist modes of representation. If anything, the culture of the Popular Front can be read as an attempt to bring modernist techniques back to a form of figural representation that will now address itself to the status of popular labors and struggles, employing what might indeed be termed a "subaltern modernism," or "social modernism," to borrow the phrasing of Michael Denning, "as writers abandoned established family plots and the individual *Bildungsroman* to create an experimental collective novel based on documentary and reportage."[49] Modernism and realism alike are stretched to their limits in the face of working-class experience. The broad alliance that characterized this cultural formation stretched from working-class writers and artists to modernists and bourgeois antifascists, many of whom were concerned less with an overcoming of modernism than with a deepening of modernist techniques to grasp the crises of the 1930s.[50] While turning away from the avant-gardism of the 1920s, Popular Front culture was nevertheless dependent on modernism and indeed in many ways responded to the crises of modernity itself. In this sense, to borrow a phrase from Miriam Hansen, Popular Front culture might be thought of as a kind of "vernacular modernism," which mapped complicated cultural responses to modernization through the negotiation of the increasingly contested boundaries between mass culture and high culture.[51] Popular Front culture reframes modernist techniques within more traditional epic forms, hewing closely to the experience of everyday life. Indeed, Hansen's characterization of 1930s and 1940s Hollywood cinema as a fusion of neoclassicism and Fordism could be applied to social realism of the Popular Front as well (and indeed also to Socialist Realism proper), as a modern aesthetic attempting to lend a sense of historical presence to the experiences of modernization, industrialization, and mass communication technologies that were reconfiguring the lives of people under both capitalist and socialist modernities.

This observation also sheds light on the oft-noted shift from a cultural politics based on a compact and militant working-class identity and milieu to one that takes as its primary rhetorical terms the "people" and the "nation."[52] If the Popular Front itself was a largely defensive tactic at the political level, the culture of the Popular Front was no less a response to the tenacity of the modes of subaltern behavior in social life, and as Eric Hobsbawm points out, even the victories of the

Popular Front represented the failures of the revolutionary politics that had anticipated it, dramatizing "the costs of past disunion" within the workers' movement.[53] Indeed, I will argue, rather than turning away from the working class, much of the Popular Front literature produced by writers affiliated with the revolutionary left of the Weimar Republic locates the popular itself within the everyday experience of proletarian modernity and within the sites of labor, exploitation, violence, and confinement that shaped the working-class experience of industrial modernity. In some ways, then, the work of left avant-gardists and proletarian authors can be understood as following a trajectory from a modernist and working-class minor literature, to borrow a term from Gilles Deleuze and Felix Guattari, at once experiential and political but isolated within a particular beleaguered subgroup, to the literature with designs on something like a Gramscian social hegemony. Thus, Denning writes of the U.S. context of the Popular Front, "the turn to a populist rhetoric was less a retreat from radicalism than an emblem of the shift from an embattled subculture to a significant mass social movement."[54] But this marks a key difference in the U.S., Soviet, or French Popular Fronts on the one hand and the German on the other, since German writers shared this rhetorical inclusiveness without on the other hand representing a mass movement in any sense.

Within the official discourse of the KPD, as is often pointed out, an insistence on the continued militancy of the German working class prevailed, even after the collapse of the workers' parties and labor organizations, a process largely completed in the early months of Hitler's reign. As Jean-Michel Palmier notes, "there was no theoretical analysis at this stage of the defeat suffered by the working class and the KPD, and no in-depth analysis of National Socialism, which was simply seen as the logical development of capitalism in crisis."[55] Even after the turn to the strategy of the Popular Front in 1935, discussion within the party continued to emphasize the progressive role of the working class as the true representative of antifascist resistance. This theory was expressed in an "Appeal to the German People" from the Central Committee of the KPD issued in 1941 from the Soviet Union, which stated: "There are two Germanys: the Germany of the Nazi-parasites and the Germany of the working masses."[56] At the same time, the work of the authors discussed in this volume folds the proletarian experience of modernity into the *longue durée* of plebeian oppression, attending to the long historical accumulation of *Eigensinn* in the residues of the capacities, dreams, desires, and fantasies that have remained scattered and foreclosed in the German popular imaginary over the centuries, a kind of plebeian residue ghosting the working class as the revolutionary subject of history. Alongside the attempts in the rhetoric of the German Popular Front to capture and give progressive meaning to terms like *Volk* and *Heimat*, or people and homeland, the thematics of the *deutsche Misère*, or German misery, emerge in the novels examined in this book, alongside a preoccupation with the peasant and plebeian heritage of the German proletariat, as key topoi by which these novels attempt to grasp German history in terms of the fragmented traditions of the oppressed discussed earlier in relation to Walter Benjamin's thesis "On the Concept of History." The plebeian and the peasant should be read in this literature then as figures for the prehistory of the proletariat, a class composed of the descendants of the ancien régime but itself without a feudal past.

The figure of the plebeian opens onto a particularly contested national history in German Popular Front literature. A term coined by Marx and Engels in the 1840s, the *deutsche Misère* makes a return among exile circles in the 1930s. Referring not only to Germany's claustrophobic provincialism, political authoritarianism, and a popular democratic cultural tradition, the term also gave the exiles a historical reference point for their own situation.[57] F. C. Weiskopf begins his early survey of German exile literature, *Unter fremden Himmeln* [Under Foreign Skies 1948], with a useful sketch of this term, which for Weiskopf "lies in that peculiar historical development that brought in its wake the fact that after the failure of the greatest German people's movement to date—the Peasant Wars—the rule of feudal regime was sealed for centuries, every progressive tendency was blocked, and even the constitution of the national state was prevented in anything other than an authoritarian fashion."[58] Producing only a "beggarly echo" of the bourgeois revolutions of England and France, the German subject failed to become a citizen. Against this misery, "consistently, in order to write at all, in order to breathe at all, writers had to contemplate flight and emigration," not to mention expulsion. From the "wave upon wave of German *Dichter und Denker*" who were "thrown across the borders of the homeland" in the nineteenth century the German exiles of the twentieth drew their line of ancestry, which included figures like Friedrich Hölderlin, Georg Büchner, Heinrich Heine, Marx, and Engels.[59]

For German émigrés, the *deutsche Misère* was also a way of thinking about the confluence of exile and modern German culture. Since the

Thirty Years War, German literature in particular was a pantheon of exiles, whose writings were often shaped by the lack of the institutional support around which something like the historical bloc that would tie German literature to mass movements might emerge.[60] The *deutsche Misère* served antifascist writers as a diagnostic tool for understanding fascism in Germany's long history of plebeian suffering and failed revolution going back to the Peasant Wars of the sixteenth century and the defeat of the theological communism of Thomas Münzer but also served to create a genealogy that would draw together the defeats of the bourgeois revolutions of 1848, the debacle of 1918, and the catastrophe of 1933. This concept served to bring those who had struggled against German conditions into sharper relief and to construct a German progressive tradition around which the German Popular Front might rally. It is no coincidence that one of the most important cultural institutions in the antifascist German emigration, founded in 1941 by Anna Seghers, Egon Erwin Kisch, and others in Mexico City, was named after Heinrich Heine, the paradigmatic figure of the dashed hopes of the German Vormärz period and the democratic aspirations of 1848, who himself died in Parisian exile.[61]

Heine's satirical poem "Deutschland: A Winter's Tale" [Deutschland, ein Wintermärchen 1844] is perhaps the locus classicus of the constellation of tropes that would compose the left critique of German conditions, along with perhaps Marx's famous speculations in the introduction to his "Contribution to the Critique of Hegel's *Philosophy of the Right*" from a year earlier or his early works with Engels like *The Holy Family* and *The German Ideology*. What both Marx and Heine emphasize in these works of the Vormärz is that the *deutsche Misère* is precisely not to be understood in regard to Germany's backwardness but rather in regard to Germany's embodiment of the combined and uneven development of capitalist modernity, its ambiguous status as a land of "gothic illusion and modern lie," as Heine famously put it.[62] The generalized philistinism of the German scene reveals itself, following Heine in the archaic pretensions of the semifeudal absolutist aristocracy on the one hand and a "wooden, pedantic" subaltern plebeian habitus, born of social immiseration and military drill, on the other, "as though they'd swallowed the whipping rod / That bloodied their backs last night."[63]

Heine's critique of German conditions serves as a transitional point between the laments of the failed German Jacobins of the late eighteenth and early nineteenth centuries, as in Friedrich Hölderlin's bitter travelogue *Hyperion* (1797 and 1799), where the Germans are depicted as "unfeeling, moribund, pedantic philistines," and the appropriation of the phrase *deutsche Misère* by Marx and Engels with its materialist and historical grounding.[64] Engels described the Germans as "the philistines of world history,"[65] but this was no longer a psychological diagnosis, just as little as the discourse of the German misery among KPD authors was an aspect of the discussion of the German national character and the notion of collective guilt associated with figures like Emil Ludwig or Lord Vansittart in the 1940s.[66] For Marx and Engels, German philistinism was the result of what Warren Breckman describes in terms similar to those of Ernst Bloch's theory of the noncontemporaneity of the contemporary. Germany of the nineteenth century "was neither abjectly backward nor fully modern."[67] As Marx famously put it, "we are the *philosophical* contemporaries of the present day without being its *historical* contemporaries."[68] And yet Germany is in fact a contemporary of European history but in a precisely negative sense, as a country that has "shared in the restorations of modern nations without ever sharing in their revolutions."[69] Thus Germany is not simply a provincial backwater but a zone of experimentation for the most advanced strategies of reaction, so that "the struggle against the political present of the Germans is a struggle against the past of modern nations."[70] In this sense, Germany is a palimpsest of the "sins of all the forms of state."[71]

This situation of historical impasse, as Breckman argues, leads the writers of the 1800s to particular ambiguity in their accounts of the potential for political agency on the part of the German masses, upon whose action the revolution would depend even as their political and social behavior was shaped by the misery of German conditions. In contrast to nations like France, Spain, and Poland, where the "entire *Volk* fights for its freedoms," Ludwig Börne complains in anticipation of 1848, "the German patriots will be defeated not by their enemies, but by the cowardice of their friends."[72] In Arnold Ruge's account this lack of national civil courage can be explained by the absence of a functional public sphere in the German states. Ruge takes Prussia as an exemplary case of a *res privata*, where, "excluded from public life, Germans languished in a state of political ignorance, content with private security and comfort."[73] This confinement in the private is then the defining characteristic of the German philistine, producing the apathy toward public life, that "modest egoism which displays . . . its own narrowness,"[74] which critics on the left would continue to bemoan into the twentieth century. This notion of the *Volk* as philistine, however, is still not yet one that takes account of the specificity of social class.[75] Marx was not alone among German radicals in the 1840s in the double move of opposing the proletariat to the "German," as the negation of this society that is not a society, a class of radical chains, "which has a universal character because its sufferings are universal."[76]

Indeed, the proletariat is increasingly figured in Marxist discourse as the representative of a foreclosed German universality and cosmopolitanism opposed to the parochial and narrow character of Germany as a cultural polity. After the defeat of 1933, despite the official rhetoric of the revolutionary proletariat maintained by the KPD, the neat distinction between philistine and proletariat becomes more ambiguous in the works of a number of writers associated with the party. In the wake of Germany's defeat, longtime party functionary Alexander Abusch published one of the few attempts on the part of the KPD to provide a historically rigorous account of the German misery with his 1946 treatise *Der Irrweg einer Nation* [The False Path of a Nation 1946]. Abusch begins his account of the German tragedy with the failed alliance of the peasantry with the urban plebeian classes and the petty nobility during the Peasant Wars. Abusch describes this defeat of the utopian humanism of Münzer as the "prelude to the German drama," as Germany is haunted by what Abusch sees as a missed opportunity for the beginnings of a unified democratic nation (IN 17). Instead, German history becomes a repetition of failed attempts to break the boundaries of narrowness and division, what Abusch describes as the legacy of "German discord," or *deutsche Zwietracht*, marked by the increasingly irreconcilable contradiction between national and social aims that finds its institutional expression in the unification of Germany under the semi-absolutist Prussian state rather than as part of a bourgeois revolution (20, 199). Abusch traces this legacy up to the revolution of 1918, the failure of which he traces to the reformist illusions and disunity of the German working class (226, 237). With the betrayal of 1918, the Social Democratic Party (SPD) becomes for Abusch the vehicle through which the German working class inherits the national legacy of misery, with its deeply ingrained characteristics of complacency, passivity, and obedience, leading to the total capitulation of 1933. "Led by error and treachery," Abusch writes of the Social Democrats, "they themselves lagged behind the democratic party of the petty bourgeois, which in a last hour of 1849 had at least understood the need to fight" (240). As to the KPD, Abusch decries the party's failure to learn from history and its sectarianism as errors to be corrected, its isolation both a reaction against and a symptom of the constraints of the German political imaginary (242). Although Abusch is careful to attend to and praise working-class resistance to Hitler, he points out that "certain layers of the working class have not been spared from the Nazi contamination of considerable portions of the German people" (259).

In formulations such as these, the German working class threatens to fall back into the German people from which the revolutionary aspirations of Marxist discourse had attempted to conjure it forth. This is an important problem, in fact, for the narrative emplotment of the Popular Front novel, or for a realistic literature that seeks to portray and forecast emancipatory social transformation, since "the Germans" are not capable of acting as historical protagonists by the very logic of this discourse. "The history of the German people," Abusch writes, "is the history of a people rendered politically backward by violence" (252). Ultimately the figure for the abject and creaturely character of this imaginary people is an amalgam of the peasant and the petit bourgeois, figures of the subaltern that might here be opposed to the proletariat under the guise of the plebeian, the victims of history, whom Abusch describes as the main supports of National Socialism (253). Along with the trope of the *deutsche Misère* and the growing preoccupation with combined and uneven histories and temporalities that shape the impasse of the mid-twentieth century and the economic, political, and cultural crises of modernism, the figures of the peasantry and of the plebeian become key to the historical imaginations of these novels, not to mention Brecht's *Mother Courage and Her Children* in an ambivalent fashion, both as figures for the continuing subaltern habitus and lack of agency of the German working class in the face of National Socialism and as a reservoir for the longer tradition of resistance that would link the contemporary struggles of the working class with the epochal aspirations for human emancipation that this class would redeem and avenge.

Since the literary production of the initial exile years can only be understood in the context of the debates among these authors and critics prior to 1933, *Epic and Exile* begins with a literary historical account of the discussions on the Marxist left in the Weimar Republic and the exile period on the formal questions arising from the project of socialist literary aesthetics. Chapter 1 provides the discursive context for the more interpretive engagement with literary texts in the chapters that follow and focuses in particular on the role of the novel in discussions about art, class, and political struggle that were taking place in the late 1920s and early 1930s in the Bund proletarisch-revolutionäre Schriftsteller (German Association of Proletarian-Revolutionary Writers [BPRS]), an organization aligned with the Communist Party. My account draws out the tensions between the theoretical interventions in *Linkskurve*, journal of the BPRS, by critics like Georg Lukács and Johannes R. Becher, on the one hand, and the actual production of proletarian authors like Willi Bredel and Hans Marchwitza, on the other. The status of the novel as a privileged literary form emerges as the major point of contestation between critics like Lukács, interested in the claims of Marxist theory to the representation of social totality, and many of the proletarian authors themselves, more concerned with the operative value of their works in the day-to-day struggle in the factories and streets of the crisis years of the late Weimar Republic. In particular, Chapter 1 looks at the divergence between the demands being made with increasing frequency by Marxist critics in the Weimar Republic for major socialist novels in the context of the actual writing of many working-class authors, which produced a hybrid novel form incorporating proletarian autobiography, reportage, and political theory.

Chapter 2 examines the shift from proletarian-revolutionary novel to Popular Front novel. Charting this shift involves an interrogation, this time at the level of the ways in which these novels negotiate their own formal quandaries, of the novel itself as a vehicle for the representation of the present as a historical moment, both in continuity and rupture. The relationship between protagonist and emplotment becomes central here, as these novels oscillate between eventfulness and the idyll of the Benjaminian chronicle. Hans Marchwitza's 1934 novel *Die Kumiaks* [The Kumiaks 1934], now largely forgotten, was a pivotal book for this shift (although the novel precedes the Popular Front turn of the Comintern in 1935), as Marchwitza synthesizes the proletarian autobiography and the bourgeois novel into a new epic form. *Die Kumiaks* is at once a historical novel of the present and a chronicle of proletarian everyday life in the crisis years of the early 1920s. It is a eulogy for the failed German November Revolution and a work of mourning for the defeat of 1933. Taking place in the coal-mining milieu of the Ruhr Valley, Marchwitza's novel portrays the precarity and transient conditions of living embodied by the Kumiak family, migratory miners from Polish-speaking Silesia (like Marchwitza himself). The Kumiaks are suspended between peasantry and proletariat, deeply marked by the subaltern habitus of Germany's East Elbian rural land workers and equally unaware of the recent history of revolutionary struggle into which they stumble as they attempt to make their way in the west. In their atavistic opportunism, the Kumiaks come to stand for the residue of proletarian class formation, the bearers of an *Eigensinn* that increasingly spills across the narrative to shape the reduced and confined world of proletarian everyday life and the stifled emotions of Marchwitza's working-class characters. In this way, he ambiguously situates Hitler's rise to power in a longer and more complicated history of plebeian submission and complicity, developing a complex historical framework for what emerges as the creatureliness of the German working class at the key moment of the collapse of the German revolution in 1923.

Chapter 3 provides the literary historical background for the readings that will follow, considering the resurgence of the historical novel in the years immediately following 1933 and the modernism-realism debates among German literary émigrés of the late 1930s. The conception of literary realism on the left shifts around 1935 in terms of a larger strategic reorientation in the relationship between the proletariat and "the people" within the global Communist movement in the midst of Popular Front politics. Similarly, the debates within the German literary emigration on the notion of the popular itself must necessarily be conceptualized anew under the conditions of industrial modernity and mass cultural reproduction, as must any debate on the status of the popular in the twentieth century. This question informs the chapter's reconstruction of the so-called Expressionism Debate, the wide-ranging dispute between the key figures of Ernst Bloch, Georg Lukács, Bertolt Brecht, and Anna Seghers on the question of the relationship between the political and literary forms carried out in the late 1930s. Central here is the relationship between an intangible and abstract historical and social horizon of social liberation, that is to say, the revolution itself in all of its anticipated belatedness, and the local and synchronic dimension of the everyday life, emplotted in novels and theory of the decade. Lukács's theorization of the historical novel and Walter Benjamin's notion of the chronicle are critical attempts to address this fissured horizon, but these theoretical interventions can only be understood in the context of the narrative impasses that they are attempting to grasp.

The next three chapters read a series of historical novels of the present, written by Communist authors who found themselves transformed under the conditions of exile, from proletarian-revolutionary writers to Popular Front writers. Anna Seghers's *The Seventh Cross* shares *Die Kumiaks*' preoccupation with social space as a corollary for the historical agency of the working class, even as Seghers's novel shares Marchwitza's concern for the possibilities of solidarity and resistance in the wake of failed attempts at collective emancipation. Seghers's fugitive story turns on a complicated interplay between the fragile human attachments of her characters and the organization of social space through strategies of fascist surveillance that are designed to cut through the fragile connections still remaining from the KPD-aligned counterpublic sphere of the Weimar Republic. Landscape itself becomes a complex optic in this exilic meditation on the social topography of fascist Germany, as survival becomes a matter of the correct deciphering of signs of human solidarity in the opaque everyday life of National Socialist Germany. Chapter 4 traces out problems of legibility and narrative that emerge from Seghers's framing of the political problematics of the contested terms *Heimat* and *Volk* and the representational dilemmas that arise from the emplotment of immediate experience with more abstract modes of historical and political identification. Simply put, the fugitive story becomes a wager on the possibility of narratively emplotting history itself, as Georg Heisler's flight becomes a metaphor for the plausibility of narrative closure and of the narrative authority of the "we" voice that frames the novel as a tale of antifascist hope. *The Seventh Cross* is deeply concerned with the communication of experience across the barriers of political repression and isolation imposed by the National Socialist regime but also with the communication of popular history across the gulf of generations at the level of its form.

The formal problem of the novel is foregrounded in all three of the works read in this book, with Eduard Claudius's *Grüne Oliven und nackte Berge* (Chapter 5) sharing the episodic structure of *Die Kumiaks* and *The Seventh Cross* while at the same time laying similar claims as these novels on gathering the disparate historical experience and multiscalar temporalities of the European class struggle into some form of narrative totality. Likewise, Claudius evokes the long, discontinuous tradition of popular oppression and resistance, with Spain now serving at once as a backdrop to what remains a very German antifascist novel but also as an estranging vantage point of struggles that now acquire new valences beyond the German scene. For Claudius, the Spanish Civil War becomes a stage upon which central questions of emancipation and violence, exile and political commitment, are played out against the fraught political background of Europe on the eve of World War II and the collapse of the Popular Front. Claudius's novel, I suggest, appeals to the long tradition of popular resistance to oppression as a counterweight—a "countertime"—to the catastrophes of the present. Yet this countertime becomes increasingly displaced and disembodied with the foreclosure of the politics of the Popular Front, and Claudius's novel becomes a portrayal of the hardening of solidarity and discipline into the siege mentality of state socialism, even as the attempt to evoke a Spanish perspective as a point of critique of German "soldier males," both fascist and communist, involves a complicated meditation on the status of the novel as a national allegory of both Spain and Germany.

Chapter 6 shifts the formal focus of the book, examining Bertolt Brecht's drama *Mutter Courage und ihre Kinder* [*Mother Courage and Her Children* 1938/39] and Brecht's notions of epic theater as an alternative avenue of response to the same crises of historical understanding and representation at issue in discussions of the historical novel. Situating his drama in the Thirty Years War and borrowing the form of the folk play allow Brecht to reflect critically and historically on the notion of the popular, while his use of the war itself as a trope that cuts through public and private spheres effaces the distinction between history and everyday life and calls emplotment into question without abandoning it. The famed Brechtian *Gestus* thus not only becomes a historical sign but also suggests possible futures opposed to the present of exploitation and war. Brecht's *Mother Courage* can therefore be read, not coincidentally, as pushing toward the same epic tendency that Lukács sees operating, if still only as tendency, in the novels of the Popular Front. This epic tendency might be understood as the attempt to arrive at a collective historical protagonist, to conjure a "we" out of the forms that still gesture to the epic, the novel, and the tragedy. Here we return to Loren Kruger's tragedy of the commoner. This elusive "we" is tragic in that the struggles against dark times, to paraphrase Brecht, are, in Williams's terms, "necessary and incomplete" but also, as Kruger points out, "necessarily incomplete." Brecht's epic tragedy is no longer made up of "historical collisions between individual and state" but is the tragedy of the commoner, a tragic mode that points to this epic "we" precisely where historical circumstances forestall the coming into being of this plural agent, leaving in its place an ensemble of ordinary protagonists who have no fate but are instead caught up in webs of social constraint and complicity. The tragedy of the commoner,

Kruger argues, stands under the shadow of the incomplete revolution and the "experience of sacrifice . . . experienced as loss or as thwarted aspirations rather than as revolution." The shadow of the incomplete revolution, or the missing epic condition, has representational consequences in Kruger's account, though the tragic contradiction "between the experience of irredeemable loss and the desire to redeem it through representation is tragic because it both invites and eludes resolution."[77]

It is perhaps of interest here that Brecht frames *Mother Courage* as a "Chronicle of the Thirty Years War," since the tragedy of the commoner has its parallel in the epic tendency of the Popular Front novel, which is theorized by Walter Benjamin in the late 1930s in terms of the novel's formal tendency toward what he calls the chronicle. The chronicle breaks with the novel in that the coordinating "medium" of the novel, the fate of the main character, is missing.[78] Benjamin's notion of the chronicle, which also circles around the question of the possible constitution of an epic "we" and the possibility of what he calls redemption, in turn points toward the utopian or transcendent horizon of the Popular Front novel, one that is brought into relief at the moments when these novels approach the hard constraint of the failure of popular emancipation. This dimension is already implicit in Lukács's theory of the realist novel, since, as Tyrus Miller argues, for Lukács, "novels . . . can be understood as a sort of rhetorical laboratory for constituting and nominating 'the people,' exhibiting the conditions under which this succeeds or fails and with what social, political, and existential results."[79] Indeed, as J. M. Bernstein argues in *The Philosophy of the Novel*, "at the horizon of the history of the novel, just as it was at the horizon of the history of modern philosophy, there stands the question of the 'we,' the we who shall speak and make history."[80] Yet this epic "we" is not, as it perhaps was for the young Lukács, some prelapsarian utopia; it is not something that has been lost. Nor is it something that in some way is already present beneath the reified divisions of social life. Rather, as Bernstein points out, the project of an epic narrative is itself the production of an emancipated future, the narrative production of both a subject and a world in which social action and social meaning might for the first time find themselves in equipoise. For Bernstein, this project of collective narration is precisely what links representation to political practice under the sign of the Marxist project. "Praxis," he writes, "is a political narrating of experience; political experience collects experience by collecting subjects into a collective subject; that collective subject becomes itself by producing a world in which it can say who it is."[81]

Epic, then, stands in this book for a double vocation in Popular Front aesthetics. It is the impossible project of narratively producing a collective historical subject and a spatial practice of liberation. This is the epic desire of the Popular Front aesthetic, but it is not the desire for a lost golden age. Rather, the epic nostalgia in these books lies in the insight that the happy illuminated age of the epic, which Lukács takes as the constitutive lost object that makes the novel the privileged literary form of the modern, has never been. It might have been, or it might be. That is the wager of these works, which seek epic flashes of light in their own dark times. Epic is also a relationship to the forms of vernacular culture; it is, and this emerges most directly in Brecht's work, a series of operations carried out upon the forms of bourgeois literature, for example, the novel or the tragedy, in order to render them serviceable vehicles for this epic "we" that struggles to find shape and lay claims on social reality. The struggle against fascism and against Germany's history thus finds its literary expression in a complicated spatial portrayal of German modernity. If modernity can be understood in terms of the "reification of the social world" as "the becoming of non-narrativity," the *deutsche Misère*, as a trope that gestures toward both the collapse of linear historical narratives and the fracturing of the social into privation and passivity, can be grasped as an exemplary articulation of capitalist modernity itself. This constellation of impasses, blockages, and defeats whereby a horizon of human emancipation appears, like Peter Weiss's Heracles, in the form of an empty space, lends the novels of the German Popular Front their pathos. Thus in their deep engagement with the opacities of the historical, the ambiguities of everyday life, and the impasses of social agency, they are to be understood as attempts to construct this collective subject, the people as historical subject, in the face of the catastrophes of fascism and capitalist modernity.

CHAPTER I

Epic Forms and the Crisis of the Novel

This chapter lays out the key terms of the debates around the juncture of political practice and narrative form as they unfolded from the Weimar Republic in the late 1920s that continued to set the stage for the early years of the antifascist literary emigration. In the Weimar Republic, this debate was given institutional form in the BPRS and its journal, *Linkskurve*, and continued in the first years of antifascist exile in a diverse ensemble of often precarious publications. The major turning point in these debates is the transition from a collectivist leftist avant-gardism to a more explicitly realist aesthetic in the discourse of the BPRS, paralleling cultural developments in the USSR around the time of the Kharkov Conference of the International Union of Revolutionary Writers in 1931. They coincide with the arrival of Georg Lukács in Berlin in the same year and the discussions leading up to the First All-Union Soviet Writers' Congress and adoption of socialist realism in the Soviet Union in 1934.

This debate reflected a deepening preoccupation with the relationship between the KPD and modern mass culture that had already moved through several stages by the time the party was banned by the newly installed National Socialist government in 1933. The late 1920s and early 1930s saw the notorious sectarianism of the KPD in its so-called Third Period, where the party's policy toward the rest of the working class was guided by "social fascism," which saw the reformism of Social Democracy as the main support of an increasingly crisis-ridden capitalism after the crash of 1929.[1] This was, however, also the period of the emergence of a distinctive and self-referential proletarian culture, exemplified by the working-class counterpublic sphere organized around the KPD. Willi Münzenberg's impressive press empire included the high-circulation glossy *Arbeiter-Illustrierte Zeitung* [Workers' Illustrated Newspaper], the Universum Bücherei für Alle publishing house, the Prometheus film company, and the organ of the workers' photography movement, *Der Arbeiter-Fotograf*, among other outlets.[2] The paramilitary organization Rot Front Kämpferbund fought the SA in the streets of Germany's cities. The BPRS organized bourgeois writers aligned with the party and recruited authors from the working classes, while the Marxistische Arbeiterschule (Marxist Workers' School [MASCH]) in Berlin offered courses in subjects from political economy to literature, taken by both workers and intellectuals. This was all in addition to a proliferation of working-class theater groups and proletarian agit-prop choruses like Das rote Sprachrohr (Red Megaphone), supplied with songs by Hanns Eisler, himself a student of Arnold Schönberg and collaborator with Bertolt Brecht. The KPD even sponsored, if somewhat uncomfortably, a group for discussion and activism about working-class sexual issues called Sex-Pol and affiliated with Wilhelm Reich.[3] For the most part, this organizational infrastructure was destroyed by the National Socialist regime, and the German left's call to popular unity then resounds in a context where the KPD, and indeed any substantial presence of the German workers' movement, had been decisively excluded from the German public sphere despite the impressive, if improvisational, proliferation of journals, publishing houses, and cultural organizations among German émigrés.

These discussions revolved precisely around the role of culture in the context of what historian Detlev Peukert famously characterized as "the crisis of classical modernity."[4] "Classical modernity" should be understood as what Jameson calls a "culture of incomplete modernization," where elements of urban modernity and premodern village life existed simultaneously in a web of vexed circuits and relationships. "The protagonists" of classical modernism "were people who still lived in two distinct worlds simultaneously," and it was this "comparativist perception of the two socioeconomic temporalities" that accounts for the "sensitivity to deep time in the moderns."[5] Peukert notes the uneasy coexistence of authoritarian political elites and semifeudal agriculture east of the Elbe on one hand and the advanced concentration of German capital, rationalization of industry, and explosion of mass culture and mass political mobilizations on the other. Much has been written on the caesura of World War I in European politics and culture, and indeed on the war as a break with the very notion of a bourgeois subjectivity grounded in notions of interiority, experience, and development, in other words, of the subject as the hero of something like the classical bildungsroman. "The collapse was not only military and economic," noted critic Erich Knauf in 1929 looking back on the war, "the old ideological structure collapsed as well, leaving many 'carriers of culture' lying like defective caryatids in the dust."[6] Benjamin's 1933 essay "Experience and Poverty" generalizes this notion of collapse, invoking the political, economic, and social crises of the Weimar Republic. "Never has experience been contradicted more thoroughly," Benjamin writes, "strategic experience has been contravened by positional warfare; economic experience, by inflation; physical experience, by hunger; moral experience, by the ruling powers."[7]

Of course, the insight into the widening incommensurability between individual experience and the social forces in which that experience is imbricated, between self and world, is precisely the terrain of the novel as a genre, as Lukács had already pointed out in his *Theory of the Novel.* This text continued to inform the discussion of the genre during the exile of many of its practitioners, influencing, for example, Benjamin's genealogy of the rise and fall of the bourgeois novel in his 1936 essay "The Storyteller" and informing Anna Seghers's thinking on the genre.[8] In this account, it is the incommensurability between self and world—and between what Lukács calls life on the one hand and form on the other—that marks the novel's outward form as biographical, since only "in the organic unity which is the aim of biography" can the contradiction between the immanence of the world and the abstractness of social conventions, values, and forms be objectivized (TN 77). This opposition between the passions and plans of individuals and the hard objectivity of the world that had structured the novel from its beginnings according to Lukács itself was increasingly nullified by the impoverishment of experience characteristic of the mental life of the modern metropolis, to paraphrase Georg Simmel. As many critics of the Weimar period insisted, the bourgeois subject was no longer adequate as a means of framing this contradiction, and the novel as a bourgeois epic seemed equally unsuited to mapping even the limited terrain of individual experience itself.

As Siegfried Kracauer wrote in an essay on the popularity of biography during the Weimar Republic, "it is no accident that one speaks of the 'crisis' of the novel. This crisis resides in the fact that the reigning compositional model of the novel has been invalidated by the abolition of the contours of the individual and its antagonists."[9] For Kracauer, the post–World War I experience of the social, and hence narrative, insufficiency of the individual undermines the notion of the sovereignty of the subject upon which the bourgeois novel as a form is predicated. Kracauer notes in the popularity of the biography a turn on the part of bourgeois literature from subjective experience to the passage of history as such, a turn that remains abstract and escapist as long as bourgeois literature remains focused on the lives of great men rather than daring to "step in any direction beyond the border it has reached, out into the world of class." Kracauer asserts the confrontation with "the forces that embody social reality today" can only be given a properly epic form from the perspective of the advanced consciousness that can only arise at "the breaking point of our societal construct," which is to say at the juncture of class struggle.[10]

Commenting on Kracauer's essay, German Democratic Republic (GDR) critic Silvia Schlenstedt points out that "the crisis of the novel" had been a staple of literary discussion since the late nineteenth century. In addition to the crisis of the bourgeois subject, the crisis of the novel form posited during the Weimar Republic was characterized by its incontrovertibly political valence; in these years the novel was explicitly interrogated by authors across the political spectrum in connection with the crisis of capitalism and with the corresponding fragmentation of bourgeois ideologies of subjectivity and form.[11] Epic was a key term in this discussion of the crisis of the novel during the closing years of the Weimar Republic, becoming a contested term for attempts to think about the possibility of a technologically mediated collective voice that might emerge through the use of new aesthetic techniques of montage and the report, or to put it another way, through a dynamic and synthetic employment of social documentary. One sees this in the popularity of Egon Erwin Kisch, the "raging reporter," who popularized the reportage internationally in the 1920s and 1930s, or in such well-known films as Walter Ruttmann's *Berlin: Symphony of a Metropolis* (1927), where urban space, traffic, and the masses become the protagonist of the film. This documentary *Gestus*, though, was also very much present in the art, literature, and film of the time, lending even fictional works some of the aspects that Rudolf G. Wagner identifies in Kisch's reportage, from its commitment to topicality and social authenticity to its focus on urban modernity and the functional.[12] This commitment is also found in the architecture and design of the period, as exemplified by the work of the figures associated with the Bauhaus school. Here one might also want to mention a parallel turn in art and photography, associated with such diverse figures as Georg Grosz, Hannah Höch, August Sandler, and Alfred Renger-Patzsch.[13]

Mobilized by various figures to various ends, the concrete meaning of the term "epic" remains somewhat opaque in these debates. On the one hand, in German, epic, or *die Epik*, simply means narrative as such, and in this sense the revived notion of epic in the Weimar Republic simply partakes of the generally detached and cold approach of New Objectivity or Neue Sachlichkeit, which turns away from the lyrical mode of Expressionism toward a more distanced style of objective reporting.[14] Yet one could argue that a generic take on epic gestures back to the older sense of epic as the poetry of an intact world where the totality of social life is sensuously perceptible and in which the individual stands in an easily legible relationship to the social structure as a whole. Taking Greek antiquity as his example, Lukács writes of this epic unity,

> it determines all lived experience and all formal creation, there exist no qualitative differences which are insurmountable, which cannot be bridged except for a leap, between the transcendental loci among themselves and between them and the subject a priori assigned to them. . . . Hence the mind's attitude within such a home is a passively visionary acceptance of ready-made, ever-present meaning. (TN 32)[15]

For Lukács, the coming of modernity shatters this unity, and the novel becomes the epic form that expresses the opening of a rupture between subject and transcendental locus, between the horizon of collective life and the making of meanings and individual everyday experience. The novel is thus, as Lukács puts it so famously, the "expression of transcendental homelessness" (41). This transcendental homelessness is the expression of the growing opacity of social life, which can now only be felt and thought as a whole negatively, as the absence of this unity impinges upon the subject. "The novel," Lukács continues, "is the epic of an age in which the extensive totality of life is no longer directly given, in which the immanence of meaning in life has become a problem, yet which still thinks in terms of totality" (56). The novel is already the articulation of a crisis of meaning but one that remains centered on the individual subject in relation to the world. In the context of the social fragmentation of the Weimar Republic, the theme of a new epic form encompasses the desire both to remap the complexity of social relations in a way that would render them navigable and to resuture the individual into a legible sphere of social significance, but one where the individual would be cut through and decentered by the great transindividual realities of mass communication, social class, and the unconscious. The discussion of epic in the Weimar Republic was then also a discussion of modernist narrative techniques and their relationship to emergent media technologies.

Two important signposts in this discussion of epic are Alfred Döblin's 1929 novel *Berlin Alexanderplatz* and Bertolt Brecht's epic theater. Döblin articulates his project for a new epic in his well-known essay "Der Bau des epischen Werks" [The Construction of the Epic Work 1929]. He argues that the report is the fundamental form of the epic, that is, it is grounded in practical use value for groups of listeners, based on the exemplary character of events and characters (BB 106). The epic is not a description of a real event but of a true event, or "hyper-reality" (*eine Überrealität*), which encompasses reality and fantasy (108). The work of art has two functions: *erkennen* and *erzeugen*—to perceive and to create (109). Fictionality in the form of the report is a play with the terms of reality: "The form of the report suggests the sovereign will of man, or at least of the author, to play with reality despite knowledge and science" (110). The report, then, for Döblin, does not stand in opposition to the work of fantasy but incorporates it, and the epic of the future must be lyrical, dramatic, and reflexive (113). The gap between the archaic collectivism of the epic and the new collective horizon of the epic is bridged by the subjectivity of the writer, which expands through observation to contain the people. The writer becomes a site for the heteroglossic reproduction of the polyphony of urban space that shapes and fragments subjectivity—slang, advertisement, official discourses, cliché, myth—which moves toward the "depersonisation" of characters and authorial persona (120). As critic Peter Jelavich points out, "the trick for modern writers was to employ the vernacular styles of popular and mass culture, and even be carried away by them, in a productive and critical manner."[16] In Döblin's account, then, the author becomes itself a collective *locus* through the subordination to the various registers of language itself, overcoming the "book": "Los von Buch!" In his work on Döblin, Devin Fore points out that this project for a new epic was centered on the attempt to overcome the incommensurability of language *and* experience by casting the technologically mediated multiplicity of language *as* experience.[17] As such, Döblin's work is essentially concerned with the technologies and forms through which modern speech is transmitted and those forms through which the senses are organized socially. For Döblin, epic is a narrative form that refuses the differentiation between story and fact, art and science, joining literary production and consumption into a kind of "auto-referential plentitude" and ultimately inaugurating a new rapprochement between authorship and reception. The model for this kind of literature would be the newspaper, which concentrates not on character but on *Elementarsituationen* and *Elementarhaltungen*, or basic situations and basic attitudes.[18]

If Döblin's notion of a renewal of epic form was predicated on a notion of realism that posited the sign systems of urban modernity as a refoundation of collective experience, Bertolt Brecht was similarly concerned with the formal techniques required for a realist aesthetic to be adequate to new mass media like radio and the newspaper but also to the extended webs of social causality and subject formation articulated through the increasingly dispersed economic networks of industrial capitalism. For both writers, epic is a term that should signify a break with what Peter Bürger calls the institution of art in bourgeois society, where the aesthetic functions as a realm free of use value and as a compensatory formation for values, desires, and needs that are suppressed or foreclosed within the dominant instrumental rationality of the capitalist life world.[19]

Without rehashing the theory of epic theater in its entirety, it is worth pointing out that for Brecht, the central question that arises for such a mode of realism—and this a theme that will be taken up famously by Benjamin as well, as we shall see later—is the relationship between cultural producers and the apparatuses of cultural production. This is a question of the social function of culture as much as it is one of technique. What Brecht means by the apparatus is the entire social and institutional organization of art. As Brecht puts it, "great apparati like the opera, the stage, the press, impose their views, as it were, incognito." Artists, writers, and cultural producers in general thus become reduced to content providers for these apparati, as it were, behind their own backs. Operating under the belief that "the whole business is concerned only with the presentation of their work" and "imagining that they have got hold of an apparatus which in fact has got hold of them, they are supporting an apparatus which is out of their control."[20] The problem here is that "the individual's freedom of invention," already rendered obsolete through the increasing collectivization of the aesthetic means of production, becomes, under the increasing commodification of culture, a fig leaf for cultural apparatuses that work for profit.[21] Brecht links this profit-driven functionality of the aesthetic in bourgeois society to a wider critique of the division of labor between the producer and consumer of culture:

> primarily the sharp contrast between work and relaxation particular to the capitalist manner of production divides all mental activities into those that serve work and those that serve relaxation and turns the latter into a system for the reproduction of labor . . . in the interest of production, relaxation is dedicated to non-production . . . the mistake consists not in the fact that art is pulled into the sphere of production, but rather in the fact that this happens so completely and that art is intended to create an island of "non-production."[22]

Brecht's term for the nonproductive or culinary attitude of the spectator of bourgeois and mass culture is "imploitation" (*Einbeutung*).[23] This demobilized spectator is the counterpart of the "artist" who does not understand the apparatus and means of production in which he is imbricated. As Brecht points out, "to restrict the individual's freedom of invention is in itself a progressive act. The individual becomes increasingly drawn into enormous events that are going to change the world." The thrust of Brecht's critique is directed toward the form taken by this restriction of individual innovation, that "at present the apparati do not work for the general good, the means of production do not belong to the producer."[24] This means that the result is merchandise, rather than fusing the apparatus of culture with "with the educational system or with the organs of mass communication."[25] As Brecht points out in his "Three-Penny Trial," this fusion itself would imply "a society that operates according to plan and divides labor in order to make what is to be seen visible to everyone."[26] This in turn implies for Brecht the collectivization of the technological means of communication.

There is a formal implication to this line of thought as well, since, for Brecht, older aesthetic forms—the theater, the novel—cannot be left unchanged by the emergence of newer mass media: "The old forms of communication do not remain unchanged by newly emerging ones and do not continue to exist next to them."[27] Film, for example, imposes a new formal logic upon the novel, since film enables the observation of people from the outside. Whereas the bourgeois novel "today still shapes 'one world' at a time" and remains constrained within the ideological and aesthetic conceptions of its author, film does not shape a world or allow expression but "provides useful clues about human behavior in detail." If the novel continues to appeal to character for its formal coherence, film offers another model, in which "all motivation proceeding from the character is missing; the inner life of people never provides the primary impetus and is seldom the primary result of the action; the person is seen from the outside." This external gaze, Brecht asserts, is directly tied to the transformation of the social function of literature. "Literature needs the film," Brecht writes, "not only directly but indirectly. The decisive extension of its social duties which follows from the transformation of art into a pedagogical discipline entails the multiplying or the repeated changing of the means of production."[28]

At the same time, as opposed to the aesthetics of New Objectivity, which Benjamin critiqued for their resigned and culinary fetishizing of surface and fact, Brecht's techniques are predicated on the insufficiency of the image. As Brecht famously observed, "a photograph of the Krupp works of AEG yields nearly nothing about these institutions. Actual reality has slipped into the functional. The reification of human relationships, such as the factory, no longer produces the latter."[29] Brecht derives the continued necessity for artistic technique from this insight into the insufficiency of what can be visually or sensuously grasped, which is, as with the example just quoted, often simply the frozen appearance of reality. If modern mass communication technologies have rendered the older conceptions of art untenable, "it is similarly a fact that art is necessary."[30] From the recognition of this necessity, Brecht developed what by the 1940s was termed the "estrangement effect," which mobilized the tools of demonstration offered by the theater for an aesthetic of quotation based on techniques of montage, gesture, and the transposition of events into an epic past. These techniques serve to frame objects and relationships in the world so that, taken out of context representationally, they might be contextualized socially.

The techniques of "complex seeing" introduced by Brechtian theater enable a transindividual, or prosthetic, mode of perception. Brecht is not so much attempting to forestall spectatorial identification as to draw the consequences of its absence. The basic stance of quotation here then transposes the first person into the third person, demonstrating that "what we call our 'self' is itself an object for consciousness, not our consciousness itself," as Jameson points out.[31] The epic "we" implicit in Brecht's project is in the pedagogical emphasis on historicizing modes of subjectivity and perception. At the same time, however, as Roswitha Mueller has noted, the aesthetics of epic theater required that the audience "be literarized, that is, informed and trained especially for the theatrical event in order to be productive."[32] The epic aspect of Brecht's practice in the Weimar Republic was not only a question of techniques for a narrative rather than a dramatic theater but also depended to a certain degree on the high level of cultural mobilization of the German working class, for example, the workers' theater groups and choirs in the orbit of the KPD.[33] These organizations were aspects of the elaborate proletarian counterpublic sphere of cultural organizations that grew up around the revolutionary left during the Weimar Republic, and in the field of literature, none of these was more important than the BPRS.

The BPRS formed in October 1928 under the aegis of the Communist International's International Union of Revolutionary Writers (IURW) and was affiliated with the Russian Association of Proletarian Writers (RAPP) in the USSR.[34] In addition to giving an organizational structure to Marxist aesthetic debate and production in the Weimar Republic and providing a conduit for the German reception of Soviet discussions, the BPRS brought together and consolidated two important trends in German literature after World War I.[35] The first was the growing movement of workers' literature, for example, the Workers' Theater troupes that proliferated in the Weimar Republic and the Workers' Correspondence movement fostered by the Communist daily press. Many authors like Hans Marchwitza and Willi Bredel began their careers as worker correspondents.[36] The other side of the BPRS was composed of radicalized left-bourgeois authors like Johannes R. Becher and Anna Seghers.[37] Many left-bourgeois authors connected political commitment to the KPD and its revolutionary program to their sense of the anachronistic character of traditional aesthetic norms; their conclusion was that the victory of the proletariat would bring in its wake a transformation of the arts (ML 25). What both groups shared, according to Helga Gallas, was an interest in the "breaking-up of traditional genre forms in the direction of anti-psychologizing, documentary modes of representation and the suppression of traditional principles of literary construction, like the individual protagonist, the artificial plot, individual conflicts, dramatic tension, etc." (96).

From the worker correspondents to the left-bourgeois authors who came together in the BPRS, as indeed in post–World War I German literary discourse more generally, there was a sustained critique before this time of the novel form as being both inherently bourgeois and anachronistic. In a 1930 radio conversation between F. C. Weiskopf and Kurt Hirschfeld, "On the Proletarian Novel," Weiskopf declared that the traditional novel was already a genre in dissolution, at best providing a forum for the public decomposition of bourgeois ideology and for the ventilation of social frustrations that could find no political expression, as in the case of Döblin's *Berlin Alexanderplatz*.[38] The proletarian novel tended toward a documentary style and the "capturing of collective actions and collective feelings" instead of individual psychological portrayals.[39] Likewise, the plots of proletarian novels were driven more by social than individual processes.[40] The third important innovation that Weiskopf saw in the proletarian novel was the "widening of the realm of language" to include the language of the political movement, trade union, and factory culture and working-class speech in general.[41]

Realism was the central notion underpinning both the proletarian-revolutionary novel and the critical discourse around it. In his "Antwort eines 'Radikalen'" [A Radical Replies], a programmatic reply to an article by Willy Hass published in 1928 in *Die Literarische Welt*, poet Johannes R. Becher, the KPD's leading literary intellectual, describes proletarian-revolutionary literature as a guide through the "environment of schematic, abstract, impenetrable relationships" that constitute bourgeois society.[42] At stake in the development of proletarian-revolutionary literature were not only a challenge to traditional bourgeois aesthetic and ideological norms but also an attempt to remap social reality from the point of view of the proletariat. The question of the forms of realism appropriate to this endeavor was hotly debated in *Linkskurve*, the organ of the BPRS, as well as the KPD and bourgeois press of the Weimar Republic. During its first phase, *Linkskurve* sought to distance proletarian-revolutionary literature from left-bourgeois writers like Heinrich Mann and Döblin, whom the *Linkskurve* criticized for clinging to "the traditional isolated position of the bourgeois writer, with its pretension to the status of 'opinion leader' for the bourgeois intelligentsia" (ML 48). The critique of left-bourgeois writers dealt mostly with the politics of those writers rather than their aesthetics. Indeed, the aesthetics of many BPRS members coincided with broad currents of international modernism, although often with reservations. Although the debates in *Linkskurve* are often framed in terms of the gradual liquidation of the positions of socialist modernism in favor of Lukácsean orthodoxy, Helga Hartung points out that there remained a number of theoretical positions in play during these years and that there was a shaky consensus on the BPRS, stretching from figures like Johannes R. Becher to Seghers, F. C. Weiskopf, and others, that "the possibilities of aesthetic figuration accrued in the first place from social reality in transformation and could not be extrapolated from 'finished' works of literature."[43] This socialist modernism is taken to its furthest point in Anna Seghers's work before 1933, notably in her stream-of-consciousness account of a German solidarity march in support of Sacco and Vanzetti, "Auf dem Weg zur Amerikanischen Botschaft" [On the Way to the American Embassy" 1930], and the chronicle of exiles from the Hungarian Soviet Republic, *Die Gefährten* [The Wayfarers 1932], which employs a collage technique of interrelated narrative strands reminiscent of the novels of John Dos Passos.[44]

Such socialist modernism did not in many ways appear so far from the New Objectivity. Yet even where BPRS literature most closely approaches an aesthetic of the factual, for example, the reportages of Kisch and the workers' correspondents of the Communist press but also in the reportage novels of authors like Ernst Ottwalt, whose investigative novel on the Weimar judiciary came in for special condemnation from Lukács, the writers of the BPRS never adopted the observational stance of this larger movement. In contrast to much of Neue Sachlichkeit, which was content simply to reflect reality as a given, members of the BPRS like Kisch, Becher, Weiskopf, and the theater director Erwin Piscator stressed a "documentary literature that would provide a Marxist analysis of the segments of reality depicted." This emphasis on the role of social analysis of connections and contexts in the documentation of reality also differentiated these authors from the discourse of the Soviet avant-garde group Left Front of the Arts with its journal *LEF*, which advocated "a literature without a subject, the writing down of details, the montage and assemblage of true facts" (ML 93). If, under the conditions of Soviet socialist construction, literature could become a "factory of facts," as was advocated by figures like Sergei Tretyakov and Boris Arvatov in the 1920s and 1930s, in the Germany of the Weimar Republic, "the facts" themselves were still ideologically veiled by capitalist social relations and would thus require polemical treatment, or at the very least, authorial commentary.[45] Indeed, the attitude of BPRS members could be summarized with the title of the Communist dramatist Friedrich Wolf's manifesto of 1928, "Art Is a

Weapon!" which advocated an art grounded in working-class daily life and political struggle and a style that was partisan, to the point, and accessible.[46]

During this period, writers in *Linkskurve* challenged traditional literary discourse not only on the level of form, that is, by opposing the documentary to the fictional, but also by opposing the collective nature of the proletarian subject to the individual protagonist of bourgeois literature. Thus in her article "On the Tasks of Revolutionary Literature," the critic and dramatist Berta Lask, drawing on the mass performances of Proletkult in the USSR, argued for the "mass hero" as the ideal protagonist of working-class literature. With the category of the mass hero, Lask focused on the horizon of collective thinking, feeling, and action. As Gallas notes, the concept of the mass hero was based on the recognition that the individual is a generically inadequate basis for comprehending social transformation. Furthermore, Gallas writes, the "proletarian becomes an exemplary figure in capitalist society only through the role played by his class as a historical subject, not through the unfolding of personal abilities that he has no opportunity to cultivate" (ML 88). For Lask, collective experience was the basis of any possible characterization of the working class, and proletarian literature had the role of protecting the working class against the "poisoning of bourgeois ideology," which would work to interpellate proletarians, falsely, as individual bourgeois subjects.[47]

Critics in *Linkskurve* also attempted to lay the theoretical groundwork for a proletarian class literature by emphasizing the role of the Workers' Correspondence movement. This movement was officially founded in 1924 but had antecedents both in the Soviet Union and in the pre–Weimar Republic SPD press. These short pieces, written by workers themselves, were intended to describe concrete and exploitative working conditions and to report on strikes, demonstrations, union work, women and youth problems, the effects of unemployment, and fascist provocations in the workplace and neighborhoods. The main forms of this activity were the reportage and brief commentaries on events. The importance of the Workers' Correspondence movement was complemented by theories like Andor Gábor's *Geburtshilfertheorie*, according to which the role of the intellectuals within the BPRS was to act as "midwives" to the rising proletarian literature. As opposed to creating such a literature themselves, intellectuals should facilitate proletarian literature through securing publication venues for, supplying theory to, and tutoring writing workers on matters of literary technique (ML 50).

For Gábor, literature was inherently class based, serving a particular group of people whose "thoughts and feelings it depicts, organizes, and develops."[48] Gábor argued that a proletarian literature could emerge only from workers themselves, since such a literature must be "experienced from the standpoint of the proletarian-revolutionary class struggle."[49] Whereas Gábor called for the recruitment of writers from the working class, in other words for the literary training of the workers' correspondents, others saw proletarian-revolutionary literature as already present in the texts of the worker correspondents. It was this type of literary production that Erich Steffen declared in *Linkskurve* to be the essence of proletarian literature. Steffen's view represented that of many of the worker correspondents in the BPRS, arguing that, as Gallas puts it, "proletarian literature could only be created from the experience of the workplace, in constant contact with the material production process" (ML 50). What was at stake in these discussions was the elaboration of a specifically working-class literature, emplotting the working class not as a psychologically differentiated grouping of individuals but as a collective protagonist, and aiming to consolidate the class consciousness of this group through the organization of their experience using small, operative forms (ML 82).

From mid-1930 through the fall of 1931, the direction of the *Linkskurve* debate shifted to a critique of this initial focus on proletarian-specific operative genres and the beginnings of a Hegelian-influenced theory of Marxist aesthetics. Despite the opposition of the BPRS's left wing and the worker correspondents, this was the direction of the organization's evolution, culminating in an emphasis on the novel. Arriving in Berlin from Moscow in the summer of 1931, Georg Lukács was influential in criticizing leftist tendencies in the BPRS through his well-known series of articles in *Linkskurve*, which included attacks on the modernist tendencies toward reportage and montage in the works of noted BPRS authors Willi Bredel and Ernst Ottwalt. It was also during this period that discussion in the BPRS shifted from a class-specific literature to a proletarian mass literature. In his 1930 *Linkskurve* article "Against Economism in Literature," N. Kraus argued for widening the standpoint of proletarian literature in order to address other social classes and for the production of a Marxist-inflected popular literature for the broad working masses, including the petit bourgeoisie, women, youth, peasants, and other groups that might not feel themselves sufficiently addressed in the often combative and masculinist style of BPRS writing. In calling for such a mass literature, Kraus defined the proper standpoint for such literature as Marxism itself, a theory of the social totality. "The proletarian literature we need," Kraus wrote, "must reflect the entire life of human society, the life of all classes from the revolutionary proletarian standpoint."[50] Thus criteria of the previous period, such as the class origin of the author, the address to a specifically class-conscious proletarian audience, and the treatment of proletarian themes, were no longer binding (ML 83).

Kraus's article appeared as part of a general reorientation of the BPRS in the early 1930s, after the fashion of its Soviet sister organization, RAPP, toward the conventions of the traditional realist novel and its focus on individual psychological representation, breaking with previous *Linkskurve* positions on the mass hero and operative forms (ML 64). The novel form gained importance in BPRS theoretical discourse after 1929. This was due among other factors to the International Conference of Revolutionary Writers, held in 1930 in the Soviet city of Kharkov attended by several members of the BPRS. By this time, the discussions in RAPP were focused on the novel and the depiction of "the living person." The individual was to be portrayed in his or her development and change in the context of social contradictions.[51] The category of the living person, with its emphasis on psychological character development, was combined with what the 1931 BPRS draft program referred to as "dialectical realism," a mode of representation linked to "the dialectic of objective development itself."[52] This is to say that proletarian experience was theoretically subordinated to, or more positively sublated within, Marxism-Leninism as a theory of the social totality in its development. The draft program also emphasizes the novel form over smaller operative forms, like mass performances and reportage. Advocating "the great proletarian work of art," the program calls for works that "address *all* the problems of the entirety of society from the standpoint of the proletariat."[53]

The focus on the social totality in the draft program thus led to a renewed emphasis on long narrative, individuated protagonists, and the novel, and this was combined with a critique of "ultraleftism," which was understood to mean not only political sectarianism but avant-garde experimentation as well. Paralleling a similar shift in Soviet literary discussions, the call for a Marxist popular literature therefore implied a return to the literary and narrative modes of "psychologism" in the depiction of "the living person" that many BPRS authors and critics had condemned in the 1920s in order to appeal beyond the proletariat to a petit-bourgeois mass readership (ML 63).[54]

This turn toward the social totality, as opposed to a literature of proletarian militancy and class struggle, returned to the debates on literary tendency in nineteenth-century Marxism but with a crucial difference. Nineteenth-century Social Democratic critics, foremost among them in Germany Franz Mehring, were skeptical of tendentious art and tended to advocate the appropriation of German classicism as a part and parcel of proletarian *Bildung*.[55] Returning to this question of the relationship between politics and literature in the *Linkskurve*, Lukács criticized this Social Democratic position as itself undialectical. For Lukács, the very notion of tendency implies a reified opposition between tendentious art on the one hand and pure *l'art pour l'art* on the other, reflecting ideologically the capitalist division of labor in its opposition of art to morality and thus also of individual to society.[56] Against the false choice posed by this alternative, which lay in either renouncing tendency and producing a pure art rendered all the more tendentious by bracketing out the social or in straightforward moralizing, Lukács proposes the term "partisanship," or *Parteilichkeit*, as an objective grasp of the social contradictions that shape both the subjective and objective sides of life and form. For a writer proceeding from the viewpoint of dialectical materialism, in other words, the question of tendency does not arise, "for in his depiction, a depiction of objective reality with its real driving forces and the real developmental tendencies, there is no space for an 'ideal,' whether moral or aesthetic."[57] This turn from a specifically proletarian viewpoint to one of a Marxist depiction of the social totality did not necessarily imply a formal corollary, but it did accompany a shift in emphasis from operative literary forms to more traditional and closed ones.

In its final phase, from the middle to the end of 1932, conversations in *Linkskurve* and the BPRS centered on the rejection of modernist literary techniques and an emphasis on the continuity of the classical literary tradition, concentrating on issues of socialist perspective, realism, and the nineteenth-century novel form, even as opposing positions developed (ML 51–65). The year 1930 saw the first of the Red-One-Mark-Novel series published by the International Workers' Press. These novels were intended as a counterweight to bourgeois trivial literature, describing the everyday life of the masses through the viewpoint of Marxist-Leninist ideology. Introducing this series, Otto Biha evokes the threat of bourgeois "reactionary literary trash" that stalks the working class. Through the factory yards, waiting rooms, subways, tenements, and homeless shelters of the republic, "these mass novels of classless idylls and economic peace parade their slogans" of "personal diligence, love, fatherland, and property, making them "more dangerous than the so-called great literature of the bourgeoisie."[58] In order to repel this literature, the "red mass novel" will provide, Biha asserts, a kind of popular Marxism for the masses, "no less gripping and entertaining," a literature that "instead of depicting personal conflicts and private passions, gives shape to the conflicts of our time and the *struggle of the masses* by depicting the fate of individuals in their actual interactions inside the class struggle in society."[59] These novels actually displayed a considerable thematic and stylistic diversity, from thinly fictionalized protocols of the various uprisings of the 1918–23 revolutionary period, for example, Hans Marchwitza's *Sturm auf Essen* [Storm over the Ruhr 1930] and Otto Gotsche's *Märzstürme* [Storms of March 1928/29, 1962], to novels of contemporary class struggle, like Klaus Neukrantz's *Barrikaden am Wedding* [Barricades in Wedding 1931], to novels dealing with aspects of the everyday experiences of working-class women and youth, like Franz Kray's *Maria und der Paragraph* [Maria and the Paragraph 1931] about abortion law or Walter Schönstedt's book about the struggles of unemployed urban youth, *Kämpfende Jugend* [Youth in Struggle 1932].[60]

The theoretical debates within the BPRS cannot, however, be taken as a map for the actual literary production of its members. The increasing attachment of BPRS literary theory to classical aesthetic models of the novel was accompanied by criticism of the "left" in the BPRS, a label that tended to encompass both the proletarian workers' correspondents and the bourgeois left avant-gardists like Ottwalt. While insisting that the major danger to proletarian-revolutionary literature came from a "right-wing" dismissal of the political urgency of working-class literature in favor of a snobbish fixation on literary quality, he went on to insist,

> we find the "left" error today primarily in the proletarian hurrah-spirit, in spitting matches and not wanting to learn, in pitting content against form, so that content is everything and the form is just makeshift, in the denial of the heritage, in the notion that the point of our literature lies only in supplying the daily press with reportages and articles, in supplying the Agit-prop troupes with material, in activities for meetings and protest actions, or in a purely unprincipled spontaneity and pragmatism.[61]

In its invocation of the importance of the cultural heritage for socialist literature and its insistence that the daily operative forms of the newspaper and the agit-prop groups do not properly rise to the level of the aesthetic, this passage from 1932 already prefigures the doxas of the socialist realism to come. At the same time, though, the documentary techniques and episodic structure of the reportage continued to influence the actual novels of German proletarian-revolutionary writers, leading to contradictions between the epic frame of these novels and their narrative technique.[62]

The tensions within the BPRS can easily be read in Lukács's criticisms of novels by Willi Bredel and Ernst Ottwalt, as well as in the heated responses of these authors (or in Bredel's case, the proxy response of Otto Gotsche).[63] Lukács's criticism of Bredel's novels *Maschinenfabrik N&K* (1930) and *Rosenhofstraße* (1931) focuses on the inconsistencies of the novels' form, the "unresolved contradiction between the broad narrative framework of his [Bredel's] story . . . and his way of telling it, which is partly a kind of journalistic reportage, and partly a kind of public speech."[64] In these novels, which represent, respectively, a strike in a Hamburg factory and the organization of a KPD cell in a proletarian Hamburg neighborhood, Lukács links precisely this linguistic stiltedness to Bredel's insufficiently developed characters, which he faults for manifesting "a fixed and characteristic feature, which is repeated and underlined at every possible opportunity." The "abstract treatment of language" and the resulting one-sidedness of characterization in Bredel's novels prevent them from grasping concrete reality and reduce depictions of Bredel's figures to political caricature.[65] In failing to grasp the dialectical character of social reality, Bredel has reproduced the moralizing gesture of the tendency novel. Lukács's criticism of Bredel is thus easily read as a critique of elements in Bredel's novels that gesture to earlier BPRS discourses and the methods of reportage central to the Workers' Correspondence movement, where Bredel, a metalworker and KPD functionary in Hamburg, was a central figure. "A novel," Lukács writes, "simply demands a different kind of characterization than a journalistic report: what may be good enough for one is completely inadequate for the other."[66] Turning his attention to Ottwalt, whom Helga Gallas argues served Lukács and *Linkskurve* as a proxy target for Brecht (ML 125), Lukács attacked the tendency of documentary reportage on the left, mentioning Upton Sinclair, Sergei Tretyakov, and Ilya Ehrenburg.[67] In the literature of facts, Lukács similarly sees a reified elision of the social relationships that shape reality.[68]

Since in this method of depiction facts are loosened from the contexts that produce them and are forced to stand in for those contexts, there arises an arbitrary logic of connection and social necessity, "resulting in a confusion between the totality and a mere sum of facts" and leading to a more sophisticated version of socialist tendency literature.[69]

The debates in *Linkskurve* also often fail to do justice to the particular historical and psychic dynamics that are at stake in these novels. The theoretical debates of the BPRS were centered primarily on questions of ideology and form. Although replete with calls for a dialectical representation of working-class life, BPRS criticism seldom addresses the actual issues involved in such representation. The composers of proletarian-revolutionary literature acknowledged the thrust of critiques such as that of Lukács.[70] However, it was also clear that formal and methodological concerns were, if not secondary, than at least not the prime motivators of their work (ML 168). Indeed, the choice of the novel as genre was often more tactical, or even coincidental, than anything else. Willi Bredel, for example, wrote *Maschinenfabrik N&K* as a more or less extended factory report, intended for serialization in the KPD Hamburg daily paper, during his imprisonment for "literary treason" in 1930–32, with the genre distinction of "novel" employed largely for publishing purposes.[71] Karl Grünberg likewise points out in the foreword to the 1948 reissue of his 1928 novel *Brennende Ruhr* [Ruhr Valley Burning] that the choice of the form of the novel was largely motivated by the desire to elude censorship in the hostile political climate of the Weimar Republic.[72]

For the proletarian writers of the BPRS, writing was a political and social act. In his account of his authorial beginnings, Hans Marchwitza describes his isolation and need for solidarity as the catalyst of his literary production:

> A person, even one so dejected, has the need—surrounded by cursing and grumbling people, driven by profit-crazed overseers who seemed to regard us as nothing more than machine inventory—to scream out his suffering, to share with someone, to seek friends and comrades who also have an understanding of the humanity in us. . . . A small diary substituted for my much-desired comrade.[73]

Marchwitza describes how this immediate need for expression and interaction became grafted onto political discourse. Many other writers emerging from the Workers' Correspondence movement describe similar motivations, linked to the need for political and emotional solidarity under extreme pressure. In the foreword to his *Ein Prolet Erzählt* [A Proletarian Tells His Story 1930], Ludwig Turek insists on the intrinsic collective value of proletarian experience, writing that "only when all proletarians draw the right conclusions from the experiences that they have in common, then soon they will decide on common action."[74] This notion of the exemplary value of the proletarian author's experience and close connection of this authorial voice to working-class modes expression also informs BPRS proletarian writers' understanding of the mode of address of these novels as "workers writing for workers."[75] As Turek's foreword makes clear, the connection of the autobiographical and the documentary style were linked to the novels' mode of production, written by workers and KPD functionaries in moments stolen from work, family, and party obligations.[76] Otto Gotsche similarly writes of *Märzstürme* [Storms of March 1928/29, 1962], "the book became more of a report of personal experience; it was written under the influence of a present that left no time to polish each and every sentence."[77] It is precisely these elements of reportage and the pathos of immediate experience that are most often singled out for criticism (and self-criticism) in the literary discourse of German communism and that of the GDR.[78]

The question of "class" or "mass" literature revealed a central dilemma of a self-avowedly revolutionary cultural practice. From the point of view of the proletarian-revolutionary literary movement, it was not enough simply to document the proletarian milieu and its mores. Indeed, it was necessary for a literature that saw itself as a catalyst to revolution to reveal the class struggle as the constitutive, if obscured, contradiction of the social reality it set out to map. As Gallas has pointed out in her account of the theoretical debates of the BPRS, it is insufficient for a proletarian literature to stabilize the proletarian milieu through its stylization into something like a subculture:

> Even the function of literature in supplying formulas and symbols of orientation for a specific consciousness of the social situation and strengthening the group consciousness could not be understood for a proletarian literature in the sense of expressing and securing one's own context of living, but rather first and foremost as the sublation of the same. (ML 74)

Such a literature would have to contribute to the destruction of the proletarian milieu itself, along with the structures of capitalist exploitation that sustained that milieu. This necessarily implied relating proletarian experience to the social totality to be transformed by Communist activity or to risk the reduction of proletarian-revolutionary literature to the articulation of an oppositional subculture. Proletarian literature could be understood as either the production of a self-enclosed counterpublic sphere or subculture consolidating its own identity, milieu, and norms or a Marxist mass literature capable of gaining hegemony in the public sphere, a choice that in many ways paralleled the dilemma in which the KPD found itself in the late years of the Weimar Republic. By the late 1920s, it was no longer at the forefront of a broad popular movement but was increasingly isolated as a party of the unemployed.[79] Nevertheless, the KPD organized its members into a wide array of organizations, providing a sense of identity and a counterpublic sphere for many workers.[80] These counterpublic groupings were increasingly beleaguered by the explosion of "new, nonpolitical mass media" as well as new forms of leisure, not only limiting the influence of organizations of the party on the masses but also failing to connect with other classes.[81]

CHAPTER 2

After the Revolution

Hans Marchwitza, The Kumiaks

Already largely completed when Hans Marchwitza crossed into Switzerland in March 1933, *Die Kumiaks* was rewritten over the next months to reflect the extent of the fascist catastrophe in Germany.[1] Following the KPD line, Marchwitza expected Hitler's rule to quickly topple and give way to a renewed revolutionary wave.[2] As the regime consolidated, Marchwitza's book became more ambitious in its scope. Marchwitza's letters to the International Union of Revolutionary Writers in Moscow in 1933 bemoan the situation of political exiles in Switzerland and provide updates on the progress of the novel, which he initially expected to complete in September but by December envisioned as two volumes.[3] The first volume would depict the inflation years of the early Weimar Republic, while the "tendency" of the second volume was to be "the unemployed *Kumpel*,[4] who, due to continuous unemployment and impoverishment, allows himself to be ensnared by Hitler's agitators. Outcome of the second novel: contradictions in National Socialism. No way out for the proletarian." This second volume, written years later in Paris, was lost when the French interned Marchwitza on the eve of World War II.[5]

The novel that Marchwitza published in 1934 turns from narrating political struggles to charting working-class subjectivity in the wake of Germany's 1918 revolution through a thick description of working-class structures of feeling. A chronicle of the daily lives of Ruhr Valley miners during the crisis years of 1922 and 1923, *Die Kumiaks* was intended as an evaluation of the structures of feeling of the German workers' movement in the light of the debacle of 1933, highlighting the "mistakes, failings, and illusionary expectations" along the path of development of the "revolutionary self-awareness of the proletariat."[6] *Die Kumiaks* bears the aesthetic and historical debates of the German antifascist emigration within its narrative structure, developing a hybrid novel form that combines the epic concentration and social mediations of the historical novel in Lukács's definition with the operative emphasis and exemplary characterization that marked the earlier genre of the proletarian autobiography.[7] Hans Marchwitza's novel *Die Kumiaks* can be seen as part of collective effort of German Marxists after 1933 to rethink the limits of the political in relation to the triumph of Nazism. *Die Kumiaks* is often read within the turn to *Epochendarstellung*, or representations of the epoch, represented by works such as Anna Seghers's *The Dead Stay Young* (1949) and Willi Bredel's *Verwandte und Bekannte* [Friends and Relatives 1941–53] trilogy.[8] As Julia Hell has noted, these socialist *Epochendarstellungen* attempt to grasp the historical totality through the narrative coordination of the family narrative and to collect their proliferating subplots into one story, where typically, as in Bredel's trilogy, the socialist horizon marks the reunion of the family members scattered by the historical conflagrations of the century even as the surviving generations redeem the dashed hopes of their progenitors. This narrative reconciliation is often too narrow for the historical dynamics that authors like Bredel and Seghers would pack into it, leading to a conflict between the "centrifugal tendency" of the historical novel, which tends toward the elaboration of subplots and minor characters, and the centering tendencies of the family plot.[9] Indeed, Marchwitza went on to rewrite the second volume of the *Kumiaks* complex upon his return from exile and then to round it off into a Bredel-esque family trilogy, though I have chosen not to discuss the later volumes of the *Kumiak* series, *Die Heimkehr der Kumiaks* [The Homecoming of the Kumiaks 1952] and *Die Kumiaks und ihre Kinder* [The Kumiaks and Their Children 1959] in this chapter.

In this first volume, Marchwitza portrays the arrival of the Kumiak family from Silesia to the Ruhr on the eve of the French occupation of that region in 1923. Driven less by plot than by milieu, *Kumiaks*, not unlike Emile Zola's 1885 *Germinal*, chronicles the misery and petty rebellions of the striking miners, while rumors of a failed revolution arrive from afar. As opposed to the family novel that the *Kumiaks* cycle would become, this first *Kumiaks* novel is less concerned with mapping the flow of history through the generations and more concerned with the present as a complex historical palimpsest. Marchwitza does not yet aspire to the epic scope of these later volumes, both of which span decades of struggle, focusing his book on the crisis year of 1923, which marked the turning point of the post–World War I revolutionary tide in Europe, the beginning of the Stalinization of the USSR, and the rise of fascism.[10] Marchwitza's novel thus has its place alongside the work of Wilhelm Reich, particularly *The Mass Psychology of Fascism* (1933), and Ernst Bloch's 1935 *Heritage of These Times* as an attempt to understand recent German history in terms of the mutual determination of social and psychic structures. Marchwitza, too, explicates the crisis of sovereignty in the revolutionary period, yet he locates it not in the Weimar state as Carl Schmitt did in his 1922 treatise *Political Theology*.[11] Marchwitza discerns the problem in the German working class itself, using the crisis year of 1923 to illuminate a longer historical *durée* of plebeian subalternity.

This crisis can be read in Marchwitza's own paratextual framing of his novel. Published around the time of the First All-Union Writers' Congress in the USSR, *Die Kumiaks* takes Maxim Gorky's pronouncement from his keynote speech as its motto:

> We are living in an epoch of deep-rooted changes in the old ways of life, in an epoch of man's awakening to a sense of his own dignity, when he has come to realize himself as a force which is actually changing the world. As the principal hero of our books we should choose labor, i.e., a person, organized by the forces of labor. (K 8)[12]

Marchwitza omits the rest of Gorky's sentence, which refers to the exercise of labor power in the self-conscious shaping of humanity and nature under the conditions of socialist construction in the Soviet Union. Marchwitza's characters are indeed formed by labor but not necessarily by the "enthusiasm and the spirit of heroic deeds" that Andrei Zhdanov identified as central to Soviet socialist realism,[13] an enthusiasm of socialist construction that is very far from the concerns of the antifascist exile Marchwitza. The formative process of labor in *Die Kumiaks* is rather that of squalor, exploitation, and precarity, and Marchwitza's working-class characters are portrayed as subaltern, indeed creaturely, rather than as heroic fighters for socialism. Despite

Marchwitza's evocation of Gorky's vision of Soviet socialism as the threshold of a new era of human cultural development, the chronicle-like attunement of *Die Kumiaks* to the complicated and multiple temporalities and affects of everyday life reveals the political impasse that underlay the upheavals of the 1930s, which cannot be properly understood as revolutionary but rather as a playing out of social, political, and economic logics of the post–World War I revolutionary period, whether in the terroristic "normalization" of the October Revolution under Stalin or in the National Socialist solution to the latent civil war of Germany's Weimar Republic.

Despite the ample evidence of Marchwitza's unwavering Stalinist commitment, he wrote a novel of surprising political ambiguity. Critics affiliated with the Communist movement were quick to point this out. Willi Bredel, for example, praised the enormous improvement in literary quality over and above Marchwitza's earlier work, while describing the book's ideological weaknesses as a symptom of the KPD's recent neglect of its proletarian writers in favor of cultivating allies among the bourgeois literati in the years immediately preceding the Popular Front turn of the KPD.[14] Kurt Kersten, writing in the Prague-based *Neue deutsche Blätter*, describes the novel's protagonist as "an indifferent proletarian who is pushed back and forth, drifts about, never arrives at his goal, and is unable to form his life within that of his class" and as a "problematic case," and calls *Die Kumiaks* a "problematic book."[15] Similarly, Rudolf Kern's review in *Internationale Literatur* voiced a skeptical reserve toward Marchwitza's depiction of Peter Kumiak, a "boldly stupid-clever Schweik."[16] Echoing Bredel, both reviews praised the plasticity and sensual concreteness of Marchwitza's depiction, while voicing concern about the almost complete absence of the KPD or of positively portrayed Communist figures in the novel. Silvia Schlenstedt has argued that the discomfort that many Communist critics exhibited in their reception of the novel in the mid-1930s arose from a fundamentally constricted concept of literary operativity.[17] This is to say that the reception of *Die Kumiaks* was shaped by a critical paradigm that demanded protagonists whose development and ideological progress the reader could identify with and learn from.[18] Marchwitza's failure was obvious, since he had neglected to portray the positive role of the KPD in the struggles taking place around the Ruhr region in 1923. This was again perceived as a problem of foreground and background, since as Kersten pointed out, putting the politically naive figure of Kumiak at the center of the narrative relegates the decisive events of runaway inflation and the French occupation of the Ruhr to the margins. "Marchwitza has created arresting images from the struggle in the Ruhr," Kersten writes, "but not the struggle itself."[19]

What seemed to irritate Communist readers was precisely the paraleptic quality of Marchwitza's narrative. His characters are in every way marginal to "the action." Living at the edge of the city in a proletarian ghetto, locked out, unemployed, or on strike for most of the novel, politically unorganized or at the edges of debates of the period, they are beside the point from the perspective of Kersten or Bredel. There is indeed a slight irony in Bredel's critique since he had himself, in response to the critique mounted of his own novels by Georg Lukács in *Linkskurve*, called in 1932 for a proletarian-revolutionary literature that would depict not only "heroically heroic deeds" of the proletariat but also "the real, dull, contradictory, heroic *and* stupefying [*stumpfsinnig*] everyday life of the proletariat."[20] This is of course exactly what *Die Kumiaks* does, in a manner equal to Gerhardt Hauptmann's *The Weavers* (1892) or the earlier-mentioned *Germinal*.[21] Since Marchwitza forgoes the kind of proletarian *Entwicklungsroman* that was clearly expected of him (although he would supply it in the 1950s with the second two volumes of the *Kumiaks* trilogy), what we are left with is almost Brechtian in its design, more of a case study than a role model, "not an example of a hero that learns," as Schlenstedt puts it, "but rather a hero from whose depiction one can learn."[22]

The emphasis of the work lies less on identification than on distanced observation of a particular political stance and of the entire constellation of possible positions within the working class. As GDR critic Alfred Klein notes, *Die Kumiaks* uses its protagonist, a proletarian "little man" from the quasi-feudal countryside who has no sense of the recent history of revolutionary upheavals in the Ruhr,[23] as a cipher for a presentation of the "intellectual physiognomy" of the German working class at the moment when the revolutionary aspirations of the early Weimar Republic reached the impasse for which the National Socialists would provide the worst possible resolution.[24] In Marchwitza's novel, this plebeian intellectual physiognomy is shaped by the period between the November revolution and the cycle of working-class rebellion that largely ended in 1923, the year that Marchwitza's novel takes place, and the epochal defeat of the German working class in 1933. The debates among Social Democrats, Communists, anarchists, nationalists, and Christians not only fill in the politically heteroglossic frame of Marchwitza's "capaciously conceived balance of the epoch," but furthermore the interminability of this dialogue suggests the very impasse of the German revolution that Marchwitza is trying to grasp. Benjamin's remarks on the chronicle as an epic form in his review of Anna Seghers's 1937 novel *Die Rettung* [The Rescue] would seem to pertain to *Die Kumiaks* as well. He uses the term "chronicle" to grasp the crisis of the novel form that he had diagnosed as early as his 1927 essay on Alfred Döblin's modernist montage novel *Berlin Alexanderplatz* and would examine in more detail in his famous essay "The Storyteller" in 1936.[25] In these essays, Benjamin sees older, more collective forms of narration, such as the chronicle and the primer, emerging from the wreckage of a classical novel form that had been based on the isolated subjectivity of the writer.[26] Unlike the novel, "in which episodic figures appear through the medium of the main character," in Seghers's novel that medium—"the character's 'fate'—is absent."[27] The chronicle "is not organized in terms of episodes and a principal plot line," instead containing "an abundance of short episodes often building to a climax."[28] The problem of plot thus departs from the "incommensurable figure who serves as the hero of the bourgeois novel" and comes to rest on the way that these episodes are structured by the same catastrophe. Like *Die Kumiaks*, Seghers provides the stories of a community of unemployed minors, but this time on the eve of 1933 instead of 1923 and in the very Silesian mining milieu that Marchwitza's Kumiaks have fled for the Ruhr Valley. The catastrophe that gathers together these stories is, as in Marchwitza, unemployment itself, broadly construed as the underutilization of a whole array of human capacities, desires, and needs that are forced into idleness.[29] The importance of each character lies in his or her proximity to or distance from this catastrophe. In its title the novel evokes both the rescue of a group of miners from a cave-in in the book's opening pages as well as the coming of fascism, which will "rescue" these miners from their idleness "because forced labor is made legal."[30] The rescue that haunts the book is the deferred question, "will these people liberate themselves?"[31] In the deferral of this question, the tragedy of the commoner unfolds in the topos of waiting that structures the novels of both Seghers and Marchwitza. Despite *Die Kumiaks*' central protagonist, the novel's lack of a political center, its attentiveness to the claustrophobia of life on the margins of the social and its episodic narrative and lack of a clear plot all point toward the event that could draw all of this together, a German revolution that has not occurred. *Die Kumiaks* implies that Gorky's "time of deep-seated changes" evoked in its epigraph is also a time of historical blockage, of the nonpunctuality of the revolution, with it the "whole fury of the impossible."[32]

THE KUMIAK-TYPE

Marchwitza analyzes the relationship between place and everyday life from a proletarian standpoint in his 1934 essay "Heimat." Marchwitza casts *Heimat* as a site of desperate attachment and dispossession, writing of the love of the day laborer for the piece of earth he works, "which does not belong to him but costs him unspeakable effort."[33] Marchwitza links this attachment to the desire to "work up to something of one's own," a desire that is constantly negated: "all attachment to the old land is in vain: the power that degrades the worker to a dispossessed slave offers him only this: obey or leave."[34] As with the day laborers, so with the workers, who "defend their often disgusting apartments and dens of starvation when even these have been brought into dispute."[35] The alternative open to the proletariat in the face of state oppression and economic exploitation is to "fall into our misery or the merciless struggle for another way of living, for our justice." Marchwitza writes of a long learning process whereby the proletariat comes to terms with concrete and existential homelessness, arriving at the realization that only the destruction of this anti-*Heimat* can bring forth a *Heimat* of the oppressed: "from the terrible experience, from the toil that still enslaves millions, from our longing and love for a better *Heimat*, our words rise more clearly and penetratingly and shall not cease until we have arrived at the last struggle and until our trust in our justice has been fulfilled."[36] The Kumiak-type that Marchwitza develops in his novel is precisely he who refuses to listen to these words that ought to be, as Marchwitza puts it, rising ever more clearly from experience.

Exile and displacement resonate from *Die Kumiaks'* very first words: "the Kumiaks migrated" (K 9). Yet if the Kumiaks have no country, they do have the vision of one, a native land under erasure, dimly illuminating the empty present from the far corner of the past. This *Heimat* is, however, less a geographical location than it is a forming of fantasy about the peasantry. The novel opens with the Kumiak family underway from West Prussia to the mines of the Ruhr Valley, to which they have been lured by the promise of high wages and the hope of "getting something of their own" (*etwas Eigenes anzuschaffen*) in the west (K 24).[37] These hopes, as much as his poverty, have driven Peter Kumiak from the estate of Herr von Schachanowski, where generations of Kumiaks had worked as day laborers (K 11–12). Well-meaning, good-natured, and politically naive, Kumiak is no critic of the still semifeudal system of Prussian agriculture east of the Elbe.[38] Yet Kumiak has inherited from his mother "furtive hopes and wishes to acquire a modest prosperity through the work of his hands" (K 12). Despite his attachment to the land and to the paternalistic ideology of the Prussian agricultural estates, Kumiak is driven out of West Prussia by the irreconcilability of these furtive hopes and the structure of land-ownership, haunted by the specter of his own father, who died after forty years of farm labor and "couldn't leave behind even a whole acre of his own land after his demise" (K 13).

Marchwitza elaborates with energetic malice on this peasant-cum-proletarian type in a short piece titled "Do You Know Who the Kumiaks Are?" The Kumiak-type, as Marchwitza defines it, is trapped between the peasantry and the proletariat, between village and city, and these dispossessed, irresponsibly breeding nomads spread across Germany like a plague. "From this army of Kumiaks," Marchwitza writes, "the state draws its most obedient soldier, the entrepreneur his most willing and cheapest labor power, and the landowner his most obedient servant." These Kumiaks are thus doubly the remainder of proletarian class formation. On the one hand, they are the foot soldiers of what Marx called the reserve army of the unemployed. On the other hand, they embody precisely the qualities of shortsighted cunning, spontaneous acting out, and dull recalcitrance that the class-conscious worker would be asked to overcome through party discipline. It is the sly passivity of the Kumiak type that Marchwitza, no doubt from his experience as a KPD agitator, finds most frustrating. "They are those people," Marchwitza laments, "who, with knowing smiles, let themselves be lectured and enlightened for hours and days on end on how the way they act is harmful to themselves, and then nevertheless continue on in their old rut, because they don't like to part from habit."[39] Marchwitza links this evasiveness and passivity to what the Kumiaks truly do possess: the hope of finally being able to save up some money and start a better life in an imagined promised land. This pathological hope, which "proved false in the deepest misery, has driven them to the brink of starvation," is the fantasmatic kernel of the Kumiak-type.[40] The desire to get his own is one upon which a Kumiak will not compromise. It is a hope that clings to the promise held out by their own exploitation, a hope founded in the stubborn determination to have their years of exploitation mean something, to redeem the years of drudgery for the security of private property, for *Heimat*, "because in their imagination, there is a new promised land where they hope to find what has thus far been denied them—the luck of finally saving something and beginning a better life." This fantasy of the promised land leads the Kumiaks from one catastrophe to another, poisons their sense of solidarity, and leads them to political passivity. No matter how often their dreams are shattered, the fundamental illusion remains intact. "Their very gaze," Marchwitza writes, "betrays new hopes, hopes that have been proved treacherous by the miseries they have endured." And thus is a Kumiak bound to his suffering, for to fundamentally challenge the social order that guarantees his exploitation is to foreclose the possibility of redemption. This linkage of *etwas Eigenes*, *Heimat*, and political passivity is the essence of Marchwitza's Kumiak-type, a proletarianized peasant.[41]

In the ideological short-circuit between *Heimat* and private property, it is difficult not to be reminded of the role ascribed by Ernst Bloch to the peasantry in what he called *Ungleichzeitigkeit*, or nonsynchronism.[42] "Not all people exist in the same now," Bloch writes, "one has one's times according to where one stands corporeally, above all in terms of classes" (NOD 22). *Ungleichzeitigkeit* denotes for Bloch the mode in which ideologies and aspirations from past modes of production are absorbed but not fulfilled by capitalism, allowing the "motives and reserves from precapitalist times and superstructures" that were supported by these previous modes of production to persist into the present. Because of its own uneven political and economic development, Germany was for Bloch the "classical land of nonsynchronism . . . of unsurmounted remnants of older economic being and consciousness" (NOD 29). These declining remnants of anachronistic but incomplete historical stages project the motives, desires, and needs of the past into the present, where they stand in contradiction to the logic of capital but not in productive contradiction that might lead to revolution; rather they render incomprehensible the firmly synchronous language of communism (NOD 28). The peasantry, for Bloch, stand in contradiction to the Now, the capitalist modernity of the Weimar Republic, both subjectively in the form of pent-up anger, frustration, and turpitude and objectively in the "aftereffects" and "declining remnants" of the "uncompleted past, which has not yet been 'sublated' by capitalism" (NOD 30). These remnants of archaic ideological superstructures will thus become the building materials of National Socialist ideology:

> House, soil, and people [*Haus*, *Boden*, und *Volk*] are examples of such *objectively* delineated contradictions between the traditional and the capitalist Now, within which they are increasingly being destroyed and not replaced. They are both contradictions of the traditional with the capitalist Now as well as elements of the old society which are not yet dead. They were contradictions even in their origins, contradictions to past forms, which never did realize the intended contents of house, soil, or people. Therefore, they were already contradictions of unfulfilled intentions *ab ovo*, quarrels with the past itself.

Nonsynchronous contradictions (and the affective and ideological commitments and investments in these modes of attachment to place that Bloch invokes) may take the form of nostalgic longing, but the imagined past, as Bloch points out, was never equal to the promise held out by the fantasies that it nurtured in its own contradictions. The archaisms of the nonsynchronous are thus also valences of protest "against a Now in which even the last inkling of fulfillment had disappeared" (NOD 32).

From a Marxist viewpoint, this conception of fulfillment through an organic conception of property and place is nothing other than a commitment to one's own subjugation. As Engels wrote in his series of articles on the housing problem in the 1870s, under conditions of industrial capital, the house and garden at the center of the Kumiak fantasy become the "greatest misfortune for the whole working class, the basis for an unexampled depression of wages below their normal level, and that not only for separate districts and branches of enterprise but for the whole country."[43] In more orthodox descriptions of class-based structures of feeling, it is precisely this freedom from the fantasy of liberation that lends the proletariat, as the synchronous class, its revolutionary stance. Engels, for example, writes in *The Housing Question*:

> Only the proletariat created by modern large-scale industry, liberated from all inherited fetters, including those which chained it to the land, and driven in herds into the big towns,

> is in a position to accomplish the great social transformation which will put an end to all class exploitation and all class rule. The old rural hand weavers with hearth and home would never have been able to do it; they would never have been able to conceive such an idea, much less able to desire to carry it out.[44]

The contemporaneity of the proletariat, in this account, arises from the freedom of this class in the form of its very dispossession. The proletariat is, as Marx put it in *Capital*, "Vögelfrei," stripped of rights but also free from attachments,[45] and it is then for this reason that the proletariat, unencumbered by tradition, is in the position to "draw its poetry from the future."[46]

If modern large-scale industry and the revolution in economic conditions that it has wrought have "turned the worker, formerly chained to the land, into a completely propertyless proletarian, liberated from all traditional fetters, a free-outlaw," as Engels has it,[47] then the peasantry, according to Bloch, is one of the primary bearers of *Ungleichzeitigkeit* (along with youth and the petit bourgeoisie).[48] The peasantry are marked by the twin nonsynchronisms of their possession, no matter how paltry, of the means of production and their rootedness in the traditions of work on the land: "they remain attached to the old soil and the cycle of the seasons" (NOD 24). Bloch stresses that the peasant "sobriety as well as property sense and peasant individualism (property as an instrument of freedom, the house as castle)" are essentially precapitalist (NOD 24–25). This "alert sense of property" is directed toward the second element, the agricultural construction of cyclical temporality, based in the seasons, what Marx refers to in his discussion of precapitalist economic formations as the relation of the individual to nature as his own inorganic body.[49] This prelapsarian relationship to land and nature, "the inorganic conditions of human existence"[50] can only be thought within capitalist relations of production in terms of private property, but that juridical relationship does not do justice to this precapitalist identification of the earth not as the property, or *Eigentum* in German, of a legal subject but rather as an aspect of self, or *Eigenschaft*. This sense of a nonantagonistic relationship between one's own activity to one's "natural conditions of production, to land and community" as an "extended body," to paraphrase Marx, is what Negt and Kluge refer to as "originary property" (*Ursprüngliches Eigentum*) (GE 29).[51] This points to a more historically sedimented interpretation of Peter Kumiak's desire to "get something of his own" (*etwas Eigenes anzuschaffen*). Thought of in this way, to have *etwas Eigenes* would mean to have some measure of autonomy over the disposal of one's labor, and in Marchwitza's novel we see that in fact the Kumiak-type is not yet fully integrated in the regime of abstract factory time and discipline.[52] Here property is a defense of peasant time against rationalized labor time, the time of the land against the time of the factory, or as Bloch puts it, property is conceived as "an instrument of freedom" from the industrial discipline and immoderation of the proletariat (NOD 24). Bloch cites the peasant proverb "a job is no good if you have to obey a whistle." This proverb is an index of the collective memory of a process by which the proletariat is constituted through the imposition of regimented labor time and the separation of previously unified work and home as integral modes of experience, a loss that was experienced as a calamity for the working class during its formative period in nineteenth-century Germany.[53]

The peasant relation to property, however, has a deeper relationship to the cyclical construction of temporality, one that evolved not as a defense *of* this temporality but as a defense *against* it. This is the center of the nonsynchronous conflict, which is not that between land and the factory but the ways in which the peasant's desire for land serves as a defense against the precarity of peasant life itself, insofar as property represents the fantasy of security against want and exploitation. As Fredric Jameson points out, "peasant time is *par excellence* the time of oppression."[54] The history of the peasantry, Jameson writes, reflecting on Marxist attempts to define the peasantry as a class, "is to have no history." Jameson is basing his discussion on Marx's notion of the Asiatic mode of production, locus classicus of the oppressed peasant, but he identifies a crucial aspect of the Marxist imaginary when it comes to the land-hungry tenant farmers of the twentieth century, who, following Lenin, make history behind their own backs. Peasant life is figured in the Marxist tradition "as cyclical, as rife with catastrophes of all kinds which cannot, however, lead to genuine historical change."[55] Against the cycles of catastrophe the bit of one's own is precisely a reactionary utopia, a fantasy of return to an imagined "distant epoch when men knew neither death nor toil nor suffering and had a bountiful supply of food merely for the taking."[56]

The structure of feeling organized around these nonsynchronisms of property and temporality not only contradicts a more properly proletarian temporality grounded in the rhythms of machine labor, marked by the segmentations of rationalized time, by strikes and demonstrations,[57] but more specifically it contradicts the Marxist-Leninist construction of history as the progressive unfolding of class struggle and social productive forces. If, as Schlenstedt suggests, we are to take Kumiak as a literary case study rather than as a figure for identification in the sense of the conventional socialist realist hero, a number of insights emerge. First, the Kumiak-figure allows Marchwitza to present us with a genealogy of the historical process of proletarianization in Germany, and one that not only is brought into the "human" scale of an individual life story but demonstrates the unevenness of this process itself in the interactions between the initially naive and rustical Kumiak and the more experienced miners. At the same time, the peasant structure of feeling that Marchwitza diagnoses at the core of the Kumiak-type allows for a practice of representational abjection, where precisely those attitudes, affects, and qualities contributing to the political inertia of the working class can be narratively ascribed to the remainders of peasant ideology that attach themselves to the working class through the Kumiak-type that Marchwitza elaborates. For all the negativity attached to the Kumiak-type in Marchwitza's rendering, there remains an irreducibly utopian kernel to this structure of feeling, for it is the Kumiak-type that insists, in a moments where the loss of *Heimat* has become a mass experience, on happiness.[58]

Like Bloch's texts of this period, *Die Kumiaks* locates much of the appeal of National Socialist ideology in Germany's uneven social and political development, particularly in the tension between the cities and the countryside. Bloch's writings in the crisis years of the Weimar Republic and directly following the fascist seizure of power, collected in *Heritage of Our Times*, come back repeatedly to this question. Thus in texts like "Saxons Without Forests" and "Rough Night in Town and Country," Bloch speaks of fascist ideology as a collapse of urban sensibilities into a rural imaginary that is both a simulacra and a symptom of objective nonsynchronicity; writing "from the country old sap rises into long forgotten shoots, it nourishes National Socialists and folkish mythologists, in short arises as *pastorale militans*" (HT 48). Bloch describes a secret archaic Germany, rooted in the chthonic myths of the soil, as "a giant container of the past; it pours forth from the country towards the town, towards the proletariat and bank capital 'simultaneously,' it is suitable for every terror bank capital needs" (51). This *Blut und Boden* ideology might be anti-urban, but it is produced in cities and consumed by the proletarianized urban middles classes, or *Angestellten*: "Today the town and country are beginning to become superstitious together; even in the town the soil has triumphed over motion and a very old space over time" (52).

Bloch's analysis of nonsynchronicity as a political problem led him to propose a kind of temporal alliance politics, which would "liberate the still possible future from the past by putting them both firmly in the present" (NOD 33). For Bloch, the proletariat represents the absolutely synchronous contradiction of labor and capital, of productive forces and the relations of production, or, as Bloch writes, "its objective manifestation . . . is not a perishing remnant or even an *incomplete past*, but rather the *impeded future*" (33). And yet, precisely for this reason, the language of communism fails to address the kinds of popular fantasies that National Socialism is capable of mobilizing. For Bloch, the constitutive failure of KPD politics in the Weimar Republic was its "lack of any opposite land to myth, any transformation of mythical beginnings into real ones, of Dionysian dreams into revolutionary ones" (HT 60). Marchwitza's novel, on the other hand, dwells on the nonsynchronicities present *within* the German working class, a topic that Bloch's work largely sidesteps.

THE PROMISED LAND

As the novel opens, the Kumiaks enter the industrial landscape of the Ruhr Valley. Marchwitza provides a series of images through the narrative focalization of Peter Kumiak and his wife. The first is the landscape of industrial production, rendered biblically apocalyptic through the eyes of the Kumiaks:

> Then rose the first chimneys. Stark and blacked with smoke, they stretched into the sky, belched up clouds of smoke and darkened the sun. And more and more chimneys grew from this terrain, cramped with great masses of houses, which lost its fresh radiant face and became steadily more hateful. . . . Soon, the suffocating city and the flaming halls, where, immersed in the fiery glow, meager figures ran back and forth, surrounded them. (K 15–16)

This image is followed by the scarcely less bleak image of the miners themselves:

> Then men forced their way into the car, all of them carried the marks of this strange work. Their faces thin and scalded looking, their hands scaly and laced with scars. . . . Their eyes, deep in the sockets, inflamed, lids ringed with black, out of breath, tin flasks over their shoulders, cursing and spitting black filth, they forced their way in. They changed at every station. And if it wasn't crude squabbling provoked over and over on some pretext or another that rang out in the tobacco filled wagon, then it was mockery and laughter. (17)

Finally, the initial description of the miners' housing colony on the outskirts of the city:

> Accompanied by swarms of barefooted children they drew into the massive square of barracks, whose tall and wide house-fronts closed off their inhabitants from the rest of the city like a fortress wall. The miners [*Kumpels*] squatted against the houses, bearded, the rims of their eyes still black from the completed shift. Next to them the women, chattering, children all around them, children on their breasts and already back in the family way. The streets that divided the colony into four great blocks teemed like an anthill. . . . They [the Kumiaks] felt a silent refusal, since the colony was crammed full with people, and each one coming in took away a little something of the remaining space. (20–21)[59]

In all three of the passages just cited, Marchwitza is mobilizing fairly standard descriptive conventions of Weimar proletarian literature.[60] Evocations of the demonic landscape of industry were a staple of the older German *Arbeiterdichtung* of the late nineteenth and early twentieth centuries, where they stood for the destruction of traditional life worlds and paternalistic social relationships in the countryside, expressing a melancholy attachment to a mythical pastoralism. On the other hand, the Weimar Republic produced a proliferation of images of proletarian tenements and back courtyards, or *Hinterhöfe*, which were the primary venues of working-class squalor and sociability alike. These depictions of the so-called Zille milieu "of the human fauna crowding Berlin's proletarian quarters," with their "undernourished children, workers, wretched girls, organ grinders in ugly backyards, destitute women and nondescripts idling away their time," were a staple of Weimar cinema and Neue Sachlichkeit literature and journalism.[61] Indeed, such depictions often served Weimar Germany's culture industry as picturesque backdrops for more traditional mass entertainment genres. This is the basis of Walter Benjamin's accusation against Neue Sachlichkeit that "it has made the struggle against poverty an article of consumption" (AP 776).

Marchwitza's landscape descriptions in these opening passages interrupt the dynamic of foreground and background, canceling out the "safe perspective," the "aestheticizing distance" that would enable Marchwitza's characters to contemplate this landscape as an aesthetic object.[62] This is not a landscape at all but an event and a network of relationships that Marchwitza is describing (but not narrating; that will come later), rendered here as a site. Following Raymond Williams's observation that "a working country is almost never a landscape," W. J. T. Mitchell argues that if landscape, as a matrix of representation, corresponds to something like the symbolic order, which is concerned with establishing boundaries and normative ways of looking and seeing, place itself can be regarded "as the location of the Lacanian Real, the site of trauma or the historical event."[63] Place is where something has happened, and this is what the Kumiak family sees from the window of the train: the traces of the social revolution of modern industrial capitalism. It is precisely the relation between the fire-spewing factories and the squalor of the Zille milieu that is the historical break that they have not yet experienced but into which they are now drawn. The uncanny nature of this traumatic inscription into modern industrial labor, an event that has happened, but for Kumiak himself is still to come, is evoked when Kumiak encounters another man who bears his name on the train. Frau Kumiak compares her husband with this "haggard and twitchy" stranger: "like night and day, so different were the two men. There, the healthy life overflowing with vitality, here a meager heap of bones" (K 18).

Focalizing these scenes through the Kumiaks, for whom this world is anything but the already commodified image of Neue Sachlichkeit montage, Marchwitza renders these scenes of proletarian life not from the eye of the worker but from that of the peasant-foreigner. These scenes highlight what Jacques Rancière discusses as the shock effect of the factory upon the gaze of the foreigner:

> what the foreigner perceives, in the noise and dirt of the factory, as the intolerable itself, is the assault upon the gaze. The factory is in the first place an uninterrupted movement that hurts the eyes, that gives you a headache. It is a constant and unceasing procession of sensory shocks, in which, along with the ability to look, the possibility of thoughtfulness and respect is lost.[64]

In Marchwitza's novel, the factory as the site of this assault on perception is generalized outward to embrace the totality of the proletarian life world. The factory explodes the concentrated gaze; it is a space of distraction, which, like the modern mass media of film for writers like Kracauer and Benjamin, sets in train a complicated dynamic of shock and interpretation that seeks to reinscribe the spectacle of production into some sensible frame of representation, to reestablish a sense of scale and the minimal distance required to make sense of this sight.[65] For Rancière, the question is not one of representation, though; it is the question of the proper gesture, the relationship to practice that would "liberate the gaze from the assault that both shock and interpretation lay to it."[66] Here one is reminded of Benjamin's thesis that distraction as a mode of perception marks a shift from contemplation, absorption, and visuality to the tactile and corporeal, for example, in the heightened and "twitchy" attentiveness of the stranger-Kumiak that our protagonist had encountered on the train, which becomes a form of bodily habituation to the mechanized rhythms of industrial labor.[67]

Marchwitza's novel suggests that something like a proletarian affective constellation, or structure of feeling, can be read out of the labor process itself. Along with this structure of feeling, a specific proletarian stance, or gestural habitus, would be implied as well. This habitus is itself caught up in the play of shock and interpretation described by Rancière, and the trope of the rural foreigner entering the world of the factory allows Marchwitza to recapitulate in the first chapters of *Die Kumiaks* the fraught experience of what could be described as a cultural revolution, whereby the peasantry was transformed into the industrial proletariat through the reshaping of the perception and habitus of the worker in the complicated interplay of the discipline of the factory and the pressures of proletarian everyday life.[68] Kumiak's first shifts in the mine are depicted as a sort of breakdown of his relation to his own body and the instruments of labor, a crisis of habituation, reducing Kumiak to a "dream state" where his corporeal disorientation, his inability to grasp the signs and signals of the mine as a semiotic system, is experienced as a being in the way:

> Kumiak stumbled, holding his lantern clumsily in front of him with his right hand, behind the advancing boarders. A band of ragged characters ran in front of him and behind him. He was pushed heedlessly aside. The many lanterns blinded him. He was unable to see a meter in front of himself, bumped his feet against the controls for the tracks, and his body ran with sweat, despite the sharp draught of air that swept through the long and dark passage. (K 34)

The labor of mining is described here as monotonous and dangerous, a task of managing constant physical shocks, whereby the laborer must conform to the labor process itself in order to avoid injury and death, as Kumiak narrowly escapes being run over, crushed, and blown up in the hectic shafts of the mine. Through these shocks, the labor process is inscribed into the perceptual faculty of the worker. Thus after a few weeks,

> [Kumiak] had . . . adjusted to the work. After the first shift he was so sick of it that he considered fleeing, even suicide. Now, however, it was different. With time he had copied a lot from the *Kumpels*, adapted himself to their routine, learned to walk crouched over, watched for obstacles so that he didn't bang up his legs, he noticed each wood splinter so as not to poke his eyes out, could soon deal with the wagons that were badly greased, and knew how he had to prop them. (K 53)

Marchwitza describes this dulling and hardening of perception and consciousness with a relatively elaborate affective typology, the central term of which is *Stumpfsinn*, a word carrying connotations of both boredom and stupefaction. He draws out this affective stance in the contrast between the newly arrived Kumiak, "burning with expectation," and the other *Kumpels*, who "trotted along sleepily, indeed almost in a stupor [*fast stumpfsinnig*]" (K 31). Similarly, the labor of mining itself is described as "years of stupefying molestation and torment [*stumpfsinninge Schindenmüssen*]" (179). *Stumpfsinn* is adaptive armoring, mimetic precisely in the sense evoked by Adorno: "mimetic behavior does not imitate something but assimilates itself to that something."[69] Thought of in these terms, *Stumpfsinn* becomes a sort of code of conduct, or body armor, for the worker and, in that capacity, indeed a way of marking the boundary between worker and creature.

For Klaus Theweleit, the armored body, or body ego, is an attempt to construct psychic boundaries by a subject whose own ego is conditioned not by the classical Freudian Oedipal complex but rather from outside, which is to say directly by social disciplinary agencies.[70] The resulting ego is a bodily ego, taking the rigidly drilled body of the militaristic subject as its ideal and taking as its vocation the violent annihilation of whatever threatens its integrity.[71] While Theweleit develops this notion in relation to writings published by protofascist former Freikorps members in the Weimar Republic, Michael Rohrwasser refunctions this notion to apply to the "hard Communist" types in the novels of the BPRS, not least the early works of Marchwitza, in his *Saubere Mädel: Starke Genossen*. Rohrwasser argues that the proletarian novels of the Weimar Republic had tended to valorize proletarian interests in the sphere of workplace action and state politics, echoing what Wilhelm Reich had criticized as the "fetishization of high politics," and hence either excluded the private lives (domesticity, sexuality, leisure activities, etc.) of the characters or portrayed these elements as structurally unrelated to the properly political conflicts that drive the plots of these novels.[72] According to Rohrwasser, the tendency to downplay not only private life but also the production of subjective fantasy is expressive of a deeper psychic structure at work within the ideological matrix of both German communism and the novels of proletarian authors: the disavowal of subjective alienation in the face of capitalist production and social relations.[73]

Thus the repression of the experience of alienation in the direct labor process makes it impossible to recognize alienation in other social relations, particularly family life. The result is a one-sided division of progressive and rational political discourse on the one hand and "private clichés" on the other. Thus as Communist discourse appropriates wholesale the values of the capitalist production process, and "the virtues of the factory owner: punctuality, discipline, the maximizing of functions were also the virtues of the Communists," in these books, abstract politics banish other human and social needs to the "private sphere," where they vegetate as kitsch.[74] *Die Kumiaks* differs from this model in that it lacks this dimension of high politics and party discipline to secure the borders of its characters; instead, Marchwitza locates the process of bodily armoring directly in the spontaneous conditions of working-class life. In this, Marchwitza's characterization of the miners' milieu in *Die Kumiaks* approaches Hannah Arendt's theorization of *animal laborans* in her study *The Human Condition* (1958). For Arendt, the laborer is reduced through labor to the condition of "toil and pain" and rendered creaturely through the subordination to brute necessity and the inability to decide. Yet whereas Arendt sees this as a subjection to "necessity," Marchwitza's novel suggests that this state is less a property of labor itself than the exploitation of labor through capital.[75]

Helmut Lethen argues that the code of conduct indicates a mode of behavior that is externally directed, one that is attuned to patterns of signal and response; it is a mode of response that Lethen identifies with Neue Sachlichkeit in its radical exteriority and orientation toward surface at the expense of depth.[76] Ultimately the code of conduct is a technique for regulating gesture and affect, for avoiding shame and exposure.[77] The creature, on the other hand, is the figure of broken and exposed being, which cannot read the signals and regulate its behavior accordingly. If the code of conduct allows mastery over affect and appearance, an intentional and artificial staging of self, the creature is precisely the figure for a subjectivity that is involuntary, an "organic bundle of reflexes, in mortal need."[78] The creature evokes terror and pity precisely in its abject lack of self-control. It is given over wholly to suffering and to expression. Lethen further remarks that the "great achievement" of the Weimar Republic's proletarian-revolutionary literature "was to sever the worker's image from the creature's."[79] And yet this achievement itself comes at a price. Nor is it irrevocable: in *Die Kumiaks*, *Stumpfsinn* is described as an affect that barely contains a dangerous smoldering tension. Beneath this apparent stupefaction lie "hostility, rage, and hate" (K 134).

In order to understand the emphasis that Marchwitza places on *Stumpfsinn*, however, we must turn to another familiar affective category, that of claustrophobia, or *Enge*. The motif of *Enge* unifies the various descriptions of privation and exploitation in Marchwitza's novel. There is the overcrowding of the colony, the closure of the horizon by the massive tenements, the thick, toxic air full of the sounds of industry bearing down. *Enge* is not simply a fact of the environment but emanates from the characters themselves, as the blocked desires and needs of the proletarian milieu colonize every aspect of the workers' social lives through "enmity, rage and hatred," born of helplessness and deprivation.[80] It mediates between domesticity and the world of labor, missing in the novels of the BPRS during the Weimar Republic, since both spheres are determined by the same logic of claustrophobia, where, to paraphrase Marchwitza's description of the miners' colony, the satisfaction of any particular need or desire is to be had only through the renunciation of another.

As Klein notes in his reading of the novel, "the spheres of work and the proletarian family life are so intertwined with one another, that an almost classically proportioned image emerges of the reciprocal conditionality and dependency of these two poles of working class everyday life."[81] Mother Kumiak curses her apartment as an *enges Loch*, a narrow hole, where she can barely move (K 81), and the mine shaft where Kumiak works first as a hauler and then as a hewer's apprentice is no different: "in the stifling mountain, each man was in the other's way" (138).

Indeed, the proletarian milieu of Marchwitza's novel becomes a zone of the creaturely precisely insofar as it is the place in which the distance between life and the immediate needs of the body is most brutally canceled out. *Enge* in this sense is the reduction of the self to bodily need, so that every interaction with the crowding masses of *Kumpels*, neighbors, and boarders takes on the aspect of a bitter struggle for survival. The intractability of these crises leads to a sense of entrapment and hopelessness that cuts across the territorial division between the private and the public. As Messerschmidt puts it in her reading of *Die Kumiaks*, the impasse of proletarian daily life and the urgency of revolutionary change "no longer occur solely in the political realm, but now penetrate the entire proletarian way of life."[82] But as we shall see in the next section, Marchwitza largely amputates the dimension of political struggle from this working-class milieu. As crisis after crisis unfolds, the *Enge* of life in the miners' colony becomes ever more acute. "Something had to happen to free them from these surroundings," Frau Kumiak ruminates, waiting in vain for a "clue to a way out" (K 79, 82). The lines of escape are blocked from "this dog's life," and nothing remains but for Kumiak to gird his loins and "carry on in his misery and hope for the bit of luck that would save him from all of this" (K 108).[83]

What Marchwitza denotes as *Stumpfsinn*, this affective and material confinement at the core of proletarian experience, the impossibility of *avoiding* solidarity in these close quarters, corresponds then to what social historian Alf Lüdtke theorizes as the typical proletarian *Gestus* of *Eigensinn*, or obstinacy: a "brusque and contrary behavior directed against 'everybody' and 'everything'"; a stance that served as a "partial compensation" for the deprivations of proletarian life.[84] The behaviors encompassed by *Eigensinn*, from idiosyncratic hobbies to unauthorized work breaks and horseplay, allowed workers to distance themselves from the alienating effects of industrial production and work discipline. Lüdtke argues that in a situation where solidarity and cooperation were unavoidable, "workers often demonstrated a mutual distance in a variety of ways. They played harmless or nasty pranks on each other, and practiced a willful *Eigensinn*, a mixture of self-affirmation and prankish obstinacy."[85] *Eigensinn* must also thus be understood as a form of appropriation, or *Aneignung*, making one's own, in German, of alienated social structures. Horseplay, for example, which was based on displays and challenges of physical strength and dexterity, simultaneously interrupted the rhythm of labor and dramatized its conditions, allowing workers to stage and rehearse the proletarian body ego.

Eigensinn should not be understood as an oppositional politics. Lüdtke stresses the system-integrating function of *Eigensinn*, writing, "no praxis developed from it which might have saturated everyday life with a basic tone of resistance." *Eigensinn* for Lüdtke thus reinforces the wage-labor system by providing it with an outlet for "relieving the pressure of daily distress."[86] *Eigensinn* is not a political stance but rather a structure of feeling that is characterized by a lack of cognitive relation between the personal and the social, what Lüdtke describes as an experientially noncontradictory patchwork between the private and the political.[87] In the behaviors of *Eigensinn*, the political sphere is approached from the individualizing perspective of "formulating and gratifying *one's own* interest,"[88] or "etwas Eigenes anzuschaffen" to quote again Marchwitza, which often led workers to political activism in defense of their own personal priorities but just as often caused them to greet political agitation with indifference. In Marchwitza's novel, however, it is precisely the fantasy of escaping from this *Enge* that sustains it, since in the dreams of a bit of one's own that cause the workers to be beholden to the drudgery of the mine any hope of solidarity is eviscerated. This constraining hope, we have seen, is the kernel of Marchwitza's Kumiak-type. Through this association with the peasantry, Marchwitza gestures to the long history of dispossession and disappointment of the German masses, the *deutsche Misère* discussed earlier, but shows through the figure of the Kumiak-type how the nonsynchronous expectations of a history of exploitation persist in stubborn insistence, how they return to haunt the proletariat. For as the novel unfolds and the fantasy of the promised land congeals into the stupor of *Stumpfsinn*, the peasant structure of feeling of the Kumiak-type crosses a specific proletarian structure of feeling, where the desire for *etwas Eigenes* surrenders to a dull resignation and a stance of passive hostility. For Marchwitza, this is the meaning of such commonsense bits of advice passed around the mine and colony as "the weaker one always has to give in, and he can shoot off his mouth as much as he wants, the one that's stronger always gets the upper hand."[89]

PASSIVE RESISTANCE

As we have seen, from the point of view of a certain mode of the Marxist imaginary, the relation to history as a collective process or as a cyclical unfolding of personal disasters is one of the primary oppositions between the consciousness of the proletariat and that of the peasantry. In his analysis of the Kumiak-type precisely through the tropes of proletarian daily life, Marchwitza's text is not so much a critique of the ideological backwardness of the German peasantry as it is gesturing to what Oskar Negt and Alexander Kluge would refer to in *Geschichte und Eigensinn* as "the peasant in me," implying an irreducible kernel of nonsynchronism inhering within experience itself as a category of historical perception, which they theorize as a collective obstinacy, or *Eigensinn*. Like Lüdtke, Negt and Kluge use *Eigensinn* as a term that cuts across the division of individual and group in relation to social forces. Here *Eigensinn* represents the ensemble of capacities, needs, and potentials that are simultaneously generated and foreclosed through the development of the division of labor.

As Christopher Pavesk notes, Negt and Kluge's deployment of *Eigensinn* relies on their notion of separation, or *Trennung*, as the driving force of the division of labor and the reifying processes of capitalist society. Pavesk writes, "the repeated acts of separation thus demand and create new labor capacities at the same time that they render others obsolete and sunder them from the contexts in which they had their meaning."[90] The fragmentation, partial annexation, and repression of the subject and of precapitalist modes of life, labor, and perception by commodity-mediated social structures create modes of subterranean resistance, the stubborn insistence of qualities and desires that can find no outlet in the social field. "*Eigensinn*," Negt and Kluge write, "is no 'natural' quality, but rather arises from a bitter plight; it is the protest, drawn together at a single point, against expropriation, the result of the appropriation of one's own senses and meanings that lead to the outside world" (GE 766). *Eigensinn* is thus the mode in which labor power exceeds its constitution as a commodity, in which there is always something more or less to a person than her capacity to generate value, and it is at the same time the inarticulate collective memory of dispossession.[91] "If *Eigensinn* is founded in the expropriated human senses," Negt and Kluge write, "it nevertheless lives on under the earth, as collective memory" (767).

Geschichte und Eigensinn grounds this mode of collective memory in a particularly German context, and Negt and Kluge elaborate the concept through a reading of a well-known Grimms' fairy tale, "The Obstinate Child," or "Das eigensinnige Kind." The fairy tale belongs to the context of the feudal German peasantry. If classical Greek mythology represents the collective history of the colonist and the capitalist, holding up the virtues of guile and manipulation, the German fairy tale is the record of those who will be dispossessed, related to capacities of labor and differentiation, the skill to tell friend from foe (GE 752–54). Here the central problem is how to discern the enemy who would annex one's labor and its instruments, to outwit the forces of expropriation in whatever guise they may appear, to see through whatever cunning they might deploy. This is the mythology of the house, a defensive position (754). In this sense, *Eigensinn* is the persistent claim of a precapitalist mode of originary property not as an alienable thing but as a relationship to one's own activity, to the earth, and to the community. Yet for Negt and Kluge, neither primitive accumulation nor original property is to be understood in a strictly historical sense, as things and events, but as a continuous process of differentiation where new capacities for cooperation come into being and are expropriated, fragmented, or suppressed in the continuing social dynamics of accumulation and reification. It is in fact rather analogous to the particularly German notion of *Heimat*, the irreducible kernel of Marchwitza's Kumiak-type.

In both Negt and Kluge and Lüdtke's accounts, *Eigensinn* is a paradoxical formation. It is an affect that manifests itself in specific behaviors, a memory that is only legible in seemingly disconnected and unrelated practices. It is collective yet acted and experienced by isolated individuals.[92] As an adaptive rebellion or a spontaneous explosion of rage, *Eigensinn* moves between Michel de Certeau's "ways of operating," tactical everyday practices designed to secure one's own space in a pre-given system,[93] and what Otto Rühle describes as plebeian protest, spontaneous uprisings against the order of exploitation that surge with radicalism that quickly dissipates into apathy upon defeat.[94] Although *Eigensinn* arises from the potentials for cooperation inscribed within the process of separation, it appears in isolated modes. Negt and Kluge write, "the motives extracted from society do not simply disappear from the entire economy of qualities, but rather work on there where they are best protected, in the subject. The *Eigensinn* of rebellion appears, in pupation so to speak, in the form of the private" (GE 765).

Yet as we have seen, the form of the private is precisely what precludes any collective overcoming of the proletarian context of living. *Eigensinn*, though, is neither public nor private, neither individual nor collective; rather, like affect and habit more generally, it marks the instability of these categories for describing subjectivity. Lüdtke, for example, comments on the "lack of contexts" that characterizes *Eigensinn* as a structure of feeling consisting of a patchwork of politicization and privatization, where the personal and the social exist next to one another in the mind of the worker without any necessary relation.[95] Finally, *Eigensinn* is a *proletarian* affect in both of these accounts. For Lüdtke, this is so in the historical and sociological sense, whereas for Negt and Kluge, proletarian denotes "all interests, desires, and labor capacities that cannot find their realization in the bourgeois public sphere."[96] In this sense, *Eigensinn* is a way to conceive of precisely the *Ungleichzeitigkeit* of the proletariat itself and, contra Bloch, the multiple and overlapping temporalities that have attached themselves to the long cultural revolution of proletarianization. As Pavesk points out, these are precisely the "historical and moral" elements of labor power, "those aspects of subjective identity, of subjective productive capacity, which exceed the reduction of labor power as a commodity."[97] This also, though, implies a history, "a subterranean historiography of aborted utopias."[98]

Marchwitza situates his novel precisely in the shadow of aborted utopia, which is to say in the wake of the 1918 revolution and its violent suppression by the SPD and the Freikorps. Locating his novel in the crisis year of 1923, Marchwitza supplies the reader less with a definition of this specifically proletarian structure of feeling than with a historical synecdoche: "passive resistance."[99] The policy of passive resistance allows Marchwitza to depict the political positions being articulated by various characters in the mine and the colony, including the aptly named anarchist Schwarz and the nationalist saboteur Baum (both of whom are eventually executed by French occupation forces), the Rhineland separatist Klein, and the Bible study group that forms around the pious miner Martin Fuchs. The novel lays its main emphasis on the arguments between Social Democratic miner Schumann, who wants to avoid violence and preserve the union, all the while knowing that the policy of passive resistance is in itself senseless, since "the currency devaluation would have to degenerate into a hunger catastrophe" (K 189), and Schwarz, an anarchist who condemns passive resistance as a game played by the SPD and unions to paralyze the workers' resistance to the occupation, telling Schumann, "you can suck up to your union bosses, but they won't stop us from saving our necks," and urging direct action against the French (172). The KPD's perspective remains curiously unarticulated, as the works councilman Saletzki, one of the novel's few presumably Communist characters,[100] is given to consider only that the cowardice of the German government and the unions has left no room for maneuver and nothing remains but to support the policy of passive resistance, despite the obvious fact that the French will "come up with their own people, who will only have to unload the coal and coke inventory" (174).

There is no possibility given in the novel of taking an active political position in the face of the French occupation, only for outbursts of spontaneous violence and sullen resignation. As the plot unfolds, Marchwitza gives examples of the miners acting out each of these affective stances and shows them to be mutually conditioned and conditioning. Thus, following the French occupation of the mine and arrest of the works' councillors, Schwarz is able to convince the enraged miners to destroy the mine shaft, over the feeble protests of Schumann. The wrecking of the mine itself is figured less as an act of resistance than as a childish acting-out, conflating political crisis and the rage and desperation of daily exploitation and privation. "It seemed," writes Marchwitza, "that even in those who had always been among the most reasonable among them, the hatred for the long years of tedious [*stumpfsinnig*] excoriation raged" (K 179). Only Lewandowski and Kruschin stand aside, Kruschin scolding, "that doesn't help us in the least, when we destroy the shaft. The gents will stay up on top all the same, and the slave-driving will just start right back up" (179). After the sabotage of the mine, the everyday rhythm of passive resistance sets in, an idyll of sorts, despite the misery and hunger of the Ruhr miners. "People had gotten so accustomed to the passive resistance," Marchwitza writes of the miners, "that some wished in secret that it might stay this way forever" (186). The *Kumpels* lie around the wrecked shaft, joking and racing mice, and yet all of this is colored by a rising boredom and rage:

> the monotony and stupor [*Stumpfsinn*] in the pit grew ever stronger. The *Kumpels* lay or sat around at the brake center, which for a while now had been the meeting place of everyone from the various coalfaces. In their derisive jests was a boundless bitterness, a self-mockery intended to cover up the restlessness in which they all found themselves. They were consumed by a barely contained rage over their hardship, which seemed to have no end. They irritably attacked one another at the slightest excuse. (188)

Earlier in the novel, *Stumpfsinn* had been the affect proper to the work in the mines; here it becomes that of an idleness enforced by the political impasse of passive resistance. When the mine's management attempts to compel the *Kumpels* back to work in disregard of the policy of the German government, there is a brief loosening of the *Stumpfsinn* that the politics of passive resistance "had allowed to breed mutely and drowsily" (233) while in Berlin the government falls and the mine erupts into daily political meetings. Saletzki sees at this point that "passive resistance could only end in failure unless they went over to the attack," and this is precisely what happens (233). As prices soar and the government runs out of money, the *Kumpels* lie about in the mines and wait, worn down by hunger and uncertainty.

The political stupor of the *Kumpels* emerges in stark contrast during the one moment of their active intervention in the book. This occurs when the workers learn that petit-bourgeois elements in the city have proclaimed a separatist Rhineland Republic under the protection of the French occupation. The workers assemble and quickly disarm the separatists, storm the city hall, and "[return] to the colony as victors." "They felt," Marchwitza writes with reference to the Red Army of the Ruhr, "the way they had felt in 1920, in that month of March when, storming ahead as a workers' army, they took city after city" (K 241). Toppling the Rhineland Republic, however, has little impact on the miners' own situation, and the conditions of passive resistance quickly reassert themselves. The tension of the miners' waiting finally culminates in a macabre bit of horseplay that seems intended to force the impasse after the German government announces that it will no longer pay out wages and the mine management demands an unconditional return to work. The ensuing strike has little effect, and the hunger demonstrations at city hall likewise yield no results.

In the midst of this misery, the workers are surprised one morning by a makeshift gallows erected in front of the mine administration building. "A restrained tension prevailed," Marchwitza writes, "as if in the next moment something out of the ordinary had to happen" (K 243). What follows is precisely a compensatory staging of escape from the double bind of *Enge* and *Stumpfsinn*, where the fantasized murder of the exploiter supports the fantasy of a life without exploitation:

> one could recognize in the gleaming eyes and the dark expressions how each one wished to conjure his worst tormentor, so as to bring him to the gallows. Oh, for many it was a glorious pleasure in their thoughts to savor the terror and moaning of such an antagonist. . . . They began to joke, but in this joking lay a dangerous gravity. (244)

The truth behind this play is that the worst tormentor is none other than oneself: "at first, he [Kumiak] felt the need to lay the noose around his own neck" (K 244). The identification of the production supervisor Kanopka as the first victim of the mock execution is a substitution motivated by Kanopka's recognition of the "deadly earnestness" of this game. This is to say that Kanopka places himself outside the circle (or more literally inside it) of this game by displaying fear instead of rage, thus marking him as a suitable stand-in for this self-directed eruption of violence (244–45). Before Kumiak's attention is redirected to Kanopka, it is the ensemble of defeated expectations and unemployed capacities, from the hopes of the peasants to the properly political dimension of the largely absent KPD, from the disorder of proletarian living conditions to the skills developed in partial and alienated forms in capitalist production, that collapse upon themselves within Kumiak. At this moment, it becomes clear that the Kumiak-type is an inadequate basis for portraying the broader narrative of class struggle that now breaks through its periphery, since this last desperate moment of self-annihilation is the only act of rebellion of which Peter Kumiak is capable.

Again it is Saletzki who voices Marchwitza's vague political gloss of the situation. "Hanging some little tormentor isn't enough," he points out, "to force better working conditions and bread" (K 248). Saletzki is able to talk the miners into taking down the gallows by invoking the importance of political discipline, but he is unable to offer them anything other than the insight that "this is not how our struggle should look" (250). The gallows episode is the dead end of *Eigensinn* in Marchwitza's novel. "Everything's finished for me," mumbles Kudiatzeck, the "executioner" in the game that Saletzki has ended. Far from channeling the energy of the *Kumpels* into the realm of political action, Saletzki's intervention results in further listlessness and disillusionment, as the miners wander home:

> Kumiak, who couldn't cope with all of this, followed them utterly defeated. So even this meager joy was done with. No one could have moved him to remain for the meeting that was to follow. Just go home and not think about anything. If people were so little in agreement about all of it, what was left other than simply to lie down and wait to die of starvation? (251)

In this passage, passive resistance crosses into pure passivity, as Marchwitza has led the Kumiak-figure to what would seem to be the renunciation of *etwas Eigenes*. Passive resistance, at least for Marchwitza, is in fact the truth of *Eigensinn*. All of the episodes of *Eigensinn* in the novel are immediately coded as essentially passive, as the mere appearance of activity, political or otherwise. Undisciplined and undirected, *Eigensinn* in *Die Kumiaks* resembles nothing so much as what Slavoj Žižek denotes as "interpassivity," wherein "the subject is incessantly, even frantically active, while displacing onto another the fundamental passivity of his/her being."[101]

Marchwitza's evocations of *Eigensinn* are not restricted to the mines. Even the tenuous bonds of social order have broken down in the colony as well, as the miners, their wives, and their children loot the supply trains and prostitute themselves to the soldiers of the occupation. As Alfred Klein notes, the breakthrough that Marchwitza achieves with *Die Kumiaks* over and against his previous books lies in the portrayal of a situation in which "public and private, personal and social, collective and individual become so closely interwoven that one continues to cross over into the other."[102]

Nevertheless, the novel itself expresses the epic connection between the political and the personal through a common affective register rather than through any specific politics. *Die Kumiaks* provides "an uncompromising phenomenology of the hatred born from privation and powerlessness."[103] This affective register itself, Marchwitza suggests, responds to the impasse of working-class daily life as the ongoing crisis or trauma of its own all-embracing immediacy, which is to say that like the assault of the factory upon the gaze of the foreigner evoked earlier by reference to Rancière, this life is always too close and too much; one cannot gain a point of purchase on it. This is to say that the crisis does not end, and neither the crisis nor the novel offers a possibility of resolution, just as they offer no lines of escape. Frau Kumiak seeks in vain "advice, sympathy, some indication of a way out" (K 81), just as Kumiak himself despairs of this "dog-like life" (108). This question of immediacy and *Enge*, the inability to achieve a minimal distance from the conditions of existence, is indeed repeatedly figured in *Die Kumiaks* in terms of the creaturely. The miners cringe before the mine's director "with the timidity of animals accustomed to being beaten" (68), a drunken Kumiak arriving home is described as an "evil animal" (124), and so forth.

We have seen how *Eigensinn* can itself be understood as a code of conduct, a forestalling of creatureliness. The Kumiak-type that Marchwitza develops seems to be precisely a threshold between these terms, a zone of undecidability. This threshold is a guiding thread to Marchwitza's oeuvre, and it is usually read through the lens of the Marxist humanism that no doubt informed Marchwitza's conception of what a life deserving to be called human might look like. At the same time it marks out what

> personhood means for the worker at the given historical stage, nothing less than an inhuman existence, wherein the hatred of one's own work and the hatred of the workers among one another develop into an everyday phenomenon, wherein naked existential fear triumphs over the will to revolt, and wherein isolated outbreaks of desperation only increase misery.[104]

Humanism here is arrived at negatively, through the exploration of the realm of the creaturely. The creaturely is not the frontier of but a zone within the human. This is as true of Marchwitza as it is of Kafka, in whose work, as Eric Santner has argued, "creatureliness is a by-product of exposure to what we might call the excitations of power, those enigmatic bits of address and interpellation that disturb the social space—and bodies—of his protagonists."[105] In other words, we have to regard the creaturely in this sense as a dimension of the social, or more precisely, in Santner's psychoanalytically informed formulation, a state that is called into being through the contradiction between the explicit content of the law and the surplus violence through which law is materially grounded, it arises at the "threshold of law and non-law."[106]

Marchwitza's novel situates its narrative two years after the defeat of the Red Army of the Ruhr in April 1920 and closes with rumors of the disastrous "German October" of 1923, when the KPD staged an abortive uprising in Hamburg (K 250). The unarticulated narrative frame of *Die Kumiaks* is the endgame of the post–World War I revolutionary period, when the political energies and socialist aspirations of the German working class were being violently suppressed.[107] Marchwitza's book places its characters in what Walter Benjamin refers to as the "state of emergency" in his theses on the concept of history, where he writes, "the tradition of the oppressed teaches us that the 'state of exception' in which we live is not the exception but the rule."[108] Yet rather than reading *Die Kumiaks* as an illustration of a Benjaminian ontological truism, Benjamin's claim, precisely in its historically unanchored generality, calls for a look at the way that Marchwitza handles the question of periodization in his novel. After all, the crisis period of the early Weimar Republic was of course the moment in which Carl Schmitt, in his 1922 *Political Theology*, framed his own discussion of sovereignty as precisely the capacity to "decide on the exception," to determine "whether there is a state of emergency as well as what must be done to eliminate it."[109] Schmitt's notion of the state of exception is connected to his notion of dictatorship elaborated the previous year. The problem that Schmitt is addressing with these concepts was the crisis of sovereignty of the Weimar state. During this period of unrest, the state made excessive use of violence and terror to force the revolutionary workers into passivity. The white terror was largely successful, and in the aftermath of the confusing and violent loss of the revolution, most workers were driven into resignation and attempted to retain what little private advantage was to be had from the new political dispensation.[110]

The effects of this violence have been described by Susanne Schöberl as a growing sense of isolation and the breakdown of working-class solidarity.[111] Similarly, Erhard Lucas describes the effects of the Terror in terms of repression and isolation. Not only the fear of the possible consequences of collective political activity but also a sense of shame and guilt among those who had survived the rampages of the Freikorps and the arrests and torture (not only of active Communists and radical workers but whole working-class populations) isolated the workers both from politics at large and from each other.[112] The creatureliness of the working-class characters in *Die Kumiaks* is, by implication, the fruit of a failed revolution, or more precisely, it arises in the gap between the power of the working class and its inability to exercise sovereignty in the Schmittian sense, insofar as it is unable to seize the state of exception brought on by the crisis of the republic and dispose over it by articulating a clear political field of friend and enemy. The impasse, in other words, remains at the level of the Schmittian state of exception, which is understood as suspension of law for the sake of its preservation, the violent installation of a "normal everyday frame of life" that would allow "the legal order to make sense."[113] It is precisely this norm that from the point of view of the oppressed, pace Benjamin, is the reigning *Ausnahmezustand* of the oppressed, which is to say that the oppressed are oppressed insofar as they are unable to bring about the "real state of emergency," the suspension of the logic of sovereignty itself.[114] Marchwitza's miners are unable to be at once proletarian and sovereign.[115]

If Santner's definition of creaturely life is one that is shaped by a "signifying stress," an exposure to indiscernible and opaque interpellations, it becomes clear that more than state violence is at stake in the postrevolutionary affective constellation of the German proletariat as it is portrayed in Marchwitza's novel. The crisis of sovereignty at the core of *Die Kumiaks* is not that of the Weimar state but the nonarrival of the German revolution. It is not the violence of the state that renders the workers creatures but their own shame at defeat, the shame that draws together the exceptional experiences of political terror with the quotidian subaltern condition of exploitative labor and existential fear. It is shame in the form that Santner, following Levinas, describes as "an animal nakedness" that is also a form of being "riveted to one's self," reduced to one's own body, to its hunger and its stupor.[116] Marchwitza's novel acquires its proper pathos from this shame. "Our eternal glorification of bondage is to blame," proclaims the anarchist Schwarz at a union meeting, "we had the reins in our hands in '18, in our decency we let the exploiters get away scot-free" (K 117). The anxiety given voice in Marchwitza's novel is that the defeats of the early 1920s might not simply be a state of exception but rather one of catastrophe, of the reduction of the political agency of the working class to "only the horror of a destructive will which periodically stirs in the manner of forces of nature"[117] or, as the events that punctuate Marchwitza's chronicle of the French occupation illustrate, oscillate between apathy and spontaneous revolt.

The question of periodization in *Die Kumiaks* turns around this question of the revolution's nonarrival. The working class does not simply stand back up and continue to struggle but is marked by its failures in ways that can be productively applied to further struggle or can contribute to apathy, isolation, and disagreement. As Negt and Kluge write, echoing Luxemburg's thoughts on the eve of her death, the history of the labor movement is marked by defeats that have had progressive, galvanizing consequences, such as the Paris Commune, and defeats that "remain wholly without experience; they have destroyed experience and left only traumatic fixations."[118] For Negt and Kluge, the defeats of 1918 to 1923 are examples of the second. Rather than representing a "store of experiences for all subsequent periods," these defeats enforced in the working class the commonsense lesson that "the only plausible reaction to the experience of defeat is for it to avoid the situation with which the defeat was associated."[119] For Marchwitza, then, *Eigensinn* becomes a form of what Negt and Kluge, following Adorno and Horkheimer, call "social stupidity," "the scar tissue of historical defeats," where, to quote from *Dialectic of Enlightenment*, "coercion suffered turns good will into bad."[120] In his essay on Negt and Kluge, Jameson points out:

> it is not therefore some primal "self" that has *Eigensinn*, but rather a whole range of historically developed skills, drives, and capacities, each of which with its own "stubborn" demands and its own distinct "meaning." Such forces, however, can be residual or emergent; they often fail to be used to capacity, and their unemployment generates specific pathologies, as does their equally possible repression, alienation, or diversion.[121]

The energies, drives, and capacities that were directed toward political action from 1918 to 1923 are portrayed in *Die Kumiaks* in the moment where they are crushed by the forces of reaction and collapse upon themselves, becoming pathological in the sense of *Eigensinn*, marking the directionless work of blocked desires and needs. "We have wasted our strength on partial struggles and passive waiting," declares Saletzki following the collapse of the miners' strike, which coincides with the defeat of the KPD-led German October (K 261). The catastrophe at which Marchwitza's novel gestures is then perhaps nothing but the proletariat itself, reduced to its own subaltern habitus.

Die Kumiaks is a novel that derives its epic principle from the collective experience of the impossibility of collective action. Marchwitza's 1934 novel, written in a precarious exile in Switzerland, closes with images of the state of siege imposed on the Ruhr in October 1923. As the French occupiers and the German police make arrests and conduct house searches, the *Kumpels* learn that the workers' uprisings in central Germany and Hamburg have been crushed and that "the state of emergency reigns in the insurgent territories" (K 260). This state of emergency will not be a transitional moment. One is reminded here again in the rhythm of inconclusive events and empty waiting structuring the narrative of *Die Kumiaks* of Benjamin's reading of Seghers's *Die Rettung*, which brings out precisely the lack of "temporal perspective" in Seghers's novel.[122] As one of Seghers's characters muses in a moment of crisis, "this was not at all the beginning of the end, this would go on like this for a long time still."[123] Marchwitza's novel, then, chronicles the structures of feeling of a German working class in disarray, stumbling from defeat to defeat in the impasse of a failed revolution and under the shadow of the future, the catastrophic defeat to come in 1933. In this *Zwischenzeit* or indeterminate temporality, the Kumiak-type of Marchwitza's novel becomes a figure for the *Ungleichzeitigkeit* itself, the scattered affective histories, desires, and capacities that are thrown up in the wake of the revolution's collapse and the closure of the present into an open-ended "state of siege." In the final pages of the novel, Marchwitza repeats the opening sentence, "the Kumiaks migrated" (263). Kumiak (who has been blacklisted for political agitation by the mine's management) has found another promised land, this time in Holland, and he again sets off to find his living by his "industrious hands" and God's grace (264). Paradoxically it is here, in Kumiak's quixotic hopefulness, in his shameless optimism that catastrophe might possibly still harbor the chance for a new beginning, that *Die Kumiaks* reaches out toward what Benjamin calls the "weak messianic power" of the fractured tradition of the oppressed in the face of the historical continuity of the oppressors.[124]

CHAPTER 3

The Tasks of Emigration

For both those in the antifascist underground and those in the many host countries of the antifascist emigration, the fascist period meant the loss of the political and literary organizations through which Communist authors had attempted to create a counterpublic sphere in the Weimar Republic. Communist writers were largely separated from their reading publics and, indeed, from contact with Germany itself.[1] Nevertheless, German exiles managed to create an impressive, if always unstable, literary infrastructure, including theater troupes, publishing houses, literary journals, and art exhibitions in the countries to which they, often illegally, fled the fascist terror.[2] These literary networks were animated by the political imperatives of exile. As KPD functionary Fritz Erpenbeck, a novelist and publicist who was a major protagonist in the literary debates of the exile period, puts it in his novel *Die Emigranten* [The Emigrants 1937], "our emigration cannot be a flight from the battlefield of the class struggle, it is merely a retreat from a particularly endangered position, a retreat, so to speak, with our weapons in hand. . . . Our emigration cannot become a purpose unto itself!"[3] Rather, Communist émigrés saw their task in the analysis of conditions in Germany, the consolidation of their own organizations, and the ideological and material support of the antifascist resistance within the Reich. Through this commitment, exiles sustained the politicization of daily life learned in the KPD of the Weimar Republic.[4] The strategic shift to the strategy of the Popular Front at the Seventh

World Congress of the Communist International in 1935, the Spanish Civil War, and the so-called Expressionism Debate of the late 1930s was carried out in the pages of various émigré journals and formed a series of exchanges between figures like Georg Lukács, Anna Seghers, Bertolt Brecht, and Ernst Bloch.[5] This debate, ostensibly one about the status of realism and modernist aesthetic techniques for a socialist literary practice, soon became, as Fredric Jameson has pointed out, one that "quickly extends beyond the local phenomenon of expressionism, and even beyond the ideal type of realism itself, to draw within its scope the problems of popular art, naturalism, socialist realism, avant-gardism, media, and finally modernism—political and non-political—in general."[6]

This deployment of a Popular Front rhetoric in the absence of an elaborated public sphere through which writers and intellectuals on the German left could create reciprocal relationships with German audiences accounts for some of the particularity and moral pathos of German exile literature. Such an emphasis on the national dimension marks a correspondence between the German literary exile and the more broadly construed horizon of the Popular Front as a cultural horizon in the 1930s. As Katerina Clark argues, "the cultural arms of the Popular Front had begun invoking precisely authority and tradition. . . . Many intellectuals had begun to reject the avant-garde experimentalism as jejune and self-indulgent in the face of the world crisis. In their stead, writers were gravitating back toward the grand narrative."[7] If, for the French Popular Front, the major event grounding such narratives was the French Revolution, in the USSR this pride of place was taken by the civil war, chronicled in such films as the Vasilyev brothers' *Chapaev* (1934) and Nikolai Ostrovsky's 1936 socialist realist epic novel *How the Steel Was Tempered*. In the German case, with progressive national traditions harder to discern, there was a notable turn to the legacy of Weimar Classicism. Nevertheless, thinking about Popular Front culture purely in terms of nation and tradition fails to do justice to the cultural constellation of the 1930s. As Clark stresses, this was not a culture of insular nationalism, especially not in the Soviet Union or among the geographically dispersed German exiles. "Arguably," she writes, "in the 1930s the causes of nationalism, internationalism, and even cosmopolitanism were not distinct, but to a significant degree imbricated with each other in a mix peculiar to that decade."[8] But if other Popular Fronts could appeal culturally and politically to a kind of local popular progressive tradition, the German exiles could only appeal to the so-called better Germany through an analysis of the misery of German popular life, the poverty of the German progressive tradition, and their own exclusion from a thoroughly Nazified public sphere.

Likewise, lacking in a mass basis or anything equivalent to the CIO in the United States or the Popular Front governments of France and the Spanish Republic of the early civil war years, the German emigration coalesced around cultural organizations in the emigration like the refounded SDS (Schutzbund deutscher Schriftsteller or Protective Union of German Writers) in Paris, the various groups organized around the KPD by people like Willi Münzenberg, and the later Committee for a Free Germany in Mexico City.[9] Indeed, as Lion Feuchtwanger has pointed out, the exiles were hardly in a position to contest the cultural, let alone political, hegemony of the National Socialist regime inside Germany. Feuchtwanger describes the "emigrant" as rather an undesired shared identity, one based in precarity and *déclassement*, in the foreclosure of the very horizons of everyday life around which Popular Front culture revolves, with its supports of work, place, and collectivity. For Feuchtwanger, however, this negative identity is itself the basis of a new and more forceful mode of political engagement for German antifascist writers. "Indeed," he writes, "exile broke us down, made us small and miserable, but exile hardened us as well and made us great."[10] Heinrich Mann, an integral figure to both the cultural and political gestures toward a German Popular Front, makes similar points in his essay "Aufgaben der Emigration" [The Tasks of the Emigration 1933], where he argues that the precarity and dispersal of the exile can only be ameliorated by the German émigrés themselves organizing their own safety, and this in turn implies casting the exile itself as a political project. The exile must act as a conduit for protest from inside Germany and represent to the world "the passionately feeling section of the German people."[11] Rather than casting themselves as victims, they must publicly claim their superiority to the writers who have remained in Germany. "The émigrés alone," Mann writes, "may speak of facts and contexts. They are the voice of their people, who have fallen silent, they must be this for the world."[12] The question, however, of what form this voice might take remained a contentious one, and the debates around this question stretched back to the fractious discussions of the Weimar Republic.

THE POPULAR FRONT AND EXPRESSIONISM DEBATE

The discourses of antifascist exile were largely shaped by two significant shifts in the tactics and cultural politics of the Communist movement. The first was the official codification of socialist realism at the 1934 First All-Union Writers' Congress in Moscow.[13] The second was the adoption of the Popular Front policy at the Seventh Congress of the Communist International the following year. In 1932, the Soviet government, which had so far avoided direct involvement in literary debates, dissolved RAPP. Initially this move seemed to promise increased cultural openness by eliminating "the old RAPP line of proletarian and Communist exclusiveness" in order to "make room for literary diversity." The doctrine of socialist realism was thus intended in part as reconciliation with the old bourgeois literary intelligentsia by removing the class status of the writer as a criterion of literary criticism.[14] As Sheila Fitzpatrick has written, socialist realism, as Maxim Gorky largely posited it, fit in with "the firm establishment in Soviet ideology of the concept of a classless and apolitical 'classical heritage' in culture."[15] This literary turn fits with a general reorientation in Soviet culture after the First Five-Year Plan toward *kul'turnost*: the turn to explicit bourgeois norms of culture, dress, family, behavior, and so forth.[16] Thus the dissolving of RAPP and introduction of socialist realism between 1932 and 1934, while preserving many positions and figures from that organization, marked a reconciliation with the bourgeois literary intelligence, both within the USSR and among potential allies abroad, authors like André Malraux, Heinrich Mann, and Lion Feuchtwanger, for example.[17]

Socialist realism is a more complicated literature than it may initially appear, since it is both a literature of "normalization" and an attempt to overcome the distinction between high culture and mass culture, which Adorno famously described as "torn halves of an integral freedom, to which however they do not add up."[18] As Boris Groys has famously argued, socialist realism marked a liquidation of the historical avant-garde but one that continued with the avant-garde project of shaping life through art.[19] Groys points out that socialist realism is in opposition to the historical avant-garde on the question of whether a new reality requires new artistic forms, or whether an art that stands for social transformation is better served through adaptation of popular forms, be they those of high culture or those of mass media.[20] The apparent traditionalism of socialist realism, Groys argues, is an expression of its status as a "style and a half," a bridge between high modernism and postmodernism. What appears as kitsch to a modernist sensibility was socialist realism's appropriation of ready-made forms in the name of a certain avant-garde impulse, but now separating its aesthetic premises from its social premise.[21] If high modernism sought freedom from the market and the political through a retreat from representation, Groys sees socialist realism as an articulation of Sovietness:

> Socialist realism was . . . a style and a half: its proto-postmodernist strategy of appropriation continued to serve the modernist ideal of historical exclusiveness, internal purity, and autonomy from everything external . . . the definition of "Sovietness" was achieved by separating it from everything which questioned the fundamental project of the world's transformation by the autonomous will of man . . . from the point of view of Soviet culture, the modernist artist merely served the market, unlike the Soviet artist, who participated in the collective project of restructuring the world.[22]

This collective restructuring of the world is a project that socialist realism pursues through a practice of pastiche and citation. Socialist realism therefore was an aesthetic that was uniquely concerned with cultural traditions, seeing itself as both the inheritor and appropriator of all that had come before. At the same time, the categories of socialist realism always remained somewhat vague and, as Leonid Heller has argued, were marked by endless repetition of fundamental antinomies, for example, the opposition between realism and romanticism, between the depiction of social conflict and social harmony, and so forth. The system and practice of socialist realism were thus "always at once static and constantly changing."[23]

As Devin Fore has argued, the protean character of socialist realism's categories allowed in principle for an almost infinite stylistic variation, "since this new practice positioned itself as heir to all of the various movements and to the panoply of aesthetic techniques they had at their disposal."[24] Thus, as opposed to the "relentless *de*coding" performed by the historical avant-garde, socialist realism can be read as a "zealous *over*coding" of the conventions of mimetic illusionism and the various devices of realist representation.[25] Given this inbuilt eclecticism, as Fore points out, it was not surprising that the question of the *Erbe*, or cultural heritage, which is to say the question not only of national cultural idioms but also the catalogue of serviceable techniques, became a central question not only in the USSR but among the German émigrés within and outside the Soviet Union.[26] At the same time, precisely because of this eclectic citationality and total appropriation of the traditions of the past, many critics have seen socialist realism as an aesthetic that, echoing critiques of postmodernism, aims toward an ahistorical timelessness, a kind of restitution of an "absolute epic past" in the Bakhtinian sense of a closed and univocal world.[27] A persistent dilemma for German writers in antifascist exile would be negotiating the appropriation of traditional aesthetic forms and foregrounding of the urgencies of the present in the midst of the crises of the 1930s.

If one could locate a break between socialist realism and the tendencies expressed in *Linkskurve*, it might lie precisely in this uncanny admixture of eclecticism and an insistence on traditional forms. The BPRS, even as it came increasingly to emphasize the great forms of the novel and the drama in its discussions, always continued to emphasize formal innovation and the class basis of literature, whether bourgeois or proletarian. Socialist realism should therefore be understood in the context of the Popular Front that it somewhat anticipates. It links up the positions Lukács had been developing since the late 1920s, an emphasis on the classical realist novel, national cultural traditions, and the political significance of perspective rather than the class origin of the work.[28] In many ways, the relative openness of the debate at the Moscow conference, with Willi Bredel making a plea for the continued vitality of proletarian-revolutionary authorship and Wieland Herzfelde's emphasis on the usefulness of modernist techniques, set the tone for a broad antifascist literary alliance.[29] The result of this, organized largely by Becher, Mikhail Koltsov, and Sergei Tretyakov, was the first International Congress of Writers for the Defense of Culture, which took place in Paris in June 1935.[30] This was the high point of the literary Popular Front, with 235 speakers from 38 nations representing a wide spectrum of the literary left.

The tone of the event was conspicuously focused on a broad alliance politics, with many of the speeches concentrating on the preservation of Enlightenment values and the moral responsibilities of the writer in the face of fascism.[31] As Clark points out, the congress worked to define the function, style, and goals of an antifascist world literature, based on notions of reason and humanism.[32] For Clark, the reciprocal connections between a reinvestment of national traditions on the one hand

and a commitment to internationalism on the other were key to the structure of feeling of the Popular Front, and the Paris congress represented its high tide.[33] Becher repeatedly declared, "this congress stands under the sign of humanism" and praises proletarian-revolutionary literature for its commitment to truth and peace, locating this stance as a more authentic mode of antifascist patriotism.[34] Furthermore, Becher sees this working-class literature as a concretization of the notion of "world literature" that remains abstract in bourgeois culture. For Becher, this "new articulation of the concept of world literature" is enabled by the construction of socialism in the USSR, which makes possible a gaze upon the past, present, and future from the heights of a perfected human history.[35] Becher criticizes the lack of a theory of cultural heritage, or *Beerbungslehere*, on the part of the literature of the working class. Like the German *Heimat* itself, the German cultural tradition is cut through with "barbed wire fences and high walls" and awaits its liberation.[36] He links the question of heritage to the question of class but largely elides an analysis of fascism itself. Some speakers, notably Anna Seghers and Bertolt Brecht, who critically introduced the idea of property relations, challenged this vague humanistic consensus. If much of the congress was taken up by the question of civilization versus barbarism, Brecht and Seghers at least attempted to bring the discussion around to questions of fascism as a symptom of the crisis of mid-twentieth-century capitalism.[37] At the same time, both the All-Union Writers' Conference in 1934 and the Paris congress in 1935 crystallized around a certain formal consensus that tracked the implicit conservatism of the literary debates we have been following thus far. Largely eclipsed were the production aesthetics of figures like Brecht, Benjamin, and Tretyakov. While GDR literary criticism insisted into the 1980s that the mid-1930s saw a turn away from the "collectivism" syndrome of the 1920s to a more subtle analysis of subject formation and society, for many, the Paris congress marked a decisive break between aesthetic and political avant-gardes.[38] But it failed to articulate a practical strategy for Popular Front cultural politics, and the alliances that found expression at this congress quickly dissolved as the Popular Front itself began to unravel in the late 1930s.[39]

The years of exile were also the time of the so-called Expressionism Debate, carried out between 1937 and 1939 largely in the pages of *Das Wort*, a journal founded in Moscow in the wake of the Paris congress. Edited jointly by Lion Feuchtwanger, Brecht, and Willi Bredel, the journal was intended as a forum for wide-ranging cultural debates on the left. Ironically, largely under the de facto editorship of Fritz Erpenbeck, since none of the ostensible editors was in fact in Moscow, *Das Wort* became, not without controversy, a tool for enforcing what was quickly becoming party orthodoxy on matters of literary technique.[40] Behind formal questions, however, lurked political ones. For the German exiles, the categories of partisanship and popularity took on special significance under the conditions of antifascism and the Popular Front. The Expressionism Debate, which has become codified as the Brecht-Lukács debate, circled around the status of modernism and realism within Marxist aesthetics. A primary factor of the debate dealt with the question of popularity, or *Volkstümlichkeit*, of how a Communist literary culture that was literally separated from the German people through exile but also now through ideology and through contesting reconstructions of the German cultural tradition, or the *Erbe*, could nevertheless maintain a connection to that people.[41] The central cultural question of this debate involved what was ultimately serviceable from the bourgeois cultural tradition, from classicism through modernism, not only for a socialist cultural project but to contest fascist cultural hegemony.

Lukács had tackled this subject in his 1934 essay "'Größe und Verfall' des Expressionismus" [Expressionism: Its Significance and Decline] in *Internationale Literatur*.[42] According to Lukács, Expressionism was a reflection of the ideological confusion of left-wing elements of German Social Democracy, especially the Independent Social Democratic Party (USPD), around the time of World War I.[43] From the standpoint of this class analysis, Lukács critiques Expressionism's shallow Bohemianism and elitist anticapitalism, its abstract notion of pacifism, and its unreflected formal characteristics of fragmentation.[44] Although Lukács's article had little resonance in 1934, its salient points were taken up again in 1937 in an article by Alfred Kurella under the title "Nun ist dieses Erbe zuende" [Now This Heritage Has Its End] that sparked the debate.[45] Writing under the name Bernard Ziegler, Kurella attacked Expressionism through the works of Gottfried Benn as belonging to the intellectual patrimony of fascism—part of the process of bourgeois ideological decay and decomposition of bourgeois relation to the so-called classical heritage.

As a leading exemplar of Expressionism, Benn, who had been a central participant in the *Gleichschaltung* of the Prussian Academy of the Arts in the early days of the Hitler regime and who had recently written an open letter denouncing German antifascist exile authors, was an excellent target for Kurella. Indeed, one of the first debates in the literary exile was provoked by Klaus Mann's open letter denouncing Benn for his role in the cultural consolidation of the National Socialist regime, to which Benn responded with a blistering critique of the literary emigration and a declaration of partisanship for the new German state.[46] Benn may have exemplified much of what Alfred Kurella condemned in Expressionism, however, the author's choice of pen name, eerily similar to that of Adolf Ziegler, Hitler's president of the Reich Chamber of Arts, as well as the date of Kurella's intervention, coming shortly after the opening of the notorious *Entartete Kunst*, or degenerate art, exhibition of summer 1937, which featured the works of most of the leading German Expressionists, also revealed something of the apparent contradiction in this socialist denunciation of Expressionism.[47]

For Kurella, the decomposition of forms in the arts objectively supports the fascist ideological project of irrationalism. Locating the origins of Expressionism in the decay of bourgeois classicism, Kurella continues, "today one can clearly recognize whose spirit Expressionism was the child of, and where this spirit, carefully cultivated, leads to: into Fascism."[48] Kurella accuses Benn, and in his train Expressionism tout court, of a willed dissolution of the bourgeois cultural heritage and of antiquity into a mere background for his own irrationalist metaphysics, resulting in a cannibalization of an already declining bourgeois culture—"a corruption of a corruption" and a "montage of spiritual values" that can only play into the hands of a Goebbels.[49] At the end of the article, Kurella polemically asks three questions, the positive answer to which is obviously the criterion of approval for cultural production in the orbit of the Communist movement:

> Classical antiquity: "Noble simplicity and silent greatness" —do we see it this way?
>
> Formalism: main enemy of a literature that truly strives to great heights—do we agree with this?
>
> Closeness to the people and popularity: the fundamental criteria of every genuinely great art—do we affirm this unconditionally?[50]

These questions, with their presupplied answers, were read by many as more or less condemning any form of aesthetic modernism or avant-garde practice, with Expressionism becoming a figure for the avant-garde as such. Thus many writers rushed to the defense of Expressionism, if not Gottfried Benn, pointing out that it was the cultural crucible of the entire generation of critical artists and intellectuals born around 1900, and many of the key artists and writers on the left had begun as Expressionists—one need only name Johannes R. Becher. For many, Expressionism was a closed chapter, both biographically and culturally, but one that was useful for many artists and writers in breaking away from bourgeois norms in aesthetics, ideology, and daily life.

Perhaps more important than the local arguments about the status of Expressionism were the attempts by figures like Ernst Bloch, Hanns Eisler, Anna Seghers, Bertolt Brecht, and, from the other side, Georg Lukács to shift debate to the problematic relationship between the political and the aesthetic avant-gardes in the context of Popular Front politics. As Bloch and Eisler put it in a 1937 article in *Die neue Weltbühne*, the aesthetic avant-garde needs the Popular Front in order to give focus to their work, to prevent the most technically advanced artists from producing in a void, whereas the Popular Front needs the avant-garde to give reality "its most contemporary, precise, and colorful expression."[51] Moving away from the question of whether or not the masses could "understand" nonfigurative art, Bloch and Eisler maintain, as did Brecht, that art must keep pace with the most advanced forces of production. This implies not only the political refunctioning of mass media like newspapers, film, and radio but also the transformation of older forms like the drama and the novel to take these newer technologies into account.[52]

Eisler and Bloch argue that aesthetic and political avant-gardes march separately and often do not strike together.[53] Acknowledging the critiques that pre- and postwar German avant gardes often remained elitist, abstract, or culinary, Bloch and Eisler nevertheless insist that precisely the Popular Front should and must open up a space for a new, popular avant-garde, arguing that "today the artist only remains avant-garde when he succeeds in making the new means of art useful for the struggle of the broad masses."[54] Against the argument that the difficulty of the avant-garde isolates such art from the masses, Bloch and Eisler insist that it is precisely the question of aesthetic level that lends urgency to avant-garde art on the left, since only here, from a socially critical viewpoint, can new mass technologies, from newspaper to radio and television, be refunctioned as instruments of political engagement.[55] In a follow-up article, "Die Kunst zu erben" [To Inherit the Arts], Bloch and Eisler move to a more direct address of the *Erbe*-question, noting that the tendency to dismiss modernism as decadence has the corresponding effect of fetishizing the classics, a left version of the National Socialist canonization of a properly German tradition.[56] If the bourgeois heritage is to be engaged from the left, it must be a critical engagement that recognizes the aesthetic as historically dynamic and understands modernism as a mode of resistance to the commodification of culture and social life under industrial capitalism.[57] As Bloch and Eisler point out, the avant-garde exercises an emancipatory function, developing new ways of seeing and feeling the modern social world, a world that is not only that of the dissolution of the bourgeoisie but also the rise of the proletariat. From the very artifacts of bourgeois decay, according to Bloch and Eisler, we catch glimpses of the socialist future. "Therefore," they write, "the achievements of Picasso and Einstein acquire something of the anticipatory; they are illuminated from the world that is not yet here."[58] Rather than judge the cultural production of the day by the aesthetic standards of the past, Bloch and Eisler end their piece with this slogan: "critical acceptance of the present, and through this the facilitation of productive access to the traditions of the past."[59]

In his major repost to Kurella's article, "Discussing Expressionism," published in *Das Wort*, Bloch sidesteps Kurella himself and turns to a critique of Lukács's earlier 1934 piece on Expressionism. In addition to criticizing Lukács's one-sided account of Expressionism as a cultural formation, Bloch is concerned here with a larger point about the relationship between representation and social phenomenon. If "recent artistic experiments . . . must all be summarily condemned as aspects of the decay of capitalism," Bloch writes, "the result is that there can be no such thing as an avant-garde within capitalist society."[60] In other words, Lukács's, and Kurella's, notion of decadence would imply, as KPD critic Hans Günther put it bluntly in a review of Bloch's own *Heritage of Our Times*, that everything of value in the bourgeois tradition was already critically inherited by Marx, Engels, and Lenin.[61] The question of an open relation to more contemporary bourgeois culture, however, circles around the question of whether or not there are "dialectical links between growth and decay."[62] If, as Bloch argues, "authentic reality is also discontinuous," then there is a certain value to "art which strives to exploit the *real* fissures in surface inter-relations and to discover the new in their crevices."[63] This dialectic is precisely what Bloch had sought to clarify in his treatment of montage techniques in *Heritage of Our Times*. He dismisses a superficial montage as the highest form of distraction and intoxication, a play with the ruins of older unities of the bourgeois institution of art, a "castle restoration of the background" (HT 203). Yet there is another "constitutive" use of montage that "takes the best pieces for itself, builds other coherences out of them, and the owner of the previous coherence is pleased by the new one, if this does not remain patch work and artistic myth, no longer" (204). As an example of constitutive montage, Bloch cites the work of Brecht, whose epic theater mobilizes montage as a force of production, using interruption as a tool for carving out building blocks for a new reality among the ruins and refuse of late capitalist culture (206).

Lukács objects to this synthetic modernism in his famous riposte to Bloch, "Es geht um den Realismus" [Realism in the Balance]. For Lukács, the problem of the decadence of bourgeois culture is not the breakdown of the unity of its aesthetic forms. Modernism is decadent, in contradistinction to the contemporary realism of the brothers Mann, Roman Rolland, or Maxim Gorky, precisely through its formal reflection of the fundamentally false notion that reality is in fact discontinuous. The social world of advanced capitalism, Lukács recalls with reference to Marx, is precisely a totality. What is decadent about modernism is its renunciation of the aesthetic forms that would be capable of reflecting this totality, which is concealed behind the fractured appearance of social relations. Bloch privileges discontinuity, but Lukács argues that capitalist society forms a totality insofar as it is shaped by the mode of production. The world market appears to be discontinuous and fragmentary, but it is not (RB 31). Approaching the period of the avant-gardes, Lukács notes "the underlying unity, the totality, all of whose parts are objectively interrelated, manifests itself most strikingly in the fact of crisis." And yet "every Marxist knows that the basic economic categories of capitalism are always reflected in the minds of men, directly but always back to front" (32). Thus when crisis draws together the semi-autonomous aspects of the system, the subjective experience of this is one of disintegration. Lukács writes, "when the surface of life is only experienced immediately, it remains opaque, fragmentary, chaotic and uncomprehended" (39).

At the level of literary form, Bloch and the various pre- and postwar avant-gardes mistake ideological reflections of imperialism for the thing itself, without, as does Thomas Mann, for instance, locating ideological disintegration within bourgeois social conditions themselves (RB 34–35). For Lukács, this misprision of the appearance of reality as the reality of social conditions themselves is precisely the immediacy of which modernism in general is guilty, and it is also the source of the abstract character of much of modernism (36). He thus posits a dialectical unity of immediacy and abstraction (38), which he then contrasts with the necessary aesthetic abstraction of realist writing. Realism as a method is for Lukács precisely found in the work of mediations between underlying relationships and their false appearance. The realist writer thus moves from immediate experience to abstract knowledge of social laws but then effaces the abstraction within a "new immediacy" that is aesthetically mediated and brings totality into the field of perception (39). This second immediacy supplies the experience of formal closure as a mimesis of a social totality that itself exceeds direct representation, and therein lies, for Lukács, its value.

The debate was brought to a close by a presumptive declaration of Lukács's victory in an article by Kurella in 1939, where he modified his controversial thesis that Expressionism led by necessity to Nazism, maintaining now that Expressionism was the symptom of a process of "decadence" and "decay" that contributed to the Nazi victory in Germany.[64] Finally, in his summation of the debate, Fritz Erpenbeck attempted to shift the terms of the discussion of realism to a discussion of popularity. Asking why it was that both Nazis and Communists rejected Expressionism, the Nazis through the biologized trope of "degenerate art" and the Communists with their historicist language of "decadence," Erpenbeck argues that Expressionism had no basis in the popular life of the German masses, who "spontaneously rejected" it.[65] The Nazis, according to Erpenbeck, exploit this spontaneous rejection demagogically, condemning avant-garde art while supplying the masses with kitsch, whereas the Communists will face the difficult task of overcoming the separation of art and life in Germany. Erpenbeck sums up his argument by asserting that "the dominance of kitsch in the taste of the broad masses of the people is the flip side of the fact that the 'isms' have left the position of popularity unoccupied."[66] Though Erpenbeck is vague on this point, his definition of *Volkstümlichkeit* seems to be largely a matter of style or an accessible realism of popular conventions. Lukács uses the term in a broader vein to denote "a living relationship to the cultural heritage" of the nation, which is to say the connection to the daily life and progressive traditions of the people (RB 54). This notion of popularity is rooted more in historical experience than in contemporary reception, and it is also philosophically tied to his notion of totality. For Lukács, *Volkstümlichkeit* is intimately related to realism, in that it connotes a realm of the accessibility of the experience of a people as it has developed through history. This rendering of historical identity may take a critical form—indeed, in the German case it must do so—but a popular realism must be "based on an accurate and profound understanding of the realities of history."[67] That these realities are often themselves opaque when experienced is the thrust of Seghers's critique of Lukács's understanding of popularity, to which we shall return in Chapter 4.[68]

MODERNITY AND THE POPULAR

These aesthetic questions were part of a widespread reevaluation of Communist positions during the period between 1933 and the late 1940s. The existence of the National Socialist state encouraged what Sigrid Bock has termed the necessity of a "new conception of the epoch" that had led to fascism.[69] "Germany" as a historical problem thus comes to the fore in the exile novel in a manner that it had not during the Weimar Republic. The political defeats and marginalization of the KPD in the 1920s and early 1930s as well as the inability of the party to understand or effectively combat Nazism as a mass movement contributed to a theoretical helplessness in the face of Nazism's success, which Communists could neither understand as a mass movement nor convincingly explain as purely a tool of German capitalism.[70] At the same time, many exiled German writers turned to the historical novel as a means of grasping the epochal crisis of modernity represented by the success of National Socialism, implicitly critiquing the presentist and economist logic of the KPD's explanations of fascism.[71] Thus the 1930s saw the publication of Heinrich Mann's Henry the Fourth novels, *Die Jugend des Königs Henri Quatre* [The Youth of King Henry the Fourth 1935] and *Die Vollendung des Königs Henri Quatre* [The Fulfillment of King Henry the Fourth 1938], Thomas Mann's *Lotte in Weimar* [1939], Lion Feuchtwanger's Josephus trilogy, Alfred Döblin's *November 1918* [1933–1945], and Hermann Broch's *Der Tod des Virgil* [The Death of Virgil 1945].

It was only with the Popular Front policy that the KPD and the Communist movement turned decisively to the question of national historical traditions in their analysis of fascism, following the general shift in the International. In his address to the Seventh World Congress of the Communist International in 1935, Georgi Dimitroff argued, "fascism is able to attract the masses because it demagogically appeals to their *most urgent needs and demands.*"[72] This demagogy has a historical and a national aspect as well in Dimitroff's account. "The fascists," Dimitroff points out, "are rummaging through the entire history of every nation so as to be able to pose as the heirs and continuators of all that was exalted or heroic in its past."[73] Dimitroff implies that the rummaging of the fascists within the traditions of nations is enabled by a working-class politics that brackets out the national dimension:

> Communists who suppose that all this has nothing to do with the cause of the working class, who do nothing to enlighten the masses on the part of their people in a historically correct fashion, in a genuinely Marxist-Leninist spirit, *who do nothing to link up the present struggle with the people's revolutionary traditions and past*—voluntarily hand over to the fascist falsifiers all that is valuable in the historical past of the nation, so that the fascists may fool the masses.[74]

Such a linkage of the working-class struggles of the day with the revolutionary traditions of the past requires a popular understanding of history that would have to account for the social and spatial integration, or marginalization, of the working class from the discourse and practice of the nation. In other words, such a perspective would have to entail a shift from the great men of history to the everyday life of the people as the ground of national history.

In the German context, this shift is indicated by the renewed concern with the problematic notion of *Heimat* among antifascist émigrés. *Heimat* was of course a highly contested term in the 1930s, since it was one of the discursive pillars of National Socialist ideology. Yet the notion of *Heimat* tends to be a depoliticizing one. "*Heimat*," as David Clarke explains, "is a complex notion that implies simultaneously the regional, the provincial (in the sense of the non-urban), a resistance to the rationalized and instrumental human relationships of modernity through a recourse to a rooted, stable and homogeneous community, and a nostalgia for the secure world of childhood and home."[75] The Communist discourse on *Heimat* is built not only around the rejection of Nazi *Blut und Boden* propaganda and the militarist-nationalist discourses in which the term *Heimat* is mired. It is also an expression of loss and longing for the landscapes and social networks of the proletarian milieu, from which Communists were decisively excluded after 1933. In the discourse of German communism, this separation of the real, existing state of proletarian dispossession from the utopian space of *Heimat* is achieved through the opposition of *Heimat* to the term *Vaterland*. As Peter Blickle points out, if *Heimat* is already a tendentially utopian concept, marking the fantasy of a nonalienated space of collective identity shielded against the hard winds of modernity, the concept of *Vaterland* generally represents the public and political construction of the state and thus, in our context, class domination.[76] *Vaterland* thus represents a context of exclusion vis-à-vis proletarian interests. Marx and Engels famously wrote in the *Communist Manifesto*, "the worker has no fatherland."[77] From a proletarian perspective, *Vaterland* signified a negative, nationalistic, and militaristic concept that allowed German elites to simultaneously mask the exploitation of the working class and mobilize the working class for nationalistic objectives. "Occupied territory," laments the narrator of Adam Scharrer's proletarian-revolutionary novel *Vaterlandslose Gesellen* [Fellows Without a Fatherland 1930], conflating the landscape of war with the world of labor, "that is the proletariat in all countries."[78] Thus Klaus Weber cites an SPD pamphlet from 1870 that explicitly negates the nationalistic usage of *Vaterland* and gestures toward a notion of proletarian *Heimat*, declaiming: "Where we are secure, which is to say where we can be human beings; that is our fatherland."[79] This notion of *Heimat* as a collective project and aspiration for the building of a just world finds its philosophical articulation in Ernst Bloch's *Principle of Hope*, which closes with the assertion that once the "working, creative human being . . . has grasped himself and established what is his, without expropriation and alienation, in real democracy, there arises something that shines into the childhood of all and in which no one has yet seen: homeland."[80] The utopia of the socialist homeland, as Weber stresses, is a dialectical play of the marginalization and deprivation of proletarian everyday life and a collective desire for a better life.[81]

This socialist notion of *Heimat* depends on what Peter Blickle calls "anti-*Heimat*." Blickle argues that notions of anti-*Heimat* dwell on the processes of violence, exclusion, and domination that operate within the fantasy of *Heimat*. Images of the anti-*Heimat*, however, are, as Blickle points out, nevertheless already inscribed within the notion of *Heimat*, since *Heimat* is an idea that paradoxically only finds its elaboration in the exploration by the now homeless subject of its absence or loss.[82] The proletarian writer Hans Marchwitza explores this problematic from a proletarian standpoint in his 1934 essay "Heimat." Writing from the perspective of exile, Marchwitza casts *Heimat* as a site of desperate attachment and dispossession. Marchwitza writes of the love of the day laborer for the piece of earth he works, "that does not belong to him but costs him unspeakable effort."[83] Marchwitza links this attachment to the desire to "work up to something of one's own," a desire that is constantly negated: "all attachment to the old land is in vain: the power that degrades the worker to a dispossessed slave offers him only this: obey or leave."[84] As with the day laborers, so with the workers, who "defend their often disgusting apartments and dens of starvation when even these have been brought into dispute." The alternative open to the proletariat in the face of state oppression and economic exploitation is to "fall into our misery or the merciless struggle for another way of living, for our justice."[85] Marchwitza writes of a long learning process whereby the proletariat comes to terms with concrete and existential homelessness and arrives at the realization that only the destruction of this anti-*Heimat* can bring forth a *Heimat* of the oppressed: "from the terrible experience, from the toil that still enslaves millions, from our longing and love for a better *Heimat*, our words rise more clearly and penetratingly and shall not cease until we have arrived at the last struggle and until our trust in our justice has been fulfilled."[86] This fulfilled *Heimat* is only suggested by the proletarian geography of the actual nation. Following a description of Hamburg's harbor in Willi Bredel's novel *Die Prüfung*, with its ships rotting on their moorings during the Great Depression, Bredel writes of the coming socialist Germany:

> And all of this will one day belong to us, to the people. The leaders of the socialist planned economy will work in the houses of commerce. The harbor will be the trading center of a socialist Germany. The ships will not need to rust; rather they will bear the products of socialist industry throughout the world.[87]

Bredel's invocation of a socialist Hamburg opens onto a dimension of *Heimat* as a liberation of the proletariat through the liberation of labor itself, echoing Brecht's famous invocation of socialism as the "Great Production."[88] At the same time, it marks this novel that, like most of the Communist exile literature, depicts no actual work, as a workers' novel. Labor is for the most part negatively written into the exile novels of KPD members, as a longing for activity and self-objectification. It is a literature of unemployment, not, like the books of the Weimar-era BPRS, a literature of work.

The opposition of actual anti-*Heimat* to a perhaps concretely utopian *Heimat* is a common trope in the discourse of German communism in the exile years and evolves into a historiographical discussion based in the notion of the *deutsche Misère*. Against this reactionary tradition, a feeding ground for German fascism, Communist intellectuals elaborated the theory of a second progressive, humanistic Germany. The capacity of the exile to identify with the lost homeland splits that homeland into a reactionary-fascist element and a progressive socialist one, a distinction reminiscent of Lenin's famous two cultures thesis, which postulates that each national culture is split by a cultural struggle between forces arranged basically across class lines.[89] At the same time, the attention of many on the left turned from what Ernst Bloch might term the synchronous contradiction of labor and capital in Germany to a consideration of the eruptions of the past into the present. Bloch thus links the revolutionary struggle of the German working class to a genealogy of plebeian resistance to oppression in Germany stretching back to the Peasant Wars. Evoking these past struggles opens a vantage point on the noncontemporaneity contradictions between the multiple time frames of German social life that are synthesized by fascism (HT 105), which Bloch implies is rooted in the essentially archaic subjectivity of Germany's petit bourgeoisie.[90] Likewise, in a 1934 article titled "Das Große Bündnis" [The Great Alliance], Becher writes, "what the Nazis call heroism is nothing but the bravery of the *Landsknecht*," linking fascism to the early modern German tradition of roving plebeian and peasant mercenaries and inserting Hitler's reign into the continuity of the *deutsche Misère*.[91]

But to return to the problematic implied by the introduction to this chapter, what do these concerns have to do with the epic and the novel? As we have seen, for Lukács, the popular is a capacious and historically grounded category. While this is also the case for Brecht, Brecht's writings on popularity are more sensitive to the historical as a problem of technology and form. Schematically, one might say that while Brecht is more concerned with reception and production of cultural forms, Lukács is more focused on the question of cultural heritage. For Lukács, the popular is to be defined precisely in distinction to mass culture, and this on two fronts. "Retrograde traditionalism," Lukács writes, "such as regional art [*Heimatkunst*], and bad modern works, such as thrillers, have achieved mass circulation without being popular in any true sense of the word" (RB 164). The popular in Lukács's sense is eroded both by capitalist mass culture and by fascist folkish-ness and nationalist kitsch. To this phenomenon, Lukács juxtaposes the cultural heritage, or *Erbe*. For Lukács, "wherever the cultural heritage has a living relationship to the real life of the people it is characterized by a dynamic, progressive movement in which the active creative forces of popular tradition, the suffering and joys of the people, of revolutionary legacies, are buoyed up, preserved, transcended and further developed" (53–54). As opposed to the "great jumble sale" to which modernism reduces this tradition, Lukács insists, "the life of the people is a continuum" (55). This historical continuum is itself, however, "the living dialectical unity of continuity and discontinuity, of evolution and revolution" (55). Realism, as the grasp of the mediations that provide the continuity to conflicted historical formations, thus arises for Lukács "organically" from correct formulation of the notion of popularity; it is the narrativizing of the people. Lukács is properly skeptical of the rootedness of the progressive popular tradition in Germany but insists that the historical isolation of Germany's humanist intellectuals, writers, and artists from the everyday concerns of the people will be, or at least could be, overcome by the radical democratic politics of the Popular Front (HN 262–67).

Bertolt Brecht took issue with this notion of popularity read as the continuity of national traditions in an essay, "Popularity and Realism," written in 1938 but not published until decades later. For Brecht, the popular cannot simply be the socialist adoption of classical forms but must entail an active reconception of accepted aesthetic modes and practice, warning, in an implicit reference to the "popularity" of fascist *Blut und Boden* literature, that "it is precisely in the so-called poetical forms that 'the people' are represented in a superstitious fashion or, better, in a fashion that encourages superstition" (PR 80). Nevertheless, the socialist appropriation of key terms of fascist discourse, such as the concept of the people and of *Heimat*, was central to German Popular Front discourse. In his 1935 essay "Five Difficulties in Writing the Truth," Brecht had suggested a counterterminology for these fascist keywords, substituting, for example, the inclusive term "population" for "the people" and "human dignity" for "honor."[92] Brecht's notion of an antifascist counterdiscourse sat uneasily with Erpenbeck's, and to a degree Lukács's, commitment to a pre-given notion of the popular. Brecht notes first that the term "popular" is problematic in the German context precisely because exile has concretely severed the links between antifascist writers and a German literary public. "The term popular," Brecht points out, "as applied to literature thus acquires a curious connotation" (PR 79). Furthermore, the reality of exile is not so much a state of exception as it is an exacerbation of the norm. "The prevailing aesthetic, the price of books and the police have always ensured that there is a considerable distance between writer and people," Brecht notes (79). This distance is not for Brecht, as it is to a degree in Lukács, the product of a false immediacy or the inadequate grasp of the popular tradition but of concrete determinations of the public sphere of a modern class society. At the same time, Brecht insists that it is impossible to put the terms "popularity" or "the people" to productive use unless these terms are understood in a materialist manner and salvaged from their central mystifying roles in bourgeois and fascist ideology. "The history of the many deceptions which have been practiced with the concept of the people is a long and complicated one," Brecht reminds us (81).

The concept of "the people," then, must be specified in terms of its use, and Brecht goes on to supply a definition of the popular that would both be intelligible to the broad masses and represent their standpoint but at the same time engage pedagogically with this standpoint, "confirming and correcting it" (PR 81). This notion of the popular would seek to establish the cultural hegemony "of the most progressive section of the people," that is, the working class, while also appealing to the interests of broader social strata. For Brecht, this in turn implies a more capacious notion of realism. Realism cannot simply be taken over wholesale from the nineteenth-century classics, and at any rate, Brecht is careful to insist, realism is not a question of form but of method. For Brecht, realism encompasses those historically specific techniques that allow for the discovery of the "causal complexes of society" and that emphasize "the element of development," while "making possible the concrete, and making possible the abstraction from it" (82). The two considerations informing these definitions are historical specificity, for, as Brecht points out, "what was popular yesterday is not today, for the people today are not what they were yesterday" (83), and the notion of the useful. The value of utility comes across for Brecht in his experiences in the workers' theater of the Weimar Republic:

> the workers judged everything according to the truth of its content; they welcomed every innovation which helped the representation of truth, of the real mechanism of society; they rejected everything that seemed theatrical. . . . Anything that was worn out, trivial, or so commonplace that it no longer made one think, they did not like at all. (83–84)

To put this in terms of Brecht's famously invoked *plumpes Denken*, then, the terms "realism" and "popularity" can be thought of as valences of usefulness, the first asking perhaps useful for what and the second asking useful for whom. This notion of usefulness lies at the base of Brecht's critique of Lukács's positions, in particular the critique that Brecht mounts of the reification of the classical realist novel as the model for socialist realism, and it likewise lies at the base of a notion of popularity that for Brecht is rooted more in the transformations of class relationships in the midst of the crisis of capitalist modernity than in national tradition. If Balzac masterfully portrayed the differentiated individual characters, or "monstrosities," which grow from the organic formation of the bourgeois family, the "soviets and factories" of the present that "shape individuals today are precisely—compared to the family—products of montage."[93] Montage thus acquires its status as a realist technique precisely through its hermeneutical usefulness amid the dispersals and concatenations of modern everyday life. Here Brecht has not turned his back on realism but has developed an aesthetic adequate to the fact that the human figure is itself constituted through the techniques of montage and mechanical reproduction as much as human subjectivity arises from complex social interactions rather than organically.[94] Indeed, as Fore argues, for both Brecht and Döblin, in different ways, the project of reviving the "archaic paradigm" of the epic in the twentieth century involves precisely a notion of the technologically and socially mediated character of modern subjectivity as "a function that . . . circulates through the various *Grundmodelle* (or primary situations) of social intercourse."[95]

Benjamin addresses this question of utility directly in his 1936 essay "The Storyteller." Noting that the story as a form is dying out because of the increasing attenuation of face-to-face and individual experience in modernity, Benjamin points out,

> all this points to one of the essential features of every real story: it contains, openly or covertly, something useful. In one case, the usefulness may lie in a proverb or moral; in another, in some practical advice; in a third, in a proverb or maxim. In every case, the storyteller is a man who has counsel for his readers. But if today "having counsel" is beginning to have an old fashioned ring, this is because the communicability of experience is decreasing. (ST 145).

The novel, and here Benjamin echoes the early Lukács, arises precisely from this breakdown in the communicability of experience. "The birthplace of the novel," Benjamin writes, "is the individual in his isolation . . . who himself lacks counsel and can give none. To write a novel is to take to the extreme that which is incommensurable in the representation of human existence" (ST 147). All of the various attempts to recuperate the term "epic" in the 1920s and 1930s seem to circle around this notion of the utility of literature for social practice, and this is true of Döblin as much as it is for Brecht. If the novel is formally incommensurable to experience, what kind of forms would allow for a restoration of the counseling function of the epic in a context where immediate community is no longer the site of the production of experience?

Benjamin himself attempted to supply an answer to this question in his earlier essay "The Author as Producer." Benjamin's focus here is on the formal question of the political adequacy of literary work. As he famously formulates it, "The politically correct tendency includes a literary tendency" (AP 768–69).[96] In other words, how does a work stand in relation to the social relations of its period? The question, as Benjamin puts it, is one of technique and the relation to the forces of production, not one of the subjective attitudes of the writer. Benjamin's example in this essay is the newspaper, and particularly the reportage of Sergei Tretyakov. In this operative literature, the barrier between public and writer breaks down, and the worker gains access to authorship as expert—"Work itself has its turn to speak" (AP 772). In the absence of this kind of productive engagement with the apparatus of literature itself, political engagement remains subjective. This, for Benjamin, is the problem with the German left-bourgeois writers of the 1920s, for example, Döblin. "A political tendency," Benjamin writes, "however revolutionary it may seem, has a counterrevolutionary function so long as the writer feels his solidarity with the proletariat only in his attitudes, not as a producer" (777). Here Benjamin juxtaposes what he sees as Döblin's fatalism to Brecht's work in refunctioning the apparatus of the theater. Epic theater does not seek to produce the "great work" but rather to seize hold of the organizing function of art (777). What is epic about the epic theater is its orientation to scene rather than to plot. It does not invent but rather maps through montage and interruption of social contexts. "What emerges is this," Benjamin tells us, "events are alterable not at their climaxes, not by virtue and resolution, but only in their strictly habitual course, by reason and practice" (779).

In taking hold of the apparatuses of culture in such a way, to reveal social contexts, the artist joins the proletariat at the level of the means of production; the revolutionary artist is one who works on socializing the intellectual means of production (780).

Understood in this way, Benjamin's notion of progressive literature implies a notion of popularity that sidesteps the question of the national. At the same time, however, the literature of the Popular Front period will find itself increasingly preoccupied with the narration of what might be thought of as the historical texture of the everyday life of the common people. Benjamin, Bloch, and Brecht underscore that a cultural formation concerned with the common, the popular, and the everyday is not in fact inimical to modernism. At the same time, the return to the novel in this period should not be understood as a retreat from the experimentation of the 1920s but rather as an attempt to recoup the techniques of modernism to illuminate realms of collective experience in a moment of historical catastrophe and political defeat. As Lukács framed it in *The Historical Novel*, the great task of German literature in the 1930s was to "reveal those socio-historical and human-moral forces whose interplay made possible the 1933 catastrophe in Germany" (HN 342). Lukács himself knew that these forces were in a sense not to be grasped by the novel. One might argue that Lukács's theory of the novel, like Benjamin's, is entirely grounded in the realization that the individual level of experience, upon which the novel is in some sense irreducibly dependent, is inadequate, incommensurable, to the representation of the larger historical, social, and ideological constellation that he is here tasking literature with exposing. "Society," he writes, "is the principal subject of the novel, that is, man's social life in its ceaseless interaction with surrounding nature, which forms the basis of social activity, and with the different institutions and customs which mediate the relations between individuals in social life" (139). Key concepts in Lukács's work such as the typical, or realism itself, are theoretical tools for harmonizing this rupture.[97] Both of these concepts are, for Lukács, rooted in the understanding that the crises of history are located in popular everyday life and that they do not necessarily unfold in the form of punctual and recognizable breaks but over long durations.

The novel, precisely through its attunement to the everyday and the affective constellations of history as an indirectly lived process, is able to "show how the *direction* of a social tendency becomes visible in the small, imperceptible capillary movements of individual life" (HN 145).

For Lukács, of course, these capillary movements of individual life are mediated through the objectivity of the social, or what he refers to, following Hegel, as the "totality of objects" that is the basis of epic forms (146), and this is precisely what narrative allows through what Lukács terms the retarding aspects of duration. "Here then," Lukács writes,

> is a form of action which is alone suited to solve the basic stylistic problem of epic, namely to translate into human activity that great series of natural circumstances, human institutions, manners, customs, etc., which taken together form the "totality of objects." . . . The regressive motif is only an expression of those general objective forces which are necessarily stronger than the will and resolve of the individual. (146–47)

For Lukács, then, there is a tragic aspect to the epic as well, since here, as in tragedy proper, "social-historical necessity must triumph over the will and passions of individuals" (149). Following Lukács, the historical novel is not in fact to be regarded as an independent practice of the novel proper. Echoing Döblin's famous formulation that "every good novel is a historical novel," Lukács insists that on the one hand the novel as a genre is itself centrally concerned with the relationship between the present and the past and that on the other hand, the historical novel both rises from and returns to the social novel (83).[98] As Agnes Heller notes, the historical character of the novel has less to do with any direct depiction of historical figures and events than it does with the sensitivity of the modern novel to "a very special kind of kairos: social character, personal fate, story, historical moments, all of them need to be interwoven in a unique pattern, since what can happen with a particular social character cannot happen with another."[99] The novels—and, for that matter, the dramas—discussed in the following chapters[100] will deploy various strategies to develop a mode of historical representation in light of the catastrophe of National Socialism that at once "brings the past to life as the prehistory of the present" and opens onto the "portrayal of the past as history" (53, 83). It is this notion of the epic portrayal of the past as history, enabled by the durational and capillary form of the novel that both grounds Lukács's critique of novels that use historical settings merely as backdrop and unexpectedly draws his account of the novel within range of Benjamin's notion of the chronicle, that will be discussed further in the following chapter.

In other words, the debate around the historical novel in the German antifascist emigration was a debate about the relative serviceability of the novel itself. While none of the works analyzed in this book can be considered a historical novel in the proper sense, they are all attempts to fulfill the novel's vocation of historical orientation and localization. In different ways they present popular genealogies of fascism and antifascist resistance as embedded in the present of the 1930s. For Jameson, these are the axes of contradiction of the historical novel: on the one hand the opacity of the mediations between the level of experience and the givenness and institutionality of the world, and on the other hand the discrepancy between power and events, since neither the center of power nor popular life can be represented.[101] One could say the same about the great cataclysms of history, in the sense that, as Lukács points out, it is a mistake to think of these catastrophes as being punctual. "In reality," Lukács writes, "'sudden' catastrophes are actually long in preparation." Indeed, Lukács asserts, such crises and catastrophes arise from a "complicated, uneven evolution . . . in objective reality the false, subjective and abstract contrast between 'normal' and 'abnormal' vanishes."[102] The novel, then, reemerges as a privileged genre in the 1930s as a tool for coordinating the uneven time scales and nonlinear histories of everyday life in Germany that underlie the National Socialist political and social synthesis.[103] Thus, Lukács writes, "epic gives a broadly unfolded, entangled picture of the varied struggles—great and small, some successful, some ending in defeat—of its characters, and it is through the totality of these that the necessity of social development is expressed" (HN 146). At the same time, despite Lukács's stylistic preferences, his book on the historical novel closes with an invocation of a new epic tendency expressed by the novel of the Popular Front, which would reach beyond the prose of capitalist society, where "the only result of the people's colossal heroic efforts was the replacement of one form of exploitation by another," to the "heroic upsurge" of the "revolutionary liberation of the people" (346–47). Nevertheless, for Lukács, this is only a tendency, one that would find its realization only in fully developed socialism (48). What is interesting here is that Lukács is implicitly enfolding the Popular Front novel within a more general argument that the novel is in fact a genre that is centrally concerned with charting not so much the emergence of the new as the slow decay and disintegration of the old (144). This collective experience of disintegration undergirds the crisis of modernity in the 1930s. The German Popular Front novels that I will be examining in the next three chapters can be read as an epic adaption of the novel, and the historical novel in particular. In the conditions of exile where authors were largely separated from the means of production for the modernist, industrialized, mass cultural experimentation that had marked the 1920s in the Weimar Republic, the epic aspect moves from montage and technological reproduction to a subtle deployment of affect as a tool for grasping the present as a historical moment.

CHAPTER 4

Place and Plot

Anna Seghers, The Seventh Cross

In September 1938, Anna Seghers wrote a letter to the head of the Soviet publishing house for foreign literature in which she announces her plans for *The Seventh Cross*: "I will finish a little novel, about 200 to 300 pages, based on an event that recently took place in Germany, a story that provides an opportunity to learn about very many levels in fascist Germany through the fate of a single man."[1] The novel narrates the escape of seven prisoners from a concentration camp near the cities of Mainz and Frankfurt. While six fugitives are soon killed or captured, one, Georg Heisler, escapes down the Rhine to Holland with the help of the underground Communist Party but also through the more or less spontaneous assistance of a number of people acting from any number of motivations. Seghers had herself escaped from Germany after being briefly arrested and interrogated in the wake of the Reichstagsbrand.[2] She spent much of the 1930s living outside Paris, where she was deeply involved in the cultural and political life of the German emigration.[3] Seghers would later tersely sum up her activity in French exile from 1933 to 1940 as "work, write, study, fight against the Nazis."[4] With *The Seventh Cross*, Seghers develops an exilic meditation on the social topography of fascist Germany, so that landscape becomes a complex optic in this novel through which Seghers attempts to discern a fragile network of solidarity and resistance beneath the grid of National Socialist surveillance. This chapter traces out the problems of legibility and narrative that emerge from Seghers's framing of the political problematics of the contested terms *Heimat* and *Volk* in *The Seventh Cross*, a novel that foregrounds the limitations of the Popular Front politics of the 1930s in its concern with the narrative coordination of everyday life and emplotment.

Internationale Literatur published the first chapter installments during the summer of 1939. In September of that year the serialization of *The Seventh Cross* ceased, as the novel's antifascist politics were no longer welcome in the Soviet Union after the signing of the non-aggression pact with Germany.[5] Publication plans in western Europe collapsed as well, as the struggling Querido Verlag, among the most important of the German exile presses in western Europe, dragged its feet until the German invasion of France and the Netherlands made the publication of Seghers's novel impossible in Europe. By 1940, with Seghers herself on the run from the invading German troops and her husband, László Radványi, interned by the French as an enemy alien, Seghers was more concerned with saving the manuscript than having it published. Seghers later recounted:

> I had four copies: one at the house of a friend, which was bombed. . . . A French friend took the second with him when he was called up; he wanted to translate the book into his own language. This friend was sent to the Maginot Line. I have not seen him or the famous Maginot Line or the copy again. The third fell into the hands of the Gestapo in my Paris apartment. The fourth was fortunately brought to the United States, and thus the book was saved.[6]

Through the energetic intervention of F. C. Weiskopf, the recipient of that fourth copy in the United States, *The Seventh Cross* was published in English translation in 1942, quickly becoming a best seller.[7]

Previous to *The Seventh Cross*, Seghers had published three major novels during the exile period, *Der Kopflohn* [A Price on His Head 1934], *Der Weg durch den Februar* [The Way Through February 1935], a fictionalized account of the Austrian February uprising of 1934, and *Die Rettung*. These novels focused on the proletarian milieu and the dynamics of everyday life as a site of political struggle.[8] During the 1930s, Seghers developed her distinctive mode of novelistic composition, which she was to pursue and refine in her later great panoramic novels of the GDR, characterized by "an extensive character ensemble, . . . scenic and episodic narration, . . . montage, and simultaneous and independently progressing plotlines" that aspired to create a kind of prismatic totality by way of the structural concentration of these narrative elements around a clearly delineated place or event.[9] This narrative structure, which dominates *Die Rettung* [The Rescue 1937] and *Die Toten blieben jung* [The Dead Stay Young 1949] in particular, was first developed by Seghers in her early novel *Die Gefährten* [The Wayfarers 1932], a multistranded narrative that follows a number of émigrés from the Hungarian Soviet Republic through the white terror of 1920s in southern and eastern Europe, which Siegfried Kracauer had already described as a contemporary martyr chronicle in a review of the book for the *Frankfurter Zeitung*.[10] This novel is heavily influenced, as Kurt Batt points out, by the techniques of Dos Passos, echoing in its "montage construction . . . [and] interspersion of authentic reports into a fictional plot" novels like the *42nd Parallel*. At the same time, Batt insists, whereas Dos Passos uses these techniques to underlie the anomie of individual life in the modern metropolis, in Seghers's novel "the apparent amputation of one character from another, which corresponds to the separated parallel plotlines, is abrogated by a connecting ethos, the oneness with the avant-garde as international force."[11]

While sharing formal similarities with *Die Gefährten*, *The Seventh Cross* also borrows from popular genre-literature to tie its various narrative strands and thematic concerns together around a classical fugitive story, producing a kind of Popular Front thriller.[12] In many ways indebted to the modernist experimentation of the 1920s, the novel is less formally experimental than some of Seghers's earlier works. Alexander Stephan has described the book's form as a kind of "moderate modernism," which incorporates and mediates between modernism and realism, fiction and reportage elements, and episodic episodes and a traditional linear plot.[13] Seghers herself has stated that her model for the novel was less the work of Dos Passos than the Italian author Alessandro Manzoni's 1821 novel *The Betrothed*. In Manzoni's work, Seghers found a model for her own *Gesellschaftsroman* fascist Germany around an "event" that would allow "the author to show all of the conflicts of his people in all strata, in all individuals."[14] As Bernard Spies points out, the escape is less the theme of Seghers's novel than its narrative principle. The book "uses the movement of the fugitive in space as a corridor allowing insight into various strata and mentalities of National Socialist Germany, and simultaneously as a structuring element that creates linearity and integration."[15] Continuity and discontinuity in this narrative structuring are punctuated by the repetition of moments of decision; confronted by the fact of Heisler's flight, what do characters do?

If, in the first period of antifascist exile literature, reports from Hitler's Germany had aimed to shock their readers with the truth of Nazi barbarism, by the late 1930s Seghers was attempting to portray a Germany in which, to again quote Spies, "the outrage of National socialist rule had become the norm."[16] The escape story is thus a means of mapping what the novel repeatedly invokes as *das gewöhnliche Leben*, which is to say the terrain where consent for the National Socialist state is daily produced, and it is in this quotidian production of consent that Heisler's escape provokes "a breach" in which fascist interpellation is momentarily suspended or placed in question (SC 71). Heisler is therefore the figure of an excess or lack in everyday life, the token of the immanent political dimension of the everyday that the Nazis have suppressed, and as he moves through the lives and spaces of fascist Germany, he must conceal himself at the same time that the narrative will invest in him and his escape the symbolic meaning of antifascist struggle. Georg thus represents what Seghers liked to call *das gefährliche Leben*, the life of fugitives, criminals, and revolutionaries, which brushes up against the everyday and produced that uncanny moment where the violence concealed beneath the surface of the quotidian briefly flashes into view.[17] Heisler is described in the novel as "a man who is ready to lose in order to gain" (SC 253). The trope of the *gefährliches Leben* is not merely a thematic preoccupation in Seghers's work but is at the same time an expression of the understanding of the epic form itself, which as Lukács had already asserted in his *Theory of the Novel*, effaces itself before the fact of the world that it depicts, "throwing away in order to win" (TN 53).

The epic cuts through the partial narratives of the normal and reveals their shared exposure to what Lukács calls "the fundamental dissonance of existence" (TN 62). In *The Seventh Cross*, the poles of the normal and the dangerous, however, become hopelessly confused in the oscillation of terror and idyll that characterizes daily life under the Nazi regime, and this thematic contradiction parallels the novel's formal preoccupation with the epic form as such. If, for Lukács, "the totality of life resists any attempt to find a transcendental center within it" (54), the *gefährliches Leben* represented by the fugitive Heisler casts the immanent and empirical worlds of atomized *gewöhnliches Leben* suddenly as themselves so many allegories of the possibility of a Popular Front politics within the total closure of daily life under National

Socialism, while Heisler's flight, the operator of this turn, gives itself over to the contingencies of this everyday life.

The attempt to bridge the gap between modernist techniques and more popular literary genres at a formal level is paralleled by the novel's deep preoccupation with the everyday life and what might be called the social imaginary of Germany under National Socialism. Stephan makes a case for the novel as a precursor to more contemporary directions in the writing of history from below, revealing history as a "product of collective fabrication" of narratives, symbolic forms, and social imaginaries, rather than some kind of objectively unfolding process.[18] With its subtle admixture of literary fiction, documentary fact, and eyewitness accounts of life under the National Socialist regime, *The Seventh Cross* shifts the stakes of resistance and complicity from the kind of explicitly political exposures of fascism and resistance familiar from documents like the famous *Brown Book of the Hitler Terror* to the more thickly graduated shadings of everyday experience:

> Resistance is defined in the novel not as the murder of tyrants or as the centrally directed action of a political association like the KPD, SPD, or the unions, rather as a complex meshwork of punctual dissatisfaction, self-preservation, non-conformity, opposition, and more or less open protest in the everyday realms of family, workplace, and milieu.[19]

For Stephan, the intervention that Seghers makes into the so-called modernism-realism debates lies in its practical demonstration "that realistic literature is historiography from below."[20] To this would have to be added that historiography from below must also wrestle with those same dilemmas of emplotment and chance, of immanence and transcendence, that underlie the literary narrative.[21]

Both in its vernacular modernist form and in its constellation of characters from various classes and social strata of German society, *The Seventh Cross* was in consonance with the turn toward the Popular Front and realist forms in the latter part of the 1930s among artists and writers in the orbit of the Communist parties.[22] In a number of speeches and essays throughout the 1930s, Seghers would develop her own theory of how the figure of the popular should be understood and of what a literary practice in line with the politics of the Popular Front might look like. Among her better-known interventions is the exchange of letters that Seghers initiated with Georg Lukács in the pages of

Internationale Literatur at the time that she was working on *The Seventh Cross*. In this correspondence, Seghers defended the experimental character of much contemporary socialist prose against Lukács. With reference to the generation of Kleist, Hölderlin, and Büchner, variously destroyed by the misery of the post-Napoleonic German reaction, Seghers wrote that aesthetic immediacy is not always to be linked, as Lukács would have it, to cognitive immediacy, that is, mistaking social appearances for deeper contradictions that produce them.[23] Rather, in times of crisis, revolution, and extreme reaction, aesthetic immediacy represents the urgency and trauma of the present. Thus, for writers like Kleist, "the reality of their time and their society did not exert a gradual and persistent influence on them, but rather a kind of shock effect,"[24] producing not so much a mirror of the social whole but rather "splinters," fragmentary reflections of an epoch that could not yet be thought or represented.[25]

As Lukács rejoins, the question here is less one of the shock of the new than it is of what he refers to, citing Gorky, as the "social backing" of literature, "the unity of democratic tradition in social life and realist tradition in art,"[26] a unity that both Seghers and Lukács agree has never existed in Germany. Yet whereas for Lukács, the lack of this popular tradition is the justification for rejecting what he dismisses as the aesthetics of immediacy, from Kleist to Expressionism and beyond, Seghers sees the "social backing" of Germany's popular tradition precisely in the tragic and head-on confrontation with the conflicts and antagonisms that have historically disfigured German culture and society.

The popular is thus less to be found in a given progressive tradition or heritage than in a social engagement that allows for the "making conscious of conflicts."[27] Throughout the 1930s, Seghers argued that the key terms of the Communist Popular Front discourse, terms like *Volk* and *Heimat*, cannot be regarded as self-evident unities but can be approached only through the searching out of the contradictions that they are used by fascist demagogy to conceal. *The Seventh Cross* is centrally engaged with both of these terms, but it arrives at them by way of a close attentiveness to everyday life and those moments where the false closure that fascist ideology and practice impose on these terms breaks down. Walter Benjamin, as we have discussed, uses the term "chronicle" to grasp the complicated ways in which Seghers refracts the opacities of the notion of popularity through the very architecture of her narratives. The chronicle, as we know from his thesis "On the Concept of History," has a special place in Benjamin's thought as an epic form that "narrates events without distinguishing between major and minor ones" in accord with the principle that "nothing that ever happened should be regarded as lost to history."[28] Thus Seghers's epics are "not organized in terms of episodes and a principal plot line," instead containing "an abundance of short episodes often building to a climax."[29] *The Seventh Cross*, I will argue, is a novel that poses this problem on a formal level, but at the same time Seghers explicitly thematizes this narratological question of emplotment and open-ended narrative as a formal allegory of the problem of the popular itself. The question animating the novel, then, is how one is to make legible, to bring into the realm of visibility, the contradictions, connections, and resources for resistance in everyday life under fascism and how to summon something like a Popular Front plot out of the fascist present from these scattered moments. The doubling of the narrative into a third-person narrator and the *Wir-Stimme*, or "we," of the plural singular narrator that frames the novel as a fragile and flickering epic possibility pose this question on the formal level.

The Seventh Cross frames this question in terms of a tension between plot and coincidence. Will the escape (that is, the plot both in the sense of the narrative and the conspiracy to get Georg Heisler to safety) succeed and become a sign of the vitality of antifascist solidarity and the inevitability of National Socialism's demise, or will it become just another random and anecdotal happening in the daily life of Nazi dictatorship? Hanging in the balance is the question of whether it is possible to introduce a historical break into the mythical time of fascism. This question will be decided not within any of the episodes that the narrative will relate but in the very relation between them. In this relationality, a spatial dimension opens within the novel's formal structure such that again here, the construction of the novel reflects its thematics. As a story of flight and detection, the novel is inevitably entangled in the dynamics of place and space, and Seghers uses this aspect of the plot to contest the National Socialist framing of *Heimat*. *The Seventh Cross* is thus a novel of place in the sense that "all attempts to institute horizons, to establish boundaries, to secure the identity of places, can . . . be seen to be attempts to stabilize the meaning of particular envelopes of space-time."[30] It inscribes the landscape between Frankfurt and Mainz with two legibilities, both revealed in Georg Heisler's flight from the Westhofen concentration camp. Seghers provides a fascist conception of social space, which she identifies with the metaphor of the grid. Against this fascist mapping, Heisler's escape depends on his ability to establish a different sense of place, one delimited by the "confidence" (*Vertrauen*) that binds antifascists and decent Germans in small-scale acts of resistance and defiance against the Nazi regime, which the novel variously describes as a network or a circuit and which links these small acts with the great struggles of the day, from the Spanish Civil War to the resistance of Chinese workers to Japanese imperialism. The novel lays out these modes of the grid of surveillance and the net of *Vertrauen* but also narrates the interpenetration of these two modes of reading the social space of Germany under National Socialism. This ambiguity drives the obstinate undecidability of plan and chance in the book's preoccupation with emplotment and thus opens onto the condition of exile itself through the instability, the revocability—in either its fascist or its antifascist variant—of stabilizing space into place.

PLACE AND SPACE

Consider a well-known depiction of the city as a gridded space from the Weimar Republic, Fritz Lang's 1931 film *M*.[31] Early in the film Lang uses a telephone conversation between the *Polizeipräsident* and a government minister as scaffolding for a communications montage of the police investigation of the rash of child murders creating mayhem in Berlin. Perhaps the most notable image of this montage is that of the concentric circles radiating out from the crime scene onto a map of the city. Tom Gunning notes apropos of this scene, "the investigation converts the city into a series of charts and maps, a rational order . . . viewed from above, the city becomes a pattern of lines and forms, intersections and borders, placed within the hard-edged geometry of the compass."[32] For Edward Dimendberg, this scene marks the emergence of film noir at the moment that technologies of seeing developed by the German avant-garde (one thinks of the *neues Sehen* school of photography or the photomontage of Hannah Hoch and John Heartfield) are appropriated for the purposes of surveillance of what he refers to as the "centripetal city" of classical modernity, "a navigable metropolis" "of neighborhoods, public landmarks, and zones of safety, danger, and transgression."[33] In many ways, as Anton Kaes reminds us, *M*. provides the founding imagery of what he calls, following Ernst Jünger's famous 1930 essay "Die totale Mobilmachung," the mobilized city, a space increasingly shaped by modern technologies of war and perception.[34] For Jünger, the urban landscape was increasingly one where the line between war and peace, everyday life and martial mobilization, was effaced by the growing interpenetration of war, industrial labor, and technologies of mass communication in the frisson of ceaseless traffic and "merciless discipline." In total mobilization, the boundary between the everyday and the state of emergency is disabled, as everyday life itself becomes a militarized battle of materials and a "gigantic labor process" at once, war and work indistinguishable.[35] "With a pleasure-tinged horror," Jünger swoons, "we sense that here, not a single atom is not in motion—that we are profoundly inscribed in this raging process."[36]

This mobilized and mediatized city can be thought of then as the production of a representation of space, in the sense that Henri Lefebvre uses the term, as the conceptualized realm of systems of power and control.[37] What is being produced in this scene, both on the diegetic level of the film and on the level of the film as discourse, is, however, not simply the abstract space of the segmented, mappable city, "dominated by technological mediations, commodification, conceptualization, and visual stimuli,"[38] but rather a cognitive mapping of two incommensurable yet overlapping orders of spatial practice. Dimendberg conceptualizes the film as a contestation of urban space between two orders of practice, that of vision and reading on the one hand (the police) and that of verbal discourse and seeing on the other (the underworld).[39] It is important to note that Lang's film does not allow one of these modes of spatial production to dominate the other. Thus the *Polizeipräsident*'s elaboration of the investigative methods being put to work is cut short by the minister's exasperated cry, "But what good is all this!?" As Gunning notes, the film is less a gridding of the city into abstract space than an exposure of the "blindness" that "defeats its rational order of investigation." This blindness is literal in the film, since it is a blind panhandler who identifies Beckert to the underworld, but in a broader sense, blindness is a figure for the remainders left over from the production of abstract space that Gunning describes as the "monstrous shapes and distortions" of a desire driven underground by a rationalized spatial order.[40] Here, in the interstices of competing mappings of the city—those of the police, the underworld, and of course the media—Lang's film undermines the notion of a single abstract space gridding the modern metropolis, dissolving it into the palimpsestic multiplicity of *Eigensinn* and contested and partial totalizations.

Like *M.*, *The Seventh Cross* is a story of flight, detection, and forensic mapping. The Nazi pursuit of the seven escapees from Westhofen is mobilizing and spatializing of the pathways of the *gewöhnliches*, producing a network of signals that will lead to the fugitive out of the aggregation of conversations, activities, and relationships that appear to their subjects as the contingent ephemera of their everyday lives. The search for Heisler is conducted by the Gestapo across a "network that covered the entire country, to all the railroad stations and bridgeheads, all the police stations and guards, all the landing places and inns" (SC 212). The entire urban landscape is quickly mobilized, and all means of transportation "closely watched, as if war had broken out."[41] In other words, the search itself transforms the region into a map centered upon "the red dot marked CAMP WESTHOFEN" and the "three concentric circles" surrounding it, which mark the sphere of possible itineraries of the seven escapees (25). Indeed, this network not only links the frontier, the bridges, and traffic flows of the Rhineland but Heisler's own life history, catalogued in police files. In other words, it is not a matter of territory and borders alone but also of the spatialization of experience. By the fourth day of his escape, Heisler finds "his home town and all the people who had ever been connected with his life, that circle which sustains every being and surrounds him with blood relatives, lovers and teachers and masters and friends transformed into a network of living traps" (212). In this moment, Georg realizes that life itself has become a spatial grid, "a triangular network within which the man would have to be trapped unless he were the devil himself" (391). However, as in Lang's film, the representational space of surveillance is literally shaped by that which eludes it. "The tightest net consists mainly of holes," the narrator reminds us (216). Indeed, even at the outset of the escape, the narrator juxtaposes the clean extension of the map's grid to the dense fog surrounding the camp, which in turn corresponds to Fahrenberg's vertiginous sensation of reality itself slipping away at the news of the escape. "This whole ghastly business was not even a bad dream," Seghers writes, "but merely the memory of one" (23).

Fahrenberg's sergeant Zillich is overwhelmed by the image of absolute extension when he ponders the escape and the "precious seconds during which seven little dots moved further and further out into an infinity where they could no longer be overtaken" (SC 24). At the close of the novel, as Fahrenberg ponders what he considers to be the impossible possibility that Heisler might actually have escaped, Heisler's body, refusing to resolve itself into a discrete point on the grid, expands in Fahrenberg's own mind to fill the map, becoming "not an individual but a featureless and inexhaustible power" (392). Another way to think about these maps and the problems they bespeak is the distinction that Michel de Certeau draws in his essay "Spatial Stories" between the map and the itinerary as spatial trajectories or syntaxes.[42] For de Certeau, the itinerary is the principle of mobility and practice; it is going rather than seeing. The map, on the other hand, describes the proper and the named. The map belongs to the order of the place, of the fixed and bounded space of power and surveillance. The itinerary, conversely, opens up space, which de Certeau describes as "intersections of mobile elements" or as "practiced place."[43] With this distinction in mind, de Certeau describes the story as the movement between these determinations of the mobile and the inert; it is "the identification of places and the actualization of spaces."[44] The problem represented by the map with its concentric circles in both *M.* and *The Seventh Cross* would then appear to be the relationship between map and itinerary; indeed it is in a sense the problem of narrative itself, if we follow de Certeau's definition of story as the introduction of "the dynamic contradiction between any given delimitation and its mobility."[45]

While it is tempting to read the mobility of Heisler's body through space as a transgressing or undoing of Nazi place in *The Seventh Cross*, Seghers's narrative in fact confounds the binary terms of "map" and "itinerary." Heisler's itinerary is also a map, even if at first glance it appears more opaque than that of the Gestapo. It is the network of the underground Communist Party, which by the late 1930s had been largely destroyed by the Nazi regime. What remained of a KPD resistance was scattered and well concealed, as many former party activists retreated into a private sphere that was itself, as Stephan remarks, compromised by "fear and mistrust, betrayal, and passivity."[46] The notion of the connection, or *Verbindung*, becomes essential in *The Seventh Cross* as a kind of circuit through which the party might maintain itself beneath the surface of fascist everyday life. This kind of connection is neither an intimate relationship nor simply involvement in the party. It is neither public nor private, and it both cuts across and shapes Seghers's characteristic distinction of the *gewöhnliches* and the *gefährliches Leben*. When Franz Marnet hears of Georg's escape, he realizes it is not simply "the firm bond of the common cause" but also still "that other bond which at the time had bitten so painfully into their flesh and at which they had both tugged so violently" that ties him to Georg (SC 17). This is the bond that produces what Jameson describes in his essay on *The Aesthetics of Resistance* as a particular kind of space that arises in the interrelations of the confined spaces of clandestinity and imprisonment on the one hand and the urban map on the other, between isolation and a heightened receptivity to the signals and signs of the world outside. "These enclosed spaces," Jameson writes of the rooms and cells that feature so prominently in Weiss's novel, "have their own specific dialectic: a perception and a groping reading of the outside of themselves . . . can only be organized by and projected onto some larger grid; just as the very movement of the clandestines from one room to another demands advanced planning and spatial foresight."[47]

Among the most important of these enclosed spaces in *The Seventh Cross* is Franz Marnet's room, in which the ensemble of the thematics is captured in a tableau of reminiscence. The novel associates Franz with the realm of the *Gewöhnliche* and Georg with its opposite number, *das Gefährliche*. Georg is portrayed as a disruptive outsider, arrogant and contemptuous of others, while Franz is a deliberate and thoughtful young man. In the winter they live together, Seghers writes, "they worked, studied, and went to political demonstrations and meetings" (SC 65). This relationship that is at once political and intimate is anchored in its pedagogical valence: "the mere fact that Georg asked questions and Franz answered them created their common world, which grew younger the longer one dwelled on it and expanded the more one took from it." This common world is not only Georg and Franz but the intimacy between them that arises through their party work and study, through their connection to the wider project they are caught up in, reminding the reader of the famous evocation of the "Common Cause" in Brecht's *The Mother*: "he and I were two; the third it was, the common cause commonly driving us, that is what united us."[48] That other bond, the bond of betrayal, subtends this bond of the common cause. For Georg, moving in with the young Communist Franz was very precisely an escape from *das gewöhnliche Leben*: "living with Franz meant not only studying, absorbing certain thoughts, and taking part in certain struggles, but also carrying oneself differently, wearing different clothes, hanging different pictures, and judging different things to be beautiful" (233).

But the "unintentional but impassable chasm" that opens between Georg and his old family and friends through his friendship with Franz and his adoption of the latter's Communist asceticism soon opens between Georg and Franz as well. The pedagogical relationship between the two thus finds its complement in the bond of betrayal, as

Georg seduces Franz's girlfriend, Elli Mettenheimer. This betrayal is itself a kind of question addressed to the world that Franz represents. "You're no friend of mine," he tells Franz, "you never say anything of yourself" (SC 67). Georg's feeling that there is something essential that Franz is concealing, that Franz "has something up [his] sleeve" (66), turns into Georg's motivation for stealing Elli, but one suspects that this problematic has less to do with Elli than with the enigmatic surplus of intimacy between Franz and Georg that somehow cannot be squared with the common cause. The moment of betrayal, "the first one in their life together in which they understood each other completely," is the moment of recognition between the two (67).

Verbindungen then in Seghers's sense are a form of intimacy that exceeds both the personal and the political, and Georg, precisely in his notorious "unpredictability" (SC 233), is the operator of these connective associations. After the Nazi seizure of power, Georg becomes the man in underground party work who "held all the threads in his hands" (70). In the wake of his arrest, Hermann, an underground KPD functionary, must change all those connections of which Georg was aware, in case Georg should break under the duress of his internment. The connection thus stands in an ambiguous relationship to the problem of visibility. It must be concealed and invisible to the surveillance and mapping operations of the fascist state apparatus. Yet the very possibility of antifascist solidarity depends on the capacity of the novel's characters to recognize the traces of this "common cause" that has been forced beneath the visible surface of experience. The plot of the novel thus relies on motifs that in their very intangibility were to become central to Seghers's work in exile and in the GDR: the affective bond of *Vertrauen*, meaning trust, confidence, dependability, and increasingly a figure for a social solidarity that exceeds the territory of the narrowly political to invest the *gewöhnliches Leben* in a sense similar to Brecht's development of the term *Freundlichlkeit*, a willingness to "make common cause with whatever is unobtrusive but relentless like water," in other words to ally with the forces for change within the everyday.[49]

The problem associated with *Vertrauen* in *The Seventh Cross* is therefore one of legibility, and this in turn introduces an element of contingency into the plot, since the novel's emplotment is driven by the capacity of its characters to recognize this nebulous quality, which not only is a sense of shared past experiences but is burdened with a predictive power to answer the question of what will someone do now that they are isolated from the third thing, the common cause. *Vertrauen* is thus inevitably shadowed in the novel by its opposite, mistrust and suspicion. Seghers reminds us as Heisler spies a once loyal comrade palling around with the SA, "there was no sign on [his] head to identify him as trustworthy" (SC 197). Likewise, when Heisler's old soccer friend Paul Röder begins looking for someone with KPD connections to help Georg, he thinks to himself, "the bad ones will betray me, and the good ones are hiding" (322). When Röder finally approaches his colleague Fiedler (a former party member) on Georg's behalf, Fiedler's reaction is one of shock that Röder has seen something in him that he had taken such good care to hide and muses, "in spite of every precaution and without any intention . . . something must have remained" through which Paul Röder was able to perceive that, despite having lost all connection with the party, he is "not entirely callous and indifferent" and that he "still belongs to the movement, for how else could Paul have found [him] out" (327). Asking Röder why he has come to him of all people, Fiedler receives the answer, "confidence [*Vertrauen*] I guess" (325). Whereas the gaze of National Socialist mapping sees "the luscious everyday world that is not transparent and without core" (186), the Communist characters in the novel are those to whom it is revealed "how ruthlessly and fearfully outward powers could strike at the very core of a man, but at the same time . . . at the very core there was something that was unassailable and inviolable" (395).

The topoi of confidence and connection become hermeneutic tools in a different mode of mapping, one based on memory rather than vision, as Heisler's flight catalyzes a fleeting resuturing of the sundered connections of the KPD's Weimar-era counterpublic sphere, bringing together people who had been forced into isolation by fear and persecution.[50] Even in the absence of immediate relations, these connections allow themselves to be felt, exercising a kind of objectivity of their own. With an eye to facilitating his escape, Franz thus attempts to anticipate Georg's itinerary through another kind of representation of space:

> Just as the police used their documents and card indexes and records to acquire knowledge of the fugitive's former life and enable them to draw a net over the whole city, so Franz too laid a net that from hour to hour became tighter as his memory conjured up everyone who to his knowledge had at one time been connected with Georg. Among them were some who had never left a trace on any registration blank or any other official

> document. It needed knowledge of a different kind to get on their track. (SC 216–17)

This different kind of knowledge comes from a capacity to read the seams where *das gewöhnliche Leben* and *das gefährliche Leben* overlap, and it is a mode of spatial practice that is less invested in the itinerary and map dynamics that de Certeau theorizes than it is in a reframing of the map and its borders themselves. Franz's practice of place is concealed but no less binding in its mapping function, as expressed in the envelope that Georg finally receives to enable his passage across the Rhine and out of Germany, containing a false passport and some banknotes, the "result of a vast amount of dangerous and painstaking work; it represented innumerable errands, information, lists, the work of past years, old friendships and connections . . . a whole network that spanned across oceans and rivers" (368). The envelope represents, then, a network of connections that links the underground resistance inside Germany to an antifascist Popular Front politics outside Germany; it is the circuit of the common cause. As the interned first-person plural narrator explains in the novel's opening passage, Heisler's escape, precisely because it could not be done alone, is "a small triumph, assuredly, considering our helplessness and convicts' clothing, but a triumph nevertheless . . . which suddenly made us conscious of our own power" (6).

In other words, what appears perhaps from the perspective of Fahrenberg and the Gestapo as a contingent flight across boundaries is in fact less of an "actualization of place" in de Certeau's sense of introducing some delinquent, mobile, unplaceable element than it is a contestation of place, a countermapping. The establishment of place is at stake in the novel. If we might briefly return to the image from *M.*, what is notable in *The Seventh Cross* is that in contrast to the modern metropolis portrayed in *M.*, the space of Seghers's novel is very much centered. This is no less true for the antifascist circuit of *Vertrauen* than it is for the National Socialist network of surveillance and terror. The map in *M.* is anchored by the *Tatort*, the scene of the crime, a contingent point in the infinite extension of the urban grid, which though it anchors a particular map is not itself really a place. The camp in *The Seventh Cross*, on the other hand, authorizes urban space from the outside, lying in the countryside but connected to the cities of Mainz and Frankfurt through "the electric lines and telephone apparatus" to which the commandant is so partial (SC 24).

In this sense, the camp is, as Agamben puts it, a "dislocating localization,"[51] an exceptional site that shapes and produces the space around it. Westhofen functions in Seghers's novel as a kind of heterotopia in the sense that Michel Foucault uses this term to denote a place where given social relationships are "at one and the same time represented, challenged, and overturned: a sort of place that lies outside all places and yet is actually localizable."[52] Centered on the Dance Ground, which "resembled an intermediate landing station," a "place . . . hardly of this earth, nor . . . part of the beyond" (SC 383), where prisoners are beaten, harangued, and humiliated, the camp represents an "effectively realized utopia"[53] of National Socialism in Seghers's book. Precisely in its enigmatic centrality, the camp provides a symbol of the regime's coercive power, for example, in the reaction of the village in the first days of the National Socialist regime, "when the Westhofen camp had been opened more than three years before, when barracks and walls had been built, barbed wire put up and guards posted, when the first column of prisoners had passed by to the accompaniment of jeers and kicks . . . when screams could be heard at night, and howling" (82). An enclosed, occluded nonplace, which, like the apparatus of Kafka's penal colony, provides a conspicuous but illegible spectacle of judgment and punishment, Westhofen is the site where Nazi discourse of masters and creatures is produced. For the SA and the SS, the camp is the realized place of the *Alles ist erlaubt* ideology of Nazism,[54] where they are given the opportunity to "have full-grown vigorous men lined up before oneself and be permitted to break them, quickly or slowly; to see their bodies, erect only a moment ago, become four-legged" (SC 143).

Nevertheless, in *The Seventh Cross*, creatureliness is produced not through direct violence but through discourse, as we see in the multiple scenes of interrogation in the novel. Overkamp, the police commissioner in charge of investigating the escape, is described as having the manner and bearing of "a man whose profession it is to get something out of someone else: diseased organs, secrets, confessions" (SC 49). The extraction of secrets, confessions, and discourse is based on the production of fear, which works as a kind of lubricating agent. In separating fear from the "useless material" of conflicting emotions, not only is evidence revealed, but the subaltern imaginary of fascism is produced as well: "the feeling of fear became separated from secondary feelings; visualizations of a painful death from the fact of actually being alive. . . . Evasions and irrelevancies became separated from the true record" (264). In the affective idiom of the novel, fear is a realm of immobilization and atomization; it is, as Seghers tells us, "the condition in which a certain idea begins to overrun everything else" (107). Fascism creates, through fear, an almost mythical temporality in which the subject is reduced to the single idea of its own subalternity, its own exposure, and is inscribed into a timeless space of domination and submission:

> But the fear that had gnawed at her heart at that time was still in her blood: the fear that is entirely dissociated from the conscience, the fear of the poor, the fear of the chicken before the hawk, the fear of being pursued by the state. It is the age-old fear, indicating more exactly who the state served than all the constitutions and historical works in the world. (300)

It is precisely this mythical temporality of fear into which Heisler's escape introduces a breach. Already in Westhofen, Heisler becomes an example of resistance and a demonstration that "nothing can break a man of his stamp" (70). His successful escape carries this breach beyond the grounds of the camp itself into the public sphere, catalyzing doubts, conversations, and speculation. The camp is thus estranged in an almost Brechtian sense, which Seghers captures through the young boy who helps Georg by lying to the Gestapo about a stolen jacket. "Ever since he had begun to think independently," Seghers writes, "the camp had been there, and so had the explanations for its being" (83). Precisely in a context where National Socialism has become normalized, Heisler's escape calls its regime into question. "It was," Seghers writes, as if "the camp, to which they had long ago been accustomed, was erected all over again" (83).

If the gaze of the fascist apparatus of surveillance is totally mobilized, it is also obsessively discursive. It cannot maintain or countenance silence or opacity. Overkamp, it is said, "could get information from a corpse" (SC 183). The countervailing principle is that of the book's Communist characters, particularly Georg and his mentor, Ernst Wallau, who represent an uncanny silence that by virtue of its very perseverance becomes "a delicate slippery thing . . . supple like a lizard," which "slipped between one's fingers, elusive and unseizable, unkillable, invulnerable" (143). Seghers portrays Overkamp's session with Wallau as the storming of a fortress, with Wallau's face as the "scene of the approaching action" (184–85). The stakes of the engagement are the production of a reaction that could be decoded into a semiotics of fear or surprise, and Overkamp watches "the prisoner's face as an officer watches a terrain" (185).

Wallau counters with a gaze "directed straight ahead, right through the affairs of a world that had suddenly become glassy and transparent . . . right through to the core of what is impenetrable and able to withstand the gaze of the dying." Whereas Nazis see only what presents itself to vision, Wallau's gaze is the one able to step out of history; it is the gaze of the dead. Wallau falls silent before the questioning of Overkamp, and he will not speak again. "Once there had been a man named Ernst Wallau," Seghers writes, "that man was dead. Hadn't we just heard his last words?" (SC 187). What follows is a strange double framing of Wallau's life as a Communist partisan, of an exemplary biography of the German workers' movement from the November revolution to 1933, as the parallel accounts of Overkamp's questions find their silent refutation in a narration that is no longer Wallau's but also no longer that of the novel's narrator. When Overkamp poses the question of whether Wallau still clings to his old ideas, this voice addresses us: "They should have asked me that yesterday. . . . Yesterday I should have been compelled to shout Yes! Today I keep silent. Today others are answering in my place; the songs of my people, the judgment of posterity" (188). Wallau's "ugly little face" and the "icy flood of silence" that issues forth from it mark the threshold of another voice, concealed beneath the disconnected and accidental stuff of the everyday world. This silence, Seghers implies, if one were to truly listen to it, would be the transcendental horizon of liberation itself, the possible happy end of history, but this voice is also the voice that is beyond all terrestrial bonds.

The Westhofen of 1937, the "wild camp" four years into National Socialism, is not yet the extermination camp of the 1940s.[55] That we are not yet at the threshold of bare life is clear from the initially odd fact that the antifascist discourse of the novel is also centered on the camp, and this in the form of the book's narrative frame, the *Wir-Stimme* or first-person plural voice of the Westhofen inmates who narrate the novel's frame. The camp is thus, as Foucault remarks of heterotopias generally, a juxtaposition of incompatible spaces.[56] Just as the fascist network of mapping and surveillance centers on Westhofen, so does the Communist circuit that shadows that network, but it also extends beyond the German frontier. "Neither electrically charged barbed wire nor long lines of guards nor machine guns had been able to prevent events that happened on the outside from finding their way into Westhofen," Seghers writes. "A certain natural law, or a mysterious circuit, seemed to connect this group of chained up miserables with world centers" (SC 219). This mysterious circuit is itself a breach in the National Socialist representation of space; it is a circuit at the heart of the fascist project that generates plans and visions of another Germany, tales and legends of escape and resistance. One might in fact read Seghers's depiction of this indigestible Communist remainder in the bowls of the fascist torture apparatus as the materialization of the irreducible utopian element that persists in National Socialism in the displaced forms of its betrayal and persecution, the traces of heaven on earth that cannot quite be driven from hell, to evoke the spirit of the contemporaneous work of Ernst Bloch.[57]

The Westhofen camp, then, is paradoxically both the privileged site of the production of fascist masters and subjects as well as the site of the persistence of the common cause, the principle of connection, to which Seghers gives voice. This first-person plural voice is not so much an attempt to summon forth a voice of witness, but it is very explicitly the voice of a kind of future-perfect tense in which fascism will have been defeated.[58] This is the voice that reaches from the barbed wire of the Westhofen camp to the battlefields of Spain and China. That circuit is at once less perceptible but more substantial than the Nazi network of surveillance that it eludes or exceeds would then be the polemical point of Seghers's novel; it is that power that, precisely because it cannot be fully reduced to spatial extension but retains a trace of duration and chance, "is the only force suddenly to grow immeasurably and incalculably" (SC 8).

HEIMAT, OR, THE LEGIBILITY OF EVERYDAY LIFE

Commenting on Lukács's *Theory of the Novel*, Fredric Jameson notes the contradiction inherent to the novel form between poles that Jameson designates with the Kantian language of transcendence and immanence.[59] The uniqueness of the novel, then, lies in its fusion of form to content: "*Episch* is immanent," Jameson writes, "in the sense that meaning is inherent in all its objects and details, all its facts, all its events."[60] In this sense, Seghers is using Lukács against himself in their correspondence, where her notion of immediacy is not to be confused with the kind of immediacy that Lukács never tired of pillorying as a fixation on "the objective immediacy of the social surface."[61] For

Seghers, immediacy is not a question of cognitive misrecognition but rather one of immanence in this sense of the question of the legibility of the world in terms of its immanent meaningfulness, and the possibility of what Jameson refers to as an epic mode of "immanent transcendence," wherein "the transformation of being would somehow be implicit in being itself" as a kind of transcendental horizon of the inert factuality of everyday life.[62] To the degree that *The Seventh Cross* is an antifascist novel, then, it occupies itself with the hermeneutics of the quotidian in Hitler's Germany, searching for openings that might betoken some subterranean movement beneath the frozen surface of everyday life and spatial practice. Throughout the 1930s and 1940s, Seghers articulated such a project in her own elaboration of a counterdiscourse of *Heimat*, locating this fissure historically. In her 1941 essay "Germany and Us," Seghers develops an analysis of the *deutsche Misère*, arguing that the nineteenth-century industrialization and unification of Germany were not achieved under the banner of an ascendant bourgeoisie but by the reactionary Junker aristocracy. Particularly after the revolutions of 1848, social demands in Germany were no longer articulated in concert with national ones. This rupture between personal experience and the political, generally thought to be one of the defining characteristics of modernity, is pathologically accentuated in the German context, and "therefore the life experience of the Germans is also fissured, burdened by its history."[63]

Seghers's address to the 1935 International Congress of Writers for the Defense of Culture in Paris had already explored this fissure in terms of the German relationship to place, opposing the notions of blood and soil deployed by National Socialism with a vision of a different mode of spatial identification inscribed with the history of class struggle and the divisions of German society:

> If one of our writers travels crossways through Germany, more or less from the north-east to the south-west, and he caught sight of the grandiose, dreadful, sulfur-yellow Leuna factory-landscape, the pumping heart of our fatherland, where tens of thousands of workers realize peculiar inventions for the frugal country, is he then proud of this sight? Is he proud of Leuna, the national asset? He is not proud of the national asset, and yet he is proud of the labor power of fifty thousand workers, proud of the achievement of this landscape saturated with the blood of the central German uprising, proud of the future of

> Leuna. Ask first of the weighty word *Vaterlandsliebe* what it is about your country that is cherished. Do the holy goods of the nation console the dispossessed? . . . Does the "holy earth of the homeland" console the landless? Yet he who has worked in our factories, who has demonstrated in our streets, who has struggled in our language, he would not be human if he did not love our country.[64]

The presence of this other Germany inscribed into the landscape is a concretization of the "progressive" German culture that might anchor an antifascist discourse of the nation during the exile period. This notion of *Heimat* reverses the naturalization of social relations through National Socialism's idealization of biology and destiny. Leuna is not evoked here as a landscape for contemplation as much as it is conjured as a symbol for the very possibility of a different emplotment of German history than that offered by Hitler's ideologues, of a popular antifascist politics that might emerge given a shift in optics. Thus Seghers returns to the ambiguity of the Leuna landscape in "Germany and Us," writing,

> Leuna means at once a painful phase in Germany's history, memories of the central German uprising, struggle and sacrifice, and the vengeance of those who are today the rulers of Germany and already then had shown their true faces, tortured and murdered. Leuna means the unfailingly precise labor power of tens of thousands of workers, today frightfully misused, employed tomorrow no longer against, but rather for the people, of which it is a part. Just like Leuna, every square kilometer of our country attests to the ability, to the labor power, of the resistance of its people and at the same time of the flashpoints of its history.[65]

Here, rather than a naively crypto-fascist relation to the landscape as a type of mythical origin, the notion of *Heimat* is political and historical, based in the shared experiences of work and struggle that link the generations.[66] *Heimat* is a way of addressing the complicated thickening of place and emplotment that animates both the novel form and an antifascist conception of history. The problem that occupies many of Seghers's works of the exile period is one of the legibility of *Heimat*, which is to say, by what discursive, aesthetic, and political practices can this substratum of resistance be made to appear?

Seghers opens *The Seventh Cross* with a well-known historical and geographic panorama of the Rhineland viewed from the Taunus mountain range bounding the Rhine-Main lowlands in which the novel is set. These lowlands initially appear in a pastoral vision, neither rural nor urban, where the fields and fruit trees stand side by side with the railroad tracks and smoke of the nearby factory (SC 8 9). But this apparent idyll is, as Seghers portrays it, a moment of repose for a region that has in fact been shaped by a long history of struggle. "This is the land," she writes, "of which it is said that the last war's projectiles plow from the ground the projectiles of the war before the last." In a sweeping historical panorama, Seghers emplaces the Rhine-Main lowlands at the border between empires, religions, and revolutions:

> For a long time, though, this chain of hills meant the edge of the world; it was here that the Romans drew their *limes*. So many races had perished here since they burned the Celts' sun altars, so many battles had been fought, that the hills themselves might have thought that what was conquerable had finally been fenced and made arable. . . . Here camped the legions, and with them all of the Gods of the world: city gods and peasant gods, the gods of Jew and Gentile, Astarte and Isis, Mithras and Orpheus. Here, where now Ernst of Schmiedtheim stands by his sheep . . . here the wilderness called. In the valley at his back, in the soft and vaporous sun, stood the peoples' cauldron. North and south, east and west, were brewed together, and while the country as a whole remained unaffected by it all, yet it retained a vestige of everything. Like colored bubbles, empires rose up from that country, rose up and as soon burst again. They left behind no *limes*, no triumphal arches, no military highways; only a few fragments of their women's golden anklets. But they were as hardy and imperishable as dreams. (9)

Seghers then proceeds to provide the reader with a thumbnail sketch of the history of the Rhineland, from the invasion of the Franks at the close of the fifth century AD to the arrival of Nazi regiments into the Rhineland in 1936, writing of the fireworks "the other day" as the "the 140th Infantry Regiment once more marched across the bridge behind its merrily playing band" while "thousands of little swastikas twistedly reflected in the water." The history of empires is briefly interrupted by moments of resistance, for example, the Mainz Republic founded by German Jacobins inspired by the French Revolution, reminding us of the fractured and discontinuous character of Germany's progressive tradition (9).[67]

The landscape bears this history but remains, as GDR critic Kurt Batt has put it, "the emblem of continuity in the midst of historical change."[68] "In this land," Seghers writes, "something new happened every year, but every year the same thing: the apples ripened, and so did the wine under the gently befogged sun and the care of man" (SC 10). Critic Bernard Spies similarly points out that Seghers's account dwells less on the singularity of the succession of historical powers that have crossed over and tarried in this landscape than on "a continuum of historical acts of violence."[69] Spies notes that here Seghers casts history itself as "the progress of violence" in a rather Benjaminian vein. Only against the continuum of domination does the "eschatological point" of Seghers's historical understanding come into view, "which does not after all expect salvation at the end of historical upheavals, but rather beholds it in its immanence: what asserts itself in the continuum of violence in other words is in the long run not the violence itself, but rather humanity, which each power tramples underfoot without being able to destroy."[70]

Regarded from this epochal vantage point, the pageantry of the Nazis already augurs their downfall, the ephemeral quality of their rule when measured against the mute solidity of the quotidian and the persistence of nature itself: "in the morning," Seghers writes, "when the stream left the city behind beyond the railroad bridge, its quiet bluish-gray was in no way altered. How many field standards had it lapped against? How many flags?" (SC 12). This fundament of the natural aligns itself in Seghers's novel with the stories and legends of revolt and resistance from the peasant uprisings, from the Mainz Republic and the workers' movement, and, as Spies points out, with the great leitmotifs of human culture (understood now in the broad sense of the cultivation of nature), "culled from the natural wealth of the region, refined through the labor of centuries: apples and wine."[71]

Heimat in *The Seventh Cross* embraces occurrences that themselves signify both the unrepeatability of the historical properly understood and at the same time the persistence of the everyday. For Seghers, to be in the midst of both of these dimensions is to belong. Thus, riding across through the valley of the Rhine, Franz is struck by "an overpowering feeling that he belonged here. People of feeble sentiments and feeble actions will not understand him easily. To them, 'belonging' means a definite family, or a community, or a love affair. To Franz it meant simply belonging to that piece of soil, to those people, and to that early shift bound for Höchst—above all, to the living" (SC 8). In this sense, to be in *Heimat*, to be among the living, is to be in this punctuated but nonpunctual eventfulness. This simple mode of belonging, though often under duress and brought to the vanishing point, is the ground of *Vertrauen*, which is to say trust, confidence, and intimacy, but an intimacy that springs not from organic relatedness but from "commonly experienced social processes, through work, culture, and language."[72] As Erika Haas writes of this metanarrative, "*Heimat* . . . is there where one belongs, where trust [*Vertrauen*] dominates and where there are collective goals."[73] In another essay of her exile period, "The People and the Writer," Seghers speaks of *Heimat* as an "*Originaleindruck*, the first and therefore inimitably deep impression of all areas of life, of all social conditions, an impression to which we unconsciously and forever compare and measure."[74] *Heimat*, this original impression, is then what we might call the *mémoire involuntaire*, which flashes up as an "instant" and is, as Benjamin reminds, "much closer to forgetting than what is usually called memory,"[75] of the uncanny remainder of the possibility of freedom and togetherness that is always already torn asunder.

The original impression that Seghers evokes could thus be thought of as an expression of the gathering function that Edward Casey ascribes to the "event of place." For Casey, "places gather," and the power of place "consists in gathering these lives and things, each with its own space and time, into one arena of common engagement."[76] This arena of common engagement, however, gains its "eventmental" character not only from the discrete bringing together of time and space into place and date, of locating eventfulness hic et nunc,[77] but also, it is important to note, "gathering" evokes a labor of demarcation and exclusion. We never entirely belong, in other words. The "hold of place," as Casey theorizes it, "is a holding *together* in a particular configuration," but precisely for that reason it is also a "holding *in* and a holding *out*."[78] This function of gathering, of holding together "those things that are radically disparate and quite conflictual" and of the modes of containment and mobilization that follow from this gathering lend place its eventmental character, since holding in and holding out are not ontological givens but are themselves events that occur in space and in time.

Like place, *Heimat* is at once local and evental, spatial and temporal. If the event of place is the event of a dialectical opening and closure, a marking of inside and outside, then this event mentality itself calls forth the urgent question of the legibility or opacity of this event itself. If we think of *Heimat* as a "local" variation of the place problematic, it is a variation that foregrounds the uncanniness of place, its *Unheimlichkeit*, "that class of frightening which leads us back to what is known of old and long familiar,"[79] insofar as *Heimat* is only really there, present as an object of longing, when it is absent.[80]

Heimat as an aspect of the German social imaginary is deeply anchored in what Freud describes as the ambiguity of the word *heimlich*, whose meanings range from familiar to secret and indeed uncanny. In its conservative deployment, *Heimat* is an imagined wholeness that disavows the increasingly spectral and phantasmagoric quality of modern space, which increasingly becomes a domain of pure abstract extension and exposure.[81] *Heimat* in this sense is haunted by the disavowals it entails, by its bad faith in the light of the simple truism that we have never been at home. For a Popular Front aesthetic the problem acquires a somewhat different valence. Recall that Seghers's panoramic description is one of the borders that are both historical and geographical: the Rhine itself, the Taunus range, the *limes* of the Romans. These borders, however recordable and tangible, seem in the novel less of note in themselves than as complicated spatial and historical metaphors pointing to the less tangible boundaries that arise from and are imposed upon everyday practice, just as the uncanniness of *Heimat* in Seghers is less psychological than a problem of the remnants of the historical caught up in the mythical time of the fascist present. The uncanny understood in this sense is not the return of this or that repressed content but the sudden experience of the border that traverses the everyday itself.

This is the dimension of the uncanny that confronts Georg Heisler, since the fugitive occupies this very border. Escaping after three years of internment in the Westhofen camp, even something as simple as walking down the street and pausing before a butcher's store catalyzes a perceptual crisis for Heisler, as he is unable to orient himself in the everyday between these poles of idyll and violence that *The Seventh Cross* sets in play:

> how in times past he had despised the strength and glamour of everyday life! Now to be able to go in instead of waiting here, to be the butcher's helper, the grocer's errand boy, a guest in one of these homes! How differently, when he was in Westhofen, had he pictured a street to himself. Then he'd felt that every

> face and every paving stone reflected shame, that sadness muffled every step and every voice, even the children's games. But this street was quite peaceful, and the people seemed to be in good spirits . . . Georg was seized with as strong an attack of sadness as he had ever known in his life. He would have wept had not that voice soothed him, the voice that even in our saddest dreams tells us that presently all will be as nothing. "And yet there *is* something," thought Georg. (SC 53–54)

The uncanniness of the familiar seems to lie in the very obstinacy of the everyday, in its indifferent normality, "that had actually gone on uninterruptedly all this time" in the shade of the Nazi terror (56). For Georg, what is uncanny about this persistence, what unsettles the familiar and renders it strange in this passage is precisely the absence of shame. This shame that should cling to every gesture of the passersby on the street (but doesn't) is the affective surplus of defeat, the light that is shown on the everyday from the vantage point of the "we" interned behind the barbed wire of Westhofen. The invocation of shame in this passage can be read in the context of a certain antifascist moral quandary, well expressed later by Seghers herself in her essay "Germany and Us," where she poses the question: "a people that throws itself upon other peoples to exterminate them, can this still be our people?"[82] It is the shame of the antifascist at the sight of a people that has thrown off shame, a people for whom "everything is allowed."

There is, however, another aspect to this shame at the shamelessness of everyday life under fascism. Thus, for example, in a passage toward the end of the novel describing the workers at Paul Röder's factory, which captures the "total mobilization" of the twentieth century from the position of the subaltern, mobilized body:

> Their bare, steaming torsos—lean or fat, young or old—bore the marks of every kind of wound a human being can sustain, some from birth, some from a fight, some from Flanders or the Carpathian Mountains, some from Westhofen or Dachau, and some from work. . . . But no wounds could have bled Heidrich as did the ensuing years of peace; unemployment, hunger, family worries, the crumbling of all rights, the cleaving of the classes, the waste of precious time, squabbling about who was right instead of doing the right thing at once, and then, in

> January '33, the most terrible blow of all. The sacred flame of faith—of faith in one's self—burned out! (SC 320)

This is the shame of exposure to an everyday life as an ongoingness of violence, war, poverty, exploitation, and terror. It is the everyday life of the *deutsche Misère*, the pressure of domination and the state of emergency that has always been the rule.[83] The terrible blow of 1933, the year of the National Socialist *Machtergreifung*, lies in the reduction of everyday life to this, the pure immanence of subalternity, which in turn marks a moment of anagnorisis in which antifascist subjects are confronted with the truth of their own social irrelevance and practical exclusion. The everyday of the fascist dispensation then becomes an almost mythical time of suffering, violence, waiting, and boredom, as the *gewöhnliches Leben* slides back into its *gefährlich* variant.

And yet, as Georg reminds himself, "there is something." The gaze upon the everyday must be attuned to those traces and remainders of resistance, traces of the struggle that lies frozen within the merciless normality of everyday life under fascism. In this sense, Heisler's escape is an almost Benjaminian archaeology of the quotidian. *Heimat* is itself nothing but the fantasmatic "link between inside and outside on the level of lived, local experience,"[84] everyday life "stands at the conjunction of past *and* present, present *and* future, past *and* future."[85] Like the historical materialist in Benjamin's formulation, the Communist circuit that Heisler is a part of and upon which his escape depends is charged with the task of "appropriating a memory as it flashes up in a moment of danger."[86] The problem of legibility, of recognizing this memory image, would then offer an avenue for reading the famous scene in the Mainz Cathedral, where the categories of time and space seem to dissolve, releasing the historical images congealed within them as Georg cowers "under the eyes of six arch-chancellors of the Holy Roman Empire" (SC 73). The cathedral presents the offering of power to the terrorized subaltern, "peace instead of fear, mercy instead of justice." Through these very images of suffering, betrayal, and torment, in the last instances expressions of power, the experience of the oppressed is preserved and given form. The cathedral projects and sanctifies the power of its patrons, the House of the Hohenstaufen, but it is also the "product of individual architects' intelligence and the inexhaustible power of the people" (80). Just as the skill and labor of the collective become visible in this insight, exceeding the edifice of power and mercy in which they are frozen like so much dead labor, the images of biblical calamity offer their own solidarity across time and space: "anything that mitigates solitude has the power to comfort," Seghers writes of the biblical images that float across Georg's semiconscious gaze, "not only other people's suffering paralleling ours, but also the suffering others have gone through in bygone days" (79).

As John Roberts points out, for Benjamin, the everyday is a "realm of alienated symptoms and signs of desire," and the interpreter of everyday life intervenes precisely through providing a history to "the symptom's apparent meaninglessness. . . . By drawing the image of the past out of its historical slumbers, the image of the past is invoked as once having been the image of the future."[87] This element of the inviolable, *das Unverletzbare*, is the border between, to paraphrase Roberts, "the homogeneity and repetitiveness of daily life" and "the space and agency of its transformation and critique."[88]

The uncanniness of the familiar arises precisely at this border between nothing and something, between the everyday as a site of struggle and transformation and the everyday as the meaningless repetition of domination and survival, just as the uncanniness of *Heimat* results from the obscured historical dimension of its openings and enclosures. Thus, to take an example, when Liesel Röder becomes aware that she is implicated in Georg's flight, she experiences this uncanny boundary of the everyday:

> Her heart was struck by a foreboding that for her even to continue her train of thought was not permissible. Nothing could ever be as it had been. Ordinarily, Liesel had no comprehension of anything outside of her orbit of life. She knew nothing of the border posts of reality, and less than nothing about the strange proceedings that take place between the border posts: when reality fades into nothingness and can never return, or when the shadows show a desire to come crowding back in order to be taken for real once more. (SC 370)

Reading Seghers's engagement with the everyday through Benjamin allows us to see that these "border posts of reality" do not lie at some exterior boundary that one can in some sense mark and either cross or not cross according to one's wish, but rather they cut through the very heart of the quotidian, flashing up at precisely these moments of danger that arrest the epochal rhythms of daily life. The uncanniness of the familiar, in other words, arises at the moment that it becomes dimly apparent that the everyday is insufficient and exposed in inscrutable ways to all of those "'objective' methods of production and domination" that also always become "'subjective' ways of life" that it cannot accommodate from its local gaze.[89] Domination is not in some fundamental sense outside of the everyday, in other words. The uncanny presence of that which appears to erupt into the everyday from without lies not in the fact that everyday life exceeds and outpaces the forces of domination but in the fact that immediate, face-to-face, directly experienced relations produce the objective, abstract modes of production and domination out of themselves.[90]

In a further twist, it is also open to those moments, to use Benjamin's terms, when a "revolutionary chance" is able to force open the door to a "chamber of the past . . . which up to that moment has been closed and locked."[91] In her reading of *The Seventh Cross* in relation to Benjamin's "On the Concept of History," Helen Fehervary points out that in his notes to these theses, Benjamin writes, "redemption is the *limes* of progress."[92] The *limes* in this sense are not simply a historical border inscribed into the landscape but a figure for the very concatenation of immanence and transcendence. "The edge of the world" and the "unknown country" in this broader metaphorical sense cut through *Heimat* and the everyday, disclosing both the unrealized projects of the past and the possibilities of future transformation. Here at the "*limes* of progress" Seghers's first-person plural narrator appears again, as she closes her panoramic description of the Rhine-Main plain with an invocation of Benjaminian *Jetztzeit* or the time of the now: "We have now arrived. What happens now is happening to us" (SC 12). This is an epic temporality that opens onto the vision of human history transfigured through its liberation, grasping hold of the resources of resistance, the "confidence, courage, humor, cunning, and fortitude" that "have effects reaching far into the past"[93] and laying them bare. Seghers's landscape thus becomes a dialectical image, which freezes the movement of time itself, laying bare the real of history. "Articulating the past historically" in this sense, Benjamin writes, "means recognizing those elements of the past which come together in constellation of a single moment."[94]

THE NO-MAN'S-LAND BETWEEN THE GENERATIONS

This moment of recognition, where "what happens now is happening to us," in which one perceives oneself as a historical subject, is something of a leitmotif of *The Seventh Cross*, punctuating the novel's various episodes. This historical ekphrasis of the Taunus Valley is not only the drawing together of *Jetztzeit* in the Benjaminian sense described earlier but also the moment where the singular plural voice of the epic "we" steps forth from the framing narrative and into the real time of the novel, an anagnorisis, a recognition of an ambiguous and sedimented collective agency. Heisler's escape catalyzes the uncanny dimension of the quotidian for the characters of the novel, recasting the constraints of the familiar into what Spies calls moments of revelation and decision, moments of the "abrupt recognition of one's own inner essence as well as the characteristic aspects of the new or newly perceived circumstances."[95] The fugitive narrative is not only a kind of hermeneutic tool for parsing the mute surface of the everyday but also a way of setting everyday life into motion, of making connections and estranging the bad familiar of fascist daily life. Heisler's escape from Westhofen is the contingent event onto which "other events are attached, without a necessary relationship being immediately visible between them."[96] The attachment of these events and the pathways and interconnections between characters and situations that they illuminate are neither predetermined nor aleatory. Rather, pace Spies,

> multiple possibilities of development lie within each event. Their attachment to one another is not organized through a meaning guaranteed at each moment, but are more often brought forth through outward circumstances or rather through the inner movements of the characters, which are not at all comprehensible to these same characters and which are also not interpreted by an omniscient narrator into some unified superordinate perspective.[97]

In other words, Heisler himself becomes the catalyst of a complex negotiation of necessity and coincidence within both the diegesis and the structure of *The Seventh Cross*, which in an almost Brechtian fashion marks out the territory of the "not . . . but" and endows each action and situation with its own virtuality such that, to paraphrase Brecht, whatever does not happen is contained and preserved within what does happen.[98] This is, as we have hinted, very much not a matter of random causality or some sort of contingent flow of events but is an effect of the way that Seghers organizes the epic space of her novel. Critic Friedrich Albrecht has shown that Seghers's narratives are typically built around the constellation of what he describes as "cave-like" microworlds of experienced space "set aside from the main lines of movement" of the plot itself. The plot of *The Seventh Cross* thus draws these microworlds into relation with one another, draws them, in other words, into a properly epic frame.[99]

The main line of the narrative itself only exists insofar as these "cave-like" microworlds can be connected through Heisler's flight and pursuit. In a narratological sense, this novel is a wager that connections will prove possible. This brings us back to Benjamin's notion of the chronicle as an epic form of connecting contingencies while at the same time preserving their difference. Again, however, this is not a matter of revealing some concealed substrata of necessity that links the many discrete stories concatenated by Heisler's escape. Rather, Seghers seems more interested in the way that the encounter with Heisler infuses the ossified surface of the everyday with the potential to be otherwise. Thus, for example, as Greta Fiedler is sent by her husband to make contact with the Röders, she experiences this surge of possibility:

> All at once everything was possible, quickly possible. For suddenly it was in her power to hasten the march of events. Everything was possible in the time that had just now begun; a sudden change in all relations, her own included, quicker than one had dared to hope, while one was still young enough to jointly partake of some happiness after so much suffering. . . . Only when nothing at all is possible any longer does life pass by like a shadow. But the periods when everything is possible contain all of life—and of destruction. (SC 351)

This breaking dawn of the possible is not arbitrary, however, which is to say that though anything might happen, it has its own conditions of possibility. It opens onto a zone of unpredictability, but "this time that had just now begun," like Benjamin's *Jetztzeit*, depends on a reactivated urgency of a particular past. "If someone had asked her this noon," Seghers writes, "about labor conditions or the prospect of the struggle, she would have shrugged her shoulders exactly as her husband would have." Despite the fact that Greta Fiedler's errand has resulted only in the exchange of a cake recipe with a tearful and terrified Liesel Röder, through this moment of danger, "she had taken her place again in the old life" of solidarity and struggle (351).

In his classic study *Reading for the Plot*, Peter Brooks writes, "plot is the structure of action in closed and legible wholes."[100] This definition of plot, derived from Brooks's reading of Freud, locates the meaning of a narrative in its closure, which shines a transcendental light back on the discrete episodes that saturate the narrative and build toward the revelation of its proper ending. For Brooks, this structure can be grasped as a play of part and whole, of the associational work of metonymy and the totalizing claims of metaphor:

> it thus must *use* metaphor as the trope of its achieved interrelations, and it must *be* metaphoric insofar as it is totalizing. Yet it is equally apparent that the key figure of narrative must in some sense be not metaphor but metonymy: the figure of contiguity and combination, of the syntagmatic relation.[101]

Narrative for Brooks is thus "a double operation on time," one that both puts time into motion and suspends it, allowing for the dilatory spaces that set the stage for the metaphorical totalization of the narrative's closure by providing a space of "retard, postponement, error, and partial revelation."[102] It is, in short, a process of metonymic repetition that allows for the mastery of metaphorical closure.[103] Binding is a working over that creates the middle, it is a postponing and transforming labor that allows for the emergence of a *sjuzhet*, a coherent story, from the protean materials of the *fabula*.

Jameson, in his extended reading of Paul Riceuor's *Time and Narrative*, provides us with another way of shifting the emphasis of emplotment from totalization to a "production of aporias" or the making visible of contradictions.[104] Thinking about the vocation of emplotment seems to bring us closer to what is at stake in *The Seventh Cross*, since the very doubling of the narrative into the omniscient third-person narrator that coordinates the novel's principal multiple strands of free indirect discourse, focusing almost cinematically in on one character and then another, is itself overlaid by yet another narrative voice framing the novel. The seemingly discorporate "We voice" that narrates the novel's frame from within the camp would seem to suggest that we are no longer on the ground of the psychoanalytic metaphors that ground Brooks's account of narrative totalization. If, for Brooks, the master-narrative renders any local and discrete narrative a sort of allegory of that larger metanarrative closure that is the finitude of human mortality and the resolution of the countervailing tendencies of Eros and Thanatos described in Freud's *Beyond the Pleasure Principle*,[105] Seghers's novel seems to be gesturing at a no less anthropomorphic narrative principle but one that takes a collective horizon rather than that of the subject. The question thus becomes less of meaning at the level of the individual story than that of "the interweaving of many plots and many destinies," each of which retains its virtual openness in the sense discussed earlier.[106] In Jameson's terms, such a move from the individual to the collective turns plot inside out and relocates the providential path of narrative toward its "proper end" from the realm of the subjective to that of the objective. Jameson's example for this type of narrative is Goethe's *Wilhelm Meister's Lehrjahre*, where the mysterious Society of the Tower intervenes at the close of the novel to suddenly reveal that what had appeared "as a series of chance happenings . . . is suddenly revealed as a plan and as a deliberately providential design."[107]

Jameson's offhanded remark that the Society of the Tower can be read as a kind providential conspiracy that in fact "anticipates the structure of the Party itself, and the dialectic of a collective leadership, which both reflects the social order and works back upon its already present tendencies to develop them," brings us to the heart of *The Seventh Cross*.[108] The notion of the party itself as a collective providence that secures the interweaving of plots and stories into an overarching narrative totalization that could gesture to something like an "immanent transcendence, in which a transformation of being would be somehow implicit in being itself," is not so much a kind of Stalinist metaphysics but points to the real presence in the Weimar Republic of a Communist Party structure and counterpublic sphere that anchored the transcendental horizon of political and social transformation in the everyday lives of many Germans. This amputated counterpublic sphere flashes up like a ghost limb at certain moments of *The Seventh Cross*, for example, in the reminiscences of the wife of the streetcar conductor Bachmann, the man who betrays Wallau to the Gestapo:

> And what a life! An ordinary, surely, with the usual struggle for one's daily bread and stockings for the children. But at the same time a bold, strong life, with a burning interest in everything that was worthy to be experienced. Add to it what they—she and the Wallau woman—had heard their fathers say when they were still two pigtailed girls who lived on the same street, and there was nothing that had not resounded within their

> four walls: struggles for the ten-hour day, for the nine-hour day, the eight-hour day; speeches that were read to even the women as they bent over the truly fiendish holes in the stockings; speeches from Bebel to Liebknecht, from Liebknecht to Dimitroff. Even their grandfathers, the children had been told proudly, had been imprisoned because they had taken part in strikes and demonstrations. Ah, to be sure, in those days no one had been murdered and tortured for such misdeeds. What a straightforward life! And now that a single question had, a single thought even, had the power to undo it all! (SC 137)

What we are given here is a quick juxtaposition of two modes of organizing spatial practices of everyday living, the first of which sees the scenes of proletarian sociality, the working-class kitchen, the pub, the courtyard, as nodes in a circuit linking the private existence of workers to larger political struggles and counterpublic spheres, and the second of which portrays the fascist depoliticization of everyday life, where the isolation of these intimate spaces is bridged not by linkages that can be positively identified but by the negativity of fascist social space, where the social is expressed through coercion, intimidation, suspicion, denunciation, and fear.

In the absence of the material institutional culture of the KPD, the providential agency of the party becomes increasingly spectral in *The Seventh Cross*, and the question of immanence and transcendence that Jameson takes to be the fundamental contradiction to which the novel addresses itself as a form is thematized through the tropes of plan and coincidence in Seghers's novel. Thus in the first scenes of the book, as Heisler is fleeing the camp into the surrounding wilderness, this providential remainder asserts its influence over and above the panic of the chase:

> Strange indeed that, wildly and unconsciously, he had stuck unwaveringly to his original plan. Plans evolved in sleepless nights—what power they retained in the hour when all planning comes to naught, when the thought occurs that another has planned for us. *And even that other one is myself.* (SC 22)

The plan in this passage becomes the operator of connections that stretch across both space and time. Through the plan, Georg is connected to this other self, which reaches out from the past toward the future while at the same time coordinating the various subplots of the novel. At the same time, the plan cannot be anchored in the narrative material of the novel, since there is no central point or narrative agency that could guarantee its success or coherence. Indeed, the trope of the plan in *The Seventh Cross* seems to move into the more precarious zone of intuition and memory, as the alternative to "making [his] way from chance to chance" (225). This is a matter of thinking through which connections might be reestablished and used, as Georg searches the realms of his own experience for someone who "had remained unchanged," which the novel informs us in a different context "actually signifies the greatest conceivable difference, whether the most important thing in man manifests itself in action or withdraws to his most secret point" (168).

Alternately, the question of the nebulously formulated "most important thing" would ask which of these characters rising up in the memory palace that Georg conjures on the streets of Frankfurt is susceptible, or open, to being put into play as proper lines of emplotment. "A multitude of faces," Seghers writes, "floated through his mind. Exhausted he peered into the conjuries he had evoked—followers half of them, pursuers the other half" (SC 226). That Georg alights on his friend Röder in this search cannot be traced back to any political logic, since Paul is more of the classical type of the cheerful and long-suffering little man, a kind of proletarian Pinneberg, than he is a determined partisan of antifascist resistance.[109] The necessity that drives Georg to Röder arises rather from the act of emplotment itself, insofar as this operation can be thought of as a kind of judgment in its own right, "a judgment without trumpet blasts," as Seghers puts it (226). As Jameson argues, emplotment is a conjugation, imposing "a feeling of necessity on the event, characters, and elements thereby configured."[110] Thus, with the sudden thought of Paul Röder, who to this point in the novel has had no presence in the narrative, a new horizon of emplotment is opened. "It was all a tangled skein of recollections from which a single smooth thread presently emerged," Seghers writes of Georg's decision (227).

The notion of plan in the novel thus seems to stand in allegorically for the possibility of successful emplotment and proper narrative closure. The capacity to plan, however, is itself the very condition that is brought into question by the novel. At a late point in the escape, Franz expresses this question quite clearly to Elli. "Either Georg is done for and is utterly incapable of thinking," he states, "in which case all our planning is useless and nothing is predictable; or else he can still think, in which case his thoughts must run parallel to ours" (SC 249). The dilemma of Seghers's novel is that of a planning or emplotment that brings together isolated microworlds, but precisely because those microworlds are atomized and isolated from one another through the terror and complicity of fascist everyday life, the logics of their potential connections remain unpredictable. In this gap, coincidence becomes the threat of a disentangling of plot into random happenstance, into nothing. This is the vision of pure immanence without transcendence that we get in Georg's oneiric fantasy of capture and interrogation at the hands of Fahrenberg and his henchmen:

> Suddenly he noticed that the flesh on Zillich's cheek that was turned toward him was apparently rotted away, one ear on Bunsen's handsomely shaped head was crumbling off, and so was his forehead in one place. Georg realized that the three men were dead and that he himself, whom they received in eternal concord, had likewise already died. (SC 363)

Georg's capture and the closure of the breach in fascist omnipotence that it represents would then result in the decay and collapse of the horizon of sense and meaning itself, in an interrogation of the dead by the dead under the sign of pure contingency.

The notion of the coincidental as a collection of unrelated and disassociated events is, however, complemented in the novel by another notion of the coincidental as itself a form of provenance:

> Coincidence, if one truly allows its rule, is not at all blind, but rather clever and witty. One must only trust in it completely. Should one tamper with its handiwork and help oneself along, the results are a bumbling for which one falsely blames coincidence. If one calmly leaves all to its power and obeys it completely, one generally achieves the right end, and quickly too, and wildly and without detours. (SC 128)[111]

What seems to be at stake here is less a binary opposition between determination and contingency but rather the dialectical tension between the two, and the uncanny reversal whereby one pole inverts into the other. In this sense, one might argue that what Seghers is describing is akin to what Benjamin theorizes in a 1933 fragment as the mimetic facility, which is to say the ability to perceive and recognize "non-sensuous similarity."[112] This is a mode of perception that is attuned not so much toward metaphoric totalization as toward the perception of those very metonymic correspondences that enable the emergence of metaphor in the first place. As Bettina Engelmann argues, "mimetic perception," like Freud's notion of dream work, operates less through the semiotic decoding of signs than through a process of translation or figuration, grasping similarities in their repetition and difference, creating not a representation (in the sense of *Abbild*) but an image in the Benjaminian sense of the insight into the relationships between things, people, and situations.[113] Seghers attributes this faculty, for example, to Elli Mettenheimer when, during her detention by the Gestapo, she finds herself in "an unreal state between expectation and recollection," a dream state that signifies precisely "her being prepared for everything" (SC 175).

If the fugitive story is the means by which Seghers links the many stories of her novel into a larger epic narrative, the kind of mimetic perception just described is the methodological operator of the gathering together of this emplotment, catalyzing the play of plan and coincidence around which the narrative is built. The mimetic capacity in *The Seventh Cross* therefore opens onto an essentially collective dimension of experience, linking characters in moments of emergency with a spatially and temporally dispersed community of survival, for example, when Georg finds himself cornered in a tool shed, only to be "reminded by his invisible advisor that once before someone in a similar situation had escaped in that manner from a house in Vienna, a farm in the Ruhr district, or a guarded street in Tshapei" (SC 36). Likewise, insofar as Franz and Hermann are able to aid Georg in his escape, it is because they are privy to this same structure of collective experience, which has emerged from the social struggle and the culture of the workers' movement. The plans developed by Seghers's characters likewise partake of this mode of correspondence and coordination, which estranges and expands the perspective of individual experience in the light of what Seghers designates as "legends." Thus Hilde Wallau decides to plan her husband's escape from Westhofen:

> She followed up this decision with the uncanny perseverance of a woman whose first step in approaching an impracticable plan is the elimination of her sense of judgment, or at least of that part of it whose function is to pass on the practicability of things. Wallau's wife was guided neither by previous

> experience nor by information vouchsafed by those around her, but by two or three legends of successful escapes. For instance, Beimler's from Dachau, Seeger's from Oranienburg. Legends, too, contain certain information and certain experiences. (134)[114]

This evocation of legend as a vehicle of experience and guide to action is of course reminiscent of the role ascribed to the story in Benjamin's well-known essay on the tales of Nicolai Leskov.[115] For Benjamin, what separates the story from the novel is that the story is still in some way connected to a notion of usefulness; if the novel is distinguished from other epic forms in that it "emerges from the individual in his isolation" and "neither comes from oral tradition nor enters into it," the story remains tied to experience, which it stores up and renders communicable (ST 146). "The story," Benjamin writes, "preserves its energy and is capable of releasing it even after a long time" (148).

What the story concentrates and passes on is what Benjamin describes as "having counsel," a usefulness that might consist in a moral, in practical advice, or in a proverb or maxim (ST 145). In each case, this usefulness lies in demonstrating a certain relation to what Benjamin calls "the way of the world." Like the medieval chroniclers, who, "by basing their historical tales on a divine—and inscrutable—plan of salvation" have "at the very outset . . . lifted the burden of demonstrable explanation from their shoulders," the story allows the place of explanation to be "taken by interpretation, which is concerned not with an accurate concatenation of definite events, but with the way these are embedded in the great inscrutable course of the world" (153). This interpretive apperception opens into the fairy tale, which Benjamin sees as secretly living on in the story (157).[116] The fairy tale is the repository of popular good counsel, teaching, "the wisest thing is to meet the forces of the mythical world with cunning and with high spirits" (157). If myth is the zone of domination, subalternity, and fate, what Bloch calls "endured destiny," the fairy tale "makes space for a different life from the one into which one was born or, spellbound, had stumbled" (HT 153). In parting ways with the state of emergency that is the norm, the fairy tale allows for an *other* story to emerge. "Instead of fate, a fable begins," writes Bloch (153).

For both writers, cunning is precisely that mimetic faculty, in the ability to seize the chance for a "magical escape" as it flashes up in the midst of mythical time, to act in a way that draws out the inscrutable plan of salvation concealed within the immanent suffering of daily life (ST 158).[117] What renders this mimetic faculty materialist rather than mystical in *The Seventh Cross* is precisely that it is the ghostly appearance of a collective political practice that had been embedded in very material institutional networks like political parties and trade unions that had shaped the experience of generations of German workers. In Seghers's novel, this spectral insight arises for characters as they are drawn into the emplotment of the fugitive narrative itself. To take another example, Paul Röder's involvement with Georg's escape allows him to perceive this previously opaque dimension in the everyday routine of the Pokorny factory. "Suddenly," Seghers writes, "Paul could understand the whispering of people, just as the man in the fairy tale can understand the birds' songs after he had eaten a certain food" (SC 321). What he understands of the whispering, though, is not the semantic content of the whispers, that is, what is said or not said, but that there *is* whispering, that there is this web of connections hidden in plain sight, if only one is looking for it. This whispering, the sudden evidence of another story that implies these three workers, Fiedler, Berger, and Emmerich, in the web of connections that then gathers into the factory the popular traditions of solidarity and resistance that make up the other world of Hilde Wallau's legends, just as suddenly draws these three whispering workers into some great as yet to be thought out plan—or plot—for Georg's escape.

The Seventh Cross is not a story in the Benjaminian sense but a novel about the connective possibility of stories. The tension of the novel lies in the vicissitudes of emplotment itself, "the interweaving of many plots and many destinies" pace Jameson. Heisler's flight as a diegetic element of the novel thus acquires an allegorical valence for the conditions of possibility of this narrative connectivity itself, and yet there is a sense in which Seghers's novel seems very much to be a kind of wager on the conditions of possibility of the story as well, and indeed to imply the necessary reciprocity between these modes. What is at stake in other words is "the web which all stories form in the end" (ST 153). The threat posed by the fascist depoliticization and atomization of everyday life is the pulling apart of this web of historical experience and the severing of stories and events from one another into meaningless and opaque coincidences. This is the threat that confronts the first-person plural framing narrator when Wallau is brought back to the Westhofen camp. "This was an event," we are told, "that made upon us prisoners about the same impression as the fall of Barcelona or Franco's entry into Madrid or some other event that showed clearly that the enemy had all the power in the world on his side" (SC 163). In the same way that Spain represents solidarity, collectivity, and open struggle in the novel (225, 262), Wallau, as we have seen, is the repository of the collective experience of working-class resistance, and it is this conjugation of the theater of struggle with the experiences and memories that animate it that justifies the framing of Wallau's capture through the collapse of the Spanish Republic, since it is in both cases the capacity for a popular politics of emancipation that is at stake:

> A whole generation had to be annihilated. These were our thoughts on that terrible morning: then for the first time we voiced our conviction that if we were to be destroyed on that scale, all would perish because there would be no one to come after us. Almost unprecedented in history, the most terrible thing that could happen to a people, was now to be our fate: a no-man's land between the generations, which old experiences would not be able to traverse. If we fight and fall, and another takes up the flag and falls too, and the next one grasps it and he too falls—that is natural, for nothing can be gained without sacrifice. But what if there is no longer anyone to take up the flag, simply because he does not know its meaning? It was then that we felt sorry for the fellows who were lined up for Wallau's reception, to stare at him and spit on him. The best that grew in the land was being torn out by the roots because the children had been taught to regard it as weeds. (165)

The catastrophe that is evoked in this passage is not only one of political defeat and physical annihilation but one of the destruction of experience and or the capacity for meaning itself, which is based on that mimetic capacity to recognize similarities and felicitous coincidences that Seghers locates in the collective memory of the oppressed. "Memory," as Benjamin argues, is "the epic facility par excellence" (ST 153). It "creates the chain of tradition which transmits an event from generation to generation" (154). Precisely this chain, in the present tense of *The Seventh Cross*, in a time "where what happens now happens to us," is drawn through the concentration camps of Hitler's Germany and from there connected to the vast circuit of the Popular Front. There are still those who, to paraphrase the German refrain to "The Internationale," can hear the signal, but these partisans are now scattered, claiming the mantle of the "better Germany" in Heinrich Mann's famous formulation, from the precarious stations of exile, hiding, and imprisonment.

For Seghers, the fugitive story is a kind of totalization aimed at bridging the gap that Benjamin diagnoses as opening up in the nature of memory itself between its singular and collective resonances since those happy times of the epic, "when," to quote Lukács, "the starry sky is the map of all possible paths" (TN 29). Thus Benjamin credits to the storyteller the facility for starting always anew, like "Scheherazade who thinks of a fresh story whenever her tale comes to a stop" (ST 154). Storytelling is its own kind of cunning, not only a giving of counsel to others but, as the invocation of Scheherazade makes clear, an art of survival in and of itself. Against this logic of succession, though, which starts the web over again through the *reminiscence* of exemplary "magical escapes," Benjamin reminds us that the novel, too, has its vocation, which becomes apparent in such "moments of solemnity" as the "invocations to the muse" in the opening lines of Homeric epics, writing:

> what announces itself in these passages is the perpetuating remembrance of the novelists as contrasted with the short-lived reminiscences of the storyteller. The first is dedicated to *one* hero, *one* odyssey, or *one* battle; the second, to many *diffuse* occurrences. . . . It is *remembrance* [*Eingedenken*], the muse-derived element of the novel, which is added to recollection [*Gedächtnis*], the muse-derived element of the story, the unity of their origin in memory [*Erinnerung*] having disappeared with the decline of the epic. (154)

Benjamin's mention of the Homeric invocation of the muses seems to resonate with Seghers's framing device for the novel, the voice of the "we" that speaks from behind the barbed wire of the camp. This is the voice that sets the recuperation of the lost epic unity of memory as a task for the present, very much in the vocation of Benjamin's chronicler, whom Michael Löwy describes as the practitioner of the *apokatasis*, the "ultimate salvation of all souls without exception."[118] The frame narration of *The Seventh Cross*, then, in this sense reaches out toward that "redeemed mankind" for whom the past "becomes citable in all its moments."[119] Even more than the novel's many foregroundings of the vital importance of antifascist pedagogy, the frame narrative of the novel makes the wager that the chain of tradition that has been woven through Hitler's concentration camps will not be broken there. This is the voice that attempts to seize the terrain of remembrance and hold it in recollection, weaving the contingent event of Heisler's escape into a plan that will only be evident from the standpoint of a providential future-perfect tense, in which everything will have been won, where one story will become legible as the dialectical image of many diffuse occurrences. In this future-perfect tense the voice of the "we" speaks when, at the close of the novel, written in 1939 on the eve of the war, an unknown liberated "outside," spatially and historically, of the National Socialist regime is held forth as the transcendent horizon of the now: "We didn't know any of this as yet then. So many things happened later that nothing that could be learned could be believed implicitly. True, we had thought it was impossible to experience more than we had already experienced; but outside, it emerged how much more was still to be experienced" (SC 394).[120] Bearing the excess of what will be experienced over and above what has been experienced, the voice of the "we," speaking from the heart of National Socialism, is the dilatory space that postpones the narrative closure of German history as the history of the Third Reich.

CHAPTER 5

Ghostly Solidarities

Eduard Claudius, Green Olives and Bare Mountains

Eduard Claudius's novelistic account of the fall of the Spanish Republic, *Grüne Oliven und nackte Berge* [Green Olives and Bare Mountains 1944], frames the collapse of the emancipatory political and cultural aspirations of the Popular Front against the fraught political landscape of Europe on the eve of war. It appeals to the long tradition of popular resistance to oppression as a counterweight—a "countertime"—to the catastrophes of the late 1930s. Yet this countertime becomes increasingly displaced and disembodied with the foreclosure of a Popular Front politics, and Claudius's novel becomes a meditation on the hardening of solidarity and discipline into the siege mentality of state socialism, even as the novel's attempt to evoke a Spanish perspective as a point of critique of German "soldier males," both fascist and communist, involves *Green Olives* in a complicated meditation on national allegories of Spain and Germany, displaced onto a nonsynchronous dialectic of the working class and the peasantry. Between these two modes, one cyclical and telluric, the other synchronous and mobile, Claudius's novel figures a collective break from the long history of exploitation and misery that Claudius implies is the basis of popular everyday life. "The modern age," as a figure in Peter Weiss's portrayal of the Spanish Civil War in *The Aesthetics of Resistance* puts it, "is a prophecy, we ourselves still live in the Middle Ages, there may be a second or two of illumination, it takes our breath away, makes us euphoric, then we slump back again" (AR 185).

Eduard Claudius, born Eduard Schmidt, began his writing career as a workers' correspondent for the KPD daily, the *Ruhrecho*. A trained bricklayer, he became a union functionary at the age of sixteen and joined the KPD in 1932 at the age of twenty-one. Shortly thereafter, Claudius fled persecution in Nazi Germany, living illegally in Switzerland until going to Spain to fight in the International Brigades, eventually becoming a political commissar for the Edgar André Battalion. In 1939, a wounded Claudius returned to Paris, and then to Switzerland, where he was interned in a series of camps for politically undesirable refugees, avoiding deportation to Germany through the intervention of Hermann Hesse. In these camps, under the patronage of the KPD, Claudius wrote *Grüne Oliven*, which was published in Zurich in 1944. Claudius would later go on to fight with the Garibaldi partisan brigade in northern Italy in the last days of the war before returning to the GDR to write the first notable East German production novel, *Menschen auf unsrer Seite* [People on Our Side 1951], and later to serve as the East German ambassador to the Democratic Republic of Vietnam.[1]

Although Claudius emerged from the same working-class milieu as Hans Marchwitza and Willi Bredel, he had no real contact with the BPRS and the literary debates that took place in and around that organization. Instead, Claudius began his serious literary career in the Popular Front atmosphere of the Swiss émigré community. Under the name of Edy Brendt, he had already published his first novel, *Umbruch einer Jugend* [A Youth in Upheaval], in 1936. In the coming years, Claudius gained the attention of figures like Bredel for short fiction pieces like "Das Opfer" [The Sacrifice], based on Claudius's experiences in the Spanish Civil War and published in 1938 in the Moscow-based *Das Wort*.[2]

Perhaps because of his distance from the official discourses of the BPRS, and later in exile from the debates on realism, Claudius's style is more open formally than is that of many of the other worker-cum-writers of the German Popular Front. While Claudius points out the importance of Hans Marchwitza and German proletarian-revolutionary literature in his own development, as well as socialist realist classics by authors such as Maxim Gorky and Fyodor Gladkov, he also stresses that his strongest influences were American leftist writers such as Jack London and John Dos Passos and early Soviet modernists such as Isaac Babel and Ilya Ehrenburg.[3] In particular, Claudius makes extensive use of flashbacks and of narrated action and free indirect discourse, a method that allows him to ground the biographies and motivations of his characters in social and historical conflicts.[4] This type of narration is well suited to his subject matter, a "picture of an engaged, partisan person, striving forwards and acting decisively," the figure of the Communist partisan fighting on the various fronts of antifascist exile.[5]

Horst Haase writes that in *Grüne Oliven und nackte Berge*, Claudius creates a "counter-image to the fascist mythos of the fighter," contrasting the "'martial morality' of an exploiting class with the morality of a class in the process of liberating itself."[6] As Erika Pick has pointed out, this thematic constellation also has a national and historical dimension, since in *Grüne Oliven* "the 'inner plot' of his protagonist builds mostly on self-analysis and on the confrontation with German history."[7]

The partisan is a firmly established character type in Germany's socialist literature, grasping a generationally defined structure of experience, a collective way of confronting the twentieth century. Wolfgang Engler describes it from the perspective of the last years of this generation in the GDR of the mid-1960s, where the grizzled partisans of the revolution often come to the aid of young reformers in their struggle with the bureaucrats of the ruling Socialist Unity Party (Sozialistische Einheitspartei Deutschlands [SED]) apparatus in works like Heiner Müller's *Der Bau* [The Construction Site 1965] or Christa Wolf's *Der geteilte Himmel* [The Divided Heaven 1963]:

> This figure . . . made its appearance in many contemporary artworks, always cross referencing the same key experiences—early memory traces of the First World War, on the homecoming of soldiers and cripples; clearer reminiscences of the struggle for a socialist German republic and of the defeat; sharp retrospection on their socialization in the Weimar Republic, on the still open struggle against the Nazis in Germany, Spain, or elsewhere; finally individually divergent, but very present memories of the Nazi dictatorship, of the camps or prisons, of underground resistance or exile. And the partisan always the partisan drew the same conclusions for socialist everyday life, placed his own judgment above the pleas of others, energy and risk-taking above pathos and ritual, so much that he at times became the most bothersome nettler, the personified bad conscience, of his compliant, disciplined contemporary, the functionary.[8]

Claudius was certainly a partisan. These figures gave a certain charisma to the antifascist claims of the East German party, contributing a patina of legitimate heroism to the workers' and peasants' state. At the same time, as Engler points out, both the partisans and the functionaries in the SED shared a generational structure of feeling shaped by the struggles of the twentieth century. The gaze upon the outside directed both partisans and functionaries, Engler argues. The shared experience of "life and death political struggle" shaped a code of conduct common to the old Communists born around the turn of the century, in which "one did not internally lower one's guard, could admit to no omission and no mistake unless one wanted to all go under together served as the premise for all thought and action." For the old Communists, "the enemy always sat at the table, the gaze upon him and his motives governed the gaze upon oneself and one's intimates."[9] Claudius gives us an example and genealogy of this type and of the contradictions between discipline and solidarity embodied in the partisan.

The Spanish Civil War was not only a symbol of the Popular Front and the "integral antifascism of the 1930s" but also a crucial international test of this and cultural political dispensation, the "decisive confrontation between democracy and tyranny, atheism and Catholic reaction, between fascism and antifascism."[10] Thus it is no coincidence that the second International Congress of Writers for the Defense of Culture of 1937 took place in Valencia, Madrid, and Barcelona. The speeches from German authors at this conference stressed the connection between the war in Spain and in the international struggle against fascism but also the connection between partisanship and military struggle and the democratization of culture. Brecht's speech at the congress puts this succinctly, asking, "if culture is something inseparable from the entire productivity of a people, if one and the same violent intervention can deprive the peoples of butter and the sonnet, if culture is something that material, what can be done to defend it?"[11] In many of the speeches at the congress, cultural production is figured as the material ground for the resistance to fascism. Thus the cultural work of the republic army was an often-evoked theme at the second congress as a vehicle of popular collective pedagogy for a people who, in the words of an anonymous speaker, "had lived for centuries under the dull pressure of the church."[12] Likewise Anna Seghers, in her summation of the congress in *Das Wort*, stresses that "today defense of culture is identical to the defense of Spain" but goes on to argue that the left must move from the defensive position of "anti" and "demonstrate what we are fighting for." Seghers continues, writing of the defense of Madrid, "we can render many more people free for the struggle if they have a better grasp what kind of city it is, what kind of a culture it is, that they are defending."[13] This emphasis on internationalism, social pedagogy, and the active intertwining of the military and the cultural was the expression of the commitment and solidarity of European Popular Front antifascism.

At the same time, the Spanish Civil War was a theater for many of the contractions that structured the Popular Front both as a political program and as a cultural constellation. As historian Ursula Langkau-Alex notes, "Spain was the highpoint of the Popular Front, but also its death blow."[14] For Langkau-Alex, the decisive conflict here was between winning the war and pursuing the social revolution in Spain. As Walther Bernecker puts it in the same interview, should the Spanish Civil War be viewed, as the Communists did, as a reprisal of the 1808 rebellion against the occupying Napoleonic troops, or was it to be understood, as the anarchists did, in the tradition of the Paris Commune?[15] If the question is one of winning the war, the emphasis falls on discipline and restraint of spontaneous revolutionary forces and movements, and this is indeed what happened particularly after 1937 as the Spanish Communist Party gained increasing influence under the Negrin government.[16]

As Geoff Eley notes, this tension was anything but arbitrary. A regular army and the restraint of certain revolutionary experiments for the sake of winning the war could be broadly accepted as necessary. For Eley, the weakness of the politics of the Communist Party of Spain (PCE) lay in making the contradiction between "prosecuting the war with a central command" and allowing the social revolution to unfold "into a dichotomy."[17] At the same time, along with the Comintern's commitment to seeing the conflict in Spain in terms of a "bourgeois-democratic revolution," the PCE and the International Brigades increasingly became vehicles for the export of the purges underway in the USSR, targeting largely anarchists and non-Comintern Communist groups.[18] This tension between solidarity and discipline in the face of political defeat was dramatically played out in the subsequent dissolution of the Popular Front following the fall of the Spanish Republic and Hitler's successes in Austria and Czechoslovakia, even as the Communist left was increasingly isolated as a result of public reactions to the Moscow show trials and the Hitler-Stalin Pact of 1939. Indeed, as Michael Rohrwasser argues, the contradictions around the Spanish

Civil War, as much as the reaction to the Moscow show trials and the Hitler-Stalin Pact in the west, contributed to the polarization of the left that contributed to the collapse of the Popular Front in the late 1930s.[19]

Eduard Claudius stages these political and social contradictions in his Spanish Civil War novel at the affective register. *Grüne Oliven und nackte Berge* both defamiliarizes and deepens the depiction of the Communist code of conduct represented in the novels of the BPRS, while also connecting this discourse to the historiographical discussion of the *deutsche Misère* in the antifascist emigration. Here the hardness of the Communist is not a given but a role that must be consciously adopted and maintained in the face of a long tradition of plebeian subalternity. *Grüne Oliven und nackte Berge* is an obsessive, yet historicizing, meditation on the armored body, to borrow a phrase from Klaus Theweleit. But this armored Communist, although bearing superficial similarities to the male fascist soldier, obeys a different logic, since the fascist identification with the armored body ego is foreclosed to the Communist, as we shall see, by the very insistence on situation and tactics that is part of the Communist code of conduct.[20] Jak Rohde, the protagonist of the novel, must assume this armored body, but he must be able to assume a stance of self-reflexivity over and against this armored body. This is to say that the principal tension of *Grüne Oliven und nackte Berge* is the necessity not only of renouncing one's own weakness and passivity but also of maintaining a conscious and critical distance from that very renunciation.

This difference registers in the linguistic usage not only of Claudius's novel but also of Communist literature in general. For Theweleit, the literary language of the soldier male is expressive rather than narrative; it charts affective intensities rather than providing description and representation of structures of feeling as they develop in duration.[21] Claudius's language, on the other hand, performs the opposite operation, attempting to situate affective intensities into a historical emplotment, to gather these affects back up into a coherent story, a narrative that would parallel the character armor of the Communist partisan. In one sense, this narrative becomes itself a kind of character armor itself, a character armor that also begins to accumulate all sorts of unmarked qualities at its margins. Claudius attends to the contradiction that arises as the Communist code of conduct, in its exclusion of the history of *Stumpfsinn* and *Enge*, paradoxically preserves these affects beside itself, leading the body armor of the Communist to become another type of *Eigensinn*, an obstinate attachment to forms of bodily and psychic discipline that mark the figure of the Communist partisan as otherworldly and strange. As the novel progresses, the discipline that was originally founded in the bonds of solidarity of the antifascist struggle takes on a darker valence, as Claudius describes how this discipline collapses upon the Communist partisan, marking him as a spectral remainder of the very historical violence against which he struggles and as a specter, a ghostly reminder of the promises of the antifascist Popular Front.[22]

THE ARMORED COMMUNIST

Like many narratives of the Spanish Civil War written by German émigrés, Claudius's novel underwrites the pathos of Communist self-discipline. *Härte*, or hardness, marks the Communist of exile literature. In describing his protagonists as having "become hard, like steel upon which one can hammer and that will never break," or invoking the hard eyes of German Communists, Claudius is employing one of the more common tropes in international socialist realism (GO 40). The quality of hardness, however, takes on particular significance in German exile literature, with its typical situations of illegality and confinement. In Willi Bredel's early concentration camp novel, *Die Prüfung*, the imprisoned Communist Reichstag deputy Heinrich Torsten repeatedly declares, "praise be to everything that makes one hard."[23] Torsten wins no small amount of respect from the SS guards for his hardness under torture.[24] In Jan Petersen's chronicle of Communist resistance in Berlin during the first year of the Nazi dictatorship, *Unsere Straße*, Petersen notes that "these times have made us all harder."[25] In both of these books, hardness is first and foremost a guarantee against betrayal. The Communist must be able to be silent under torture in a situation where "treachery lurks around every corner."[26] Thus the resolve of Torsten in Bredel's novel is contrasted with the inconsequentiality of the party activist Kriebel, who breaks under the duress of the camp. "Not every Communist possesses an armored soul," Bredel's protagonist muses.[27] At the same time, this hardness is a resource of survival for characters that are increasingly cut off from the material and institutional structures of the party. The hardness of the Communist inscribes the collectivity of the party as a visible sign on the body of its members. In *Unsere Straße,* hardness is evoked as the discipline necessary to carry out illegal KPD work without endangering other comrades, but it is also a shield against the "indifference" of ordinary Germans toward everyday life in the Third Reich.[28] For Bredel in *Die Prüfung,* hardness is a defense against the enforced idleness of life in the Fuhlsbüttel camp.[29] The psychic armor of the Communist protects him not only from external threats but from his own psyche and fear as well. Torsten, for instance, begins an aggressive gymnastics routine in solitary confinement to ward off his growing "fear of his own thoughts."[30]

Of course, the literary type of the hard Communist was already well established in the BPRS literature of the Weimar Republic, where, as Michael Rohrwasser and others have pointed out, it also serves a compensatory function. In BPRS novels narrating the German civil war between 1918 and 1923, such as Hans Marchwitza's *Sturm auf Essen*, Karl Grünberg's *Brennende Ruhr*, and Otto Gotsche's *Märzstürme*, the trope of the hardened Communist emerges clearly in relation to the white terror of these years and the ebbing of the post–World War I revolutionary tide in Germany and Europe. Discipline in these novels is not a theoretical, or ideological, layer imposed upon the composition but is at the center of the experience that they seek to narrate; it is the psychic and affective motor of these books. The proletarian-revolutionary novel presents a more or less collective and egalitarian mode of discipline when narrating the Red Army struggle itself, which then becomes more entrenched and authoritarian when the novels turn to the defeat of the insurrections they narrate. This emerges clearly in Hans Marchwitza's description of the Red Army of the Ruhr. Marchwitza juxtaposes the discipline of this army to that of the German army during the war while describing the drilling exercises of the worker-soldiers:

> "Comrades, jump!—March—march!" Like before on the parade ground, as though shot from a pulled bow,—chop-chop—in elastic, powerful leaps over the dewy ground, chop-chop—they drop down. Rifles forward and a pair of shots fired off to cover those not jumping. Not like before, with a chalk-white, trembling lieutenant behind them, no, here things went without a leader. Each man was a leader. They were soldiers with all their hearts, yet soldiers without any compulsion. Without the hated blind obedience. Without hesitation, they crashed against the death that smashed against them from dozens of machine guns. They knew why! Not for a little group of war profiteers and exploiters—for themselves! For the freedom of the working class![31]

Marchwitza's description marks a release from the coordinates of the discipline of alienated labor in that, even in military formation, the workers here partake in a kind of armoring of the collective laboring body, "the collective experience of the body in real time, in real space," that as Charity Scribner points out, apropos of Negt and Kluge, "stands at the crux of socialist solidarity."[32] This laboring body is constituted in the factories and sites of production under the reign of capital in an alienated form, but here Marchwitza portrays a refunctioning of the collective skills acquired through submission but freed of their coercive form. The emphasis on the lack of the leader is an index of the collective, nonauthoritarian quality of proletarian discipline in this moment of Marchwitza's novel. In this account, discipline becomes a collective stance of trust, or *Vertrauen*.

As these novels move to telling the story of the revolution's defeat, the status of discipline is transformed. The Communist code of conduct is the response to this historical constellation of defeat, and insofar as it fetishizes discipline, it does so not out of some ephemeral authoritarian bent of the workers' movement but as an answer to the very real problems of immediate survival and of collective political affectivity in the midst of counterrevolution by way of exemplary behavior, or a code of conduct, as Helmut Lethen might have it.[33] The BPRS author Ludwig Turek renders a characterization of this code of conduct and its inherent performativity in a scene in *Ein Prolet Erzählt* that is worth quoting at length. When the protagonist is threatened with execution by white troops while fighting with the Red Army in Lithuania, Turek contrasts the cowardly death of the pleading victim with that of the armored Bolshevik:

> This was the end, why make such a scene. But it's horribly difficult not to make such a scene. For this, one needs a scorching hatred of one's tormentor, hatred of the enemy, love of one's own cause, both too great for the temptation of disloyalty. I feel how those who beg for mercy with whimpering fearful faces murder themselves. In pleading for the life of their bodies, they strike a lethal blow against their soul, against their self-consciousness, without which a man is less than a beaten dog. . . . Now the executioner directs his words in Russian to the Russian. He questions him repeatedly, excited, his saber raised. In vain he waits for an answer. The Bolshevik stands immovable. The iron gaze is a sharp weapon. Each threat of

> the White officer is deflected by the imperturbability of the Red soldier and falls hurtfully back upon the headman. The crowd is inspired by the steadfastness of the Bolshevik.[34]

Depictions of actual struggle in these novels do not substantially individuate character. The actions of the novels are collective; characterization functions mostly as focalization, not as an attempt at psychological depth. The grasping toward an individual protagonist occurs after the defeat.[35] Much the same could be said of the stereotyped figure of the hard Communist, or what would later enter the discourse of socialist realism as the positive hero. Schöberl calls the positive hero a "voice of desperation," a narrative convention that emerges in the German proletarian-revolutionary novel under the sign of failure and catastrophe. Rather than an element of realism, the positive hero is a "medium by which to polemically recall a possible common strength" and to provide a visible sign of that common strength for those denied it.[36]

A careful reading of proletarian-revolutionary literature, then, historicizes what Negt and Kluge describe as the mentality of the camp, which could also describe the structure of feeling of the Communist partisan of Claudius's novel. The mentality of the camp derives from the proletariat's need for tangible symbols of solidarity, for example, party symbols, demonstrations, and other rituals of working-class culture. The camp mentality combines this need for solidarity with a misrecognition of the proletariat as an autonomous entity standing against the bourgeoisie, neglecting the fact that, as we noted earlier, the proletariat is in fact a part of bourgeois society, lacking in the material basis for an autonomous culture.[37] The mentality of the camp, which seeks to insulate proletarian culture from bourgeois elements, is an articulation of solidarity under the tremendous pressure exercised on any organization of the workers by both the state apparatus and the ideological superstructure of capitalist society, producing a "spiraling demand for security and delimitation" within the so-called proletarian camp.[38] According to Negt and Kluge, the public sphere of workers' organizations absorbs this need for solidarity, which lends this public sphere its substance and its appeal to proletarian interests, but simultaneously, in abstracting and fetishizing these interests, the public sphere of workers' organizations finds itself in a situation where it cannot satisfy the interests so absorbed.[39] If, as was the case with the KPD in the Weimar Republic and the SED in the GDR, this solidarity becomes severed from the experiential base of the masses and gains a partial autonomy as the expression of bureaucratic imperatives of the workers' organizations, Claudius's novel describes the entire weight of this camp mentality borne by monadic, isolated subjects. Amputated from those key sites of proletarian class solidarity, labor and the street, these partisan figures, like Claudius's protagonist, style themselves as prophets and appear as tramps.

At the same time, this hardness, so necessary for survival in illegality, in the prisons and camps of the Nazis, and in exile, must not be uncritically accepted. As Brecht wrote already in *The Measures Taken* in 1930, "he who fights for Communism must be able to fight and not fight."[40] This minimal self-reflexivity in relation to one's own psychic armor and exercise of violence is what separates the Communist from the soldier male that Theweleit analyzes. Likewise, Bredel writes of the Communists imprisoned in Fuhlsbüttel, "they have become hard here, pitiless—but not cruel."[41] This ethical problem of exercising violence without fetishizing violence, of killing without becoming a murderer, pervades Communist discourse. In the 1940s, Communist writers often used the figure of the determined Communist who struggles, but takes no pleasure in war, as a counterimage to the militarism promoted by the Nazis. Writing in the pages of *International Literature* in 1941, Johannnes R. Becher attempted to draw the distinction between the "true soldiership" of the Communist partisan and the "irresponsibility and cowardly thoughtlessness" of the fascist soldier male. This distinction is based on a self-conscious relationship to discipline and violence. "The courage to personally stand by his actions and to assume responsibility for them as his own," writes Becher, "is what has always separated the soldier from the easily bought *Landsknecht*. The honor of the soldier lies precisely in the fact that he *consciously* risks his life and is *consciously* prepared to risk his life for his fatherland."[42] The term *Landsknecht*, referring to the German mercenaries of the fifteenth and sixteenth centuries, connects Hitler's armies to an essentially plebeian and premodern dispensation of eternal exploitation and domination, whereas the Communist has assumed a collective historical subjectivity and agency.

For the German antifascist émigrés, however, this historical agency is itself more or less an armature for waiting under the conditions of exile and illegality; partisanship articulates itself in hiding and isolation, the spatial imaginary discussed in the previous chapter. Jak and his comrades thus volunteer for the International Brigades as an opportunity to emerge from the psychic armoring that had sustained them in the squalor of exile, even though this war will demand renunciation and discipline. As the Interbrigadists arrive in Valencia, Claudius describes the laughter of Albert Kühne, an exiled miner from the Saar: "It sounded like a hard shell had broken in two, the shell around a firm, ripened kernel" (GO 18). Albert later comments, as the Interbrigadists are escorted through the streets of Valencia by jubilant Spanish workers and peasants, "a skin of leather has grown around our hearts. We . . . have armored ourselves so we don't melt away, but this—this here—I've never experienced anything like it . . . we are human again" (13). The motif of reclaiming one's humanity through the war is figured as an escape from the anonymous passivity and enforced inactivity of the exile years in Claudius's rather graphic transposition of armed discipline and the opening of the armored body:

> Maybe they would puke from fear, puke in revulsion at the killing, but they would shoot and puke out the stink of all this foulness and puke out the pus of their rotten lives that they had had to swallow down. And it's good to puke, because a person isn't born to kill and takes up his rifle anyway, so he won't choke on his disgust at himself and on his cowardice. (88)

The release of the "pus of their rotten lives" is an expulsion of affect familiar from *Die Kumiaks*, of *Enge* and *Stumpfsinn*. In Spain, the exiled Germans can openly fight against what in Germany, or even in Paris, could only be resisted secretly, illegally, and under aliases. Fighting in Spain allows for the reappropriation of one's antifascist identity, since the exiles are in Spain legally and no longer have to use the false names employed in Paris. The exiles renounce these names on the ship approaching Valencia, tearing up their forged papers and becoming themselves once again by publicly revealing the bonds of Communist collectivity that had remained necessarily concealed in illegality (12). "We seemed to change with the other names," comments Albert, "but you don't forget who you are. And now we're more than ourselves. Now, going into the struggle. . . . Now I can once again say to anyone who I am" (14–15).

Recovering humanity in *Grüne Oliven und nackte Berge* is precisely the reflexive stance vis-à-vis one's psychic armoring. Claudius contrasts the hardness of the Communist to the body armor of the fascist through the character of the Jewish worker Samuel Fischbein. Jak feels an instant antipathy to Fischbein, not entirely because he is Jewish but because he does not conceal his fear: "Jak gazed into the hard bird-face of this man. Strange, how he tries to control himself. He trembles with fear, everyone sees that he desperately tries to control himself" (GO 17). Fischbein's face acts for Jak as a signifier of fear and abjection, yet at the same time Claudius gives us this face as "hard," indicating that perhaps Fischbein is there to suggest another kind of discipline, one that integrates hardness and trembling. Fischbein further antagonizes Jak through his desire to *speak* about the fear of death. During one such conversation, Jak interrupts Fischbein and grumbles, "but we don't talk about it. . . . Who cares what a man thinks about death? No one!" (32). Fischbein's reply, "sometimes talking is like having someone put his arm around your shoulders," will be sewn throughout the novel. This reply grounds discipline in discursive solidarity, a move that is central to Claudius's construction of the Communist code of conduct. At the same time, the anti-Semitism that Claudius raises only in order to dismiss it demonstrates the degree to which fascist discourses lurk in the psychological recesses of German antifascists.

Jak's dislike of Fischbein is explicitly linked to a fascist mode of expelling fear through Jak's unreflected anti-Semitism. "This damned propaganda has got to me too," Jak muses as he watches Samuel weep at the reception of the International Brigades in Valencia and ascribes it to Jewish cowardice. Yet Jak, too, is weeping (GO 42). Later in the novel, Jak realizes, "I wanted to chase away my fear with his" (203). The expulsion of fear through projection onto the racial other is contrasted to the proper Communist *control* of fear, or *sich beherrschen*, which is a complicated interplay of opening and maintaining the armored body (18). During the fighting at the Campo del Casa, Samuel holds his post when other members of his unit flee. When they run into Jak, they tell him with contempt how Samuel soiled himself in terror. "How can you laugh at people who go in their pants, but hold out," Jak snarls at these men who mock Samuel even as they flee, "when you're just pieces of shit with pants yourselves?" (126). Claudius validates Fischbein's ability to admit and control fear as the proper Communist attitude.

A Communist proves himself, notes Fernando, the head of the cadre department of the International Brigades, by how he comes to terms with these bodily breaches of his armoring. "There are people who have shit in their pants from fear," Fernando reminds us. "It's truly the case that everyone is afraid; a Communist too is afraid to die; no one loves life like a Communist. This is where the power that comes from the idea, from dialectical thinking, has to take hold" (GO 69).

This construction of the Communist places his fear at the center of his being, which is to say that here, and elsewhere in the novel, it is emphatically not a matter of the denial, suppression, or disavowal of fear but rather a matter of control: "one cannot wipe away fear through thought," Jak muses while being strafed by fascist planes, "but one can overcome it. Thinking has to be stronger, so that one can hold out even with a face pale from fear" (19). The appropriation of one's own fear guarantees the Communist against the twin temptations of a more perverse body armoring: projection and brutality. Jak renounces the expulsion of one's terror onto the figure of the Jew, just as the Communist fighters renounce the physical inscription of fear on the enemy, as it is performed by the Moroccans in Franco's army, who leave dead Interbrigadists with their own severed testicles in their mouths (132). The emphasis on collectivity and discipline separates the armored Communist from the Freikorps soldier male discussed by Klaus Theweleit insofar as the disciplinary armor of the Communist manifests itself chiefly through discursive discipline and performance as opposed to bloody massacre. If, for Theweleit, the superego of the soldier male is externalized into practices of collective transgression, and the "utopia of fascism is an edenic freedom from responsibility,"[43] the Communist variant of body armoring admits no such freedom. Communists display discipline precisely through restraint. They do not beat and torture, and the pleasure of violence for its own sake is nowhere to be found in these novels. Whereas acts of violence directly maintain the full identification of the subject with the superego of the male, the intervention of discipline blocks the full identification of Communist armoring with violence. Communist discourse stresses theoretical clarity and tactical flexibility. As Lenin argues of discipline in *"Left-Wing" Communism*, violence is a specific tactic, appropriate in specific conditions and not others. It is not a motive force of self-constitution and maintenance, as it is in fascist discourse. Communist discipline must maintain a space of self-reflexivity or, as Lenin insists, the ability to maneuver and compromise.[44]

The emphasis placed on *thinking* in this process demonstrates not only the sustaining power of Marxist-Leninist ideology but also an ethical self-reflexivity vis-à-vis the disciplining of the self. The kernel that peeks from the hard Communist's shell is less the sublime Communist body, represented by the "power of the idea," than a manifestation of belonging to the collective.[45] Dialectical thinking, as Fernando invokes it, allows for a minimal space between the subject and its activity, a space of reflection and strategy. The Communist must be able to judge and evaluate his own affect. Instead of simply executing a deserter during the siege of Madrid, Fernando submits the case to the company for discussion: "the form of the death would be decided here. . . . Their own feeling, their own reason should pass judgment over feelings that are their own" (GO 111). Those who judge the deserter and decide his fate are at the same time judging their own fear. This stance of judgment is grounded less on some fetishized objectivity than on a model of Communist solidarity. If the discourse of fascism is, for Theweleit, expressive, which is to say incapable of representing or storytelling, the discourse of Communist solidarity is precisely narrative.[46] Together they "must think a life through to its end" (111). The decision reached is that the deserter will be sent to the front precisely because "one can only erase the stigma of cowardice by living on and finding oneself again" (112). Such moments of collective judgment of individual affects, emotions, and capabilities reveal the collective nature of these emotions and thus also the collective character of Communist psychic armoring. This is what the deserter must be given the chance to recapture.

A utopian moment exists in this Communist discipline. Jameson explains the third-person narration of experienced events as an attempt to think of the self and the collective, experience and history, as mutually determining. Consciousness is not identical to self but is rather consciousness *of* the self.[47] The self at stake in Claudius's novel, like that of the agitators in Brecht's *The Measures Taken*, is, however, a relation between the first and third person, as Alain Badiou puts it in his discussion of Brecht's play. For Badiou the party itself, in Brecht's portrayal, becomes "above all . . . the organized paradigm of the articulation between the 'I' and the 'we.'"[48] It is a "deciding machine,"[49] but it is not above the individuals that constitute it; it is precisely, to recall Claudius, "their own feeling, their own reason" passing "judgment over feelings that are their own." As Badiou puts it, this is neither a totalitarian absorption of I into we nor an ecstatic fusion of the two but the more subtle "inseparate form" by which the "I" abides within the "we." It is this third-person-ness that opens up the space of political deliberation. Once the "we" has been amputated, politics is replaced with morality.[50]

A bond of solidarity holds the community of Communist partisans in Claudius's novel together that itself draws its vitality from something like a class memory of creatureliness and resistance. The material sign of this solidarity, its inscription on the Communist body and psyche, is discipline. This discipline, however, acquires its true pathos less in the scenes of battle that punctuate the novel and more in the portrayal of the collapse of the Spanish Republic once Claudius's wounded protagonist returns to Paris in time for the fall of the Popular Front government there. Already in Spain, the great collective paradigm of the party increasingly becomes a matter of necromancy. In this sense, discipline becomes a kind of signifier of memory as well. The Communist wears the martyrs to his cause in his bodily gestures and poses. Claudius supplies a dramatic image of this passion of the partisan. Toward the end of Jak's time at the front, he attends the anniversary banquet of the Edgar André Battalion, in which he is now a political commissar. "It was meant as a day of remembrance and became a day of the dead" (GO 200). Claudius describes the celebration that ensues as a coming together that is foreclosed by its own circumstance: "somewhere someone had dug up an old gramophone, and they danced like large, helpless bears, each alone for himself, and each one had a ghost on his arm, but it did not seem to them that they had a ghost on their arm" (205). Thus the dead intervene between discipline and solidarity, making their way into the body armor of the survivors. The armored body of the Communist then not only defends against the enemy but also inscribes his dead comrades into the very *Gestus* of his body as trust, or *Vertrauen*, congeals into character armor.

The Claudius novel does not bring this contradiction between discipline and solidarity to its logical conclusion, which for German Communist exile was perhaps optimized in the experience of the Great Purges.[51] Weiss brings these aspects together in his postwar novel *The Aesthetics of Resistance*. In the closing pages of Weiss's novel, the characters await evacuation in a Spanish field hospital, listening to radio reports of the great catastrophes of March 1938: the collapse of Republican fronts across Spain, the beginnings of the Trial of the Twenty-One in Moscow, in which Nicolai Bukharin, among others, were sentenced to death, and the entrance of Hitler's troops into Vienna (AP 263). "It was barely possible to distinguish between the various levels of what was happening," Weiss writes, "the images of the centers where power and violence were concentrated thronged into our steps, our actions" (253). In these discussions, discipline emerges as the refuge of the defeated, of the exile, as the necessity to defend the USSR imposes the duty to "agree with the court and turn our backs on the people we used to trust," and thus, in the bitter words of the feminist

Marxist character Mercauer, "you people, with your need for truth, recognize and defend the verdicts" (256–57). The Norwegian writer Nordahl Grieg, who asserts, "the time of voluntary action had slipped through our fingers, has already preempted this argument. Unity could be attained only through coercion, violence" (252).[52] Indeed, the Popular Front from 1936 was shaped by the great events of the Spanish Civil War and the Terror in the Soviet Union, which were often juxtaposed as poles of voluntary and coerced unity. Michael Rohrwasser points out in his reading of Weiss's novel in light of the memoirs of Regler and Kantorowicz, "Spain was the place of action, of active solidarity, where one seemed temporarily protected from what was playing out in Moscow on the theatrical stages of the courts and in the party apparatus of the various nations."[53] The growing suspicion that these poles were not as stable as one might like and that one was not in fact protected by the active solidarity of the Spanish struggle from what was occurring in Moscow was one of the most important factors in the polarization of the Popular Front, as the USSR exported the purges and the terror to Spain along with its international solidarity and military assistance.[54] At the same time, many on the left saw precisely in the show trials a guarantee that the Soviet Union would not allow itself, as had the Spanish Republic, to be undermined by the plots of conspirators.[55]

Slavoj Žižek makes this point from a slightly different direction, noting the particular fantasmatic constellations around the Moscow trials, which he describes as post-tragic sacrifice. The tragic sacrifice, and here Žižek cites Antigone, is one that destroys the individual in the service of a higher ideal or justice, for which the tragic protagonist thereafter becomes a sign in the collective memory, "of a fidelity that goes beyond (biological) life and death."[56] What makes the Communist sacrifice post-tragic is precisely the public disavowal of this tragic fidelity in the name of that very commitment: to "show your ultimate fidelity to the Revolution by publicly confessing, by admitting that you are worthless scum."[57] The logic of sacrifice is inverted in this instance, in which it is less a question of the objective truth or falsity of the charges to which one confesses but precisely a question of willfully abandoning what Žižek calls the bare "minimum of personal autonomy" through the ritual of confession. The specificity of the show trials of course is that often the victims were perpetrators, the perpetrators victims, caught up in the same discursive machinery. As Žižek notes, the stance of post-tragic sacrifice paradoxically re-creates a "perverse economy of duty."[58] The Stalinist dispensation in this sense is not pure enough but clings to the pathos of self-instrumentalization, assuming the position of one "who loves mankind, but nonetheless performs horrible purges and executions: his heart is breaking while he's doing it, but he can't help it, it's his Duty towards the Progress of Humanity."[59] In contrast to the Stalinist stance of rendering oneself the instrument of the logic of history, the Leninist stance breaks with notions of objective historical stages and demands the "throwing oneself into the paradox of the situation, seizing the opportunity and intervening."[60] What Claudius and Weiss portray is precisely the vicissitudes of this transition from the Leninist to the Stalinist stance, situating this transition at the moment of the collapse of the Popular Front, not as an ethical or ideological failing but as the closure of real historical possibilities for collective intervention. As Brecht famously wrote, "We who would prepare the ground for friendliness could not ourselves be friendly," not because of a lack of desire for friendliness but because of a lack of material and political conditions for friendliness.

By 1939, the German Popular Front was more or less in a state of decline. Émigré SPD groups had never shown much interest in working with the Communists, and the public impact of the Moscow trials only seemed to confirm the SPD's skepticism. At the same time, the persecution of anarchist groups in Spain and the hunt for Trotskyists by the KPD in the various left formations that had agreed to collaborate with it alienated the KPD from other groups on the left. All of this was only exacerbated by the collapse of the Popular Front governments in Spain and France.[61] The Hitler-Stalin Pact was a traumatic shock for many intellectuals both without and within the KPD. For many antifascists the non-aggression pact seemed to foreclose any possibility of materially resisting fascism, as party discipline and antifascist conviction were now drawn into direct contradiction by this agreement at the same time that the pact left Communists in many countries all the more exposed.[62] The full pathos of this double bind of discipline and solidarity is perhaps achieved in Stefan Heym's *Die Architekten* in an opening scene where the German Communist functionary Goltz has been deported to Nazi Germany by the Soviet authorities under the conditions of the Hitler-Stalin Pact. Goltz faces a painful dilemma vis-à-vis the German comrades in the concentration camp where he is sent. If he reveals what is happening in the USSR, he will undermine KPD resistance in Germany. He must pose before the German comrades as the traitor that he is not. "So there remained to him as alternatives, either to sweep away the support for their moral existence from under the feet of the German comrades—or from beneath his own."[63] Here discipline intervenes against the very possibility that the German comrades could express solidarity for Goltz, and his solidarity for them renders him unable to critique the Stalinist purges, which is equivalent not only to self-betrayal but to the betrayal of Stalin's victims. Trapped in a dilemma now more moral than political, Goltz, amputated from the collective of the inseparable, must take the guilt of the purges upon himself. In this moment, the trope of discipline acquires its properly post-tragic valence.

THE PARTISAN

Claudius understands partisanship in *Green Olives* under the sign of the Communist revolutionary and, what's more, the Communist revolutionary as mobile and exilic. In this sense, Claudius's partisan is a typical of Popular Front figures, which Katerina Clark describes as cosmopolitan adventurers, marked by their "fatal but authentic passion for the revolution," caught up "in the frisson of frenetic movement."[64] In this sense, the partisan is, precisely, non-telluric and sustained by bonds of solidarity that are at best precarious. Claudius writes of his protagonist, "he had been a person without a name in the years of emigration. And they were called tramps, vagrants, because one knew that they were no tramps. He had read the *Manifesto* that began with the words: 'A specter is haunting Europe,' and was a part of that specter, a person with many names, but known among everyone" (GO 25). The challenge of the exiled Communist was to maintain partisanship, discipline, and identity after the collapse of the Communist counterpublic sphere that had sustained these commitments in the Weimar Republic. The Communist must assume the mask of anonymity without becoming anonymous, to bear a name without fully assuming it, as Claudius writes of the exile. The partisan must, to paraphrase Brecht, always again erase the traces while at the same time remaining legible as a sign of resistance and futurity. Embodying this double negation of *das gewöhnliche*, the partisan is the figure outside the quotidian. The disappearance of the very possibility of telluric attachments stands between the partisan, who now can relate to normal life only as an ironic and nostalgic citation, and the "people" for whom the partisan fights.

This emphasis on mobility marks a tension in the concept of partisanship itself. Think only of Carl Schmitt's well-known account of this figure in his *Theory of the Partisan*, which also takes Spain as its point of departure, although the Spain of the 1808 revolt against Bonapartism rather than the Spain of the Civil War.[65] Here Schmitt defines the partisan by the criteria of "irregularity, increased mobility, intensity of political commitment, and telluric character."[66] The ambiguity in comparing Claudius's notion of the partisan with Schmitt's centers precisely on the question of the telluric. For Schmitt, partisans are "defensive autochthonous defenders of homeland," which remain distinguished from "globally aggressive revolutionary activists."[67] Schmitt argues that with Lenin, and particularly with the Soviet partisans of World War II, these dimensions become joined, but the question that Claudius raises of the partisan without homeland remains outside of Schmitt's frame.[68] This is precisely what produces the suspicion of the Spanish peasants alongside whom the German Communists are fighting in Claudius's novel. The Germans, a group of Spanish soldiers tells Jak Rohde, Claudius's protagonist, act like they don't love their own women and children, and continues, "there is a rattling about your people, and this rattling is also here around you people, also around you, *Comisario*. The rattle of iron, the gaze of steel in the eyes, you Germans have that" (GO 189). For the Spanish, there is something profoundly unsettling about the Germans, Communists as well as fascists, and their discipline. German discipline is all the more threatening in that it forecloses the dimension of the telluric.

The fact of this exilic mobility also raises questions for the notions of the popular that subtended the Popular Front. In the formulations of critics like Georg Lukács, "the Popular Front means a struggle for a genuine popular culture, a manifold relationship to every aspect of the life of one's own people as it has developed in its own individual way in the course of history" (RB 57). Acknowledging the fragmented character of the German popular progressive tradition, Lukács nevertheless insists on the essentially national quality of a realist aesthetic. Yet, as Weiss's working-class narrator in *The Aesthetics of Resistance* points out, this disconnection from something like a homeland is one of the constitutive aspects of the proletarian condition, in which "the changing places, the travels, the arrivals in strange cities were linked not to epic impressions but to the question of whether a job could be found there" (AR 115). The precarity of the proletariat is itself a kind of disavowed aspect of the Popular Front:

> The issues given priority in the magazines concerning realistic art, concerning workers' literature, the elucidation of

> an everyday milieu, the linkage with its inhabitants and the exchange of values with them, these elements would apply to me only in a limited sense . . . it had become obvious to me that we were at home nowhere but in our partisanship.[69]

This partisanship, and the solidarity that it founds, can only find form and expression, however, in a militant discipline, which is not yet the practice of liberation, as one of Weiss's characters puts it:

> we were en route to our own values, but overhead we carried flags, banners, coats-of-arms, insignia deriving from times that had nothing to do with us. No, we needed them in this era of war, for us they spoke about future things, about the defeat of war, about liberation, peace. (AR 183)

In the midst of the siege of Madrid, Albert and Samuel talk through something quite akin to Schmitt's theory of the partisan, noting that the old rules of wars can no longer be applied to war in the age of industrial technology and to the exterminating logic of fascism. "One should not speak of humanity in the context of war. There are wars for humanity and for humaneness, but war itself is never humane" (GO 106). Albert furthers this thought, adding that in Spain, "the lines between soldiers and civilians are becoming increasingly blurred. And that's a good thing. Everyone will be pulled into the struggle" (107). It is precisely this generalization of the struggle against fascism to the very substance of popular life that Albert sees as the redeeming quality of the kind of total warfare he is describing in a passage indirectly evoking both Schmitt's theory of the partisan and Ernst Jünger's theses on total mobilization. The fight in Spain, as we have seen, is viewed here as part of a larger struggle against fascism: "they're like snakes," says Albert of Germany and Italy, "that still have their grub in their jaws when they're attacked. . . . They will swallow up country after country, and then, when they need to defend themselves, they won't be able to use their fangs, because they'll have still have their unchewed prey in their throats and gullets, and they'll choke on it" (107). This is the logic that grounds this particular mode of partisanship—that neither the technologies of war nor the fascist threat can any longer be localized or addressed at the telluric level. Precisely in the globalization of the contemporary struggle, as Albert describes it, the war in Spain opens onto the insight that oppression and resistance have always exceeded a local frame. It is precisely this expansive and extraterritorial logic of fascism, though, in which Albert sees some measure of hope. There is no local dimension to fascism, nowhere for it tarry for digestion.

If the Communist partisan is likewise extraterritorial, it is notable that Claudius places this figure in relation to the more conventionally telluric Spanish peasantry. Upon arrival in Valencia, to the greetings of the Spanish peasants and workers, Jak declares, "We have come home!" (GO 40). In this scene, Jak is approached by an elderly fisherman, who explains that his family has been fighting for generations and gives Jak a piece of his old and tattered black anarchist flag. The old fisherman establishes continuity with the fight in Spain, which is here pictured as a sort of ancient people's struggle, less the "contemporaneous" struggle, to use Bloch phrase, between labor and capital but the eternal struggle of the oppressed against the oppressor. At the same time, this flag is the marker of Jak's non-telluric status as a Communist. "You have no flags," the fisherman points out. "Communists just came into the world yesterday," he continues (47). This moment stands the usual Marxist take on the relationship between the proletariat and the peasant on its head. Against the claims of Jak and the Communist Interbrigadists to historical contemporaneity and geographical mobility, the anarchist peasant raises the claims of the telluric. For the peasant the Communists, the privileged bearers of the historical process, have no history, and the peasantry emerges as the subject of a tradition of revolution to which the Communists are newcomers.

The Germans find the telluric quality of the Spanish soldiers difficult to comprehend. As the International Brigades arrive in Valencia, Albert is disappointed to see that the workers have come out of the factories to greet them, complaining, "*merde*, damn it, isn't there a war going on? They run away from their workbenches, they wave and act like crazy people!" (GO 38). Although Jak himself criticizes Albert for "measuring out, like a butcher measures out a piece of meat, the joy of the masses and our joy and our enthusiasm," he, too, is shocked by the Spanish conduct of the war. "This is a strange country," he muses.

> They say that on the fronts of Madrid, the *milicianos*, the volunteers from the unions and parties, go home at night and sleep in their beds. The ground is too hard in the trenches. In the afternoons, the women apparently take the tram from the Puerta del Sol to the trenches and bring lunch to the men. What was the creation of myths, what was malicious slander? (57)

This telluric quality of the Spanish engagement with combat is all the more inscrutable to Jak insofar as it is precisely through the renunciation of all of this that he has, in his own account, proven himself as a member of the guild of the specter (70). As he explains later in the novel to his Swiss bourgeois lover, Thea, whose offer of a safe home in Davos he has emphatically refused, "I have come from the war, but the war is still on. . . . I am a partisan, a part of the specter, and where the Party sends me, that's where I'm going" (300).

The thematics of exile and communism open onto a discourse on nationality in the novel, pointing to an alternate interpretation of Communist discipline. To the Communist characters in *Grüne Oliven und nackte Berge*, discipline is a defining characteristic of what it means to be part of the specter. To the Spanish, however, this discipline is no different from the iron discipline of the Nazis supporting Franco. For the Spanish, the Germans, Nazi or Communist, are the bearers of the dangerous life, cool and disciplined adventurers without families or homes. The Spanish Republicans of *Grüne Oliven* both admire and fear this trait of the exiled Germans. The young Spanish Republican soldier Juan, who has joined the largely German Edgar André Battalion because of his disappointment with the undisciplined manner in which the Spanish Republic is waging the war, explains, "discipline is something insulting for many of our people, something that oppresses them. People know about you Germans that you have it. People hate you for it, and people are jealous too" (GO 77). To the Spanish characters, it is not Communists who are disciplined but Germans. Juan is politically mature enough to realize the necessity of this quality, but this is not a widely held position among the novel's Spanish characters. At the same time, the old fisherman represents a different standpoint to discipline, one that manages to hold together the dimensions of the public and the personal that are fissured in Communist discourse. "Where are your women?" asks the fisherman. Jak replies that "one doesn't go to the front with women." The fisherman is unsatisfied. "It's a good thing to lie with a woman at night between the murder and the fighting," he tells Jak, "otherwise one comes to find joy in the taste of blood and with time becomes a murderer" (43).

This warning is less a matter of sexual politics, the feminine instrumentalized as a sort of homeopathic remedy against the excess of male subjectivity, than it is a matter of maintaining the proper balance toward struggle. Struggle is here not a thing for itself but is part of the life of the people. This is one of the central tensions of *Grüne*

Oliven und nackte Berge, that between the discipline of warfare and the capacity to integrate that discipline into the bonds of social life.

The Spanish soldiers refer to the German Interbrigadists as "los moros rubios," or blond Moroccans, equating German discipline with the putative brutality of Franco's Moroccan soldiers. Like the Kumiak-type discussed earlier, the Spanish regard the German Communist exile as a potentially dangerous outsider. It is worth noting that these Spanish characters are almost always peasants, so that much of what was said about the Kumiak-type earlier can also be said of the novel's Spanish soldiers, whose concerns center on their families and villages. The difference is that the Spanish, unlike the Kumiak-type, are still rooted in their homes and families as opposed to the fantasy of home and family, and perhaps this is why, like Juan, they realize the need to fight for them. German discipline is all the more threatening in that it forecloses these very spheres of life in Spain. The Germans, Communists as well as fascists, are without the personal, familial, and erotic attachments that the Spaniards cherish. Yet, as Jak points out, "our hardness has something self-defensive to it, we've lost our kitchens. We've lost everything that makes a normal person. A kitchen, a bed, a woman living somewhere but we've won something after all, something that makes a person in the first place: the will to relentless struggle" (GO 238–39). The critique of the telluric, then, here as in Marchwitza's novel, is the critique of *Eigensinn*, the critique of attachments that have already been rendered hollow and precarious through exploitation and war.

As in many German émigré writings on the Spanish Civil War, this suspicion of the perceived domestic and telluric aspects of the fighting in Spain leads to a literary figuration of the Spanish as children who are in need of the disciplinary pedagogy of the German Interbrigadists.[70] This becomes the direct responsibility of Jak Rohde as political commissar, "who has to make certain that others overcome their misery and the weakness of their bodies and their desire, their fear" (GO 191). As the Spaniards threaten to melt into the night during the battle of Teruel, Jak implores them not to obey but to see: "Didn't you see the two ways that there are for you? Either fight, and fight well and win, or fight badly and find yourselves in prison with no houses and no homeland" (194). In this moment, it is not the performative discipline of the Communist that Jak is bringing to bear as a persuasive spectacle, but rather it is a rhetoric of prophecy to which Jak is appealing. The Germans are hard because, and precisely because, they have been defeated. They have sat in fascist prisons, been cast across Europe, and transformed into specters. In a moment of anagnorisis, the antagonism between the telluric Spaniards and the metallic Germans is shifted to the insight that the attachment to the local, to the "defensive autochthonous" commitment, to return to Schmitt, of the Spanish characters can only be sustained through a partisanship that acquires a properly global frame. Here is it not the telluric that sustains partisanship but partisanship that holds out the very possibility of the telluric. The boundedness, however porous, of place will now have to be articulated through the mobile and non-localizable space of the European class struggle, which is to say that the local in the sense of home and hearth has been rendered mythical by the larger forces at play in the antifascist struggle. Jak, as a German, is exiled as well from the "normal life" of the countries of his exile, as the bearer of the uncomfortable fact that this "normal life" is itself an illusory idyll in the face of what is to come. Partisanship becomes abstracted from place but remains rooted in a texture of plebeian and proletarian experience of subalternity and the desire to escape the confines of this dispensation. "Humans are a race of servile dogs," Claudius writes. "When they're beaten, they whimper and lick the hand that beats them.—Is this true?—No, it is not true. Now they have rifles. And the many beatings they have taken, they're giving them back" (88). Partisanship is a struggle against this subalternity of a ruined, rotten life. As such, it becomes itself a sign of the failure of popular life, of the long historical trauma that has been the everyday. This becomes a national discourse insofar as the German émigrés represent the break with this *gewöhnliches Leben*, but Claudius has reduced this break, symptomatically, to the fantasmatic disavowal of the possibility of such a life of everyday attachments. At the same time, the visibility of the partisan as a social figure creates a representational inversion between what Žižek refers to as subjective violence and objective violence. Subjective violence is visible and can be easily tied to agents, but at the same time, this very visibility means that subjective violence is "experienced as such against a background of a non-violent zero level. It is seen as a perturbation of the 'normal,' peaceful state of things." Of course the normal state of things is precisely the durational and nonpunctual constellation of violence, confinement, exploitation, and privation of the rotten life; it is objective violence in Žižek's terms, which "is invisible since it sustains the very zero-level standard against which we perceive something as objectively violent."[71] Into this representational inversion steps the partisan, whose warnings and invocations of the objective and systemic violence of capitalism and fascism are perceived as nothing but the subjective expression of the violence of the German national character.

THE GUILD OF THE SPECTER

The gulf between *gewöhnliches* and *gefärhliches Leben* becomes truly unnavigable when Jak is sent back to Paris after a wound leaves him unfit for combat. The returning Interbrigadists are the wraiths of the Popular Front. "Jak Rohde knew the outer appearance of this emigration," Claudius writes, "which for many had become the image of their inner state. Beleaguered, threadbare, sleeping two in a bed, too narrow!" (GO 261). The poverty and precarity of the emigration is in a sense the bad conscience of the collapsing Popular Front in France. Supported by a meager pension and a small group of German émigré trade unionists, the émigrés are hounded by the French police and regarded as dangerous outsiders by the Parisian population. "One comes back from the war and goes into the new, other war," Jak muses (265). This new war is not only one of survival in the streets and cheap hotels of the French capital but one of maintaining the political impetus of the Popular Front itself in the face of what Claudius describes as the tiredness of the French. The credibility of this antifascist prophecy, however, becomes increasingly fragile in the light of the collapse of France's Popular Front government and the failure of the general strike of November 1938. Exile in Paris will be a test of perseverance in the face of this political impasse. "Few are left of the old ones," Jak muses, "and under storms time ripens the fruits. How can one fill the barns if there are no workers for the harvest? He will have to drink this cup to the dregs" (331).

In this second exile, as the fall of the Spanish Republic becomes only a matter of time and the French and German Popular Front movements are collapsing, the figure of the Communist partisan becomes a kind of dispossessed and unheard prophet, a militant Cassandra. This begins already with the fever visions of a wounded comrade whom Jak encounters during the battle of Teruel, where Jak himself becomes an oneiric figure for the unheeded warnings of Europe's antifascists, an avenging Cassandra:

> Yesterday . . . we were back in the countries that we came from. Everyone stared at us while lots of airplanes circled

> above the city . . . you couldn't count them anymore, and they flew from one horizon to another. And all the people were asking us, "why didn't you tell us this would happen?"—"Didn't tell you?" you sneered, "we drove into you with our words like whips." (GO 226)

The wounded comrade's dream vision of Jak proceeds to reproach this fantasmatic audience, which in the face of death from above might finally lend him their ears, with their previous indifference to his warnings. Their apathy, their clinging to comfort, and their disavowal of all that challenged this complacency, their hatred of the Communists, "because we made you uncomfortable and no one likes the caller in the wastes," their contrariness in the face of the essential rightness of the KPD's warnings, their love of their own fattened bellies, and finally their egoism have brought this fiasco to pass, according to the scorned Communist prophet.

Grüne Oliven figures post–Popular Front France as symptomatic of a Europe that is unwilling to acknowledge the storm clouds of war on the horizon and of a world that turns an intentionally deaf ear to the prophetic warnings of the specter. From the point of view of the French, the German émigrés are an omen of disaster, of an approaching catastrophe. Following a night of carousing, Jak finds himself discussing politics with the bartender in a Parisian café. "Spain is fighting for Europe, and Europe is leaving Spain in the lurch," he complains. The waiter brings the question back to German aggression. "I think your people," he explains, "have a machine in their backs, that when it's wound tight, brings them to marching" (GO 284). From the waiter's point of view, the twentieth century is nothing but a wearing and pointless vigilance against its eastern neighbor. "We are so tired," he tells Jak. "Look, German, for fifty years we've just had to listen for marching at the border; that makes you tired. . . . We turn in circles, and whenever your circle touches our circle, there's an explosion. Isn't that right?" (285). Jak objects that this war is not the war of 1914 but a generalized European civil war that had already begun in 1933 with the smashing of the German workers' parties and is now being fought in Spain but that will stop at the borders of neither of these nations (286–87). "Until now, we were virtually alone in Germany," Jak intones, "and in Spain we were virtually alone, because you people weren't there, instead you were happy to be content." The fascists could have been stopped in Spain, or on the Rhine, with a couple of French divisions, but now it is a total war that Jak sees on the horizon. "Oh, old man," Jak prophesies,

> your people are tired, and because you are tired, one day the flood will rise around your throats. Maybe you'll make a try at copping out, but in these days you can't cop out. You won't be able to breathe anymore, if you're tired, won't be able to eat anymore, to sleep anymore, and so you'll have to fight. And you'll need your claws and feet and your eyes and ears and to fight with your whole flesh and your whole fear; there will be nothing else left for you to do.

The waiter does not understand what Jak is unfolding before him. The French are tired, they want peace, and Jak's injunctions to fight against fascism seem little different in tone than Nazi Germany's aggressions. In the waiter's estimation, Jak is no prophet but just another German: "you are a strange people, you Germans! You always talk about fighting" (287).

Ultimately, at the base of French weariness, Claudius locates the same kernel of fantasy that Marchwitza had already elaborated in 1934 as the Kumiak-type: the valence of *Eigensinn* for which the attachment to *Heimat* as private property, as *etwas Eigenes*, has become inextricably interwoven. Thus an old French comrade, Rozat, tells Jak that the German émigrés "are like ravens in autumn. When they come into the cities, you know that now it is winter. Their cawing brings the snow." Rozat goes on to explain that in the last war, he had no land but now has a house and a piece of the earth that is his, not because he owns it but because "the ground has received from me that which it needs." Rozat continues, "I am afraid for my house and my garden, so I don't like to hear your raven's call. The way it looks now, your people will fight ours again, and we—we can't resist" (GO 316). It is precisely the lack of this telluric tie, however, that lends Jak his spectral power. When Rozat reproaches him for having no fatherland, Jak replies, "because nothing in the country belongs to me, everything belongs to me" (317). To recall Georg Heisler in Seghers's *The Seventh Cross*, this is the maxim of the *gefährliches Leben*, and of the partisan, to give up everything to win everything; it is a radical affirmation of the objectivity of social violence (SC 260).

Between the poles of partisan and prophet, Jak is fighting a war on two fronts in prewar Paris. This is a struggle that can be understood in terms of discipline and spectrality. The figure of the guild of the specter, evoked earlier, appears only in the scenes where Jak finds himself in Parisian emigration. The partisans fighting in Spain are not specters but part of a collective fighting body. In Paris and the cities of emigration, "they were called vagabonds" precisely "because everyone knew they were no vagabonds." The difficulty of being a specter, as Claudius elaborates, is that of maintaining the bonds of solidarity in isolation, of maintaining fidelity without legible signs of commitment. "Being a specter is no simple thing," Jak muses to himself.

> you are always in danger of softening. It was hard, to be honest: grueling. You wore dark glasses that were meant to conceal the fanatical looking gaze and the emaciated cheeks. You had become used to being a specter, indeed, you were proud to be a part of the great, fearful specter. You laughed when you thought about possessing no papers. . . . You often stood before the mirror, examined your always more exhausted features to see if there wasn't after all some trace of the stranger whose name you bore. You laughed when you even found yourself celebrating the birthday of the man whose papers you possessed. (GO 25)

Tiredness returns here as the threat of losing one's spectral status. This is precisely the threat posed to Jak when his bourgeois Swiss lover arrives and offers him the *gewöhnliches Leben* and "the bourgeois security of her home." "He is a specter," Jak thinks to himself, "and can it be that a specter has a wife and a family. He is a visible member of the guild of specters that stand on Europe's street corners. And will there not be, when this war is lost, a time to come when he will again have to disappear and become invisible as a specter?" (271). At the same time, Thea's offer of domesticity is an expression of her own tiredness, as she explains to Jak. To Jak's question about her commitment to the cause, she replies,

> I gave a piece of my life to the cause. It was the most beautiful and best part, and I will never regret it. But it is so hard to see no results. I've spent years and years on educating the children of the comrades; the least bit that I could do I did, and then suddenly I saw: the children grew up, they forgot the songs of our flags and of the new life that would someday come,

> and now they sang jazz songs and songs about sweet, kitschy hearts. (303)

In this passage, Thea evokes that very catastrophe feared by the collective "we" voice of the Westhofen camp, that the best of a generation will be killed and that no one will take up the flag, simply because no one will recognize it. Claudius thematizes this unbridgeable gap between the present and the past throughout the novel, and this fissure between time frames is precisely what prevents the reentry of the specter into the *gewöhnliches Leben*: "One cannot knit the present together with the future, because those years that one has lived alone are always missing" (271). This insight, which intervenes now between Thea and Jak as the life they have not shared, is generalized in various registers throughout Claudius's novel as an acknowledgment of the irrevocability of the collapse of the German left, the catastrophe of fascism, and the trauma of exile. Thus Jak recalls a conversation with a fellow émigré in Zürich. "We have suffered a defeat from which we will not soon recover," he tells Jak, "it is not so, like people sometimes say, that it wasn't a defeat. They beat us, hard and without a doubt" (309). Here the incommensurability of the present to the past is reframed in terms of a national and historical discourse, but in either sense, the specter is the figure and sign of the break between these two times.

Green Olives thus complicates Ernst Bloch's assertion that the proletarian struggle is entirely contemporaneous. While Claudius makes it clear that the figure of the Communist partisan that he is portraying is securely located in working-class experience, the novel elaborates, but does not theorize, the continuity of proletarian experience and struggle with the *longue durée* of plebeian oppression. The noncontemporaneity of the contemporary and the contemporaneity of the noncontemporary, to recall Bloch, find their natural home in the misery of the German experience. During a battle in Spain, Fernando turns to Jak and asks, "Do you love Germany?" to which Jak replies, "Love? What should I love about Germany? Maybe the prisons, all the filth and misery and wretchedness that I had to go through and the brown shirts, I should love that? . . . Is that something that one can love? Anything in our whole history? All the half measures, the revolutions that are never carried through, should anyone love that?" (GO 255–56). Fernando agrees with Jak's critique of the German misery but totalizes and contextualizes this critique by placing himself and Jak within it. Rather than the rhetoric of the fascist Germany and the better antifascist Germany that has been elaborated in the book and in much of the KPD discourse on the nation during the Popular Front period and after, Fernando frames the problem of Germany as a problem of the very failure of the popular to have any real social purchase, a failure in which the Communists find themselves also complicit:

> I know that our people are guilty too, that things have come so far, but we too are guilty, all of us in all peoples; how could one absolve oneself of complicity for everything that is, what will come? But not to love your people and your country because of it? Do you know why I love my country? Because I often see, in the gray hours, the beautiful future; when this is all past . . . and Germany is a human country; then it will be as we dreamed of it, that's why I love it. (256)

The future and the past are thus set in a reciprocal relationship that negates the present, and this becomes, for Claudius, an antifascist temporality that in some sense is particularly German, and precisely insofar as it is non-telluric. Amputated from the past and from the present, the Communist specter inhabits this future space, which paradoxically can only be envisioned in Germany, precisely because Germany as an affective place has been stripped of all humanness, of any illusion of a normal life and telluric attachments that are not sutured into the circuits of violence and terror that constitute everyday life under National Socialism. Only the German émigrés can envision a liberated future, and for that very reason they have no place and no present.

Later, wounded by a grenade, Jak has a vision of the eternal soldier. In this vision, Jak is confronted with the dead of all past wars, and, lying faceless among the dead, he finds himself, not as Jak Rohde but as a "strange dead peasant, who held an old musket on his arm, his body mutilated by a halberd." Jak asks himself if it hurt, and the reply is the voice of that history without history that defines the trope of the eternally suffering peasant who now is also his partisan interlocutor:

> what are you asking, the peasant answered, dying doesn't hurt. Living, like we have lived hurts; it was an eternal fear of the power of the lords. This life hurts, it wastes you away; you can never be what you might have been. Why are you asking? You are fighting, and I have fought; we have both fought since many centuries past. (GO 166)

In this vision, Jak is briefly reinscribed within the continuity of peasant history as a static continuum of oppression, punctuated by the occasional disaster, of temporality as a circle of scarcity, toil, and death. Bent and distorted by fear, the life of the peasant is identical to its own foreclosure—"you can never be what you might have been"—determined by the narrow confinement of an oppression so ancient as to become ontological. The fighting of this bent-over peasant is only an extension of his passivity, of his cowardice. Jak's response—"I have a rifle, and I have hand grenades, and I have the courage not to tolerate this life any longer!"—marks the break between Communist violence and the passivity of the peasant dispensation (167). This exchange marks not only the difference between the conscious partisan and the armored, yet creaturely peasant, the *Landsknecht*, but at the same time reveals that peasant heritage as the deep structure of partisan commitment. The Communist partisan fights for the very break into a human history denied to the peasantry. In the prologue of the novel, Claudius writes,

> it is only worth fighting and dying for all of the smells you have yet to smell. For each taste that you have never tasted. For all of the melodies you have not heard. For all of the things that you have never done and that you have been denied from doing. For all of the thoughts that you have not thought and that you have been denied from thinking. . . . Only for the future that they wish to deny you is it worth living and dying. (8)

The future that Claudius evokes here is very much the future of a redeemed peasant past, of the life in which one can never become what one could have become. In this sense, one is reminded of a well-nigh Benjaminian messianism, for Claudius is not here evoking a historicist model of progress, the kind of thinking that Benjamin takes issue with in his twelfth thesis on the concept of history:

> The Social Democrats preferred to cast the working class in the role of a redeemer of future generations, in this way cutting the sinews of its greatest strength. This indoctrination made the working class forget both its hatred and its spirit of sacrifice, for both are nourished by the image of enslaved ancestors rather than the ideal of liberated grandchildren.[72]

What Claudius contributes to this Benjaminian insight is that the future and the redeemed past cannot be thought of separately, just as the peasantry and the proletariat are both articulations of a *longue durée* of oppression and subalternity.

If the solidarity of partisans in Claudius's novel is legible in the discipline of these partisans, then this discipline must then absorb and redeem the historical constellation of affect of the peasantry and draw its power not only from the contemporary struggle against fascism but also from the whole history of plebeian and peasant struggle. Likewise, the disciplined Communist body remains a signifier of a principle of partisanship that is no longer telluric in the Schmittian sense but rooted in a collective affective history. As Weiss writes of the fall of Spain, "our body, the body of the country, was sheer pain, it was bloody, hacked up, yet everywhere this body developed new ways of grabbing, repulsing" (AR 271). What holds this body together, as Jameson has noted of Weiss's novel, is a network of precarious connections between spaces of isolation—hotel rooms, prison cells, battlefields—wherein the isolation and deprivation of those confined itself produces a special mode of attunement to the signals coming from outside.[73] These signals of "constant anonymous cooperation," as Weiss's narrator puts it, are the material ground of an "anticipation of the future." Weiss's narrator, himself on the verge of departing for Spain, elaborates, "Thus my activity, paltry, infinitesimal in the gigantic network of forces, led me from the underground into the stage of national war, which the class struggle had now entered." This question of isolation and reconnoitering is also one of literary form and of realism from the point of view of a proletarian authorship, since, as Weiss points out, "the motive force" behind this constant anonymous activity "had been an incessant hatred, a hatred of greed and selfishness, of exploitation, subjugation, and torture" (147).

Yet as Weiss explains, a proletarian writing is precisely the attempt to give form to this experience, to discipline it and to render it partisan. "Whatever we learned in daily work," Weiss writes, "in social life, in our investigations of painting and writing, of science and scholarship, was drawn into the chief task of overcoming the enemy world" (AR 147). We can see that this insight has implications for a literary politics of the Popular Front that might look a bit different from the epic realism promulgated by Lukács. This comes across in Weiss's narrator's complementary readings of Kafka's *The Castle* and Klaus Neukrantz's *Barricades in Wedding*, a Weimar Republic proletarian-revolutionary novel about the events of Bloody May 1929. Kafka's novel reveals the creaturely aspect of proletarian experience, the confinement, shame, resignation, and bewildered muteness of the proletarian exposed to a capitalism, which, like Kafka's castle, seems "on the verge of collapse, bizarre and despicable, and yet remaining erect, doling its mean little strokes . . . keeping us at bay with its unreliable messengers, customs officers, and sentries" (AR 153). Neukrantz's book on the other hand, with its straightforward description of working-class struggle and lack of subtext or interiority, stands for a break from the "paralysis that wore down the villagers" of Kafka's novel. Kafka and Neukrantz relate to one another in Weiss's account as two sides of a single process, or as the narrator puts it: "investigation and defensive combat were two sides of the same position" (158). What is important in this complementary relationship is precisely that Neukrantz's matter-of-fact dive into a specific historical struggle only gains its significance against the background of the almost eternal condition of popular life, less as a progressive heritage to be preserved but as a timeless and unredeemed bondage and suffering that in the work of both Kafka and Breughel, whose work Weiss also invokes, is associated with the peasant village, "a self-contained place of the ordinary and traditional if seen from afar," which in the work of these figures "became the site of nameless despair when the viewers drew closer" (151). This is the material of the partisan intervention, to which it must maintain fidelity, and *Green Olives* is an attempt to give form to this material from the perspective of the contemporaneous struggle. For Claudius, Spain presents a territory in which these disparate temporal and experiential registers can be thought together, but this moment of unity comes apart once Claudius's narrator returns to a Paris where the Popular Front is collapsing in the face of the gathering catastrophe of European fascism, rendering the very act of fidelity to a notion of the future as the redeemed past spectral and grotesque.

CHAPTER 6

Die Deutsche Misère?

Bertolt Brecht, Mother Courage and Her Children

Rather than settling in any of the major centers of the left-wing literary emigration, Paris, Prague, and Moscow, for much of the 1930s Brecht found himself in the Danish town of Svendborg.[1] Here Brecht worked largely cut off from the theatrical public sphere and workers' organizations that had been his chief venues for cultural intervention in the Weimar Republic. Brecht maintained a group of interlocutors and collaborators in Denmark and participated in Popular Front literary politics, attending, for example, the 1935 International Congress of Writers for the Defense of Culture in Paris and editing the journal *Das Wort* along with Lion Feuchtwanger and Willi Bredel. At the same time, his plays were staged with greater or lesser success, for example, the controversial production of Brecht's dramatic adaptation of Maxim Gorky's socialist realist epic *The Mother* at the Theater Union in New York in 1935 and Slatan Dudow's more successful 1937 staging of Brecht's Spanish Civil War drama *Mother Carrar's Rifles* in Paris. Nevertheless, as Brecht's exile lengthened, the tension in his work between engagement and isolation becomes more acute, as in the famous poem, written at this time, "Thoughts on the Duration of Exile":

I

Don't knock any nails in the wall
Just throw your coat on the chair.

Why plan for four days?
Tomorrow you'll go back home.

Leave the little tree without water.
Why plant a tree now?
You'll pack your bags and be away
Before it's as high as the doorstep.

Pull your cap over your eyes when people pass.
What use thumbing through a foreign grammar?
The message that calls you home
Is written in a language you know.

As whitewash peels from the ceiling
(Do nothing to stop it!)
So the block of force will crumble
That has been set up at the frontier
To keep out justice

II

Look at the nail you knocked into the wall:
When do you think you will go back?
Do you want to know what your heart of hearts is saying?
Day after day
You work for the liberation.
You sit in your room, writing.
Do you want to know what you think of your work?
Look at the little chestnut tree in the corner of the yard
You carried a full can of water to it.[2]

The structured contrast across the poem's two stanzas between the impatience of the revolutionary to rejoin the struggle and the increasing attention to the quotidian aspects of sustaining daily life in exile is separated not only by the stanza break but also by a second beginning of the poem from a much more ambivalent structure of feeling. There is no transition here but rather juxtaposition between the urgency of the first part and the indeterminacy of the second, where the work of liberation and the act of writing become themselves forms of waiting, where cultivation and passing time are no longer clearly to be distinguished. Is there a wager on the possibilities of new lives involved in watering the tree, or is it just part of the daily routine? Regardless of how one would answer the question, the poem bears a conflation with the resigned patience of the second part with an attention to the forms of life, to interiors and the rhythms of growing things, that itself seems to inform the act of writing, which now happens "day by day." In other words, the work of forms seems in this poem to be a figure for the very stance of cunning patience that Brecht increasingly cultivates after the mid-1930s and that informs his renewed interest in the apparatus of the theater itself.

As is often remarked, Brecht's work during this period is dominated by a sustained meditation on the question of literary and theatrical realism at the same time as his exile work continually returns to the historical problem of the *deutsche Misère. Mother Courage and Her Children* can be read as a practical intervention into the Expressionism Debate, which was coming to a close around the time of its composition, as well as a reaction to the collapse of the European Popular Front at around the same time.[3] Brecht wrote the play in 1938 and 1939, beginning its conceptualization in Denmark and producing the first full draft in September and October 1939 as the Hitler-Stalin Pact cleared the way for the German invasion of Poland.[4] Devin Fore thus describes Brecht's "significant tactical re-orientation within his practice as a playwright" in the mid-1930s.[5] If Brecht's experiments with the *Lehrstück* and what he called the Major Pedagogy, which would abolish the distinction between cultural production and consumption, between stage and audience, marked a "phase of radical aesthetic abolitionism," Brecht's work after 1933 was increasingly preoccupied with an explicit return to theatricality as such, "reconstructing the proscenium between the observing audience and the images that unfolded on stage."[6] As Loren Kruger points out, Brecht's turn to theatricality came at the same time that he was working out the theory of the *Verfremdungs-Effekt*, or estrangement technique, which critiques the theatricality of ideological illusions precisely through the means of theater. Central to this refocus on the stage was Brecht's concept of the *Gestus*, which for Brecht is less a gesture than a quotation of a basic social attitude.[7] An epic theater, then, as Brecht refined his practice and theory in the 1930s, was thus primarily a theater of quotation, for example, of the secondhand speech of public discourses in National Socialist Germany, as in *Fear and Misery of the Third Reich* (1938) or his exile poetry.[8] As Fore points out, in theoretical works like the *Messingkauf Dialogues*, Brecht becomes increasingly interested in the use of the theater and the "armory of aesthetics" as a means of countering what Benjamin famously called the fascist "aesthetizing of politics." If German fascism had "outbid the avant-garde's project of aesthetic deautonomization," as Fore puts it, then Brecht increasingly turned to the theater as a form of complex quotation that not only reintroduces "the apparatus of representation" but also aspires to providing a space for distanced and critical reflection on representation and spectacle itself.[9] The citational aspect of Brecht's practice from the mid-1930s onward marks an epic reworking of bourgeois forms of the theater. His becomes apparent in the work that *Mother Courage* performs on the genre of the tragedy, removing the tragic from the level of the individual and resituating it at the level of what Brecht referred to as the "dividual," in other words, "a social being whose existence is defined through the public life of the collective."[10]

Framing the Thirty Years War as an inaugural crisis of the modern at the moment of the midcentury crisis of classical modernity provides the framework for a Brechtian *Grundgestus* of the *deutsche Misère*, which, as Fore writes of this Brechtian technique, "inhabits a deep, collective temporality that defies the time-scales in which the individual experiences and wills."[11] *Mother Courage* reflects on what Kalle, the worker, describes in Brecht's contemporaneous text *Flüchtlingsgespräche* as the "unhappy history" of the German people.[12] The failures of the Peasant Wars, the revolutions of 1848, and the revolutionary insurrections of the years following World War I result for Brecht in a structure of feeling based on obedience and violence. "The German obeys," Kalle comments, "even when someone wants to turn him into the master race."[13] Brecht's depictions of fascism often turn on the quotidian aspects of obedience, submission, betrayals, and advantages won within the network of fascist power. Fredric Jameson argues that the *deutsche Misère* for Brecht is not so much a culturalist notion of a German *Sonderweg* as it is a framing of the particular national character of a subaltern structure of feeling.[14] Brecht situates this structure of feeling in the plebeian milieu of the religious wars of early modernity. In a similar vein, the Thirty Years War becomes a parable of the impasses of survival in an antagonistic social system that seems to foreclose any possibility for collectivity and change. Thus Brecht wrote in his journals, "why is courage a realistic work? It adopts the realist point of view on behalf of the people vis-à-vis all ideologies: to the people war is neither an uprising or a business operation, merely a disaster."[15]

Of all of Brecht's dramas in the exile period, *Mother Courage and Her Children* is perhaps the most pointed illustration of the contours of what the poetry of this period describes repeatedly as dark times. If, to recall, Alain Badiou describes 1937 as the metonymic turning point of the century, the fall of 1939 was certainly in many ways its low point, when, to paraphrase W. H. Auden, antifascists could observe the expiration of "the clever hopes . . . of a low dishonest decade."[16] Brecht, as we know from his conversations with Walter Benjamin in the summer of 1938, was well aware of what was transpiring in the Soviet Union in those years, as important collaborators like Sergei Tretyakov, Carola Neher, and Ernst Ottwalt among others were arrested and executed. Indeed, the transcripts from Bukharin's trial figured heavily in the composition of the first version of *The Life of Galileo*, written in Denmark in 1939.[17] At the same time, Brecht became increasingly alarmed at the cultural politics promulgated in the pages of Moscow-based journals like *Internationale Literatur* and *Das Wort*, of which he was nominally a coeditor along with Bredel and Feuchtwanger.

Speaking of Moscow and what he called the Moscow camarilla of critics like Lukács, Erpenbeck, and Kurella, Brecht remarked, "actually I have no friends there at all. And the Muscovites themselves don't have any either—like the dead."[18] By the late 1930s, Brecht saw the Soviet Union as a specific moment of noncontemporaneity, as a "workers' monarchy," a historical and political corollary of what Benjamin describes as "the grotesque freaks of nature which, in the shape of horned fish or other monsters, are brought to light from out of the deep sea."[19] Indeed, the dark times of the late 1930s were shaped by the either-or logic of the seemingly inevitable triumphs of fascism on the one hand and the need to publicly support the Soviet Union on the other. As Brecht commented to Benjamin in regard to the USSR, "we've paid for our positions; we're covered with scars." Brecht was certainly not the only antifascist intellectual for whom the German-Soviet Non-Aggression Pact was a reopening of these none-too-old wounds. Days after the outbreak of war Brecht wrote in his journal, "I don't think more can be said than that the union saved its skin at the cost of leaving the proletariat of the world without solutions, hopes or help."[20]

This world without solutions, hopes, or help is captured in the shattered Central European landscapes of war and plunder through which Mother Courage and her children and hangers-on wander in circles to increasingly diminished returns in Brecht's drama of dark times. Brecht's earlier experiments with the *Lehrstück* and the "Great Pedagogy" were intended to produce *Einverständnis* within the context of a theatrical-didactic practice directed to the production of "collective agreement about the social possibilities of humanity."[21] As Astrid Oesmann puts it:

> Brechtian *Einverständnis* (consent; agreement) has less to do with consensus than with perception and negotiated understandings of reality in the moment of its occurrence. *Einverständnis* in that moment is *verstehen* (to understand), the comprehension of reality and the commitment to change it by acting as part of this reality.[22]

In the dark times of exile, this moment of consent is stripped of its material existence, that very collective in which the recognition of the exigencies of a historical moment could be agreed upon and acted upon. *Mother Courage and Her Children*, then, can be thought of as a sort of tactical retreat, precisely in the Leninist sense that so fascinated Brecht,[23] one that works precisely through demonstrating the consequences of the absence of a collective production of historical insight.

THE GREAT CAPITULATION

Brecht famously described two modes of portraying Anna Fierling in his comments to the 1949 Berliner Ensemble production of *Mother Courage and Her Children*. The first of these was Mother Courage as Niobe, a heroic mother who is nonetheless unable "to protect her children from the fatal destiny of war." This take on Courage, Brecht tells us, allows the spectator "the enjoyment of a singular pleasure: that of triumph in view of the indestructibility of a person full of vitality who is afflicted with the rigors of war."[24] Brecht's discomfort with this way of performing and receiving Mother Courage has to do, of course, with his standing polemic against *Einfühlung*, which is to say empathy or identification. Yet here, in this text from 1952, the emphasis of Brecht's critique of *Einfühlung* is no longer, as it had been in the 1930s, on the role played by affect in the capitalist cultural apparatus but now has a decidedly more local and historical bent. Now the concern is precisely with the capacity of postwar German audiences to learn from the play, and Brecht is careful to spell out what the lesson should be: "that in wars the great business deals are not done by the little people. That war, which is a continuation of business by other means, makes human virtues fatal, for those that possess them as well. That for the suppression of war no sacrifice is too great."[25] If this lesson is to be made intelligible, Mother Courage must be played in a specific way, not as "the representative of the 'little people' . . . who 'were caught up in the war,' since 'there was nothing they could do about it. . . . They were helplessly at the mercy of the events of the war, etc."[26] Courage must be played in such a way as to not only highlight her complicity in the war but also estrange the very notion of survival itself, of persisting in the small trades and business of war: "Trade was a self-evident source of income, but a contaminated one, from which Courage drank death. The trader-mother became a great living contradiction, and it was this that disfigured and deformed beyond recognition." In this sense, it is not with Mother Courage's vitality and her canny skills of survival and perseverance that we should identify, but rather the tragedy of the play should emerge precisely through the fact that Courage is destroyed as a human being upon this contradiction, the solution to which lies outside the realm of her agency:

> The tragedy of Courage and her life, deeply tangible for the audience, lies in the fact that there is an appalling contradiction that ruins a human being, a contradiction that can be resolved, but only by society itself and in long terrible struggles. The moral superiority of this method of representation lies in the fact that the person is shown as destroyable, even the most vital![27]

In this statement, Brecht is countering a logic of identification and empathy with one of demonstration and sympathy. This is a key move in Brechtian aesthetics, as Darko Suvin points out, and what is at stake here is the relationship between cognitive distance and learning.[28] The problem with empathy in the context of Mother Courage is less that the spectator should be drawn into the illusion of the play. In fact, Brecht was aware that the reception of *Courage* was in some sense too topical, or too actual. The issue is rather that empathizing with her character confirms the spectator in an essentially passive relationship to his or her own recent experience.

Brecht notes several ways that Helene Weigel managed to estrange the character of Courage in the Berliner Ensemble performances, but in a sense the observations in the *Modellbuch* only beg the question of the intelligibility of the play's lesson. This ambiguity, Brecht acknowledges, derives from the very contradiction that would in theory provide the play's pedagogical illumination, the trader-mother. "A deeply rooted habit," Brecht notes, "allows the spectator in the theater only to pick out the more emotional statements and overlook the rest." This habit effectively neutralizes the contradiction that Brecht is attempting to portray between motherhood and commerce:

> Business deals, like landscape descriptions in a novel, are taken in with boredom. The "atmosphere of business" is simply the air that one breathes and that one does not find worthy of much comment. In the same way, war always came up in discussions as a timeless abstraction, no matter what we did to represent it as a sum of social enterprises.[29]

It becomes impossible to frame a fatal contradiction for the audience, in other words, if one side of the contradiction appears so natural as to be invisible. This in turn renders Mother Courage's own complicity in the war, her illusion that there is something to be had from it, invisible. Therefore, empathy in this case opens onto a historically specific German attitude in the postwar period. Identification in this sense becomes the alibi not only for one's own complicity in the war and the National Socialist regime but also for one's own passivity in the present:

> the spectators of the year 1949 and the following years did not see the Courage's crimes, her complicity, her desire to earn something out of the business of war; they saw only her failures, her suffering. And this is how they viewed Hitler's war: It had been a bad war, and now they were suffering. In short, it was just as the playwright had prophesied. The war would not only bring suffering, but also the inability to learn from it.[30]

This passage resonates with Brecht's comments in his journals shortly after his return to Berlin in 1948 concerning what he called the "new german misery." "Powerful influences are coming from the russians, but the germans are rebelling against the order to rebel against Nazism."[31] The Germans, this is to say, have not understood that Nazism functioned precisely through their own complicity, preferring to think of themselves as patiently suffering little people. What is perhaps more interesting in the passage on *Courage*'s German reception, however, is Brecht's own renegotiating of the stakes of the play. As opposed to the lessons of *Courage* mentioned earlier, the lesson of the play is now no longer directly about the popular experience of war but rather an explicit critique of the notion of learning from experience.

This is a question that Brecht takes up directly in his *Messingkauf Dialogues*, begun shortly after the composition of *Mother Courage* in the late 1930s. Here the figure of the Dramaturge challenges the Philosopher, who is theorizing a refunctioning of theater into a "thäetre" of social demonstration, asking, "what about learning from experience? You don't merely see things in the theatre; you share an experience. Is there any better way of learning?" To this, the Philosopher replies that experience without commentary may indeed have its lessons, but things are more complicated, since "the kind of experience the theater communicates isn't doing things yourself." He goes on to explain,

> Your audience is experiencing extremely rich, complex, many-sided incidents, comparable with those of Pavlov's dogs: food plus bell ringing. It might be that the desired reactions occurred in real life situations which only shared certain features of those they have experienced with you, secondary features perhaps. In that case, you'd be making them ill, just like Pavlov and the dogs. But of course this also happens in real life. People can experience real incidents and still go astray in this way; they have learned the wrong lessons.[32]

This passage turns on the meaning of saliva. On the one hand, this can mean simply the conditioned response of the audience to strong emotional portrayals and identification with the characters of the drama, but here, in the bad learning process that Brecht is outlining, the danger lies in the immediate identification of viewers with their own life experience through the confirming intermediary of the portrayal. The danger of *Mother Courage*, one might say, is that it tends to encourage audience members to learn from their own experiences, experiences that are in some way false or inadequate to grasping the social complexities in which they are inscribed.

To turn now to the play itself, it is apparent that Brecht is thematizing this problem of experience and knowledge largely through the discourse of virtues at the center of *Mother Courage and Her Children*. In his *Modellbuch*, Brecht introduces the children less as representatives of virtues in their own right than as demonstration objects of a sort, through which Mother Courage articulates her own understanding of how virtue functions in the dispensation of danger and opportunity that is for her the war. "Regarding the children," Brecht writes, "with the first son, she fears his daring, counts on his cunning. With the second son, she fears his stupidity and counts on his honesty. With the daughter, she fears her compassion and counts on her muteness. Only her fears will prove themselves valid."[33] The oft-noted key move of *Mother Courage* lies precisely in this plebeian inversion of values. Virtue, like the saliva of Pavlov's dogs, is a response that, for Brecht, has itself become increasingly disconnected from the situations in which it might prove useful or advantageous to survival.

The name "Mother Courage" is itself based on this inversion, as Anna Fierling famously explains to the sergeant and the recruiting officer in the play's first scene: "Courage is the name they gave me because I was scared of going broke, sergeant, so I drove me cart right through the bombardment of Riga with fifty loaves of bread aboard. They were going moldy, it was high time, hadn't any choice really?"[34] Rather than from her dogged maternity, Mother Courage's name derives from her investment in the sustaining fantasy of the war as a network of opportunity, her commitment to "sustaining her children in the war and through the war."[35] As a field of heightened opportunity and danger, or risk, to put it in the language of the commercial, the war not only is a catastrophe but also appears at first as an inversion of social norms that provides a frame for the critique of morals and virtues. It is here that Mother Courage positions herself ideologically, as the tribune of the little people, critiquing the tacit moral assumptions that lie at the base of the historical record of the rulers and great figures of history. As Franz Norbert Mennemeier points out, "the great history, which calculates its purposes above and beyond the minor history of everyday people, becomes a perverted history in the play's representation."[36] This critical inversion of the public discourses of honor, valor, and virtue that sustain the war is the key to what Hans Mayer refers to as the "plebeian tradition" in Brecht's work, which inverts the discourses of the ruling classes by articulating "a mixture of the real plebeian interests with the tinsel and trappings of the official heroic ideology."[37]

This is the sense of Mother Courage's speech on the virtues of the poor in the play's second scene, where Mother Courage comments on the Swedish commander's praise of her son Eilif's valor in plundering the local peasantry. Noting that any commander who needs brave soldiers must not be much of a leader, Courage goes on to declare that "whenever there's a load of special virtues around it means something stinks." Continuing this critique from below of the great virtues, Courage explains,

> Look, s'pose some general or king is bone stupid and leads his men up shit creek, then those men've got to be fearless, there's another virtue for you. S'pose he's stingy and hires too few soldiers, then they got to be a crowd of Herculeses. And s'pose he's slapdash and doesn't give a bugger, then they've got to be clever as monkeys else their number's up. Same way they got to show exceptional loyalty each time he gives them impossible jobs. Nowt but virtues no proper country and no decent king or general would ever need. In decent countries folk don't have to ave virtues, the whole lot can be perfectly ordinary, average intelligence, and, for all I know cowards. (MC 15)

In this passage, Mother Courage is expressing a kind of plebeian, or peasant, wisdom, one that lends itself well to the picaresque as a genre not only of spatial but also of social and, indeed, moral mobility. Here it is not the great men of the world who require virtue—in fact, as the "Song of Solomon" memorably puts it, "how fortunate the man with none" (70). The poor, on the other hand, need virtues to survive the powerful, as Mother Courage explains elsewhere:

> Poor folk got to have courage. Why, they're lost. Simply getting up in the morning takes some doing in their situation. Or ploughing a field, and in a war at that. Mere fact they bring kids into the world shows they got courage, 'cause there's no hope for them. They have to hang one another and slaughter one another, so just looking each other in the face must call for courage. Being able to put up with emperor and pope shows supernatural courage, 'cause those two cost 'em their lives. (51)

This passage outlines the dialectic of courage and cynicism shapes the gestic language of the play, conveying "the basic attitude adopted towards other men" and the social element that constitutes this attitude.[38] As Astrid Oesmann points out, attitude, or *Haltung*, is itself a form of social mimesis in Brecht's work; it is an adaptation at the level of bodily stance and behavior to a particular historical constellation.[39]

Indeed, Mother Courage's stance partakes of a particular mode of resignation, or fundamental agreement with the war, a stance that expresses "the perception of reality and the commitment to act as part of this reality without attempting to change it."[40] This fundamental agreement with a mode of everyday life structured by the exigencies of war and commerce could be said to be the fundamental gestural stance of the play, what Brecht refers to as its *Grundgestus*. In her article "Women, Space, and Ideology in *Mother Courage and Her Children*," Sarah Bryant-Bertail describes Mother Courage's relationship to the war through the same lens of strategy and tactics that Seghers puts so much narrative pressure upon in *The Seventh Cross*. However, whereas Seghers's novel attempts to bring the emancipatory aspect of popular everyday life under duress into the field of representation, to show the moments where tactics of survival might open onto alternate strategies of social organization, Brecht's play seems to be more concerned with demonstrating the boundaries and constraints of Mother Courage's experience. As Bryant-Bertail points out, tactics, "the province of those who lack political and economic power," are delimited by the immediacy of experience as *Erlebnis*, "as opposed to the distance and reflexivity of *Erfahrung*."[41] Tactics thus at once enable a certain mode of survival and mobility, but at the same time, these very tactics serve to suture those who lack power into the strategies of the powerful:

> In the case of Mother Courage, the war can be seen as a strategy directed by those with economic and political power. . . . The characters we actually see do not dictate the strategies of the war, but are engaged in tactics through which they hope to survive it. Ironically, many tactics only perpetuate the war. Sometimes characters learn a tactic that helps them survive one strategy but that proves fatal when they are confronted with another.[42]

The sense in which Bryant-Bertail discusses tactics maps onto Mother Courage's own discourse on virtues in the play, allowing us to see virtues as the stances that express any number of tactical positions and the learning processes that underlie them while at the same time demonstrating virtue itself as a historically and socially circumscribed stance.

The critical turn in *Mother Courage* lies in the way in which Brecht not only provides a series of social tableaux, as Benjamin describes Brecht's technique,[43] upon which the utility of various tactics can be measured but also constructs an implicit relationship between the immediacy of tactics on the one hand and the critique of identification on the other. Mennemeier draws attention to the empathy for the great men of history that lies below Mother Courage's critique of virtues.[44] Thus Mother Courage's eulogy for the Imperial Commander Tilly in scene six:

> Can't help feeling sorry for those generals and emperors, there they are thinking they're doing something extra special what folk'll talk about in years to come. . . . I mean he plagues himself to death, then it all breaks down on account of ordinary folk what just wants their beer and a bit of chat, nowt higher. Finest plans get bolloxed up by the pettiness of them as should be carrying them out. (MC 48)

Despite the ironic bemoaning of the smallness of everyday human motives, Mother Courage, like the commanders and emperors she pities, sees the war as a business proposition, and it is on this basis that she identifies with these figures. "A more or less concealed agreement exists between the great and the little people," Mennemeier writes, and that is "business." In this sense, the dynamic of courage and cynicism in the play is anchored in the basic *Mitmachen* of the play's characters, their going along with and complicity in the war.[45] Mother Courage is indeed, as the Chaplain reproaches her, a "hyena of the battlefield," but this cannot be seen as a moral judgment; rather the tactics of the battlefield impose upon Mother Courage the horizon of her experience. Indeed, Brecht draws attention to the ceaseless labor of Courage, itself a virtue no doubt, which must be weighed alongside her plebeian cynicism. The "unflagging willingness to work" displayed by Courage, "who is almost never seen without being at work," is what renders her "lack of success shattering."[46]

The famous "Song of the Great Capitulation" and Brecht's comments on the play's fourth scene demonstrate the extent to which, when all is said and done, Mother Courage's critique of virtues is less of a critique of the war itself than it is a measuring of virtues and tactics based on their utility from the point of view of business. The song is meant as an illustration of the futility of seeking after justice in the face of the powerful. Mother Courage and a young soldier are both waiting to lodge complaints with an officer, Mother Courage on account of the ransacking of her wagon, the young solder because he has received no reward for saving a colonel's horse. Replying to the young soldier's declaration that he will not stand for injustice, Mother Courage asks, "How long you not standing for unfairness?" This question is a warning to the young man. His rage "was a short one," and he'd need "a long one" (MC 40–41). Indeed, when the clerk tells the young soldier to be seated, he dutifully sits down, occasioning Mother Courage to comment, "You're sitting now. Ah, how well they know us, no one need tell 'em how to go about it. Sit down! And sitting and sedition don't mix" (MC 41). Here we have one of the most explicit, and self-reflexive, moments of *Gestus* in Brecht's theater, since her acute observations on the young man sitting down become her own justification for abandoning her own complaint. The discourse of virtues is shown to be a subjective deception in the face of a bodily relationship to authority. In his notes to this scene in the *Modellbuch*, Brecht describes this scene in terms of a learning process in which experience is revealed as the teacher of bad lessons:

> In no scene is the wickedness of Courage greater as it is in this one, where she instructs the young man in capitulating to the Colonel, in order to be able to carry out the same. And nevertheless the face of Weigel showed an appearance of wisdom and even nobility at this moment, and that is good. It is namely not the wickedness of her person so much as that of her class, and she at least lifts herself above this a bit, insofar as she shows insight, indeed rage, about these weaknesses.[47]

If we follow Brecht's interpretation of this scene, we have not only a complication of the notion of the *Gestus*, which now demonstrates both a concrete social attitude at the same time that it critiques precisely the failure of critique on the part of the bearer of this attitude, but also a commentary on the politics of *Einfühlung*, which leads us back to the problem of *Mother Courage*'s reception in postwar Germany. Like the German spectators who identified with her as the personification of the little people who get through the war any way they can, like survivors of a natural disaster, Mother Courage is identifying with herself in this scene but precisely insofar as she embodies a particular social network of constraints that she misrecognizes as a kind of universal destiny. This is to say that Mother Courage becomes a didactic object in her own right, as the bearer of *Einfühlung*, an identification that is bounded by her social circumstances and constrained by her own complicity in the field of force of the war itself. Her anger is also too short.

In his reading of this scene, Hans Mayer points out that much of Brecht's exile work is dominated by the theme of capitulation but that this theme is itself internally differentiated in Brecht's presentation. The first is captured by the "Song of the Great Capitulation," the cynical self-justification "of those who would so like to protest, but then quickly fall in with the choir with its 'little tone'—and sing along."

This is the capitulation from "'inner' rebellion that is not steered by real opposition and social clarity."[48] This mode of capitulation is the *Grundgestus*, the cleverness and realism, of a society that "does not allow the good person to be good without starving to death."[49] Yet for Mayer, this mode of realism is based on misrecognition, that is to say, on a static conception of society and virtue, since the question is not one of virtue at all but of a society where virtue can only appear as bad tactics, as Mayer writes of the similarly pitched "Song of Solomon": "it is thus not the fault of virtues if people can draw no use from them. Thus it must be particular social relations that bring forth calamity for the great, and very particularly the little, people. There are no '*an sich*' harmful virtues."[50] This is to say that the plebeian wisdom of Mother Courage precisely forecloses the second modality of capitulation, exemplified for Mayer by Brecht's Galileo, which is based on a kind of strategic withdrawal in the face of superior force, a "material and intellectual resistance, which falls silent in order to continue its work."[51] *Einverständnis* would thus constellate to Mayer's notion of productive capitulation. Rather than the young soldier's "sheer emotional resistance that gives in dispiritedly," this productive capitulation, rather like Brecht's own retreat into theatrical technique, consists of a strategic retreat that allows for later advance.[52] *Mother Courage*, then, could be read as a demonstration of historical conditions that do not allow for this kind of productive capitulation. The play thus becomes a historical allegory, or demonstration, of an impasse in which the resources that would allow for the processing of immediate experience into social knowledge, where in the face of a lack of a collective voice, *Einverständnis* is foreclosed. If virtue without a social basis is stupidity, there is nevertheless in many of Brecht's works a zone of engagement or intervention, what might be thought of as a strategy, which seems to be amputated from *Mother Courage*.

In *Me-ti/Buch der Wendungen* [The Book of Changes], Brecht addresses the problem of a Marxist ethics, noting that the Marxist classics did not "advance any moral teachings."[53] The Philosopher in the *Messingkauf Dialogues* connects Brecht's insight into this apparent lacuna in Marxism to the problem of theatrical representation, salvaging a decisive advantage from a seeming failure. "That doctrine," the Philosopher notes, "deals above all with the behavior of great masses of people." The problem with judging individual actions and attitudes by the criteria of Marxist theory, then, is that whereas Marxism relates these to class position and historical conjuncture, the demonstrations of the stage must in some sense call forth these larger macrostructures through the depiction of "the behavior of individuals toward one another."[54] At the same time, this apparent lacuna is at the same time an opening:

> However, the main principles of the doctrine are also a great help in judging the individual: for instance the principle that people's consciousness depends on their social existence, taking it for granted at the same time that this social existence is continually developing and that this consciousness is accordingly changing all the time.[55]

The point of the theatrical demonstration, then, if we are to remain at the level of the behavior of individuals toward one another, is less to cast these individuals as the embodiments of particular class positions than it is to demonstrate the moments and places where the subjectivity of the individual encounters the objective constraints of their social existence. In this sense, the drama is not a demonstration of Marxist categories or principles. Rather, these principles become tools, the usefulness of which is tested by their adequacy to the incidents demonstrated. This in turn implies that the incidents portrayed on stage must be adequate to social existence. "You must examine it all and prove it all," the Philosopher explains. "The only way to clarify your incidents is by other incidents."[56] In this sense, the question of ethics or morality becomes a historical question of the modes of behavior that are possible or sensible in terms "of how a particular moral system worked and what function it served in a particular social order."[57] This is the experimental aspect of Brecht's practice, which has nothing to do with the aleatory but rather with what Brecht famously characterized as the "not, but," or *nicht, sondern*, in which all that does not or could not happen is "contained and preserved" in what does occur on stage.[58]

If the criteria of the effectiveness of a demonstration involves the work necessary to "fix the sequence of incidents so as to clarify" this question of the borders of individual agency in a given social-historical and class constellation, this insight leads us back to the problem of why Mother Courage herself cannot be the subject, but must remain the object, of the play's demonstration.[59] This was the central question of the play's reception in the East German public sphere, and it was one that allowed the distinction between a socialist realist aesthetics of the example, based on *Einfühlung*, and a Brechtian method based in a stance of *Mitgefühl*, or sympathy, which itself presupposes a stance of distanced understanding and judgment rather than imitation, to come to light.[60] The well-known 1949 conversation between Brecht and the Communist playwright Friedrich Wolf illustrates this distinction well.[61] Arguing that both he and Brecht "are trying to use the medium of the stage to advance and transform humanity," Wolf poses the question thusly:

> How can our German theatres show our people what is most urgent? Specifically: How can we shake them out of their fatalistic attitude and rouse them against a new war? And in this sense I think *Courage* would have been even *more* effective if at the end the mother had given her curse on the war some visible expression in the action (as Kattrin did) and drawn the logical conclusions from her change of mind.[62]

Wolf's contention that the play lacked a positive hero and an optimistic outcome echoed a certain discomfort with Brecht's theater in the early GDR. Although *Mother Courage and Her Children* was highly successful with both audiences and critics, for some East German critics the play also provided an excuse to elaborate the principles of a Zhadonovite socialist realism through the condemnation of what were seen as formalist aspects of Brecht's method. Thus a review of the play by Brecht's old antagonist from the exile years, Fritz Erpenbeck, while praising the dramatic achievement of the play and declaring Brecht to be one of Germany's great poets, took issue with Brecht's technique of composition for a tendency toward "decadence foreign to the people," or *volksfremde Dekadenz*, a highly loaded term in socialist realist discourse with obvious fascist undertones. The implication of decadence arises through the play's structure, in which Erpenbeck sees a dangerous softening of dramatic form.[63] Erpenbeck objects that the consequence of the epic technique, with its episodic structure, prevents the formation of a properly dramatic plot, which would turn on a "dual situation" between actor and counteractor. In other words, the problem with Brecht's play is that on a formal level, it forecloses agency.

This point was made explicit in a review of *Mother Courage* by Susanne Alterman, who criticized the play's lack of a clear dramatic conflict that would "make visible the spontaneous outrage of the masses" in the face of war. She continues, "the play is lacking the idea of a revolutionary critical reshaping of the world," before going on to assert that no one is asking for a tendency drama, an obligatory gesture in 1950s East Germany if one were to demand a tendency drama.[64] "Decadence begins," Alterman writes, "where outraged human reason falls silent in the work of an artist and the impotence of humanity in the face of historical fate is confirmed."[65] As Brecht points out, the problem with Wolf's suggestion as much as Alterman's objection is that to portray Mother Courage as the exemplar of the kind of learning process that Wolf is proposing would be to remain precisely within the circumscribed radius of Mother Courage's immediate impressions of the war but could not suffice to point to some other *Haltung* or social attitude that would offer a point of purchase outside of the war or a perspective that reached beyond it. This is not a matter of capitulation before historical fate but a demonstration that from the perspective of the isolated individual, as I will argue shortly, fate can only be met through capitulation or martyrdom and that precisely the historical ground for a properly tragic dramatic collision was lacking. "The play was written in 1938," Brecht replies, "when the writer foresaw a great war; he was not convinced that humanity would necessarily learn anything from the tragedy which he expected to strike it."[66]

"WAR FEEDS ITS CHILDREN BETTER"

As Italo Michele Battafarano has pointed out, Brecht did not take much, if any, of the plot of Grimmelshausen's *Courasche* into his play, but it would be mistaken to think that Brecht owes nothing to Grimmelshausen. In his "Notes on the Realist Mode of Writing" from 1940, Brecht explicitly contrasts fascist war writing, in which "war is represented as an entirely mechanical, material battle" with "absolutely no social content," to Grimmelshausen's *Simplizius Simplicissimus*, "where war is shown to be a social phenomenon, to be civil war."[67] Battafarano argues that Brecht takes three important cues from Grimmelshausen, cues that have more to do with what might be thought of as the play's structure of feeling than with its plot, or rather with the key insights upon which Brecht builds the play's fundamental tonality, or *Grundgestus*. First, as we know, for Grimmelshausen as well as Brecht, the war is a continuation of business by other means but one in which only the rulers profit. Second, the religious claims of the Thirty Years War are shown to be ideological, and this opens up a critique of ideology as such in both Brecht and Grimmelshausen. Third, rather than a state of exception, the war is shown to be an accentuation of the normal struggle for survival that shaped the lives of the great majority of people no less in the 1930s than it did in the 1630s.[68] This last point, which casts a light on the travails of the normal, allows Brecht to relativize notions both of virtue and of burden and suffering.

The mobility of virtue in *Mother Courage*, no less than the movement of the play across central Europe in the baggage train of the Imperial and Protestant armies, marks the play as a picaresque.[69] Thinking about *Mother Courage* as a picaresque, however, raises a number of interesting questions. Ernest Schonfield has demonstrated the many affinities of Brecht's theater, and *Mother Courage* in particular, with the picaresque tradition. In particular, the picaresque is marked by a particular mode of narrative focalization, which is the partial or reduced position of the picaro herself, often a socially excluded and victimized figure. This, often first-person, point of view, precisely because of her marginalization, tends to encompass or give rise to moral and philosophical reflections on the nature of human community, which themselves are rooted in a meditation on the baser aspects of material existence and everyday life. In regard to this aspect, Mother Courage seems to fit well within this tradition. At the same time, however, there are two aspects of the picaresque that correspond less cleanly to Brecht's character and his play. The first is the question of Mother Courage's own status as the subject of a learning process. This is a point to which Claudio Guillén draws attention in his work on the picaresque. Against what he calls the "scholarly delusion" of the inherently static quality of picaro, Guillén asserts, "the hero of the mainstream picaresque novel does grow, learn, and change."[70] The second point that both Schonfield and Guillén stress is the social mobility of the picaro. The picaro's path leads her through encounters with people from diverse social groups; she moves "horizontally through space and vertically through society."[71] It is precisely this movement that allows for a wider social framing of an event than is explicitly available through the limited narrative perspective of the picaro herself. "The picaro," Guillén writes,

> is not an independent hero who may be studied *in vacuo*. . . . The picaresque is based on a situation, or rather a chain of situations. Its hero is involved from the start in . . . a "tangle." This tangle is an economic and social predicament of the most immediate and pressing nature (not a confrontation with absolute forces), an entanglement with the relative

> and contemporaneous; and it leads to further situations or "adventures."[72]

The tangle to which Guillén refers is the pressure exerted by the social on the horizon of the picaresque hero, but it is also the knotting of the vertical movements through society through which the picaro "observes a number of collective conditions: social classes, professions, *caractères*, cities, and nations."[73] Mother Courage obviously partakes of a socially horizontal and geographical mobility, as the scene titles have her moving across central Europe in the train of the armies, moving episodically from situation to situation. At the same time, the "tangle" of Brecht's play largely lacks the vertical mobility that Guillén's essay specifies as characteristic of the genre. Brecht's play departs from the traditional, or as Guillén would put it, mainstream, picaresque insofar as the social horizon of the play remains more or less circumscribed within the plebeian experience of the war; soldiers, petty officials, traders, and peasants constitute, with few exceptions, the constellation of figures within the play.

As many critics have pointed out, the Thirty Years War in Brecht's play is not a local or exceptional event. It forms rather the total system and realm of possibilities for the play's characters. It is itself the constellation of situations, or the "tangle," as it were. Rather than an aberration or state of exception, the war is itself a social form. This is already indicated in the opening dialogue of the play between the Sergeant and the Recruiter. From the Sergeant's point of view, which is that of the naturalistic battle of materials to which Brecht objects in fascist war literature, war is famously a strategy of social coordination and allocation of resources and material, both human and otherwise:

> It's been too long since they had a war here; stands to reason. . . . Peace is just a mess; takes a war to make order. Peacetime, the human race runs wild. People and cattle get buggered about, who cares? . . . I been to places ain't seen a war for nigh seventy years: folks hadn't got names to them, couldn't tell one another apart. Takes a war to get proper nominal roles and inventories . . . no order, no war! (MC 1–2)

If the Sergeant gives us the perspective of the powerful, as it were, that of rule and command, it is nevertheless notable that he, like Mother Courage herself, articulates this strategic position from below, as an enlisted man who is no more able to influence the course of events than is Mother Courage. In other words, here again we have the logic of identification and of clever adaptation to a process in which one is in some sense always already entangled. This strategic view from above is inverted by the speech delivered by the Chaplain at the moment when it seems that the war might be coming to an end:

> I'd say there's peace in war too, it has its peaceful moments. Because war satisfies all requirements, peaceable ones included, they're catered for, and it would simply fizzle out if they weren't. In war you can do a crap like in the depths of peacetime, then between one battle and the next you can have a beer, then even when you're moving up you can lay your head on your arms and have a bit of shuteye in the ditch, it's entirely possible. During a charge you can't play cards but nor can you in the depths of peacetime when you're ploughing. . . . And what's to stop you being fruitful and multiplying in the middle of all the butchery, behind a barn or something. . . . No, the war will always find an outlet, mark my words. Why should it ever stop? (MC 50)

This is a description of the war as a total system from below, from the plebeian stance in which the play seems so firmly rooted. Not only does the war supply all of the needs of peace in this account, but in fact war and peace are relativized as social states. This is a point to which Brecht returns frequently in his thinking during the exile period. Indeed, in his work journals, Brecht mentions his own satisfaction rereading *Mother Courage* on precisely this point, noting that the play allows the war to emerge "as a vast field akin to the fields of modern physics, in which bodies experience particular deviations from their courses." Rather than determining individual acts and events in a positive way, the war is a structured field of constraint:

> any calculation about the individual based on peacetime experience proves to be unreliable, bravery is of no help, nor is caution, nor honesty, nor crookedness, nor brutality nor pity: all are equally fatal. we are left with those same forces that turn peace into war, the ones that can't be named.[74]

Business as usual; like capitalism itself, war is a regime of generalized exploitation that nonetheless leaves open spaces for tactical survival and opportunities for small and uncertain profit while at the same time destabilizing the codes of conduct that at least maintain minimum purchase on peacetime experience.

The point here is not that war and peace are in some sense equivalent but that war and violence are in a sense immanent to the state of peace that capitalism would posit as the norm. Fredric Jameson's insights about Grimmelshausen's book are no less apt for *Mother Courage* when he writes, "the great and bloody rhizome of the war then becomes a representation of money, riches, wealth, taxes levied, the very sustenance of potatoes impounded from villages in flames and peasants dead or in flight."[75] This insight connects Brecht's critique of capitalism, and implicitly war, to his critique of fascism as a "battle of materials," which he lays out most clearly in his speech at the First International Writers' Congress for the Defense of Culture in 1935:

> Many of us writers who have experienced the atrocities of fascism and are horrified by them have not yet understood this doctrine, have not yet discovered the roots of the brutality which so horrifies them. For them the danger persists that they will regard the cruelties of fascism as unnecessary cruelties. They cling to the conditions of property ownership because they believe that the cruelties of fascism are not necessary for their defense. But if prevailing conditions of ownership are to be upheld, then these cruelties are indeed necessary. In this particular the fascists are not lying, they are telling the truth.[76]

The point that connects this reflection on the relationship of fascism to capitalism with *Mother Courage* seems to lie less in some sort of allegorical connection between World War II and the Thirty Years War than it does in a genealogical relationship that Brecht is attempting to posit between the origins of modernity and capitalism and the later violence of the fascist dispensation that seeks to maintain private property relations through mysticism and terror. In the note to the play, "Mother Courage Learns Nothing," Brecht gives a sketch of this genealogy. "Of the Peasant's War, which was the greatest misfortune of German history," Brecht writes, "one may say that, socially considered, it pulled the teeth of the Reformation. Its legacy was cynicism and business as usual."[77] If the religious ideologies of "the restoration of early Christian equality among members of the community" was still a revolutionary goal that sprang from the social pressures exerted on the peasantry, as articulated by Thomas Münzer, the breaking of this plebeian peasant movement shifted the ground of religious discourse into an ideological cover for the princes of Germany no less than the rising bourgeoisie. Thus the role of religion in *Mother Courage* has become one purely of cynicism, of adaptation to prevailing sovereignties and of tactical survival.[78] The status of religion in the play is less significant than the foreclosure of political horizons that derives from the defeat of the peasant uprisings, and in this sense there is a weak allegorical valence to the play indeed, linking it with prevailing analyses within the Communist discourse of the Popular Front period, which locate in the foreclosure of the post–World War I revolutionary wave the conditions of possibility for fascism.

If there is a parable lurking within *Mother Courage and Her Children*, then it can perhaps be read out of an implicit parallel between the Thirty Years War, a war of princes, popes, and emperors, seemingly lacking in any material counterforce to the strategies of power and domination, and the moment of the play's composition in 1939, as the Hitler-Stalin Pact seemed to finally put an end to the political aspirations of the struggling Popular Front and German armies marched into Poland. Indeed, Brecht's criticism of the Non-Aggression Pact was less focused on the ethics of a short-term alliance between the USSR and Germany, since he assumed that the Western allies would at any rate stand aside and allows the USSR to bear the weight of a war with Hitler in the absence of such an agreement. On the other hand, Brecht clearly condemned the manner in which the USSR concluded the pact and conducted itself under it, particularly after the Red Army had itself marched into Poland. Thus Brecht writes in his journal on September 18, 1939:

> but it is still very difficult to get used to the naked reality, which every ideological veil torn to shreds. here we have the fourth partition of poland, the abandonment of the slogan "the USSR needs no foot of foreign soil," the appropriation of the fascist hypocrisies about "blood-brotherhood," the liberation of "brothers" (of slav descent), all the terminology of nationalism.[79]

Brecht seems here to be reproaching the USSR above all with the abandonment of a clear strategic line that would allow for a material resistance to Hitler's war. As Brecht wrote a couple of months later, looking back at the USSR's declared aim in the war on Finland as an act of liberating the Finnish proletariat, one sees in the Communist justifications of the Hitler-Stalin Pact "how far the Russians are from being able to produce dialectical slogans. They have to fall back on primitive dramatizations of the facts."[80] In this context, the war becomes a matter of governments and of increasingly emptied-out ideologies masking cynical national, geopolitical, and economic interests. "It is still not the people, the masses, the proletariat that decides," Brecht writes on September 21, 1939. "Stalin finds it impossible to start a war in a revolutionary manner, as a proletarian action, as a mass war."[81] In the absence of a mass war, linked to the social and national liberation of peoples, *Mother Courage* is, as Brecht points out, a "realistic work" because "it adopts a realistic point of view on behalf of the people vis-à-vis all ideologies: to the people war is neither an uprising nor a business operation, merely a disaster."[82] The relative lack of commentary, the absence of anything like the collective voices of wisdom that we find in the *Lehrstück*, for example, the Control Chorus of *The Measures Taken*, which act to guarantee something like a Brechtian *Einverständnis*, can thus be read in the context of the "dark times" of the late 1930s. As opposed to Brecht's earlier plays, any kind of social or political collective that could take in the play's figures and give their activities a meaning beyond the war is lacking. Instead the figures of the play are largely isolated and at best form into "temporary partnerships of convenience," of which Mother Courage's family is one.[83] In this situation, the picaro, as Schonfield points out with reference to Brecht's favorite figure of the soldier Svejk, is "forced to move in a highly restricted space: threatened on all sides, he is reduced to performing '*krumme Bewegugen*,' often in ever-decreasing circles."[84] In the absence of a collective political horizon, both the 1600s and the late 1930s seem to be moments shaped by a "condition in which each action in service of survival only contributes to the worsening of the world."[85]

The circular movements that shape the dramaturgy of *Mother Courage* can thus be read as a kind of mimetic expression of the war itself as a social system that bars not only political collectives but also production itself. On the one hand, the war appears as a business opportunity, a situation of universal organization, equivalence, and exchange, where, as Marx famously wrote of capitalism itself, all fixed values are reduced to the objectivity of the cash nexus. As Mother Courage defiantly declares to the Chaplain and the Cook, "I won't have you folk spoiling my war for me. I'm told it kills off the weak, but they're a write-off in peacetime too. And war gives its people a better deal" (MC 56). Indeed, as a system that apparently has no outside, no material point of critique, the real threat posed by the war is precisely that it might come to an end, and with that all of the survival tactics that subtend it might themselves become useless. This fear, as much as plebeian irony, seems to be articulated in the speech of the Chaplain when peace does appear to threaten:

> There've always been people going around saying "the war can't go on forever." I tell you there's nothing to stop it going on forever. Of course there can be a bit of breathing space. The war may need to get its second wind, it may even have an accident so to speak. There's no guarantee against that; nothing's perfect on this earth of ours. A perfect war, the sort you might say couldn't be improved upon, that's something we shall probably never see. It can suddenly come to a standstill for some quite unforeseen reason, and you can't allow for everything. A slight case of negligence, and it's bogged down up to the axles. And then it's a matter of hauling the war out of the mud again. But emperor and kings and popes will come to its rescue. So on the whole it has nothing serious to worry about, and will live to a ripe old age. (MC 49)

The apparent space of freedom that the war opens up in Brecht's play is precisely the space of plunder, of a certain kind of accumulation without production. This freedom from the labors of peace, which are no more rewarding than the tactics of war for the "little people," is the essence of Mother Courage's famous introductory song. It is war that creates the many needs that set exchange into motion—the need for boots, the need for meat—and this is in turn what guarantees Mother Courage her minimal independence, of which the wagon is at once the source and the signifier. Thus while critics often read Courage's refusal of the Cook's offer to settle down at the inn he has inherited from his mother in Utrecht as an act of motherly devotion to her daughter, Kattrin, one might also take Courage at her word that the refusal also had to do with the wagon. The inn would seem to represent exactly the mode of domestic boundedness that Mother Courage has managed to escape through the war. One is either part of the network of plunder or the victim of it. Mother Courage's gamble is that she can outwit the warning of the sergeant, "Like the war to nourish you? Have to feed it something too" (10).

And yet, as Thomsen, Müller, and Kindt point out, Mother Courage's commercial activities seem largely irrelevant to the maintenance of the war. She needs this system of plunder, but it does not necessarily need her. The deals she makes are small ones—a belt, a capon, a bottle of liquor—and as the play progresses, even these minor transactions become less important, since "the armies supply themselves overwhelmingly through forced requisitions and pillage."[86] The play's figure for the ground on which the territorial plunder of the war operates is the peasantry. If Mother Courage's wagon does play an important part, it is that it allows her to escape this fate. Thus Eilif makes a name for himself for the Swedish general at Wallhof by tricking the local peasants into revealing the location of twenty oxen and then killing them. Eilif's virtues are cleverness and bravery, and here he has put them both to use, tricking the peasants with the promise of payment and then ambushing them. In the transvaluation of values that occurs with the brief outbreak of peace, Eilif's actions acquire a different valence, now becoming simply rapacious murder and thievery.[87] Beyond the mobility of values, and Eilif's inability to follow this trajectory, the themes of war and territoriality emerge through the figure of the peasantry. Eilif is on both sides of this relationship, himself recruited as a resource of the war. Since it does not produce, the war can persist only by expanding its territory and drawing more and more people into itself. As the Sergeant points out, "But how's anyone to a war without soldiers?" (MC 7). The war converts the peasantry into victims of plunder but also into human material, into soldiers and prostitutes.

Production is of course a central aspect not only of Brecht's aesthetics but of his political commitments. Thus Brecht famously defined socialism itself in his journals not as great order but as "great production," a program for freeing what Brecht calls the productivity of all people from all fetters and implying a notion of production that stretches from the making of material goods to the shaping of interpersonal relationships and social and cultural forms themselves.[88] This notion of productivity, which links the cultural to the economic, labor to art, and material production to social production connects Brecht to the left avant-gardes of Soviet 1920s and was a commitment to which his work maintains fidelity even through his more classical turn in exile.[89] Against this notion of socialism as great production, war is revealed in Mother Courage as "great order," a form of "entirely mechanical, material battle," to cite Brecht's critique of fascist war literature mentioned earlier, which ultimately stifles the productivity of the people through systematic plunder. *Mother Courage* not only points to this strategy of plunder as itself an overdetermined civil war between generals, soldiers, and peasants but also dramatizes the seemingly improvised social practices through which this "great order" forecloses the production of forms of understanding, critique, and collectivity. As David Bathrick points out, for Brecht, productivity must also be understood as a cognitive tool, and in this sense art as much as tools and machines "are employed 'critically' in the appropriation of the natural."[90] Thus, as a social form that precludes the use of productivity, Brecht's Thirty Years War represents a resurgence of natural history in the guise of strategies of power and plunder.

This system of war and plunder without production is the subject of a gradual wearing down as the play goes on, with the Cook declaring ominously, "The world's dying out" (MC 68).[91] Notably, even from the point of view of the strategies of power and wealth, there seems to be no real accumulation in *Mother Courage* but more of a repetitive "skinning of the peasants" and plundering of towns moving toward a gradual exhaustion. The intertitle for scene nine depicts a desolate landscape of plague and starvation, where wolves roam the streets of burned-out towns (67). "Nowt growing no more," Mother Courage laments, "just brambles. In Pomerania villages s'pose to have started in eating the younger kids, and nuns have been caught sticking people up." She and the Cook are reduced to begging as the general system of plunder and commerce breaks down: "I got nowt left to sell and folk got nowt left to buy with," Courage explains (68). As the armies become increasingly frayed, Mother Courage herself seems increasingly evacuated as a character. Her commentaries dry up, and her wit fails her. In the closing scene, Courage comes across as more dazed than determined as she pays the peasants for Kattrin's burial and hurries to catch up with the army and return to business. As Brecht points out in his notes to the play, the mechanical *Gestus* of counting out the coins for the burial is a demonstration that "the trader does not entirely forget accounting in all of her pain, since money is after all so difficult to earn."[92] The close of the play shows a world that, as the Cook puts it, is dying out, a world of plunder and trade without the possibility of production or politics, which increasing expands to engulf any imaginable spatial and social geographies. What is left are survival tactics that have become severed from any vision of an emancipatory practice.

This context of totalized plunder and survival frames the play's final scenes and the famous juxtaposition of Kattrin's heroism and Mother Courage's persistence. In the absence of a real space for intervention, Kattrin's act becomes an ethical one of martyrdom. Although perhaps more noble than Mother Courage's empty carrying on, feeding and being fed by the war, and although she saves a city, Kattrin's heroism does not in any meaningful way affect the course of the war. It is precisely the inability of such an ethical intervention carried out by necessity in isolation that enables Mother Courage to march off with the wagon at the end of the play. Thus, rather than reading these endings in contrast to one another, it seems more apt to view them as in some sense linked, less as a progression than as an unfolding meditation on the sphere of possibilities of war as a social system that persists through both the complicity and the resistance of its protagonists and victims. Here Brecht seems very far from the kind of didactic socialist humanism that colors even his own commentary on the play, since Mother Courage's failure to learn can no longer be read in terms of a politics of consciousness or social agency, or even the lack thereof. By the close of the play, Mother Courage simply has no choice. What Kattrin's final act does perhaps demonstrate, though, and here the figure of motherhood acquires a certain weight, is the one need that war does not provide for: the need for virtuous conduct and for resistance.[93] This is also, under erasure, the moment of production in Brecht's play, as indicated by his notes to this scene, which highlight the labor of drumming.[94]

This productive moment, however, fails to catalyze any larger resistance or to open any new space of practice. This insight is related to a particularity of *Mother Courage* that Wolf is quick to point out, and this is the apparent lack of any explicitly didactic framing to the play. Here we could compare *Mother Courage* to *The Caucasian Chalk Circle* (1949), with its framing scenes, which, within the context of Soviet collectivization of agriculture, themselves attempt to impart an explicit lesson on the virtues of the use and cultivation of resources as opposed to the claims of property. *Mother Courage* is without such an outside perspective; even the songs function as immanent demonstrations of the *Haltung* of the various characters rather than taking on the commentating choral function of the songs in many of Brecht's other pieces. Kattrin's act of valor in warning the city of Halle does not end, or even influence the course of the war, which will find other victims elsewhere to replace those Kattrin has saved and other cities to sack. Indeed, *Mother Courage* seems to leave us with two options, one of martyrdom and self-sacrifice, the other of weary persistence in Mother Courage's final harnessing of herself to her wagon.

To put this another way, we could say that *Mother Courage* demonstrates the amputation foreclosure of partisanship. Written in the latter months of 1938, when Brecht was contemplating the show trials in Moscow and meeting with returning Interbrigadists from the collapsing Spanish Republic, *Mother Courage* can be read as a demonstration of the foreclosure of the dimension of political efficacy with the coming apart of the Popular Front project.

WHAT IS A HISTORIC MOMENT?

Sean Carney argues that the ultimate horizon of the Brechtian *V-Effekt* is the cultivation of historical perception.[95] *Mother Courage* marks a deepening of this sort of pedagogy of historical perception precisely insofar as the play estranges the historical itself. This is most directly shown at the end of scene six, where, during Commander Tilly's funeral, Kattrin returns disfigured from an errand upon which Mother Courage had sent her. "Now they'll be burying the commander in chief," the Chaplain remarks, "this is a historic moment." Mother Courage quickly inverts this notion of the historical: "what I call a historic moment is them bashing my daughter over the eye" (MC 54–55). This recasting of the historical is of a piece with Brecht's understanding of the plebeian tradition, as Mayer refers to the inversion of official and quotidian discourses. Here the historical is precisely the mode in which the very needs, experiences, desires, and capacities that are occluded in the historical proper appear as legible objects of representation. To return to the discourse of earlier chapters, Brecht is here, as it were, reinscribing *Eigensinn* into the historical record, expanding what we understand as history to include the often opaque dimensions of the everyday precisely in the unplottable, contingent, but nevertheless structured (recall the fields of modern physics invoked earlier). The historical moment can thus be construed as one of the experience of impossibility or constraint, just as Kattrin's wound forecloses for her the possibility of the *gewöhnliches Leben* and of motherhood, placing her finally in Yvette's notorious red boots. As in many of Brecht's plays, it is the peasantry that comes to stand as a figure for this historical play of constraint and blockage. If the war is a vast field of moving bodies, the peasantry is a figure that is identified with the sort of static mobility of these bodies, always in motion but always moving over the same field. This peasant dispensation of constraint structures the play on a number of levels, since it is the peasants who are in many ways the material basis of the war, which operates mainly through its systematized plunder of their bodies and the products of their labor.

This is staged in the scenes involving Eilif's skinning of the peasants, in Yvette's "Fraternization Song," but most urgently in scene eleven as Kattrin warns the city of Halle of the approaching Catholic troops. As the peasant family realizes the city is surrounded and that they indeed will have to guide the Catholic soldiers to the city walls, the only response they are able to muster is the realization that "there's nothing we can do." They can neither refuse, since the troops will slaughter their livestock, nor give a signal, since they would be killed. There is no remedy for injustice but prayer. "Nowt we can do to stop bloodshed," the peasant woman tells Kattrin, "you can't talk, maybe, but at least you can pray! He'll hear you, if no one else can" (MC 77). As Brecht points out in his *Modellbuch*, once the war has become a system, these gestures of submission are themselves ritualized; they become citational. "The war has already lasted a long time," he writes, "the moaning, pleading, and denunciations have congealed into firm forms: this is how you do it when the *Soldateska* show up."[96] This ritualization of fear, pleading, and supplication reveals the deeper dimension of peasant misery, its meaningless and repetitive character. This is what Brecht describes as a "deeper strata of terror . . . where the common, always returning misery of the people has already compelled them to the ceremonialization of defensive gestures—which admittedly can never spare them their real fear."[97] In this scene, tactics are reduced to the helplessness of habit before a mythical power.

Jameson discerns in *Mother Courage* what he describes as the peasant temporality of much of Brecht's work, "a kind of peasant history—that is to say, the paradoxically changeless and immemorial, stagnant history, which is not yet history in our modern sense."[98] While Marchwitza's *Kumiaks* casts this peasant history as a kind of contaminated remainder within the working-class structure of consciousness, a sort of humus of *Eigensinn* beneath the contemporaneity of proletarian class struggle, Claudius's novel aims at a sort of recuperation and redemption of this peasant time precisely through that struggle. In Brecht's play, something slightly different is afoot, since Brecht does not here appeal to that other, modern, actantial, proletarian temporality that animates Marxism. What is at stake here is less the neutralization, redemption, or abjection of peasant time than, as Jameson puts it, a reconceptualization of history itself as an almost mythic continuity of "the time of oppression," what Jameson describes as "the great class struggle of human history as a whole, now defined not by specific modes of production as such but, rather, as the immemorial relationship between exploiters and exploited." Jameson points out that this is not to be construed in terms of the anarchist preoccupation with power and domination but rather in terms of production and "the general economic relationship between those who produce and those who enjoy the products of that production."[99] Indeed, even those plays that stage the struggle of capital against labor tend toward an absorption of the "actantial position of the 'proletariat'" by the "temporality of peasant life," as the working class become "reduced to Dickensian misery, lumpen-status . . . or desperate objects of charity."[100] This creatureliness of the peasantry and cyclical temporality is quintessentially one of impasse. As Marx points out, this peasant dispensation is inherently static and cyclical, giving rise at best to "dynastic" changes that affect only "the people on top, who come and go, are swept away in palace coups or by nomadic incursions, and are simply succeeded by different dynasties with the same dynamics," while popular life continues to persist in its misery.[101]

This is not a temporality that allows for revolution, for qualitative social transformation. Nevertheless, Jameson argues, "one great redemptive moment is held open by the view of History from a peasant perspective. . . . It is a vision of change as a kind of immense window." This is the moment between the collapse of the old order and the restoration of the same, a "revolt" that "is none the less the moment of Hope in the immemoriality of peasant life."[102] In these moments of provisional freedom, peasant temporality joins the logic of the fairy tale in a kind of popular utopianism, which Jameson describes, following Ernst Bloch, in terms of "everything it includes of the fable-like and of collective wish-fulfillment, which does not exclude the baleful, bad luck, oppression and death, but strikes all of this with a magic wand that also includes hope along with them."[103] These moments are preserved in the mode of melancholy legend, as "the utopian regret that tinges the contemplation of a 'golden age' that lasted but a season."[104] This golden age that appears only to vanish is at once the moment of promise in the peasant temporality and a kind of utopian interruption of its cyclical misery. Indeed, one could argue that this notion of temporality is fundamental to the technique of epic theater itself, which, as Benjamin notes, is in an important sense less about revealing the historical than it is an operation for interrupting the historical. Like a *tableaux vivant*, epic theater interrupts the flow of events in order to reveal the astonishing quality of the situations beneath the apparently natural behavior of characters. For Benjamin this technique of interruption is at the center of epic theater as a "quotable form of drama," as a theatrics of quotable gestures.[105]

Brecht's mobilization of a plebeian tradition was of course, as many critics, including Hans Mayer, have pointed out, part of his search for pre- and non-bourgeois techniques for a post-bourgeois theater. Casting Diderot and Brecht as bookends of bourgeois theater, Mayer notes that both aimed at the use of theater to "better" the spectators rather than to provide a night's entertainment. A theater of social pedagogy, however, which could "make social contexts visible and intervene into the consciousness of the viewers through its presentation" in politically effective ways, would require a formal break with the culinary forms of bourgeois theater. Yet Brecht never believed that one could break with bourgeois theater without serviceable models and traditions that could be refunctioned as countermodels.[106] Brecht's engagement with such pre-bourgeois sources as the Bible or his interest in classical Chinese theater are well-known. In many ways, this preoccupation with the Chinese theater is articulated in Brecht's theoretical work alongside his interest in popular forms such as the folk play. Thus Brecht opens his essay "Alienation Effects in Chinese Acting" by situating the estrangement effects of this acting in the context of German popular culture. "This effort to make the incidents represented appear strange to the public can be seen in a primitive form in the theatrical and pictorial displays at the old popular fairs," Brecht writes. "The way the clowns speak and the way the pantomimes are painted both embody and act of alienation."[107] This type of interruption is key to Brecht's notion of the popular, since it is in these moments that everyday experience is revealed in its historical texture. As against a bourgeois theater that emphasizes the timeless and the "eternally human" and that reduces the historical situation it employs merely as more or less exotic backdrop for the depiction of universal situations that reveal the essentially fixed character of man through the ages, the historicizing theater "concentrates entirely on whatever in [a] perfectly everyday event is remarkable, particular, and demanding inquiry."[108] What is at stake here, though, as Brecht makes clear in his notes on the paintings of Breughel the Elder, is less the historicizing of the everyday but precisely the contradictory relationship of the quotidian and the extraordinary within the everyday register of experience:

> Anyone making a profound study of Breughel's pictorial contrasts must realize that he deals in contradictions. In the *Fall of Icarus* the catastrophe breaks into the idyll in such a way that it is clearly set apart from it and valuable insights into the idyll can be gained. He doesn't allow the catastrophe to alter the idyll; the latter rather remains unaltered and survives undestroyed, merely disturbed. . . . Such pictures don't just give off an atmosphere but a variety of atmospheres. Even though Breughel manages to balance his contrasts he never merges them into one another, nor does he practice the separation of comic and tragic; his tragedy contains a comic element and his comedy a tragic one.[109]

In this quotation, Brecht is gesturing toward an interpenetration of the forms that have been separated by classical and bourgeois aesthetics, the realm of the catastrophe, of the tragic and the noble, on the one hand, and the realm of the comedy, of the quotidian and comic, on the other. For Brecht in the late 1930s, this mediation between forms would be the project of a popular theater that would infuse the *Gestus* and techniques of the folk play with accomplishments of modern art. In his "Notes on the Folk Play," Brecht writes, "a theater's cultural standard is decided partly by its degree of success in overcoming the contrast between 'noble' (elevated, stylized) and realistic ('keyhole') acting."[110] Yet what is important for Brecht in Breughel and in the folk tradition is precisely holding these dimensions in proximity, yet apart, so that their relationality can be mapped.

Brecht's notion of the popular is precisely the historicity of form, and in this sense, *Mother Courage* can be read as an attempt to write a post-bourgeois, or even post-tragic, tragedy and this in a sense that moves beyond the post-tragic stance of Stalinist subjectivity articulated in the previous chapter. If classical tragedy is about the failure of an individual's ambitions and projects in the face of a historical necessity that nevertheless allows that individual to enter into the collective consciousness as a figure for all that was utopian in those projects, the post-tragic stance forecloses that individual claim as well, as the post-tragic subject willingly submits to a fetishized notion of historical necessity. For Brecht, however, the problem seems to be inverted, focusing not on the conditions of subjective fidelity to one's own commitments but on the historical situations that structure the field of individual desires, actions, and the relations between subjects. Raymond Williams makes this point about

Mother Courage in his study *Modern Tragedy*, noting that Brecht's great exile plays are structured around "the connections and contradictions between individual goodness and social action" (MT 199). This marks a decisive break with the tragic logic of sacrifice. If, for Brecht, there is no historical necessity as such but rather the structured field of human relationships, this allows him to "reject the notion of sacrifice as a dramatic emotion." In Brecht's later work, the question increasingly turns upon what we have seen Hans Mayer refer to as productive capitulation, or what Williams here casts as the "profoundly ambiguous question: is it not a sin against life to allow oneself to be destroyed by cruelty and indifference and greed?" As Williams points out, for the individual person, "this dilemma is beyond solution" (MT 197).

The second major break with the tragic tradition that Brecht stages in plays like *Mother Courage* is to definitively separate tragedy from the register of the elevated, of the great men of history, and to suture tragic conventions into the depictions of everyday life as an oscillation of idyll and catastrophe, of continuity and interruption. This classical distinction between the low and the elevated is recuperated by more modern tragedy in the dissociation of "mere suffering," or accident, and the suffering brought upon oneself through individual action. This implies, as Williams puts it, that "the real key to the modern separation of tragedy from 'mere suffering' is the separation of ethical control and, more critically, human agency, from our understanding of social and political life." What is thus disbarred from the tragic is the wide sweep of popular everyday life and the habitual. "The events which are not seen as tragic are deep in the pattern of our own culture," Williams writes, "war, famine, work, traffic, politics. To see no ethical content or human agency in such events, or to say that we cannot connect them with general meanings, and especially with permanent and universal meanings, is to admit a strange bankruptcy, which no rhetoric of tragedy can finally hide" (MT 49). Modern tragedy, or bourgeois tragedy as Brecht might have put it, is precisely the effort to abstract the ethical from the everyday. For Williams, Brecht's move into a post-tragic mode involves the reinscription of the tragic itself with this material dimension of history, which in turn serves to estrange the ethical level of the tragic proper.

This estrangement of the ethical derives from Brecht's framing of situation and character. The action of the drama rises out of the contradictions of the characters themselves in conditions of structured constraint. "The action is continually open, through the fact of these contradictions," Williams writes. "It is not about the inevitability of tragedy, as in the traditional tragic acceptance or the modern tragic resignation" (MT 198–99). Rather, the action is continually open, and this is the key to the Brechtian notion of demonstration:

> The question drives through the continuing action: what else can we do, here, where blind power is loose, but submit, chisel, try to play safe? And then by doing these things—either submitting and pretending to virtue, or submitting and cheating around the back—a family, see, is destroyed. The question is no longer "are they good people?" . . . Nor is it, really, "what should they have done?" It is, brilliantly, both "what are they doing?" and "what is this doing to them?" (198)

What is notable in this account is that it is precisely through the amputation of the logic of tragic sacrifice that Brecht's dramaturgy reveals the materiality of the historical itself in its quotidian ongoingness, not in the sudden and catastrophic event but in the long wearing down of peasant temporality.

In other words, *Mother Courage* cannot be seen as a tragedy in the proper scene; it is an epic operation performed upon tragic forms. Indeed, like Breughel's *Fall of Ikarus* in Brecht's account, *Mother Courage* becomes a dialectic movement between the elevated level of the tragic, of the catastrophe, and of the everyday continuity of the chronicle in which, as Benjamin reminds us, everything is preserved. It is in this epic work upon the tragic that Brecht achieves his most profound estrangement of that form, which is to recover the dimension of history paradoxically through the denial of historical necessity itself. At the same time, this insight attenuates the very peasant temporality that shapes the play. This has to do with the tension between the historical moment that the play stages and the historical moment of the play itself, with the relationship between 1624 and 1939. If the Thirty Years War was, as Brecht puts it, simply an ongoing wearing down and a closed horizon of plebeian misery, the same cannot be said for the late 1930s, where the coming catastrophe can no longer be thought of in any way as necessary. Hans Mayer makes this point apropos of an exchange between Brecht and the dramatist Friedrich Dürrenmatt in 1955. In response to Dürrenmatt's question of whether or not the contemporary world could still be portrayed by theater, Brecht writes,

> In an age possessing science that knows how to transform nature such that the world appears almost habitable, people

> cannot be for very long described by people as victims, as objects of an unknown, but fixed environment. From the perspective of the cue ball, the laws of motion are hardly conceivable.[111]

If anything, the character of Mother Courage is a demonstration of this fact. At the same time, in staging the impasses of peasant temporality as an object of social pedagogy in the mid-twentieth century, Brecht is making a commentary upon what we have seen him refer to as the "new German misery," the passivity of the German masses under both the National Socialist regime and the postfascist East German socialism of the 1940s and 1950s. Indeed, it is precisely this attitude that moves Brecht's chronicle back into the dimension of tragedy, as Williams notes. "The movement of the play," Williams writes, "is from the ironic acceptance of false consciousness—what you say to get by, in an imperfect world—to the point where false consciousness becomes false action and not irony, but tragedy" (MT 201–2). The double closure of the play in Kattrin's martyrdom and Mother Courage's carrying on frames the impasse that Brecht is showing his audiences is no longer their own, hoping to interrupt the habituation of submission and survival that Brecht sees as continuing to shape the habitus of the German people even as they contrarily set about building socialism and laying the groundwork for friendliness as a social virtue and liberating human creativity from the economic, political, and historical fetters that have been laid upon it.

The play thus becomes tragic in a social and political rather than an ethical register, since the point here is very much to demonstrate the ways in which tactics of survival indirectly reproduce the very strategies of exploitation and domination that they are attempting to negotiate. "The final paradox is genuinely tragic," Williams notes, "the dumb girl, speaking for life, and being killed; the living going on with a living that kills; the final song of the soldiers" (MT 199). Again, the weak allegorical sign of the present remains in this foreclosure of a moment of intervention at the moment that Brecht was writing *Mother Courage* in 1938 and again as he was producing the play in East Berlin. If there is no historical necessity to the suffering of World War II, we have a properly post-tragic constellation, for which Brecht is searching for a proper dramatic form. As Williams puts it, "we have to see not only that suffering is avoidable, but that it is not avoided. . . . Under the weight of failure, in tragedy that could have been avoided but was not avoided, this structure of feeling is now struggling to be formed" (202). This structure of feeling has to do with a resituating of the tragic from the register of the individual and the dramatic to the dividual and the epic. If, following Jameson, we see the juxtaposition of the "the high style of the chronicle and the common one of the everyday" that is characteristic of the *Gestus* as the operator of the Brechtian *Verfremdungs-Effekt*, then by using the picaresque to estrange the tragic and the tragic to estrange the picaresque, Brecht reveals the tragedy of Germany history to be the product of the impasses of everyday life in the face of political and economic forces that both stifle the "productivity of the people" and that are systematically reproduced by these very activities of daily life under constraint.[112]

Brecht's play not only captures what he sees as the closure of political and productive horizons at the moment of the collapse of the European Popular Front but also prefigures our current moment. In a recent article, the theorist Göran Therborn characterizes the last decades of the twentieth century as a passage from the "century of the working class" to a political configuration of "the popular classes in all of their diversity—the *plebeians* rather than the proletariat."[113] Brecht's play is thus a pessimistic staging for the possibilities that remain after the suspension of the "Grand Dialectic" of the clash between the increasingly socialized forces of production and the privatized relations that canalize them.[114] Brecht's peasants and plebeians thus anticipate the contemporary "precariat." Lauren Berlant develops the trope of "the impasse" in relation to the precarity of the post-Fordist subject, to whom the "normal life" of Fordist accumulation is foreclosed but who still labors under the attachments and expectations that sustained the previous social formation. "The impasse," Berlant writes, is "a name for the transitional moment between a habituated life and all of its others . . . a rhythm people can enter into while they're dithering, tottering, bargaining, testing, or otherwise being worn out by the promises that they have attached to in this world."[115] The epic, then, becomes a framing of the temporality of *Eigensinn* itself, of the palimpsestic attachments, capacities, and needs that fail to arrive punctually in historical time. Brecht's play challenges us to imagine this habitus as the basis of a politics of the everyday while at the same time granting a tragic dimension to the impasses of the everyday, which acquires the weight of the tragic precisely because it no longer contains the horizon of this Grand Dialectic, becoming instead, to return to Loren Kruger's formulation, the tragedy of the commoner.

Epilogue

The "Immense Window of Change"?

The emergent, having failed to merge into the dominant, persists as residual.
—Nicholas Brown and Imre Szemán

In what seems an incorrect assertion to East German audiences in the early 1950s, Brecht describes the historical setting of *Mother Courage and Her Children* thusly:

> Yes, the Thirty Years' War is one of the first great wars unleashed upon Europe by capitalism. And in capitalism it is extraordinarily difficult that war is not necessary, because in capitalism it is necessary, namely for capitalism itself. This economic system is based on the struggle of all against all, the great against the small, the small against the small. One must have already recognized capitalism as a misfortune in order to recognize that the war that brings misfortune is bad, which is to say unnecessary.[1]

This is precisely the territory of Adorno's critique of *Mother Courage* in his 1962 essay "Commitment." He accused Brecht of simplifying the social and political realities of the central European seventeenth century in order "to reduce to absurdity Montecuccoli's dictum that war feeds on war."[2] Of course, what Brecht was saying to his young spectator was not that war feeds war but that war feeds capitalism. Nevertheless, Adorno is correct in implying that the play does not in fact show this, and contrary to Brecht's assertion that "the Thirty Years' War is one of the first great wars unleashed upon Europe by capitalism,"

Adorno points out that "the equation of the Thirty Years' War with a modern war excludes precisely what is crucial for the behavior and fate of Mother Courage in Grimmelshausen's novel." Indeed, Adorno insists that this anachronism corrodes the drama from within: "because the society of the Thirty Years War was not the functional capitalist society of modern times, we cannot even poetically stipulate a closed functional system in which the lives and deaths of private individuals directly reveal economic laws." At the same time, Adorno realizes that Brecht needs "the old lawless days as an image of his own, precisely because he saw clearly that the society of his own age could no longer be directly comprehended in terms of people and things."[3] Thus, Adorno argues, Brecht adopts the "old lawless days" as a setting that gives him the social opacity that he requires to portray the present and then falsifies both the bad old days and the worse new ones by rendering the Thirty Years War as a transparent allegory of the opportunism of the petit bourgeoisie.

At the same time, we have argued, following Jameson, that Brecht's use of the Thirty Years War should be thought of less in terms of comparison and equivalence than as a way of thinking about the impasses of a situation in which a proper tragedy, a tragedy without catastrophe, does not seem available as a formal template. Alberto Toscano, expanding on the work of Raymond Williams, frames the tragic in terms of "the shearing pressure of different temporal registers on political action."[4] Tragedy, in this account, is itself the form of the "determinate historical content" of transition in its noncontemporaneity, "the way in which emancipatory collective action is unsettled and displaced, distorted and undermined by the collision between different imperatives and the rifts between nonsynchronous temporalities." In order for this proper notion of tragedy to function, there must, of course, be some horizon of collective emancipation. In other words, for what Toscano describes as the line of thought stretching from Hegel through Marx, Lukács, and Williams, the tragic is none other than the form of revolution itself. "The tragic action," Williams writes, "in its deepest sense, is not the confirmation of disorder, but its experience, its comprehension, and its resolution" (MT 84).[5] If we consider order here to be roughly coextensive with what Brecht describes as "great production," we can begin to see how, in this sense, the catastrophe that Brecht is staging in *Mother Courage* is both one that inaugurates German modernity in the form of a fundamentally subaltern plebeian structure of feeling already in the seventeenth century as well as one that persists as an impasse in proletarian sovereignty in the mid-twentieth-century crisis of modernity. Toscano reads Georg Lukács's early essay "The Metaphysics of Tragedy" as marking the impossibility of the tragic form for the modern individual, for whom value and being are irreconcilably torn asunder, such that "once again, we are confronted with the paradoxical conviction that the contemporary predicament is tragic to the extent that it makes a life lived according to tragic form impossible."[6] Toscano sees this tragedy of individuality as being subsumed into a collective tragedy that still holds out hope for "the overthrow of all those conditions in which man appears as an abased, enslaved, abandoned, contemptible being," as Marx might put it.[7] "This movement," Toscano writes, "is also one from the political predicament of the modern as desolation, abstraction, evacuation to a conception of politics in terms of historical contexts of crisis and contradiction," in other words, a passage into what Göran Therborn describes as the Marxian Grand Dialectic. Brecht, on the other hand, seems to be staging a collapse of that horizon. The tragic is available in the individual form for Brecht, and we see it in different ways with Mother Courage herself and with her daughter. What is inaccessible in Brecht's epic work upon tragedy is the tragic as a historical form of crisis and contradiction that would be "discernable from the virtual vantage point of its overcoming."[8]

The plebeian thus emerges as an ambiguation of the relationship of the proletarian to the peasant, in other words, as a figuration for a proletariat stripped of historical mission. This is in a sense already the case in Friedrich Engels's account of the sixteenth-century German Peasant Wars, which Toscano characterizes as the "template for Marxist tragedy."[9] This tragedy lies again in the ambiguity of plebeian revolt. While the peasantry formed the basis of sixteenth-century German social and political life as the universally exploited class, since "every official estate of the Empire lived by sucking the peasants dry,"[10] the plebeian opposition, "ruined burghers and the mass of townsmen without rights," was the only class in sixteenth-century Germany that "stood outside the officially existing society" altogether, with neither privilege nor property.[11]

For Engels, the revolutionary party of the peasants and the plebeians was essentially led by the plebeian faction, in the form of radical clergymen like Thomas Münzer. The tragedy of the Peasant Wars then for Engels is that this plebeian uprising comes too soon; the ideological frontiers of leaders like Münzer stretch far beyond the borders of the possible. The plebeians, Engels writes, "were a living symptom of the decay of the feudal and guild-burgher society, and at the same time the first precursors of the modern bourgeois society."[12] As symptom and precursor, the "plebeian faction," in its fantasies of erecting the kingdom of God on earth,[13] bursts beyond the present and even the future, but only in its rhetoric and its aims. "On the other hand," Engels points out, "this sally beyond the present and even the future could be nothing but violent and fantastic, and was bound to slide back at its first practical application to within the narrow limits set by the contemporary situation."[14] This is then very much tragedy in the sense evoked by Toscano, "the experience of a blockage and a presentiment of being at the threshold of a revolutionary rupture."[15] Engels explores the contours of this paradox in the figure of the premature uprising, writing,

> The worst thing that can befall the leader of an extreme party is to be compelled to assume power at a time when the movement is not yet ripe for the domination of the class he represents and for the measures this domination implies. What he can do contradicts all of his previous actions and principles and the immediate interests of his party, and what he ought to do cannot be done.[16]

The premature revolution is the beheaded revolution. The twentieth century is perhaps best thought of in terms of revolutions that in coming too soon fail ultimately to arrive. The October Revolution of 1917 sets the tone, but indeed, the Thirty Years War of 1914–45, as we have argued, can be largely understood in the terms of the tragedy that Engels describes in this passage. The consequences of the Peasant Wars and the foreclosure of the German revolution in the wake of World War I are not so much parallel in this sense; rather they form a genealogy of German misery. Recall Brecht's assertion that "of the Peasant's War, which was the greatest misfortune of German history, one may say that, socially considered, it pulled the teeth of the Reformation. Its legacy was cynicism and business as usual."[17] Similarly, Heiner Müller, writing in 1985 on the eve of the collapse of the first workers' and peasants' state on German soil, describes the Germans as

> a people castrated of its civil courage by the bloody repression of a premature revolution and a resulting thirty-year war, whose spine was crushed by the beheading of its proletariat through the murder of two of its Jewish leaders forgotten by

> the majority, and a twelve-year reign of terror against the revolution. A nation with a broken spine that made it its duty to break the spines of other nations.[18]

In this genealogy of the *deutsche Misère*, Rosa Luxemburg and Karl Liebknecht thus join Thomas Munzer, the Mainz Republic memorialized by Seghers in *The Seventh Cross*, and the urban insurgents of 1848 in the gallery of severed heads of a foreclosed, virtual overcoming of German history.[19] Müller returns to this theme of beheading in a later discussion with the critic Frank M. Raddatz in the midst of the *Wende*, picking up on Brecht's comments on the Peasant Wars, noting, "since these early revolutions a tendency towards belatedness has dominated in Germany . . . and the belatedness also means that these energies can only be discharged in catastrophes."[20]

Yet rather than casting Müller as a practitioner of a kind of melancholy leftist hagiography of the type already denounced by Erhard Lucas as a demobilizing "cult of the dead,"[21] it might be more productive after all to see Müller as a diagnostician of a certain structure of feeling, that of an *Eigensinn* constituted in the constellation of war, revolution, economic crisis, and everyday violence, exploitation, and confinement that shapes the proletarian experience of the modern. In this sense, one might argue that instead of mourning the great leaders of an alternative German history, we should read comments like those of Brecht and Müller in terms of a crisis of proletarian sovereignty that articulates itself in the form of a subaltern structure of feeling. Here Brecht's plebeian survivors, as well as the creaturely peasant-cum-proletarians in Marchwitza's *Kumiaks*, and interestingly also Claudius's figure of the partisan under erasure in the aftermath of the Spanish Civil War, can all be read in terms of "the habits of obedience and respect, the stubbornness and mutism of a peasantry whose mode of resistance is utterly distinct from that of the working class."[22] All of the exile works analyzed in this book circle around this problem, which is precisely that of the German misery, so to speak: an ambiguation of the problem of collective agency that is articulated in these works in terms of the metaphors of social class. The fixation on 1918 in Communist literary work from the BPRS through the exile period highlights the precarious and disavowed outcast status of Communists in the Weimar Republic as revolutionaries in a nonrevolutionary time.[23]

In the literature of the antifascist exile, this opposition is both radicalized and brought to the fore as a political and representational problem. Marchwitza's novel *Die Kumiaks* presents perhaps the starkest vision of anti-*Heimat* within German socialist literature, suspending any utopian horizon and depicting the Ruhrland of the Weimar Republic as a space of claustrophobia, violence, and exploitation, populated by starving and superfluous urban peasants clinging to their *Eigensinn* as their last possession and only hope for survival. Eduard Claudius's Spanish Civil War novel, *Grüne Oliven und nackte Berge*, appeals to the *deutsche Misère* in order to elaborate a utopian counter-image, where it is precisely the solidarity of the struggle for a homeland and the codes of conduct of this struggle that become themselves an anticipatory signifier for a postfascist, socialist Germany.

This solidarity, however, increasing collapses upon itself in *Grüne Oliven*, as the codes of conduct developed against *Eigensinn* by the Communist "partisan" increasingly become rituals of *Eigensinn* in their own right, isolating the partisans of the International Brigades from the people for whom they are fighting and from each other. Indeed, even Mother Courage, the celebrated plebeian critic of bourgeois virtue, sits when she is told to sit. Nevertheless, in the novels of both Seghers and Claudius, this radical ambiguation of proletarian agency gestures to prophetic. In both novels oneiric accounts of the redeemed time of the oppressed in an epochal and Benjaminian sense open onto what Jameson describes as the utopia of peasant time in those moments between the collapse of order and the restoration of the same, of "change as a kind of immense window," a brief golden age of wish fulfillment that is always already in the past as much as it is in the future.[24]

Yet the difference between this utopian window in the otherwise monolithic element of peasant suffering and Jak Rohde's vision of the eternal peasant-soldier in Claudius's *Grüne Oliven* or Seghers's incorporeal collective voice of the future from within the concentration camps of the present in *The Seventh Cross* lies in the fleeting possibility that it could be held open. Thus Toscano writes of the revolution as the template for tragedy that it cannot be thought of in terms of a reconciliation, which is to say a return. At the same time, revolution is "tragedy without catastrophe,"[25] since it is the breaking with the "great order," to put it in Brechtian language, of exploitation and subalternity. This notion of tragedy as neither restoration of order nor catastrophe is instead the appeal to a tragedy "which would resist a return to order, instead advancing the recomposition of a new order."[26]

Appraising the world balance of class politics from the vantage point of our own present, Göran Therborn remarks, "while there are a number of plausible labels that might be attached to the 20th century, in terms of social history it was clearly the age of the working class. For the first time, working people who lacked property became a major and sustained political force."[27] The crises of the 1930s marked perhaps the low point of this proletarian century, as the European workers' movement found itself ground down by fascism on the one hand and the consolidation of state socialism and the rigid disciplines of the Communist parties on the other. Defeated in the USSR no less than in Germany, Italy, Austria, and Spain, the working-class organizations that entered into the Popular Front may have generated a great deal of enthusiasm but were no longer in the position to stage social revolutions. Therborn notes that today "the Grand Dialectic" that propelled the century of the working class has "been suspended, even reversed."[28]

The 1930s is the moment that the suspension of this dialectic enters into view in ways that can be symptomatically narrated but not avowed in the texts of KPD militants like Marchwitza, Claudius, and Seghers and are simply portrayed with a somewhat un-Brechtian lack of commentary in *Mother Courage*.[29] Of course this does not in any way imply that there is something like an end to a century of the working class already in the 1930s. Indeed, one should not forget that World War II ended with the triumph of a popular antifascism in which Communists around the globe played far from a minor part. As Hobsbawm notes, European Communist movements reached their peak in the years immediately following the war, emerging from the shadows as hidden and persecuted sects as popular mass parties.[30] This moment of antifascist unity marked a decisive rupture with the vestiges of the ancien régime in Europe and, with its linkages to anticolonial movements, the world itself.[31]

Nevertheless, in both East and West, the Allies dismantled local organs of self-control, from the partisans in Italy to the antifascist committees in Germany. As Geoff Eley writes, "public ownership without public participation, planning without democracy, and a welfare state without popular accountability would make reform an unfinished thing"[32] as the mass democratic aspirations of the postwar period fed the exigencies of the Cold War. At the same time, one would want to rethink the relationship between the projected "we" and the aspirations of proletarian unity that animated the Popular Front and the "anti-authoritarian, anti-colonialist, anti-imperialist" *we* of the world in the 1960s, as well as that more diffuse plural nonsingular of the multitude.[33]

Thus in the wake of the Grand Dialectic, we turn away from a substantialist notion of the working class to one that is in many ways closer to the conception of the proletariat that Marx puts forward in 1843 as the solution to the belated situation of the German revolution, writing:

> a class must be formed which has *radical chains*, a class in civil society which is not a class of civil society, a class which is the dissolution of all classes, a sphere which has a universal character because its sufferings are universal, and which does not claim a *particular redress* because the wrong which is done to it is not a *particular wrong*, but *wrong in general*. There must be formed a sphere of society which claims no *traditional* status but only a human status, a sphere which is not opposed to particular consequences but is totally opposed to the assumptions of the German political system; a sphere, finally, which cannot emancipate itself without emancipating itself from all other spheres of society, without, therefore, emancipating all these other spheres, which is, in short, a *total loss* of humanity and which can only redeem itself by a *total redemption of humanity*. This dissolution of society, as a particular class, is the *proletariat*.[34]

The proletariat for Marx in this early phase marks precisely the tragedy of transition. "For what constitutes the proletariat is not naturally existing poverty, but poverty artificially produced, is not the mass of people mechanically oppressed by the weight of society, but the mass resulting from the disintegration of society." What Marx here describes, in other words, seems very close indeed to the "plebeian faction" that Engels sees as the real losers of the Peasant Wars, that part of no part, to borrow a phrase from Jacques Rancière, that both precedes and survives the working-class century.

Volker Braun's recent text *Die hellen Haufen* [The Bright Hordes 2011] makes this clear by way of a counterfactual demonstration. Since the early 1990s, Braun has been the chronicler of the dispossessed East German working class and of the demobilized postindustrial wastelands of the former German Democratic Republic.[35] *Die hellen Haufen* is set in the Mansfeld mining region, which like the Soviet Donbas served as a principal site of the mythology of collective labor that underpinned (at great environmental and social cost) a discourse and social imaginary of the GDR as a socialist nation.[36] Braun's story brings together

1525 and 1992, as the miners of central Germany protest the selling off of the East German economy through the Treuhand under the slogan "Not Colonial Territory."[37] A group of four thousand workers, including the *Kumpels* of the Thomas-Münzer mines, gather together into *Haufen*, or armed bands, in the fashion of the insurgent peasants of the sixteenth century and prepare to march on Berlin. "The uprising, of which will be reported here, never took place," Braun writes,

> it was indeed more of a war that was only carried on by one side, and the other kept still. Its truth was that it was thinkable. One claims to know history, but it has more in it than what occurs: the not-happened, omitted, the lost also lies in that black mountain. All that was longed for and never dared, and the old desire *to act*. Resistance hidden in the depths, buried alive, sealed in concrete; the bright hordes that have not set forth to join the battle.[38]

Braun's speculative history depends on a cultural revolution very much in Jameson's sense of the term, as a break with a historically conditioned subaltern habitus. For Braun this would mean to take seriously the project of socialism, not in fidelity to but precisely in spite of the forty-year history of the German workers' and peasants' state. "The party and the government had broken them of the habit of fighting," Braun notes of the workers as they take the first steps toward insurrection.[39]

To recapture this capacity for resistance would then mean precisely an assertion of proletarian sovereignty in relation to property relations. This was for Braun the paradox of the GDR: "in the west property was sacred. In the east one was damned by it. Because it was a burden to the possessor. How was one to support it? No one wanted it. No one was attached to it, this property."[40] Following a debate among the insurgents on the character of the people's property, or *Volkseigentum* of the GDR, a miner named Mintzer asserts that "to take this into our own hands would be the real revolution."[41] What follows is the drafting of twelve Mansfeld Articles on the model of the Twelve Articles drafted by the Schwabian peasants at Memmingen in 1525, which as Engels points out articulated the political program of the Peasant Wars.[42] If the chiliastic vision of the kingdom of God on earth evoked by these sixteenth-century peasants, however, characterized a utopian anticipation of a revolution that itself could only come later, the Mansfeld Articles are an imaginary rewriting of twentieth-century socialism.

The articles of Memmingen demanded the actualization of the commons, whereas the articles of Mansfeld demand the real socialization, the making common, of labor.[43] And yet even this long-awaited stirring of the masses is in fact too late, and Braun makes much of the irony and pathos of this mob of surplus proletarians who remember that their strong fists might stop the wheels of capitalist accumulation only at the moment that capitalism no longer needs them or their labor. The mines have no claim to value in any market logic. Indeed, the GDR was already losing money in these copper pits, but

> this deficit had given work to 48,000! Not only in the pits and the foundries, in the steel mill, machine and equipment shops; it was a nest of trade and a meshwork of activities, in transport and construction enterprises, trade organizations, engineering firms, supply and finishing works. All of this had its place, and the unprofitable haulage financed these daycare centers and policlinics, libraries, theater and central heating.[44]

This passage reveals not only the ways in which the deindustrialization of the former East Germany destroyed the thick social networks elaborated around labor and the workplace, the self-confidence and solidarity of what Wolfgang Engler calls the "workerly society," or *arbeiterliche Gesellschaft*, but also the sense in which this Fordist idyll was already something like the late medieval moral economy, with its obligations, privileges, and petty illegalites.[45] In a postsocialist context, the demand for full employment and the liberation of labor seems as quaint as it does radical. The post-proletarian plebeian revolt that Braun images is thus as much of a rearguard defense of the privileges of an archaic and oppressive commons, that of socialized industrial labor, as it is a vision of the kingdom of labor realized on earth. This is, as Marx says, a revolution that takes its poetry from the past, even if that past never happened. Since the mines they defend are already closed, it is only the insurgents themselves who are surprised when the newly unified German state disperses them with military force. This is, then, perhaps the best way to read the ending of Braun's story, as the insurgent bands hold firm to the *Wende* slogan "No Violence" in the face of the helicopters and troops of the Bundeswehr, while in the background of their defeat a certain "Braun" from the Vogtland cries, "VIOLENCE, VIOLENCE, and it was not clear whether he wanted to confirm it or demand it."[46] Even in imagination, the revolution is too late, its fantasies already too intertwined in the defeats of the past generations, and yet here Braun at least attempts to render the tragedy of German socialism *as* tragedy in the strong sense of collective history, to leave it to the future as a productive defeat. This would be to lend to the *Wende* the "weak messianic charge" of the Peasant Wars themselves, or indeed the legendary defeats of the 1930s in Floridsdorf and Asturias that precipitated the Popular Front, rather than the paralyzing defeats of 1919 and 1933 or the undignified shuffling off of really existing socialism itself in 1989.[47] In attempting to return tragic form to the twentieth-century socialist project, Braun lends support to his character Mintzer's slogan: "the future is an unoccupied territory."[48] However, as Braun reminds us, "This story never happened. It was only, much abridged and unembellished, written down."[49]

Notes

INTRODUCTION

1. Eric Hobsbawm also famously frames his short twentieth century around the October Revolution and its world resonance in *The Age of Extremes: A History of the World, 1914–1991* (New York: Vintage, 1996).

2. Alain Badiou, *The Century*, trans. Alberto Toscano (Malden, MA: Polity, 2007), 22.

3. Bertolt Brecht, "To Posterity," in *Poems, 1913–1956*, ed. John Willett and Ralph Mannheim (New York: Methuen, 1976), 320.

4. Peter Blickle, *Heimat: A Critical Theory of the German Idea of Homeland* (Rochester: Camden House, 2002), 1.

5. Alf Lüdtke, "What Happened to the 'Fiery Red Glow'? Workers' Experiences and German Fascism," in *The History of Everyday Life: Reconstructing Historical Experiences and Ways of Life*, ed. Alf Lüdtke, trans. William Templer (Princeton: Princeton University Press, 1995), 212.

6. Doreen B. Massey, *Space, Place, and Gender* (Minneapolis: University of Minnesota Press, 1994).

7. Walter Benjamin, "A Chronicle of Germany's Unemployed: Anna Seghers' Novel *Die Rettung*," in *Selected Writings*, vol. 4, 1938–1940, ed. Howard Eiland and Michael W. Jennings (Cambridge, MA: Belknap Press, 2003).

8. See *The Popular Front in Europe*, ed. Helen Graham and Paul Preston (London: MacMillan, 1987). On the German Popular Front specifically, see Ursula Langkau-Alex's three-volume account, *Die Deutsche Volksfront, 1932–1939: Zwischen Berlin, Paris, Prag und Moskau* (Berlin: Akademie Verlag, 2004).

9. Arno Mayer, *The Persistence of the Old Regime: Europe to the Great War* (New York: Verso, 2010), 3.

10. Michael Denning, *Culture in the Age of Three Worlds* (New York: Verso, 2004), 32.

11. Peter Weiss, *Notizbücher, 1971–1980*, Erster Band (Frankfurt: Suhrkamp Verlag, 1981), 378. Where possible, I have tried to use published English translations of German works. Where translated editions are not cited, the translations are mine.

12. Walter Benjamin, "On the Concept of History," in *Selected Writings*, 4:394.

13. Michael Löwy, *Fire Alarm: Reading Walter Benjamin's "On the Concept of History,"* trans. Chris Turner (New York: Verso, 2005), 89.

14. Ibid.

15. Raymond Williams, *Modern Tragedy* (Peterborough, Ontario: Broadview Press, 2001), 64.

16. Friedrich Engels, *Ludwig Feuerbach and the Outcome of German Classical Philosophy* (New York: International Publishers, 1941), 57.

17. Jacques Rancière, *Disagreement: Politics and Philosophy*, trans. Julie Rose (Minneapolis: University of Minnesota Press, 1999), 77.

18. V. I. Lenin, *Two Tactics of Social Democracy in the Democratic Revolution* (New York: International Publishers, 1935), 47–48.

19. Lenin is actually careful to specify that what he sees as the Jacobin legacy of bolshevism does not lie in political aims but in a militant stance toward politics.

20. V. I. Lenin, *State and Revolution* (New York: International Publishers, 1932), 23.

21. A structure of feeling, according to Raymond Williams, is produced in the contradiction between the "official consciousness" of a period, political doctrines, legislation, public discourse, and so forth, and "the whole process of actually living its consequences." Raymond Williams, *Politics & Letters: Interviews with New Left Review* (London: Verso, 1981), 159.

22. Hans Mayer, "Die plebejische Tradition," *Brecht* (Frankfurt: Suhrkamp Verlag, 1966), 310.

23. Werner Mittenzwei, *Das Leben des Bertolt Brecht oder, Der Umgang mit den Welträtseln* (Berlin: Aufbau-Verlag, 1997), 2:406.

24. Fredric Jameson, *Valences of the Dialectic* (New York: Verso, 2009), 274.

25. Friedrich Engels, "On Realism," in *Marxist Literary Theory: A Reader*, ed. Terry Eagleton and Drew Milne (Cambridge: Blackwell, 1996), 40.

26. For an account of the plebeian as politically emancipatory precisely because of its inability to exercise power, see Martin Breaugh, *The Plebeian Experience: A Discontinuous History of Political Freedom*, trans. Lazer Lederhendler (New York: Columbia University Press, 2013).

27. Devin Fore quotes this phrase from the *Phenomenology of Spirit* in his introduction to Negt and Kluge's English-language revision of their sprawling collaborative political economy of labor power, *Geschichte und Eigensinn* (Frankfurt: Zweitausendeins, 1981). Alexander Kluge and Oskar Negt, *History and Obstinacy*, ed. Devin Fore, trans. Richard Langston with Cyrus Shahan, Martin Brady, Helen Hughes, and Joel Golb (New York: Zone Books, 2014), 36. Chapter 2 of the present volume engages with this work extensively.

28. Terry Eagleton, *Sweet Violence: The Idea of the Tragic* (London: Blackwell, 2002), 193–94. On the noncoincidence of being and the world as a fundamental issue in both the theory of the tragic and in German idealist philosophy, see Peter Szondi, *An Essay on the Tragic*, trans. Paul Fleming (Stanford: Stanford University Press, 2002).

29. Eagleton, *Sweet Violence*, 193.

30. Jameson, *Valences*, 484.

31. Loren Kruger, "On the Tragedy of the Commoner: Electra, Orestes, and Others in South Africa," *Comparative Drama* 46.3 (Fall 2012): 359.

32. Jameson, *Valences*, 553.

33. I am here using emplotment in a sense indebted to Hayden White's insights on emplotment as the lending of meaning to a narrative by rendering it in a specific formal register. Hayden White, *Metahistory: The Historical Imagination in Nineteenth-Century Europe* (Baltimore: Johns Hopkins University Press, 1973), 5.

34. Fredric Jameson, *Marxism and Form: Twentieth-Century Dialectical Theories of Literature* (Princeton: Princeton University Press, 1971), 146.

35. Geoff Eley, *Forging Democracy: The History of the Left in Europe, 1850–2000* (Oxford: Oxford University Press, 2002), 235.

36. Pierre Broué, *The German Revolution*, trans. John Archer (Chicago: Haymarket Books, 2006), 910.

37. Kruger, "On the Tragedy of the Commoner," 358.

38. Broué, *The German Revolution*, 899.

39. Cited in ibid., 780.

40. Sebastian Haffner, *Failure of a Revolution: Germany, 1918–1919*, trans. Georg Rapp (Chicago: Banner Press, 1986), 200.

41. On the Spartacus revolt of January 1919, see Broué, *The German Revolution*, 227–60.

42. Rosa Luxemburg, "Order Reigns in Berlin," in *The Rosa Luxemburg Reader*, ed. Peter Hudis and Kevin B. Anderson (New York: Monthly Review Press, 2004), 376.

43. Ibid., 378.

44. *Optimistic Tragedy* is of course the title of Vsevolod Vishnevsky's 1933 drama of the Russian Revolution.

45. Tyrus Miller, "Editor's Introduction: The Phantom of Liberty: György Lukács and the Culture of 'People's Democracy,'" in György Lukács, *The Culture of People's Democracy: Hungarian Essays on Literature, Art, and Democratic Transition, 1945–1948*, ed. and trans. Tyrus Miller (Chicago: Haymarket Books, 2013), ix.

46. Ehrhard Bahr, *Weimar on the Pacific: German Exile Culture in Los Angeles and the Crisis of Modernism* (Berkeley: University of California Press, 2008) and Bettina Engelmann, *Poetik des Exils: Die Modernität der deutschsprachigen Exilliteratur* (Tübingen: Max Niemeyer Verlag, 2001).

47. Georg Lukács, *The Historical Novel*, trans. Hannah Mitchell and Stanley Mitchell (Lincoln: University of Nebraska Press, 1983), 347–48.

48. On this point, see Devin Fore, *Realism After Modernism: The Rehumanization of Art and Literature* (Cambridge, MA: MIT Press, 2013).

49. Denning, *Culture in the Age of Three Worlds*, 67. The term "social modernism" is evoked in Denning, *The Cultural Front: The Laboring of American Culture in the Twentieth Century* (New York: Verso, 1997), 122.

50. Denning, *Cultural Front*, xvi, 28.

51. Miriam Bratu Hansen, "The Mass Production of the Senses: Classical Cinema as Vernacular Modernism," *Modernism/Modernity* 6.2 (1999): 60.

52. Langkau-Alex, *Die Deutsche Volksfront*, 1:115. See also Birgit Schmidt, *Wenn die Partei das Volk entdeckt* (Münster: UNRAST-Verlag, 2002), 64–65.

53. Hobsbawm, *The Age of Extremes*, 148.

54. Denning, *Cultural Front*, 128.

55. Jean-Michel Palmier, *Weimar in Exile: The Antifascist Emigration in Europe and America*, trans. David Fernbach (New York: Verso, 2006), 339.

56. Cited in David Pike, *Deutsche Schriftsteller im sowjetischen Exil, 1933–1945* (Frankfurt am Main: Suhrkamp Verlag, 1981), 495.

57. On the *deutsche Misère*, see Warren Breckman, "Diagnosing the 'German Misery': Radicalism and the Problem of National Character, 1830 to 1848," in *Between Reform and Revolution: German Socialism and Communism from 1840 to 1990*, ed. David E. Barclay and Eric D. Weitz (New York: Berghahn, 1998) and Jost Hermand, *Sieben Arten, an Deutschland zu leiden* (Königstein: Athenäum Verlag, 1979).

58. F. C. Weiskopf, *Unter fremden Himmeln: Ein Abriß der deutschen Literatur im Exil, 1933–1947* (Berlin: Aufbau-Verlag, 1981), 11.

59. Ibid., 13.

60. Sigrid Bock, "Roman im Exil: Entstehungsbedingungen, Wirkungsabsichten und Wirkungsmöglichkeiten," in *Erfahrung Exil: Antifaschistische Romane, 1933–1945*, ed. Sigrid Bock and Manfred Hahn (Berlin: Aufbau-Verlag, 1979), 7–11.

61. On the *Heinrich Heine Klub*, see Marcus G. Patka, *Zu nahe der Sonne: Deutsche Schriftsteller im Exil in Mexiko* (Berlin: Aufbau-Verlag, 1999), 118–38.

62. Heinrich Heine, "Germany: A Winter's Tale," trans. Aaron Kramer, in *Poetry and Prose*, ed. Jost Hermand and Robert C. Holub (New York: Continuum, 1992), 270.

63. Ibid., 236.

64. Hermand, *Sieben Arten*, 46–47.

65. Quoted in Breckman, "Diagnosing the 'German Misery,'" 34.

66. Palmier, *Weimar in Exile*, 399.

67. Breckman, "Diagnosing the 'German Misery,'" 54.

68. Karl Marx, "Contribution to the Critique of Hegel's *Philosophy of the Right*: Introduction," in *The Marx-Engels Reader*, ed. Robert C. Tucker (New York: W. W. Norton, 1978), 58.

69. Ibid., 55.

70. Ibid., 56.

71. Ibid., 62.

72. Cited in Breckman, "Diagnosing the 'German Misery,'" 39.

73. Cited in ibid., 43.

74. Marx, "Contribution to the Critique," 63.

75. This is at the base of Hermand's critique of what he sees as the essentially negative critique implicit in theories of the German misery (*Sieben Arten*, 53–54).

76. Marx, "Contribution to the Critique," 64.

77. Kruger, "On the Tragedy of the Commoner," 358.

78. Benjamin, "A Chronicle of Germany's Unemployed," 138.

79. Miller, "Editor's Introduction," xxxv.

80. J. M. Bernstein, *The Philosophy of the Novel: Lukács, Marxism, and the Dialectics of Form* (Minneapolis: University of Minnesota Press, 1984), 257.

81. Ibid., 266.

CHAPTER 1

1. For the rhetoric of the Third Period, see Ernst Thälmann, "The SPD and the NSDAP Are Twins," in *The Weimar Republic Source Book*, ed. Anton Kaes, Martin Jay, and Edward Dimendberg (Berkeley: University of California Press, 1994).

2. As the first head of the Communist Youth International and founder of the International Workers' Relief to support the embattled Soviet Republic in 1920, Willi Münzenberg was a central figure for Communist alliance politics and one of the most important organizers and publicists in the KPD until his break with the party and the Comintern in 1937, playing a central role in the cultural initiatives of the Popular Front. In this role, Münzenberg is one of the more important characters in Peter Weiss's *Aesthetics of Resistance (*Weiss, *The Aesthetics of Resistance*, vol. 1, trans. Joachim Neurgoschel [Durham, NC: Duke University Press, 2005]). See also Babette Gross, *Willi Münzenberg, eine politische Biographie* (Stuttgart: Deutsche Verlags-Anstalt, 1967).

3. On the counterpublic sphere of the KPD, see W. L. Guttsman, *Workers' Culture in Weimar Germany: Between Tradition and Containment* (New York: Berg, 1990).

4. Detlev K. Peukert, *The Weimar Republic: The Crisis of Classical Modernity*, trans. Richard Deveson (New York: Hill and Wang, 1989).

5. Fredric Jameson, "The End of Temporality," in *The Ideologies of Theory* (London: Verso, 2008), 639.

6. Erich Knauf, "Book Clubs," in *The Weimar Republic Source Book*, 515.

7. Walter Benjamin, "Experience and Poverty," in *Selected Writings*, vol. 2, part 2, 1931–1934, ed. Michael W. Jennings, Howard Eiland, and Gary Smith (Cambridge, MA: Belknap Press, 1999), 734.

8. On the influence of the early Lukács on Seghers, see Helen Fehervary, *Anna Seghers: The Mythic Dimension* (Ann Arbor: University of Michigan Press, 2001).

9. Siegfried Kracauer, "The Biography as an Art Form of the New Bourgeoisie," in *The Mass Ornament: Weimar Essays*, trans. and ed. Thomas Y. Levin (Cambridge, MA: Harvard University Press, 1995), 102.

10. Ibid., 104.

11. Silvia Schlenstedt, "Funktion und Formveränderung—Lyrik und Roman in der Debatte," in *Wer schreibt, handelt: Strategien und Verfahren literarischer Arbeit vor und nach 1933*, ed. Silvia Schlenstedt (Berlin: Aufbau-Verlag, 1983), 69.

12. Rudolf G. Wagner, *Inside a Service Trade: Studies in Contemporary Chinese Prose* (Cambridge, MA: Harvard University Press, 1992), 329–45. As Wagner points out, Kisch was a major figure in this period, not only in Europe but in the USSR and China as well.

13. For a comprehensive account of New Objectivity, which also focuses on the relationship between cultural practice on the Weimar left and the avant-garde aesthetics of the early Soviet Union, see John Willett, *Art and Politics in the Weimar Period: The New Sobriety, 1917–1933* (New York: De Capo Press, 1978). For an account of the movement in terms of the contemporary German political scene of the moment, see Helmut Lethen's classic survey of New Objectivity, *Neue Sachlichkeit, 1924–1932: Studien zur Literatur des "Weissen Sozialismus"* (Stuttgart: Meltzer, 1970).

14. For Benjamin's critique of New Objectivity, see "Left-Wing Melancholy," in *Selected Writings*, vol. 2, part 2, where Benjamin criticizes the passive stance of the objective observer as precisely the vantage point of commodification: "The metamorphosis of political struggle from a compulsory decision into an object of pleasure, from a means of production into an article of consumption—that is literature's greatest hit" (425).

15. M. M. Bakhtin develops a similar distinction between the closed and past world of epic and the open and heteroglossic form of the novel in "Epic and Novel." *The Dialogic Imagination: Four Essays*, ed. and trans. Michael Holquist, trans. Caryl Emerson (Austin: University of Texas Press, 1981).

16. Peter Jelavich, *Berlin Alexanderplatz: Radio, Film and the Death of Weimar Culture* (Berkeley: University of California Press, 2006), 21.

17. Devin Fore, "Sense, Document, and the Verbal World Picture," *New German Critique*, no. 99 (Fall 2006): 174.

18. Ibid., 202. For Benjamin, this is precisely the terrain upon which Döblin's epic technique fails. While praising Döblin's use in *Berlin Alexanderplatz* of authentic documentation from the popular culture and mediascape of the Weimar Republic and the montage structure of the novel, Benjamin condemns the traditionally novelistic closure of the book in Franz Biberkopf's resignation. "The Crisis of the Novel," in *Selected Writings*, vol. 2, part 2, 301, 303. For the BPRS reaction to *Berlin Alexanderplatz*, which the Communist writers' organization critiqued for its lack of a clear class politics, see Johannes R. Becher, "Einen Schritt weiter," in *Zur Tradition der deutschen sozialistischen Literatur: Eine Auswahl von Dokumente, 1926–1935*, ed. Alfred Klein (Berlin: Aufbau-Verlag, 1979), 1:200. On *Berlin Alexanderplatz* as a case study of the reconfiguration of class politics in the Weimar Republic in the context of the rise of what Kracauer referred to as "the salaried masses" (or *die Angestellten*), see Sabine Hake, *Topographies of Class: Modern Architecture and Mass Society in Weimar Berlin* (Ann Arbor: University of Michigan Press, 2008), especially chapter 6.

19. Peter Bürger, *Theory of the Avant-Garde*, trans. Michael Shaw (Minneapolis: University of Minnesota Press, 1984).

20. Bertolt Brecht, "The Modern Theatre Is the Epic Theatre," in *Brecht on Theatre: The Development of an Aesthetic*, ed. John Willett (New York: Hill and Wang, 1964), 34.

21. Ibid.

22. Bertolt Brecht, "The Three-Penny Trial: A Sociological Experiment," in *German Essays on Film*, ed. Richard McCormick and Alison Guenther-Pal (New York: Continuum, 2004), 122–23.

23. Ibid., 123.

24. Brecht, "Modern Theatre," 35.

25. Ibid., 34.

26. Brecht, "Three-Penny Trial," 112.

27. Ibid., 113.

28. Ibid., 114.

29. Ibid., 117.

30. Ibid.

31. Fredric Jameson, *Brecht and Method* (New York: Verso, 1998), 51.

32. Roswitha Mueller, *Bertolt Brecht and the Theory of the Media* (Lincoln: University of Nebraska Press, 1989), 25.

33. On workers' theater in the Weimar Republic, see Gundrun Klatt, *Arbeiterklasse und Theater* (Berlin: Akademie Verlag, 1975).

34. For a comprehensive history of the organizational politics and literary debates within the BPRS, see Helga Gallas, *Marxistische Literaturtheorie: Kontroversen im Bund proletarisch-revolutionärer Schriftsteller* (Neuwied: Hermann Luchterhand Verlag, 1971). The GDR perspective on the BPRS is sketched in Alfred Klein, "Zur Entwicklung der sozialistischen Literatur in Deutschland, 1918–1933," in *Literature der Arbeiterklasse: Aufsätze über die Herausbildung der deutschen sozialistischen Literatur (1918–1933)*, ed. Irmfried Hiebel (Berlin: Aufbau-Verlag, 1976). James F. Murphy situates the BPRS debates in the context of developments in the USSR and the American left in the 1920s and 1930s in *The Proletarian Moment: The Controversy over Leftism in Literature* (Urbana: University of Illinois Press, 1991). Michael Rohrwasser offers a psychoanalytically inflected reading of the works of a number of BPRS authors in his *Saubere Mädel: Starke Genossen—proletarische Massenliteratur?* (Frankfurt am Main: Verlag Roter Stern, 1975). The BPRS had twenty-six local chapters when the Nazi seizure of power ended its legal existence, arresting many members and sending others into exile. Some BPRS members continued to operate illegally, distributing antifascist literature and maintaining contact with the exile centers of Paris and Prague, until the organization was dissolved by the International Bureau of Revolutionary Literature (IBRL) in December 1935. *Lexikon sozialistischer Literatur: Ihre Geschichte on Deutschland bis 1945*, ed. Simone Barck, Silvia Schlenstedt, Tanja Bürgel, Volker Giel, and Dieter Schiller (Stuttgart: Verlag J. B. Meltzer, 1994), 97–102.

35. Many members of the BPRS, including Georg Lukács himself, were writers and intellectuals from southern and eastern Europe, with those who had fled from Hungary after the collapse of the Hungarian Soviet Republic playing a substantial role. This was also the case at the MASCH, or Marxist

Workers' School, under the direction of Anna Seghers's husband, László Radványi, living under the alias Johann-Lorenz Schmidt. On the MASCH, see *Lexikon sozialistischer Literatur*, 322–25, as well as Gabriele Gerhard-Sonnenberg, *Marxistische Arbeiterbildung in der Weimarer Zeit (MASCH)* (Cologne: Pahl-Rugenstein Verlag, 1976).

36. Although organized by the KPD press, the Workers' Correspondence movement was something of a mass phenomenon, and by 1930, the KPD national paper *Rote Fahne* alone had fifteen thousand worker correspondents in 336 factories, and this number does not even account for worker correspondents publishing in regional KPD papers. On the Workers' Correspondence movement in the Weimar Republic, see Simone Barck, "Arbeiterkorrespondenten-Bewegung," in *Lexikon sozialistischer Literatur*, 28–31. Willi Bredel, a metalworker from Hamburg, became one of the most celebrated proletarian-revolutionary writers with his militant reportage novels of the German class struggle, notably *Maschinenwerk N&K* (1930). Already in prison for "literary high treason" when the Nazis took power, he published *Die Prüfung* [The Test], one of the earliest accounts of German concentration camps, upon his release in 1934. Bredel spent the exile in the Soviet Union and served as a commissar in the Ernst-Thälmann Brigade in the Spanish Civil War. Bredel returned to Germany in 1945, where he became an important figure in the cultural and political life of the GDR. *Lexikon socialistischer Schriftsteller*, 79–81.

37. Johannes R. Becher was one of the most influential and interesting figures in the cultural politics of the KPD, the German Popular Front, and later in the GDR, as the founder of the Kulturbund zur Demokratischen Erneuerung Deutschlands (Cultural League for the Democratic Renewal of Germany) and the GDR's first minister of culture. Raised in the bourgeois milieu of prewar Munich, Becher made a name for himself as an Expressionist poet, joining the KPD in the early 1920s and quickly becoming an important functionary in the International Bureau of Revolutionary Literature and chairman of the BPRS in 1928. Becher spent the exile years in the Soviet Union. On Becher, see Jens-Fietje Dwars, *Abgrund des Widerspruchs: Das Leben des Johannes R. Becher* (Berlin: Aufbau-Verlag, 1998).

38. F. C. Weiskopf and Kurt Hirschfeld, "Um den proletarischen Roman," in *Zur Tradition*, 1:211. A Communist journalist and playwright from Prague, Weiskopf settled in Berlin, where he edited the *feuilleton* section of the left-wing *Berlin am Morgen*. Weiskopf spent the exile period in Prague and then the United States, where he was a central figure in holding together connections between the antifascist émigrés. Weiskopf returned to Czechoslovakia after the war, where he served in the diplomatic core before again settling in Berlin in 1953. *Lexikon sozialistischen Literatur*, 517–19.

39. Weiskopf and Hirschfeld, "Um den proletarischen Roman," in *Zur Tradition*, 1:215.

40. Ibid., 1:216.

41. Ibid.

42. Johannes R. Becher, "Antwort eines 'Radikalen' auf den Artikel 'Wir und den Radikalen' von Willy Haas," in *Zur Tradition*, 1:144.

43. Helga Hartung, "Sozialistischer Humanismus—Sozialistischer Realismus," in *Literatur der Arbeiterklasse: Aufsätze über die Herausbildung der deutschen socialistischen Literatur (1918–1933)*, ed. Irmfried Hiebel (Berlin: Aufbau-Verlag, 1976), 644.

44. On Seghers's "Auf dem Weg zur Amerikanischen Botschaft" as an exemplary text of left modernism in the Weimar Republic, see Katie Trumpener, "On the Way to Socialist Realism: Teleology, Subject Formation, and Anna Seghers's 'On the Way to the American Embassy,'" *Rethinking Marxism* 7.3 (1994): 45–52.

45. See "Soviet Factography," special issue, *October* 118 (Fall 2006) and *Russian Futurism Through Its Manifestoes, 1912–1928*, ed. and trans. Anna Lawton and Herbert Eagle (Ithaca, NY: Cornell University Press, 1988), 189–280.

46. Friedrich Wolf, "Art Is a Weapon!" in *Weimar Republic Source Book*, 230. Wolf was a founding member of the BPRS, the author of a number of well-regarded plays during the Weimar Republic and his exile in the Soviet Union, and involved in the proletarian theater movement. Wolf's sons, raised in the Soviet Union, would go on to have influential careers in the GDR, Konrad Wolf as the premier auteur filmmaker of the East German DEFA studio and Markus Wolf as the head of the Stasi's foreign intelligence service. On Wolf, see *Lexikon sozialistischer Literatur*, 530–33.

47. Berta Lask, "Über die Aufgaben der Revolutionären Dichtung [1929]," in *Zur Tradition*, 1:153. Lask allows that the emphasis on proletarian individuality, that is, the positions adopted by RAPP by 1929, is necessarily greater in the Soviet Union because of its progress in building socialism, insisting that it is precisely the pre-revolutionary situation in Germany that calls for the focus on the class itself as a literary protagonist (155).

48. Andor Gábor, "Über proletarisch-revolutionäre Literature [1929]," in *Zur Tradition*, 1:171.

49. Ibid., 1:177.

50. N. Kraus, "Gegen den Ökonomismus in der Literatur," in *Zur Tradition*, 1:203.

51. Murphy, *The Proletarian Moment*, 30–31.

52. "Entwurf zu einem Programm des Bundes proletarisch-revolutionärer Schriftsteller," in *Zur Tradition*, 1:435. The authorship of this work is unclear, although markings on the original text indicate that Becher, Gábor, and Lukács composed it and Becher edited it by hand. *Zur Tradition*, 4:62.

53. Ibid., 1:432.

54. Becher theorized the shift in address from class to mass in an article introducing the draft program laying the basis of a Marxist counterproduction to bourgeois mass literature. "Unsere Wendung [1931]," in *Zur Tradition*, 1:413.

55. On the cultural politics of the SPD before 1914, see H. J. Schulz, *German Socialist Literature, 1860–1914* (Columbia, SC: Camden House, 1993).

56. Georg Lukács, "Tendency or Partisanship," in *Essays on Realism*, ed. Rodney Livingstone, trans. David Fernbach (Cambridge, MA: MIT Press, 1980), 36–37.

57. Ibid., 41.

58. Otto Biha, "The Proletarian Mass Novel," in *The Weimar Republic Source Book*, 239–40.

59. Ibid.

60. On the Red-One-Mark-Novel, see Rohrwasser, *Saubere Mädel*, and Hanno Möbius, "Der rote eine-Marke-Roman," *Archiv für Sozialgeschichte* 14 (1974): 157–212.

61. Johannes R. Becher, "Kühnheit und Begeisterung. Der 1. Mai und unsere Literaturrevolution," in *Zur Tradition*, 1:454.

62. Ibid., 1:120–21.

63. Otto Gotsche defends the actuality of Bredel's novels for proletarian everyday life in his essay "Kritik der anderen—Einige Bemerkungen zur Frage der Qualifikation unserer Literatur" through the recounting of discussions with workers about Bredel's novels and Lukács's critiques of them, prompting a reply by Lukács under the title "Gegen die Spontanitätstheorie in der Literatur." See Alfred Klein, *Im Auftrag ihrer Klasse: Weg und Leistung der deutschen Arbeiterschriftsteller, 1918–1933* (Berlin: Aufbau-Verlag, 1972), 731–40. Gotsche was the author of the novel *Märzstürme*, an account of the so-called March Action uprising in the industrial region around the cities of Halle and Mansfeld, which was the location of the massive Leuna chemical works, a center of Communist militancy in central Germany. The crushing of this proletarian uprising was a turning point in the German revolution. On the so-called March Action, see Broué, *The German Revolution*, 491–504. Following his activities in the antifascist resistance under the National Socialist regime, Gotsche eventually served as the personal secretary of Walter Ulbricht in the GDR. See *Lexikon sozialistischer Literatur*, 176.

64. Georg Lukács, "The Novels of Willi Bredel [1931/2]," in *Essays on Realism*, 24.

65. Ibid., 26.

66. Ibid.

67. Georg Lukács, "Reportage or Portrayal?" in *Essays on Realism*, 45.

68. Ottwalt's 1931 novel *Denn sie wissen was sie tun* [For They Know What They Do] used documentary material to portray the corruption of the German judicial system. Ottwalt's response to Lukács's article is a spirited defense of the reportage as technique and a trenchant critique of Lukács's own aestheticism. Ernst Ottwalt, "Tatsachenroman and Formexperiment," in *Zur Tradition*, vol. 1. Ottwalt, a member of the BPRS, also cowrote, along with Brecht, the screenplay for the Communist feature film *Kuhle Wampe*. Emigrating to the Soviet Union after 1933, he was caught up in the purges and died in a Soviet work camp in 1943. *Lexikon sozialistischer Literatur*, 367–69.

69. Lukács, "Reportage or Portrayal," 74.

70. Willi Bredel, for example, wrote a reply to Lukács's attack on his novels asserting the "absolute legitimacy and correctness of such criticism and the necessity of the further qualitative development of our literature." Willi Bredel, "Einen Schritt weiter: Ein Diskussionsbeitrag über unsere Wendung an der Literaturfront," in *Im Auftrag ihrer Klasse*, 728.

71. Friedrich Albrecht, "Gespräch mit Willi Bredel," *Sinn und Form* 28.2 (1976): 414. See also Bredel's afterword to the reedition of *Maschinenfabrik N&K: Ein Roman aus dem proletarischen Alltag* (Berlin: Dietz Verlag, 1960), 185.

72. Karl Grünberg, *Brennende Ruhr: Roman aus der Zeit des Kapp-Putsches* (Berlin: Aufbau-Verlag, 1959), 7.

73. Hans Marchwitza, "Von der ersten Arbeiterkorrespondenz zur ersten Kurzgeschichte," in *Im Auftrag ihrer Klasse*, 775.

74. Ludwig Turek, "Vorwort zu 'Ein Prolet Erzählt,'" in *Im Auftrag ihrer Klasse*, 678.

75. Otto Gotsche, "Über die Entstehung des Romans 'Märzstürme,'" in *Im Auftrag ihrer Klasse*, 709.

76. Turek, "Vorwort zu 'Ein Prolet Erzählt,'" 679.

77. Gotsche, "Über die Entstehung des Romans 'Märzstürme,'" 712.

78. Thus the GDR critic Alfred Klein, echoing Lukács, describes the failings of proletarian-revolutionary literature precisely in terms of the tendency toward autobiography, as well as the perceived flatness of a style derived from the journalistic report. "Zur Entwicklung der sozialistischen Literatur in Deutschland," 77–79.

79. Eric D. Weitz, *Creating German Communism, 1890–1990: From Popular Protests to Socialist State* (Princeton: Princeton University Press, 1997), 260.

80. Ibid., 257–59.

81. Peukert, *The Weimar Republic*, 152.

CHAPTER 2

1. Beate Messerschmidt, "Neue Wege, von Arbeitern zu erzählen, Hans Marchwitza: *Die Kumiaks*," in *Erfahrung Exil*, 79–80. See also, by the same author, "Zur Entwicklung der ästhetischen Konzeption Hans Marchwitzas am Beispiel der 'Kumiaks,'" *Weimarer Beiträge* 26.8 (1980): 112–29 and "Sozialistische Literatur im Exil, das Beispiel Hans Marchwitza," *Internationales Archiv für Sozialgeschichte der deutschen Literatur* 12 (1987): 213–36. For other critical accounts of *Die Kumiaks*, see Klein, *Im Auftrag ihrer Klasse*, 544–611 and Matthias Bertram, "Literarische Epochendiagnosen der Nachkriegszeit," in *Deutsche Erinnerung: Berliner Beiträge zur Prosa der Nachkriegsjahre (1945–1960)*, ed. Ursula Heukenkamp (Berlin: Erich Schmidt Verlag, 1999), 76–84. Author of the pioneering proletarian-revolutionary novel *Sturm auf Essen*, Marchwitza was already a leading figure of working-class literature during the Weimar Republic (*Sturm auf Essen: Die Kämpfe der Ruhrarbeiter gegen Kapp, Watter und Severing* [Vienna: Internationaler Arbeiter Verlag, 1930]). Marchwitza had been born and raised in the German Polish miners' milieu of Upper Silesia, where he began working in the mines at the age of fourteen, a childhood he describes in his autobiographical novel *Meine Jugend* [My Youth 1947]. In 1910, he migrated to the Ruhr Valley. Politicized through his experiences in World War I and the November revolution, Marchwitza joined the Independent Social Democratic Party of Germany

(USPD) in 1919 and fought with the Red Army of Ruhr against the Kapp Putsch in 1920. That same year, Marchwitza joined the KPD. Blacklisted from the mines in 1924, Marchwitza began writing fiction and poetry for KPD publications, becoming a leading figure in the BPRS with a series of proletarian-revolutionary novels in the early 1930s. Upon the fascist seizure of power, Marchwitza fled to Switzerland and then France. After fighting in Spain in the Chapayev Battalion of International Brigades, Marchwitza returned to Paris and eventually fled to the United States in 1941, where he worked in construction until returning to the Soviet Occupation Zone (SBZ) in 1947. In the GDR, he became an important figure in literature and cultural life. *Lexikon sozialistischer Literatur*, 314–16.

2. The position that Hitler's assumption of power constituted a defeat for the German workers' movement was dismissed politically in the KPD as a Trotskyist position and seen as a sign of "emigration panic" and defeatism. Dieter Schiller, *Der Traum von Hitlers Sturz: Studien zur deutschen Exilliteratur, 1933–1945* (New York: Peter Lang, 2010), 45.

3. Cited in Messerschmidt, "Neue Wege," 80–81. On Marchwitza in Swiss exile, see Werner Mittenzwei, ed., *Exil in der Schweiz*, Kunst und Literatur im antifaschistischen Exil, 1933–1945, Band 2 (Leipzig: Reclam, 1978), 77–82 as well as Jonny Rieger, "*Die Kumiaks*, wie sie entstanden sind," *Büchergilde* (January 1935): 12–14.

4. *Kumpel* is a familiar term among miners in Germany, meaning roughly "pal," or "mate" in British English.

5. Messerschmidt, "Neue Wege," 81.

6. Ibid., 84.

7. On proletarian autobiographies, see Wolfgang Emmerich, ed., *Proletarische Lebensläufe: Autobiographische Dokumente zur Entstehung der Zweiten Kultur in Deutschland*, 2 vols. (Reinbeck bei Hamburg: Rowohlt, 1974–76) and Jürgen Kuczynski, *Probleme der Autobiographie* (Berlin: Aufbau-Verlag, 1983). As Messerschmidt notes, "with the portrayal of a politically ignorant and inexperienced worker whose revolutionary development still lies before him, the pregnant point was found from which Marchwitza could raise the uncomfortable questions regarding the causes of fascism's victory in Germany in relation to his own autobiographical events and experiences" ("Neue Wege," 84).

8. Whereas Bredel's trilogy follows the working-class Benthen family from the Hamburg of the Kaiserreich through the defeats of the twentieth century and then into the founding years of the GDR, Anna Seghers's *The Dead Stay Young* covers the period between 1919 and 1945, linking the family narratives of a number of right-wing *soldateska* with that of the fiancé and son of the Sparticist they murdered on the outskirts of Berlin in January 1919.

9. Julia Hell, *Post-Fascist Fantasies* (Durham, NC: Duke University Press, 1997), 38. On the family novel as socialist literary historiography, see Bertram, "Literarische Epochendiagnosen der Nachkriegszeit."

10. On 1923 as a historical caesura for theories of revolution and everyday life, see John Roberts, *Philosophizing the Everyday: Revolutionary Practice and the Fate of Cultural Theory* (London: Pluto Press, 2006), 56.

11. Carl Schmitt, *Political Theology: Four Chapters on the Concept of Sovereignty*, trans. Georg Schwab (Chicago: University of Chicago Press, 2005).

12. *Die Kumiaks* was originally published in 1934 in Zurich by the Büchergilde-Gutenberg, a Social Democratic subscription-based press, with editions appearing simultaneously with affiliated organizations in Vienna and Prague. Marchwitza revised the novel slightly for its 1948 republication in the Soviet Occupation Zone. *Lexikon sozialistischer Literatur*, 315. For the quote, see also Maxim Gorky, "Soviet Literature," in *Problems in Soviet Literature: Reports and Speeches at the First Soviet Writers' Congress*, ed. H. G. Scott (Westport, CT: Hyperion Press, 1981), 54, 56. Messerschmidt reads the quote as Marchwitza's attempt to claim a socialist realist pedigree for a novel that did not sit easily within the formal categories of this evolving aesthetic. "Sozialistische Literatur im Exil," 225–30.

13. A. A. Zhdanov, "Soviet Literature: The Richest in Ideas, the Most Advanced Literature," in *Problems in Soviet Literature*, 20.

14. Bredel's comments were made in a letter to BPRS critic Andor Gábor, cited in Sylvia Schlenstedt, "Literaturkritik im Lernprozeß," in *Wer schreibt, handelt*, 255. This essay provides a general overview of the novel's reception. Marchwitza in fact found himself, perhaps unknowingly, at the center of the controversy within the BPRS in the context of the shift to the strategy of the Popular Front around 1935. Whereas already in 1934 Johannes R. Becher and others were eager to reach out to "bourgeois" left-wing antifascist authors like Heinrich Mann and Lion Feuchtwanger, others, like Bredel, were concerned that this turn would bring with it the neglect of KPD and proletarian authors like Marchwitza and Bredel himself. In fact, Bredel implied that Becher's own more liberal literary politics were partially to blame for the lack of a clear ideological line in Marchwitza's novel. Bredel also blamed Becher for not bringing Marchwitza to the USSR, which Marchwitza sincerely desired and requested as late as 1939 in a letter to Bredel himself. According to Bredel, Becher discouraged Marchwitza from emigrating to the Soviet Union, telling Marchwitza that he would not be able to make a living there as a writer and would have to mine coal in the Donbas. Schiller, *Der Traum von Hitlers Sturz*, 288–90. For Marchwitza's letter to Bredel, see Willi-Bredel-Archiv, Signatur 3575, 14, Academy of the Arts Literaturarchiv, Berlin.

15. Kurt Kersten, "Bücher von der Ruhr: Hans Marchwitza: 'Die Kumiaks,'" in *Kritik in der Zeit: Antifaschistische Literaturkritik, 1933–1945*, ed. Klaus Jarmatz and Simone Barck (Halle and Leipzig: Mitteldeutscher Verlag, 1981), 365.

16. Rudolf Kern, "Hans Marchwitza: Die Kumaiks,'" in *Im Auftrag ihrer Klasse*, 798.

17. Schlenstedt, "Literaturkritik im Lernprozeß," 254. Anna Seghers specifically cited Marchwitza's novel in her defense of the immediacy of experience in respect to aesthetic production in her letter exchange with Georg Lukács, published in 1939 by the Soviet-sponsored German exile journal *International Literature* (Lukács, "A Correspondence with Anna Seghers," in *Essay on Realism*, 174). Seghers also expressed her dismay at the treatment of the novel in the Communist press in a 1936 letter to Becher. Anna Seghers, *Ich*

erwarte Eure Briefe wie den Besuch der besten Freunde: Briefe, 1924–1952, Werkausgabe V/1, ed. Christiane Zehl-Romero and Almut Giesecke (Berlin: Aufbau-Verlag, 2008), 32–33.

18. Schlenstedt, "Literaturkritik im Lernprozeß," 254–55.

19. Kersten, "Bücher von der Ruhr," 365.

20. Cited in Messerschmidt, "Neue Wege," 86.

21. The German workers' movement in the nineteenth century indeed received naturalism with a certain ambivalence. Popular among proletarian readers and often published in SPD journals, naturalism was also denounced by leading SPD critic Franz Mehring, as it would later be by Georg Lukács, as depicting a frozen world of misery and proletarian creatureliness. "They found the lumpenproletariat in the brothel and the corner bar," Mehring wrote of the naturalists, "but they don't know where the class conscious proletariat is working and fighting" (cited in Murphy, *The Proletarian Moment*, 43; on the naturalism debate in the SPD in the 1880s and 1890s, see Schulz, *German Socialist Literature*, 74–80). This critique of naturalism, which echoes Engels's own objections to Margaret Harkness's East London novel, would be echoed in *Die Linkskurve*, which was at pains to distance itself from the suffering pathos of the older *Arbeiterdichtung* and the naturalism that influenced it. On the *Arbeiterdichtung* of the late nineteenth and early twentieth centuries, see Frank Trommler, *Sozialistische Literatur in Deutschland: Ein historischer Überblick* (Stuttgart: Körner Verlag, 1976). By the early 1930s, figures identified with *Arbeiterdichtung* were moving into the ideological orbit of Nazism. The BPRS energetically condemned *Arbeiterdichtung* as, in the formulation of Johannes R. Becher, "poor people poetry [*Armeleutepoesie*] or sympathy literature [*Mitleidsdichtung*]" ("Unsere Front," in *Zur Tradition*, 1:157). Marchwitza himself identifies Zola as a model for *Die Kumiaks* in his speech at the Paris Congress ("Wir schreiben nur unsere Erfahrungen," in *Zur Tradition*, 1:860), and as we have seen, it was more or less naturalism of which Marchwitza was accused in the KPD reviews.

22. Schlenstedt, "Literaturkritik im Lernprozeß," 256.

23. Klein, *Im Auftrag ihrer Klasse*, 598.

24. Ibid., 579. I am using the term "intellectual physiognomy" here in the sense developed by Lukács in "The Intellectual Physiognomy of Characterization," where he describes this question in terms of the historically constrained, but not entirely determined, "vitality" of the character: "how he confronts a problem, what he accepts as axiomatic, what he seeks to prove and how he proves it, the level of intellectual abstraction he attains, the sources of his examples, what he underplays and how he does so" (*Writer and Critic, and Other Essays*, ed. and trans. Alfred Kahn [London: Merlin Press, 1970], 150). Indeed, if one brackets Lukács's emphasis on the "intellectual," this definition seems very close to Williams's notion of the structure of feeling discussed earlier.

25. This essay will be discussed in detail in the next chapter.

26. Benjamin, "A Chronicle of Germany's Unemployed," 131.

27. Ibid., 128.

28. Ibid., 131.

29. The classic sociological account of the effects of unemployment from this period, originally published in 1933, is Paul Lazarsfeld, Marie Jahoda, and Hans Zeisel, *Die Arbeitslosen von Marienthal: Ein sozingraphischer Versuch über die Wirkungen langdauernder Arbeitslosigkeit* (Frankfurt am Main: Suhrkamp, 1975).

30. Benjamin, "A Chronicle of Germany's Unemployed," 130.

31. Ibid., 133.

32. Anna Seghers, *Die Rettung* (Berlin: Aufbau-Verlag, 1973), 101.

33. This piece was originally published as promotional material for *Die Kumiaks* in the newsletter of the Büchergilde-Gutenberg. Since Marchwitza was prohibited from working or publishing in Switzerland, the article originally appeared credited as "Vom Verfasser der Kumiaks." Quoted in Messerschmidt, "Zur Entwicklung," 117.

34. Ibid.

35. Ibid.

36. Ibid.

37. This journey parallels Marchwitza's own migration from Upper Silesia to the Ruhr before World War I. See Marchwitza, "Wir schreiben nur unsere Erfahrungen," 860–64.

38. Eric D. Weitz provides a concise summary of the state of German agriculture in the interwar years in *Weimar Germany, Crisis and Tragedy* (Princeton: Princeton University Press, 2007), 159–61.

39. "Wissen Sie wer die Kumiaks sind?" This piece was also originally published as promotional material for *Die Kumiaks*. Quoted in Messerschmidt, "Zur Entwicklung," 115–17.

40. Ibid., 116.

41. In the late Weimar Republic, recognizing the strength of the National Socialist German Workers' Party (NSDAP) in the countryside, the BPRS encouraged writers to turn to rural themes. See "Resolution zur Frage der proletarischen und revolutionären Literatur in Deutschland," in *Zur Tradition*, 1:331–33. The most notable novels to emerge from this turn were Anna Seghers's *Der Kopflohn* and Adam Scharrer's *Die Maulwürfe* [The Moles 1933], both of which cover much of the same affective terrain as Marchwitza's novel. In the Marxist theoretical tradition, the peasant has a long history as a trope of the proletariat's bad other. In the *Communist Manifesto*, Marx and Engels famously praised the dynamism of capital for having led to the expansion of the urban population and thus having "rescued a considerable part of the population from the idiocy of rural life" (Karl Marx and Friedrich Engels, "Manifesto of the Communist Party," *The Marx-Engels Reader*, 477). Furthermore, the peasantry functions as the key to Bonapartist dictatorship. Marx writes that dictatorship is the necessary political expression of the ascendancy of this class, which forms a class only insofar as it stands opposed to other classes (Karl Marx, *The Eighteenth Brumaire of Louis Bonaparte* [New York: International Publishers, 1963], 124). The peasantry is embedded in an isolated mode of production, with "no diversity of development, no variety of talent, no wealth of social relationships" (123). Thus the attachment to the land binds the peasant to a reactionary historical orientation, "not his future, but his

past" (125), or what Marx calls the "underside of history" (126). Similarly, Lenin identifies the Russian peasantry at the dawn of the Russian Revolution as a mass caught up in history without realizing it. In his articles on Tolstoy, Lenin identifies a confused peasant structure of feeling, "the pent-up hatred, the ripened striving for a better lot, the desire to get rid of the past—and also the immature dreaming, the political inexperience, the revolutionary flabbiness" (V. I. Lenin, "Leo Tolstoy as the Mirror of the Russian Revolution," *On Literature and Art* [Moscow: Progress Publishers, 1970], 28). For Lenin, the peasantry's commitment to the reactionary utopia of a precapitalist smallholding agrarian society is the key to its stubborn and arbitrary oscillation between rebellion and exaggerated subservience (32).

42. The essay was originally written in 1932 and later included in *Erbschaft dieser Zeit*, published in 1935.

43. Friedrich Engels, *The Housing Question* (Moscow: Progress Publishers, 1970), 13.

44. Ibid., 23–24.

45. See Marx's discussion of the doubled character of free labor, which arises from the separation of the worker from the means of production, be it land or craft tools, in the chapter "The So-Called Primitive Accumulation," in *Capital*, vol. 1, trans. Ben Fowkes (New York: Vintage, 1976), 873–76.

46. Marx, *Eighteenth Brumaire*, 18.

47. Ibid., 23.

48. Here Bloch seems to conflate the traditional Marxist description of this class (shopkeepers, civil servants, and professionals) with the emergent white-collar labor force that Siegfried Kracauer describes as *die Angestellten*, or "the salaried masses," as the English translation of Kracauer's study would have it. Siegfried Kracauer, *The Salaried Masses: Duty and Distraction in Weimar Germany*, trans. Quintin Hoare (New York: Verso Press, 1998).

49. Karl Marx, *Pre-Capitalist Economic Formations*, ed. Eric J. Hobsbawm (New York: International Publishers, 1964), 85.

50. Ibid.

51. Richard Langston's excellent translation of this work, titled *History and Obstinacy* (see introduction, note 27), appeared as the present work was in the final stages of publication. Given that fact, as well as the substantial textual differences between the translation and the German edition, I have taken the German text as my source (with a few exceptions dealing with passages added to the Langston translation and not included in the German text) and provided my own translations.

52. The Kumiak-type can be read as a partially urbanized peasant, the persistence of an older mode of rural proletarian, or what Mary Nolan refers to as "peasant workers," "who identified neither with class nor with craft," and "even those forced to work in industry all their lives often clung to the illusion of returning or commuted to the countryside daily or weekly." Mary Nolan, "Economic Crisis, State Policy, and Working-Class Formation in Germany, 1870–1900," in *Working-Class Formation: Nineteenth-Century Patterns in Western Europe and the United States*, ed. Ira Katznelson and Aristide R. Zolberg (Princeton: Princeton University Press, 1986), 376.

53. Jürgen Kocka, "Problems of Working-Class Formation in Germany: The Early Years, 1800–1875," in *Working-Class Formation*, 320. On the intersections of the displaced peasant and factory discipline, see E. P. Thompson, "Time, Work-Discipline and Industrial Capitalism," *Customs in Common* (London: Merlin Press, 1991) and *The Making of the English Working Class* (New York: Vintage, 1963).

54. Jameson, *Brecht and Method*, 138.

55. Ibid.

56. Mircea Eliade, *The Myth of the Eternal Return, or Cosmos and History*, trans. Willard R. Trask (Princeton: Princeton University Press, 1954), 91. There is of course a more differentiated theorization of the historical role of the peasantry in Marxist thought stretching back at least to Lenin's evocations of the revolutionary peasantry and extending through the present. See, for example, Alexander F. Day, *The Peasant in Post-Socialist China: History, Politics, and Capitalism* (Cambridge: Cambridge University Press, 2013). At any rate, this argument is not one that attempts to fix, in some essentialist manner, peasant and proletarian temporalities, but rather it is an argument about the ways in which these class ascriptions, as ways of describing structures of feeling, are attached to different temporal imaginaries in the particular historical and social context of the German antifascist emigration.

57. Jameson, *Brecht and Method*, 139, 151.

58. Messerschmidt, "Neue Wege," 88.

59. *Kumpel* is a familiar German term for miners.

60. See, for example, Marchwitza's own 1930 novel *Schlacht vor Kohle* [Battle at the Coalface] with its description of barefoot children playing in open sewers, or the claustrophobic descriptions of Berlin's working-class tenements in Klaus Neukrantz's *Barrikaden am Wedding*. Hans Marchwitza, *Schlacht vor Kohle* (Berlin: Verlag Tribüne, 1980), 10; Klaus Neukrantz, *Barrikaden am Wedding* (Berlin: Verlag des Ministeriums für nationale Verteidigung, 1958), 14–18. Of course, here one could also add Franz Kafka's descriptions of the crowded tenements, with their washing lines and hordes of dirty children, where the Court is located in *The Trial*.

61. Heinrich Zille was an illustrator and photographer of working class Berlin around the turn of the century, known for his illustrations for the satirical journal *Simplicissimus*. On the Zille films of the Weimar Republic, see Siegfried Kracauer, *From Caligari to Hitler: A Psychological History of the German Film* (Princeton: Princeton University Press, 1947), especially 143ff. See also Walter Benjamin's essay on the aesthetization of poverty in the Neue Sachlichkeit, "Left-Wing Melancholy," 2:2.

62. W. J. T. Mitchell, "Preface to the Second Edition of *Landscape and Power*: Space, Place, and Landscape," in *Landscape and Power*, 2nd ed., ed. W. J. T. Mitchell (Chicago: University of Chicago Press, 2002), viii.

63. Ibid., xi.

64. Jacques Rancière, *Short Voyages to the Land of the People*, trans. James B. Swenson (Stanford: Stanford University Press, 2003), 125.

65. For Benjamin film is a proving ground of distraction, or *Zerstreuung*, in that it breaks up the very capacity for contemplation by its structuration

through shock effects (in other words, editing and montage). Walter Benjamin, "The Work of Art in the Age of Reproducibility (Third Version)," in *Selected Writings*, 4:268–69. From a more sociological perspective, Kracauer sees the spectacles of mass culture as at once a mimesis and disavowal of the disorder of Weimar society. Siegfried Kracauer, "Cult of Distraction," in *The Mass Ornament*, 327. Following Kracauer, Bloch identifies distraction (translated by the Plaices as intoxication) as the characteristic mode of a petit bourgeoisie seeking "escape from revolution and from death" (HT 26). Where Marchwitza's account of distraction, although he does not employ the term, differs is his location of this mode of perception in the labor process rather than in the effects of mass media, which are curiously absent from *Die Kumiaks*.

66. Rancière, *Short Voyages*, 126.

67. Benjamin, "The Work of Art," 268.

68. On the notion of cultural revolution in the sense that I am employing the term, see Jameson's entry on this topic in *Valences*, 267–78.

69. Theodor W. Adorno, *Aesthetic Theory*, trans. C. Lenhardt (London: Routledge and Kegan Paul, 1984), 163. This discussion of mimesis as a form of stimulus shield is of course initiated by Georg Simmel's well-known 1903 essay, "The Metropolis and Mental Life," in *On Individuality and Social Forms*, ed. Donald N. Levine and Edward A. Shils (Chicago: University of Chicago Press, 1971).

70. Theweleit's notion of the body ego developed here is influenced by the notion of character armor, developed in the late 1920s by Reich, which Theweleit nonetheless criticizes for its attempt to recontain clinical material that clearly exceeds the Oedipal schema back into that schema. Klaus Theweleit, *Male Fantasies*, vol. 1, *Women, Floods, Bodies, History* (Minneapolis: University of Minnesota Press, 1987), 222.

71. Ibid.; Klaus Theweleit, *Male Fantasies*, vol. 2, *Male Bodies: Psychoanalyzing the White Terror*, trans. Stephan Conway (Minneapolis: University of Minnesota Press, 1989).

72. Rohrwasser, *Saubere Mädel*, 26–27.

73. Ibid., 10.

74. Ibid., 10, 55. Susanne Schöberl presents a somewhat more differentiated version of this argument in *Kontinuität im Bruch: Proletarische-revolutionäre Romane in der Weimarer Republik und Betriebsromane in der DDR-Aufbauphase, zwei Beispiele zur Literatur im gesellschaftlichen Prozeß* (Frankfurt am Main: Peter Lang, 1986), arguing that this bracketing of the private is in fact proper to a literature of militant public engagement. Schöberl nevertheless attends more closely than Rohrwasser to those moments where domestic space does become important in proletarian-revolutionary novels.

75. Hannah Arendt, *The Human Condition*, 2nd ed. (Chicago: University of Chicago Press, 1988), 48, 84. Alfred Klein has pointed out that the sensitivity to the creatureliness of the laboring body is a red thread throughout Marchwitza's work, and the notion of a regime of labor that would support human dignity is the key to his socialist conviction. Klein, *Im Auftrag ihrer Klasse*, 545–46.

76. Helmut Lethen, *Cool Conduct: The Culture of Distance in Weimar Germany*, trans. Don Reneau (Berkeley: University of California Press, 2002).

77. A classical primer on cool conduct is of course Bertolt Brecht's "Reader for Those Who Live in Cities" with its injunction to "erase the traces" of intimacy and interiority. Bertolt Brecht, "Ten Poems from a Reader for Those Who Live in Cities," in *Poems*.

78. Lethen, *Cool Conduct*, 204–5.

79. Ibid., 198.

80. Bertram, "Literarische Epochendiagnosen der Nachkriegszeit," 79.

81. Klein, *Im Auftrag ihrer Klasse*, 558.

82. Messerschmidt, "Neue Wege," 93.

83. This is the same vague hope that leads Kumiak to work double shifts, earning him the enmity of his fellow *Kumpels* (K 66).

84. Lüdtke, "What Happened to the 'Fiery Red Glow'?" 227–28.

85. Ibid., 226.

86. Ibid., 227.

87. Ibid., 228.

88. Ibid., 231. Emphasis in the original.

89. The link between *Eigensinn* and political passivity is not limited to Marchwitza but is in fact made in contemporary historical discourse as well by Alf Lüdtke in addressing the relationship of the German proletariat to the National Socialist state. After some initial curiosity, Lüdtke argues, the attitude of German workers toward the Nazis was essentially one of what Lüdtke calls *Hinnehmen*, or acceptance, a sort of wait-and-see position ("What Happened to the 'Fiery Red Glow'?" 199). Even after 1937, when discontent with the National Socialist state among workers grew, it was a passive discontent that was vented in an inward turn, in the withdrawal from politics into the private sphere and attempts to "get hold of something that was their own" (233–34).

90. Christopher Pavesk, "Negt and Kluge's Redemption of Labor," *New German Critique* no. 68 (Spring/Summer 1996): 52. Devin Fore's introduction to the English version of *History and Obstinacy* gives a comprehensive account of these questions.

91. Pavesk, "Negt and Kluge's Redemption of Labor," 147.

92. Thus the mass phenomenon of retreat into private gardening in the aftermath of the defeat of the German revolution of 1918–23 noted by Lüdtke ("What Happened to the 'Fiery Red Glow'?" 206).

93. Michel de Certeau, *The Practice of Everyday Life*, trans. Steven Rendell (Berkeley: University of California Press, 1984), xix.

94. Otto Rühle, *Illustrierte Kultur- und Sittengeschichte des Proletariats* (Frankfurt: Verlag Neue Kritik, 1971), 28.

95. Lüdtke, "What Happened to the 'Fiery Red Glow'?" 228.

96. Pavesk, "Negt and Kluge's Redemption of Labor," 149. On Negt and Kluge's theoretical inflection of the term "proletarian," see Miriam Hansen's foreword to Oskar Negt and Alexander Kluge, *The Public Sphere and Experience*: Toward an Analysis of the Bourgeois and Proletarian Public Sphere,

trans. Peter Labanyi, Jamie Owen Daniel, and Assenka Oksiloff (Minneapolis: University of Minnesota Press, 1993), xvi.

97. Pavesk, "Negt and Kluge's Redemption of Labor," 160.

98. Ibid., 158.

99. This was the official policy of Germany's central government under Wilhelm Cuno when French troops marched into the Ruhr in January 1923 on the pretext of Germany's falling into arrears in its reparations payments under the Treaty of Versailles and with the further goal of separating this economically and strategically important area from the rest of the republic. The German government thus ceased reparations payments and called for a general strike, which the government supported by paying the wages of workers. This was in turn financed by printing more money, which led to the collapse of Germany's currency and unleashed mass unemployment and hunger riots (but also allowed for both the German government and industrial elites to shed much of their debt). As the crippling inflation undermined the government's support of the Ruhr miners, the French brought in their own workers to extract coal from the mines. By the summer of 1923, a new German government under Gustav Stresemann was forced to acknowledge the impasse of the passive resistance campaign and called it off. Peukert, *The Weimar Republic*, 59–61. On the inflation of the crisis years, see ibid., 62ff. For Broué's account of the 1923 crisis and the policies of the KPD toward the French occupation and its hope that the workers' governments in Saxony and Thuringia could be used as springboards for a general insurrection and revolution, see *The German Revolution*, 647–835.

100. Again, in distinction to the conventions of socialist realism, these politically enlightened figures function less as carriers of the plot's action than as an internal commentary on the developments of the novel, in other words as minor characters. Nowhere is it explicitly stated that Saletzki is a member of the Communist Party, but one can tell by his actions. *Kumpels* Lewandowksi and Kruschin also fall into this category. It is not until *Die Heimkehr der Kumiaks* (1952) that these characters emerge with fully articulated Marxist-Leninist personae, taking Peter Kumiak to his first Ernst Thälmann speech. Hans Marchwitza, *Die Heimkehr der Kumiaks* (Berlin: Aufbau-Verlag, 1964), 53ff.

101. Slavoj Žižek, *The Specter Is Still Roaming Around: An Introduction to the 150th Anniversary Edition of the Communist Manifesto* (Zagreb: Bastard Books, 1998), 55.

102. Klein, *Im Auftrag ihrer Klasse*, 599.

103. Bertram, "Literarische Epochendiagnosen der Nachkriegszeit," 79.

104. Klein, *Im Auftrag ihrer Klasse*, 597.

105. Eric L. Santner, *On Creaturely Life: Rilke, Benjamin, Sebald* (Chicago: University of Chicago Press, 2006), 23.

106. Ibid.

107. The revolutionary years of the Weimar Republic were also the years of the white terror discussed by Theweleit in both volumes of *Male Fantasies*. In this context, see most notably Emil Julius Gumbel, *Vier Jahre politischer Mord* (Berlin: Verlag der neuen Gesellschaft, 1922).

108. Benjamin, "On the Concept of History," 4:392.

109. Schmitt, *Political Theology*, 5, 7.

110. Schöberl, *Kontinuität im Bruch*, 81–82; Lüdtke, "What Happened to the 'Fiery Red Glow'?" 206–7.

111. Schöberl, *Kontinuität im Bruch*, 91.

112. Erhard Lucas, *Vom Scheitern der deutschen Arbeiterbewegung* (Frankfurt am Main: Stroemfeld/Roter Stern, 1983), 39–42.

113. Schmitt, *Political Theology*, 13. Santner notes, "creaturely life is just life abandoned to the state of exception/emergency, that paradoxical domain in which law has been suspended in the name of preserving law" (*On Creaturely Life*, 22).

114. Benjamin, "On the Concept of History," 4:392.

115. For this point, I am indebted to John Urang.

116. Santner, *On Creaturely Life*, 23.

117. Walter Benjamin, *The Origin of German Tragic Drama*, trans. John Osborne (New York: Verso, 2003), 89.

118. Negt and Kluge, *The Public Sphere and Experience*, 243.

119. Ibid., 244.

120. Ibid., 245–46. See also Max Horkheimer and Theodor W. Adorno, "The Genesis of Stupidity," in *Dialectic of Enlightenment*, trans. John Cumming (New York: Continuum, 1972), 257–58.

121. Fredric Jameson, "On Negt and Kluge," in *The Phantom Public Sphere*, ed. Bruce Robbins (Minneapolis: University of Minnesota Press, 1993), 51–52. Pavesk echoes this observation, writing, "as Negt and Kluge make clear, obstinacy lives on underground, where it threatens to seize into melancholia" ("Negt and Kluge's Redemption of Labor," 107).

122. Benjamin, "A Chronicle of Germany's Unemployed," 130.

123. Seghers, *Die Rettung*, 144.

124. Benjamin, "On the Concept of History," 4:390.

CHAPTER 3

1. Bock, "Roman im Exil," 7–11. See also Palmier, *Weimar in Exile*, chapter 4, "Exile as Everyday Tragedy."

2. See the series Kunst und Literatur im antifaschistischen Exil 1933–1945 in sieben Bänden, ed. Simone Barck and Klaus Jarmatz (Leipzig: Verlag Philipp Reclam jun., 1989).

3. Fritz Erpenbeck, *Die Emigranten* (Berlin: Verlag Volk und Welt, 1955), 131, 135. Erpenbeck began the novel in Prague in 1934, and it was published in 1938 in the USSR.

4. Bock, "Roman im Exil," 32.

5. Brecht was in fact an editor, along with Willi Bredel and Lion Feuchtwanger, of the Moscow-based journal *Das Wort*, where the Expressionism Debate was carried out. His contributions to this debate, however, were never published at the time, appearing only with the posthumous publication of his "Volkstümlichkeit und Realismus" [Popularity and Realism 1938] in the GDR journal *Sinn und Form* in 1958 and his *Schriften zur Literatur und Kunst* in 1966. See *Lexikon sozialistischer Literatur*, 143.

6. Fredric Jameson, "Reflections on the Brecht-Lukács Debate," in *The Ideologies of Theory*, 434–35.

7. Katerina Clark, *Moscow, the Fourth Rome: Stalinism, Cosmopolitanism, and the Evolution of Soviet Culture, 1931–1941* (Cambridge, MA: Harvard University Press, 2011), 171.

8. Ibid., 5.

9. On the structure of the German Popular Front, see Langkau-Alex, *Die Deutsche Volksfront*, 1:143ff. For the cultural institutions and publishing networks of the German antifascist emigrations, see Ernst Fischer, "Literarische Institutionen des Exils," in *Hansers Sozialgeschichte der deutschen Literatur: Nationalsozialismus und Exil, 1933–1945*, ed. Wilhelm Haefs (Munich: Deutscher Taschenbuch Verlag, 2009).

10. Lion Feuchtwanger, "Größe und Erbärmlichkeit des Exils," in *Exil: Literarische und politische Texte aus dem deutschen Exil, 1933–1945*, ed. Ernst Loewy (Stuttgart: JB Metzlersche Verlagsbuchhandlung, 1979), 595.

11. Heinrich Mann, "Aufgaben der Emigration," in *Exil*, 603.

12. Ibid., 605.

13. The speeches at the First All-Union Writers' Congress are reproduced in *Problems in Soviet Literature*. See also Hans-Jürgen Schmitt and Godehard Schramm, *Sozialistische Realismuskonzeptionen* (Frankfurt: Suhrkamp Verlag, 1974).

14. Sheila Fitzpatrick, *The Cultural Front: Power and Culture in Revolutionary Russia* (Ithaca, NY: Cornell University Press, 1992), 243.

15. Ibid., 250.

16. Ibid., 247.

17. On the cultural pull of the Soviet Union on leftist intellectuals across the world in the mid-1930s and socialist realism as an appeal to bourgeois intellectuals in particular, see Clark, *Moscow*.

18. Theodor W. Adorno, "Letter to W. Benjamin," in *Aesthetics and Politics* (London: Verso, 1977), 123.

19. Boris Groys, *The Total Art of Stalinism: Avant-Garde, Aesthetic Dictatorship, and Beyond*, trans. Charles Rougle (Princeton: Princeton University Press, 1992), 9.

20. Boris Groys, "A Style and a Half: Socialist Realism Between Modernism and Postmodernism," in *Socialist Realism Without Shores*, ed. Thomas Lahusen and Evgeny Dobrenko (Durham, NC: Duke University Press, 1997), 78. Katerina Clark demonstrates how Soviet socialist realist novels both emerge from and reshape the traditions of Russian culture in *The Soviet Novel: History as Ritual* (Bloomington: Indiana University Press, 1981).

21. Groys, "A Style and a Half," 78.

22. Ibid., 79, 80.

23. Leonid Heller, "A World of Prettiness: Socialist Realism and Its Aesthetic Categories," in *Socialist Realism Without Shores*, 56–57.

24. Fore, *Realism After Modernism*, 244.

25. Ibid., 247.

26. Ibid.

27. Clark, *Soviet Novel*, 40.

28. For a discussion of the role of Lukács and the German émigrés in the USSR in the formation of a Popular Front discourse, see Clark, *Moscow*, chapter 4.

29. Simone Barck, "Die Mission des Dichters, 1934," in *Wer schreibt, handelt*, 520.

30. On the Paris congress, see Johannes R. Becher, *Paris 1935: Erster Internationaler Schriftstellerkongreß zur Verteidigung der Kultur*, ed. Alfred Klein (Berlin: Akademie-Verlag, 1982). See also Wolfgang Klein and Silvia Schlenstedt, "Wirkungstrategien auf dem Pariser Schriftstellerongreß 1935," in *Wer schreibt, handelt.*

31. Clark, *Moscow*, 178.

32. Ibid.

33. Ibid., 5.

34. Becher, *Paris 1935*, 177, 178.

35. Ibid., 174.

36. Ibid., 180.

37. Klein and Schlenstedt, "Wirkungstrategien auf dem Pariser Schriftstellerongreß 1935," 548.

38. Clark, *Moscow*, 198–99. GDR critics see less of a split with the avant-garde than a critical overcoming of avant-gardism in the arts. Klein and Schlenstedt, "Wirkungstrategien auf dem Pariser Schriftstellerongreß 1935," 536–38.

39. Klein and Schlenstedt, "Wirkungstrategien auf dem Pariser Schriftstellerongreß 1935," 552–53.

40. There is a copious literature on the so-called Brecht-Lukács debate, or Expressionism Debate. Among the better accounts in English is the classic collection of essays by Theodor W. Adorno et al., *Aesthetics and Politics*. See also Eugene Lunn, *Marxism and Modernism: An Historical Study of Lukács, Brecht, Benjamin and Adorno* (Berkeley: University of California Press, 1982). Important German work on this debate includes the collection edited by Hans-Jürgen Schmitt, *Die Expressionismus-Debatte: Materialien zu einer marxistischen Realismuskonzeption* (Stuttgart: Suhrkamp, 1973). See also, from a GDR perspective, Werner Mittenzwei, ed., *Dialog und Kontroverse mit Georg Lukács* (Leipzig: Reclam, 1973) and Schiller, *Der Traum von Hitlers Sturz.*

41. The Expressionism Debate was also a vehicle for importing key concepts and positions from the antiformalism campaigns in literature and art that paralleled the Great Purges from 1936 to 1939 in the Soviet Union. Alexander Stephan, *Die deutsche Exilliteratur, 1933–1945* (Munich: C. H. Beck, 1979), 161; Pike, *Deutsche Schriftsteller im sowjetischen Exil*, 388; Clark, *Moscow*, 210–12.

42. Georg Lukács, "Expressionism: Its Significance and Decline," in *Essays on Realism.*

43. Ibid., 93. The USPD split from the SPD in 1916 on the issue of parliamentary support for World War I. A majority of the USPD joined with the KPD in 1920, whereas the remainder of the party rejoined the SPD in 1924.

44. Ibid., 96.

45. Alfred Kurella had already made a name for himself as a leading KPD functionary and publicist in the Weimar Republic. Kurella spent his exile in the USSR, where he served as secretary to Comintern leader Georgi Dimitrov before returning to the GDR, where he remained until his death a staunch defender of the orthodox cultural line against modernism and decadence in the arts. See *Lexikon sozialistischer Literatur*, 274–76.

46. Palmier, *Weimar in Exile*, 81–82.

47. Ernst Bloch, "Discussing Expressionism," in *Aesthetics and Politics*, 17. Schiller's account of the debate draws out the degree to which German antifascist émigrés in Paris and Prague were alienated by its tone and direction, while many German intellectuals in Moscow also felt that the debate was unhelpful and should be cast in the more productive terms of realism and popularity, which both Lukács and Fritz Erpenbeck attempted to do through their interventions. At the same time, Schiller shows how Erpenbeck, who was the de facto editor of *Das Wort* in light of Bredel's absence from Moscow during his service in the Spanish Civil War, hoped to use this debate both to export Soviet literary positions to the west and to "draw out" Brecht, whom he saw as influencing the arguments of Bloch and Eisler. Brecht, of course, did respond to the polemics of Lukács in particular, but these responses remained unpublished until after Brecht's death. Schiller, *Der Traum von Hitlers Sturz*, 352–58. Brecht's responses to Lukács will be discussed in the next section and in Chapter 5. Erpenbeck would return to the GDR with the group around Walter Ulbricht to participate in the theatrical life of the new socialist state as a constant antagonist of Brecht and his circle, before turning in the 1960s to writing detective novels. *Lexikon sozialistischer Literatur*, 138–39.

48. Bernhard Ziegler, "Nun ist dieser Erbe zuende," in *Zur Tradition*, 2:390.

49. Ibid., 2:396–99.

50. Ibid., 2:399–400.

51. Ernst Bloch and Hanns Eisler, "Avantgarde-Kunst und Volksfront," in *Zur Tradition*, 2:401.

52. Ibid., 2:406.

53. Ibid., 2:404.

54. Ibid., 2:406.

55. Ibid., 2:407.

56. Ernst Bloch and Hanns Eisler, "Die Kunst zu erben," in *Zur Tradition*, 2:411.

57. Ibid., 2:412.

58. Ibid., 2:414.

59. Ibid., 2:415.

60. Bloch, "Discussing Expressionism," 20.

61. Hans Günther, "Erbschaft dieser Zeit?" *Internationale Literatur* 3 (1936): 101. Cited in David C. Durst's excellent discussion of *Heritage of Our Times*, in David C. Durst, *Weimar Modernism: Philosophy, Politics, and Culture in Germany, 1918–1933* (New York: Lexington Books, 2004), 1–32. Hans Günther was a KPD publicist and functionary who had already been delegated to Moscow in 1932 to serve as the representative of the BPRS to

the IBRL. He was the author of one of the KPD's few attempts at a rigorous theorization of Nazi ideology, *Der Herren eigener Geist: Die Ideologie des Nationalsozialismus* [Of the Gentleman's Own Mind: The Ideology of National Socialism 1935]. Arrested as a Trotskyite in 1936, Günther died in a Soviet transit camp. *Lexikon sozialistischer Literatur*, 185.

62. Bloch, "Discussing Expressionism," 22.

63. Ibid.

64. Bernard Ziegler, "Schlußwort," in *Zur Tradition*, 2:574.

65. Fritz Erpenbeck, "Volkstümlichkeit," in *Zur Tradition*, 2:604–5.

66. Ibid., 2:608.

67. Ibid., 2:58.

68. Georg Lukács, "A Correspondence with Anna Seghers," in *Essay on Realism*. On the Seghers-Lukács correspondence, see also Dieter Schiller, "'Etwas Anständiges, das auch was Wind macht': Zu Anna Seghers' Briefwechsel mit der Redaktion der Zeitschrift 'Das Wort,'" in *Der Traum von Hitlers Sturz*; Kurt Batt, "Erlbenis des Umbruchs und harmonische Gestalt: Der Dialog zwischen Georg Lukács und Anna Seghers," in *Dialog und Kontroverse mit Georg Lukács*.

69. Bock, "Roman im Exil," 51.

70. Palmier, *Weimar in Exile*, 339. In addition to Bloch's *Heritage of Our Times*, the most ambitious contemporary attempt to grasp fascism as a mass social phenomenon is Wilhelm Reich, *The Mass Psychology of Fascism*, trans. Mary Boyd Higgins (New York: Farrar, Straus and Giroux, 1970).

71. Stephan, *Die deutsche Exilliteratur*, 195–204. See also Hans Dahlke, *Geschichtsroman und Literaturkritik im Exil* (Berlin: Aufbau-Verlag, 1976).

72. Georgi Dimitroff, *Against Fascism and War* (New York: International Publishers, 1986), 5–6. Emphasis in the original.

73. Ibid., 76.

74. Ibid.

75. David Clarke, "Introduction: Place in Literature," in *The Politics of Place in Post-War Germany: Essays in Literary Criticism*, ed. David Clarke and Renate Rechtien (Lewiston, ME: Edwin Mellen Press, 2009), 18.

76. Blickle, *Heimat*, 3. On the concept of *Heimat* in German culture, see also Alon Confino, *The Nation as a Local Metaphor: Württemberg, Imperial Germany, and National Memory, 1871–1918* (Chapel Hill: University of North Carolina Press, 1997) and Elizabeth Boa and Rachel Palfreyman, *Heimat: A German Dream, Regional Loyalties and National Identity in German Culture, 1890–1990* (Oxford: Oxford University Press, 2000), as well as Karl Weber, "Heimat," *Historisch-kritisches Wörterbuch des Marxismus* (Hamburg: Argument Verlag, 2004).

77. Marx and Engels, "Manifesto of the Communist Party," 488. Translation slightly altered.

78. Adam Scharrer, *Vaterlandslose Gesellen* (Berlin: Aufbau-Verlag, 1960), 164.

79. Cited in Weber, "Heimat," 2.

80. Ernst Bloch, *The Principle of Hope*, vol. 3, trans. Neville Plaice, Stephen Plaice, and Paul Knight (Cambridge, MA: MIT Press, 1995), 1376.

81. Weber, "Heimat," 2.

82. Blickle, *Heimat*, 142.

83. Cited in Messerschmidt, "Zur Entwicklung," 117.

84. Ibid.

85. Ibid.

86. Ibid.

87. Willi Bredel, *Die Prüfung* (Berlin: Aufbau-Verlag, 1976), 207.

88. Bertolt Brecht, *Journals, 1934–1955*, trans. Hugh Rorrison (New York: Routledge, 1993), 136.

89. See V. I. Lenin, "Two Cultures in Every National Culture," in *The Lenin Anthology*, ed. Robert Tucker (New York: W. W. Norton, 1975).

90. For a good account of Bloch's theory of noncontemporaneity and his analysis of fascism as a political synthesis of the multiple class time scales of Weimar Germany, see Anson Rabinbach, "Unclaimed Heritage: Ernst Bloch's *Heritage of Our Times* and the Theory of Fascism," *New German Critique* 11 (Spring 1977): 5–21.

91. Johannes R. Becher, "Das Große Bündnis," in *Zur Tradition*, 1:735.

92. Bertolt Brecht, "Five Difficulties in Writing the Truth," in *Brecht on Art and Politics*, ed. Tom Kuhn and Steve Giles (London: Methuen, 2003), 149.

93. Bertolt Brecht, "Remarks on an Essay," in *Aesthetics and Politics*, 79.

94. Fore, *Realism After Modernism*, 148.

95. Ibid., 176.

96. For two good accounts of the anachronistic status of Benjamin's essay, coming as it did after the substantial foreclosure of the left avant-garde techniques he is advocating, see Maria Gough, "Paris, Capital of the Soviet Avant-Garde," *October* 101 (Summer 2002): 53–83, as well as Clark, *Moscow*, chapter 1, especially pp. 43–50. On Tretyakov and Soviet factography, see special issue on Soviet Factography, ed. Devin Fore, *October* 118 (Fall 2006).

97. Eagleton, *Sweet Violence*, 201.

98. While Lukács agreed with Döblin that there could be no hard line between the historical novel and the novel proper, he did take issue with the other thesis of Döblin's essay on the historical novel, which is that the historical novel is irreducibly partisan at the cost of historical accuracy. For Lukács, such thinking partakes of an artificial separation between partisanship and truth. See Lukács, *The Historical Novel*, 274. For Döblin's position, see "Der historische Roman und wir," in *Aufsätze zur Literatur.*

99. Agnes Heller, "History and the Historical Novel in Lukács," in *The Modern German Historical Novel: Paradigms, Problems, Perspectives*, ed. David Roberts and Philip Thomson (New York: Berg, 1991), 27.

100. As Chapter 5 of this volume argues, Brecht's *Mother Courage and Her Children* is an attempt to apply the techniques of epic theater to the historical novel.

101. See Fredric Jameson, "A Monument to Radical Instants," foreword to Weiss, *The Aesthetics of Resistance*, 1:xviii, xx.

102. Georg Lukács, "Narrate or Describe? A Preliminary Discussion of Naturalism and Formalism," in *Writer and Critic*, 122.

103. See Bertram, "Literarische Epochendiagnosen der Nachkriegszeit," 61.

CHAPTER 4

1. Cited in Dorothy Rosenberg's afterword to Anna Seghers, *The Seventh Cross*, trans. James A. Galston (Boston: David R. Godine, 2004), 408. Unless otherwise noted, citations in this chapter follow this translation. The standard edition of the novel is Anna Seghers, *Das siebte Kreuz: Roman aus Hitler-deutschland*, Werkausgabe I/4 (Berlin: Aufbau-Verlag, 2000).

2. The authoritative biographical work on Seghers is Christiane Zehl Romero, *Eine Biographie, 1900–1947* (Berlin: Aufbau-Verlag, 2000). Still among the best presentations of Seghers's work is Kurt Batt, *Anna Seghers: Versuch über Entwicklung und Werke* (Leipzig: Reclam, 1980). Alexander Stephan gives a detailed and systematic account of the composition, reception, construction, and adaptations of *The Seventh Cross* in his book-length *Anna Seghers "Das siebte Kreuz": Welt und Wirkung eines Romans* (Berlin: Aufbau-Verlag, 1997).

3. Seghers took a lead in the refounding of the writers' association Schutzverband deutscher Schriftsteller im Ausland (SDS) in response to the book burnings in Germany in 1933, acting as the coordinator of the BPRS in western Europe and participating in both the movement for a German Popular Front and the International Writers' Conferences for the Defense of Culture in 1935 and 1937. In addition, Seghers was a regular contributor to exile journals like *Neue deutsche Blätter, Das Wort*, and *Internationale Literatur* as well as to the French press. On Seghers's exile years in Paris, see Zehl Romero, *Eine Biographie*, 270–381 as well as Alexander Stephan, *Anna Seghers im Exil: Essays, Texte, Dokumente* (Bonn: Bouvier Verlag, 1993). On the German literary emigration in Paris more broadly, see Palmier, *Weimar in Exile*, as well as Dieter Schiller et al., *Exil in Frankreich*, Kunst und Literatur im antifaschistischen Exil, 1933–1945, Band 7 (Leipzig: Reclam, 1981). On Seghers's collaboration with exile journals, see Schiller, *Der Traum von Hitlers Sturz*, 41–64, 517–36. Seghers would later find refuge in Mexico City, participating in the Heinrich-Heine-Klub and the Bewegung Freies Deutschland before returning to East Berlin in 1947.

4. Cited in Rosenberg, afterword, 408.

5. Numerous sources recount the devastating impact of the Hitler-Stalin Pact on German émigrés, and this in political, moral, and material terms. For German Communists in the Soviet Union, many of whom had been caught up in the Great Purges of the mid-1930s, the pact meant being handed back over to the Nazis. See Pike, *Deutsche Schriftsteller im sowjetischen Exil*, 352–416. For German Communists in France, the pact meant that suddenly they were classified as enemy aliens and interned. See Palmier, *Weimar in Exile*, 436–42. Seghers's 1944 novel *Transit* is a fictionalized account of the chaotic circumstances surrounding the attempts of émigrés of various nations to escape Europe ahead of Hitler's advancing armies. Although the Hitler-Stalin Pact is not given much treatment in the book, Seghers's sense of the pact, which she publicly supported, can be perhaps extrapolated from the novel's dominant

trope of *im Stich lassen*, or to leave someone in the lurch. Anna Seghers, *Transit*, Werkausgabe I/5 (Berlin: Aufbau-Verlag, 2001). For Seghers's escape from occupied Europe, see Zehl Romero, *Eine Biographie*, 347–81 as well as Seghers's letters to F. C. Weiskopf and Wieland Herzfelde from 1939 to 1941 in Anna Seghers, *Briefe, 1924–1952*.

6. Cited in Rosenberg, afterword, 414.

7. The novel was eventually adapted as a film by MGM studios, and excerpts from the book appeared in venues from the left-wing *New Masses* to the Book-of-the-Month Club. Critical reception in the United States, which had entered the war with Germany a year before, was generally positive, empathizing the book's antifascist humanism while playing down the Communist politics of its author. Stephan provides a detailed account of the U.S. reception of the novel (*Anna Seghers im Exil*, 208–80). Reception in Communist circles was also enthusiastic, although Lukács would write of the novel in his 1950 *Deutsche Literatur im Zeitalter des Imperialismus* [German Literature in the Epoch of Imperialism], "the deep Wherefore, the development of its social-historical meaning out of individual experiences, relationships, conflicts of living people remains here as well concealed behind an—to be sure poetically first class—veil." Friedrich Albrecht, "Anna Seghers in der Literaturkritik des Exils," *Bemühungen: Arbeiten zum Werk von Anna Seghers, 1965–2004* (Frankfurt am Main: Peter Lang, 2005), 318.

8. Everyday life had been a central concern of Seghers throughout her career. See, for example, "Revolutionärer Alltag," her 1927 review of Fydor Gladkov's socialist realist classic *Cement* in *Aufsätze, Ansprachen, Essays 1927–1953*, Gesammelte Werke in Einzelausgaben XIII (Berlin: Aufbau-Verlag, 1984), 5–6.

9. *Lexikon sozialistischer Literatur*, 432.

10. Fehervary, *Anna Seghers*, 95. As Fehervary points out, Seghers's husband, László Radványi, had been part of the Budapest Sunday circle led by Lukács in 1918 and had played a role in the Soviet Republic. As an exile in Germany, Radványi earned a doctorate at the University of Heidelberg on chiliasm in the work of Karl Jaspers. *Die Gefährten* thus features thinly fictionalized accounts of the postwar experiences of members of this circle, including Lukács, Karl Mannheim, Radványi himself, and Bela Balász. Fehervary argues that the intellectual diaspora following from the defeat of the Hungarian Soviet Republic is key to understanding Seghers's work in the Weimar Republic, and it certainly goes a long way in explaining what might otherwise seem a prophetic dwelling on exile and defeat in Seghers's early work (8).

11. Batt, *Anna Seghers*, 62–63.

12. For the notion of a "moderate modernism" in *The Seventh Cross*, see Stephan, *Welt und Wirkung*, 79–93. In this sense, Seghers's novel can be seen as an example also of the kind of "vernacular modernism" theorized by Hansen in "The Mass Production of the Senses."

13. Stephan, *Welt und Wirkung*, 83.

14. Cited in Rosenberg, afterword, 409.

15. Bernard Spies, "Kommentar," in *Das siebte Kreuz*, 474.

16. Ibid., 455. See also Stephan, *Welt und Wirkung*, 42.

17. See Batt, *Anna Seghers*, 42–43; Stephan, *Welt und Wirkung*, 63–64, 74; Zehl Romero, *Eine Biographie*, 261–62, 271.

18. For example, the New Historicism in the English-speaking academy or the German turn toward *Alltagsgeschichte* identified with figures like Jürgen Kuczynski and Alf Lüdtke; Stephan, *Welt und Wirkung*, 10.

19. Ibid., 11.

20. Stephan details Seghers's use of oral testimony from friends and refugees from Germany, newspaper articles, and other reports as materials for the book. Stephan, *Welt und Wirkung*, 22–24. See also Spies, "Kommentar," 453. Seghers's more direct intervention into the Expressionism Debate was her open letter to Georg Lukács, published in 1939 in *Internationale Literatur*. On the Seghers-Lukács correspondence, see also Schiller, "'Etwas Anständiges,'" in *Der Traum von Hitlers Sturz* and Batt, "Erlebnis des Umbruchs und harmonische Gestalt."

21. On this point, see Fredric Jameson, "The Experiments of Time: Providence and Realism," in *The Novel*, vol. 2, *Forms and Themes*, ed. Franco Moretti (Princeton: Princeton University Press, 2006).

22. For Seghers's relationship to the Popular Front, see Zehl Romero, *Eine Biographie*, 282–304 and Batt, *Anna Seghers*, 106–19.

23. Georg Lukács, "A Correspondence with Anna Seghers," in *Essays on Realism*. Lukács gives the example of mistaking the "essence of capitalism in lying in monetary circulation" rather than the extraction of surplus value in production (177).

24. Lukács, "A Correspondence with Anna Seghers," 170.

25. Ibid., 186.

26. Ibid., 193.

27. Seghers, "Volk und Schriftsteller," in Seghers, *Aufsätze, Ansprachen, Essays 1927–1953*, 116.

28. Benjamin, "On the Concept of History," 4:390. Bettina Engelmann makes the argument that the kind of mimetic faculty, or capacity for recognition of non-sensuous similarities, that Benjamin associates with the chronicle as an epic mode is in fact at the basis of the modernity of Germany's exile literature. See Engelmann, *Poetik des Exils*.

29. Benjamin, "A Chronicle of Germany's Unemployed," 131.

30. Massey, *Space, Place, and Gender*, 5.

31. Seghers was an avid filmgoer, and Zehl Romero makes a compelling argument for the influence of filmic montage on Seghers's compositional style (*Eine Biographie*, 218, 265).

32. Tom Gunning, *The Films of Fritz Lang: Allegories of Vision and Modernity* (London: BFI, 2000), 177, 180.

33. Edward Dimendberg, "From Berlin to Bunker Hill: Urban Space, Late Modernity, and Film Noir in Fritz Lang's and Joseph Losey's *M*," *Wide Angle* 19.4 (October 1997): 70, 72.

34. Anton Kaes, "The Cold Gaze: Notes on Mobilization and Modernity," *New German Critique* 59 (Spring–Summer 1999): 105.

35. Ernst Jünger, "Total Mobilization," in *The Heidegger Controversy: A Critical Reader*, ed. Richard Wolin (Cambridge, MA: MIT Press), 126, 136.

36. Ibid., 128. Seghers was very much aware of Jünger's essay, as is evidenced by her exhortation for a militant Communist ideological struggle against fascism in a 1938 essay: "there, where fascism begins its total mobilization, namely in people's heads, we must be there before it is, with the total mobilization of forces of a completely different order." Seghers, "Und jetzt muss man arbeiten," in *Aufsätze, Ansprachen, Essays 1927–1953* , 68. Similarly, Benjamin saw Jünger's essay as symptomatic of what he conceived of as modern industrial labor and war as a "slave revolt of technology" (312), opposing this to Jünger's battle of material to the only necessary struggle: "the one, fearful last chance to correct the incapacity of peoples to order their relationships to one another in accord with the relationship they possess to nature through their technology." The horizon of this struggle would be technology as a "key to happiness" rather than a "fetish of doom," and this discovery must in turn be used to "transform this war into a civil war." Walter Benjamin, "Theories of German Fascism," in *Selected Writings*, vol. 2, part 1, 320–21.

37. Henri Lefebvre, *The Production of Space*, trans. Donald Nicholson Smith (Oxford: Blackwell, 1991), 38–39.

38. Dimendberg, "From Berlin to Bunker Hill," 74. On abstract space, see Lefebvre, *The Production of Space*, especially 48, 281ff.

39. Dimendberg, "From Berlin to Bunker Hill," 70.

40. Gunning, *The Films of Fritz Lang*, 180.

41. Ibid., 212.

42. De Certeau, *The Practice of Everyday Life*, 115–16.

43. Ibid., 117.

44. Ibid., 119.

45. Ibid., 126.

46. Stephan, *Welt und Wirkung*, 135. As Stephan points out, the KPD's own lack of preparation for illegality was a factor in the party's vulnerability to Nazi terror (140–41).

47. Jameson, "Monument to Radical Instants," xxx–xxxi. This spatial imaginary of the room or the cell and the map is not particular to Weiss's novel, or indeed to Seghers, but is a shared characteristic of much of the resistance literature of this period, exemplified by Willi Bredel's novel about political prisoners in the early days of the Nazi terror, *Die Prüfung*, and Jan Petersen's *Unsere Straße* [Our Street 1936], which narrates the daily lives of the antifascist underground in Berlin in the same period (*Unsere Straße: Eine Chronik, geschrieben im Herzen des faschistischen Deutschlands, 1933/34* [Berlin: Aufbau-Verlag, 1974]).

48. Bertolt Brecht, *The Mother*, trans. Lee Baxandall (New York: Grove Press, 1965), 105.

49. Erika Haas, "Heimat und Vaterland: Beobachtungen und Überlegungen zum Stellenwert im Werk von Anna Seghers," *Argonautenschiff: Jahrbuch des Anna-Seghers-Gesellschaft* 8 (1999): 129. *Das Vertrauen* [Trust 1968] was of course the title of Seghers's final novel, a continuation of her 1959 novel *Die Entscheidung* [The Decision 1959], an ambitious account of the postwar period culminating in the riots of June 17, 1953. On friendliness, see Walter

Benjamin, "Commentary on Poems by Brecht," in *Selected Works*, 4:247–48. Benjamin is writing here of Brecht's exile poem, "Legend of the Origin of the Book *Tao-te-Ching* on Lao-tzu's Road into Exile."

50. Spies, "Kommentar," 460.

51. Giorgio Agamben, *Homo Sacer, Sovereign Power and Bare Life*, trans. Daniel Heller-Roazen (Stanford: Stanford University Press, 1998), 175.

52. Michel Foucault, "Of Other Spaces," in *Architecture Culture, 1943–1968*, ed. Joan Ockman (New York: Rizzoli, 1993), 422.

53. Ibid.

54. Seghers, "Deutschland und wir," in *Aufsätze, Ansprachen, Essays 1927–1953*, 92.

55. On the "wild camp" at Osthofen, see Stephan, *Welt und Wirkung*, 149–207. Stephan gives a thick historical account of the Osthofen KZ near Mainz that Seghers was aware of from her various sources inside Germany and in the exile press but also remarks that in certain ways, Seghers's Westhofen is closer to Dachau than to Osthofen in its brutality (197).

56. Foucault, "Of Other Spaces," 424.

57. In "Amusement Co., Horror, Third Reich," Bloch gives an account of the utopian valences that have attached themselves to the term "Third Reich" since the peasant revolts of the Middle Ages, noting that in Hitler's Germany, "age-old regions of utopia are thus being occupied with St. Vitus dancers" (HT 59).

58. In "Deutschland und wir," Seghers writes, "Germany: that is the concentration camps, fuller than ever, more imperiled than ever. What is the meaning of our freedom if we do not insist on naming again and again the nameless, we who can speak and can write. There, behind barbed wire the future teaching corps of the German nation is being formed, under consistent threat, in mortal danger, Germans, sufficiently proven to 'reeducate' the German youth" (94).

59. Jameson, "The Experiments of Time," 109.

60. Ibid.

61. Lukács, "A Correspondence with Anna Seghers," 179. This is in essence the Marxist critique of de Certeau, which John Roberts formulates by giving de Certeau his due for having developed a theory of the micropolitical acts of recoding and appropriating the structures of domination embedded in the everyday through discrete tactical "ways of operating" but then going on to point out that "the subaltern voice" thus theorized "is divorced from any materialist analysis of its social base and therefore from an assessment of collective levels of class consciousness." Roberts, *Philosophizing the Everyday*, 97. See also de Certeau, *The Practice of Everyday Life*, xix.

62. Jameson, "The Experiments of Time," 114.

63. Seghers, "Deutschland und wir," 91.

64. Anna Seghers, "Vaterlandsliebe," in *Aufsätze, Ansprachen, Essays 1927–1953*, 35. The central German uprising to which Seghers refers is the March Action in 1921.

65. Seghers, "Deutschland und wir," 95.

66. Haas, "Heimat und Vaterland," 123.

67. As we have already mentioned, the generation of writers who "went aground" on the post-1815 German restoration was an important touchstone for Seghers, and she also returned repeatedly in her exile writings and publicity to the Mainz Republic as a moment where German history could have taken another path. See "Freies Deutschland 1792," in *Aufsätze, Ansprachen, Essays 1927–1953*.

68. Batt, *Anna Seghers*, 128.

69. Spies, "Kommentar," 464.

70. Ibid.

71. Ibid., 465.

72. Seghers, "Volk und Schriftsteller," 117.

73. Haas, "Heimat und Vaterland," 129.

74. Seghers, "Volk und Schriftsteller," 120.

75. Walter Benjamin, "On the Image of Proust," in *Selected Writings*, vol. 2, part 1, 238.

76. Edward S. Casey, "How to Get from Space to Place in a Fairly Short Stretch of Time," *Getting Back into Place: Toward a Renewed Understanding of the Place-World* (Bloomington: Indiana University Press, 2009), 327, 329.

77. Ibid., 339–40.

78. Ibid., 328.

79. Sigmund Freud, "The 'Uncanny,'" in *Psychological Writings and Letters*, ed. Sander L. Gilman (New York: Continuum, 1995), 121.

80. Blickle, *Heimat*, 55.

81. On this point, see Johannes von Moltke, *No Place Like Home: Locations of Heimat in German Cinema* (Berkeley: University of California Press, 2005), 12–13.

82. Seghers, "Deutschland und wir," 91.

83. Benjamin, "On the Concept of History," 4:392.

84. Von Moltke, *No Place Like Home*, 14.

85. Roberts, *Philosophizing the Everyday*, 63.

86. Benjamin, "On the Concept of History," 4:391.

87. Roberts, *Philosophizing the Everyday*, 60–61.

88. Ibid., 67.

89. If, as Alf Lüdtke programmatically argues, "the 'objective' methods of production and domination always also become 'subjective' ways of life" (cited in Stephan, *Welt und Wirkung*, 11), the question that Seghers's novel seems to be posing is what these "subjective ways of life" might reveal about the deeper social and historical genealogies of the "objective" strategies of National Socialist rule on the one hand and of the incapacity of the German workers' movement to contest this rule on the other. The question of the larger historical particularity of a given constellation of everyday life and its modes of differentiation and connection to those larger political, economic, and social structures that form both its "outside" and its substratum is thus only put off in this formulation, or in other words, this remains the problem to be solved.

90. Thus, in a debate with contemporary philosophers of communism, Slavoj Žižek points out that the true question confronting a politics of the multitude is less how to free its flows from the structural totality that attempts

at all points to canalize it but rather "why do immediately produced relations still need the mediating role of capitalist relations?" A similar question, obviously, could be asked about political domination. Slavoj Žižek, "How to Begin from the Beginning," in *The Idea of Communism*, ed. Costas Douzinas and Slavoj Žižek (New York: Verso, 2010), 223.

91. Benjamin, "On the Concept of History," 4:402.

92. Ibid., 4:404. Fehervary, *Anna Seghers*, 155. Fehervary makes a compelling argument that Benjamin's work from this period, including "The Storyteller" and the theses on the concept of history, were strongly influenced by Seghers. Noting the many intertextual parallels between the theses and *The Seventh Cross*, Fehervary points out that the first chapter of the novel, which contains this description of the *limes* that Benjamin seems to be quoting in his theses, appeared in serialized form in *Internationale Literatur* during the summer of 1939, before Benjamin began his theses in the winter of 1940 (155–64).

93. Benjamin, "On the Concept of History," 4:390.

94. Ibid., 4:403.

95. Bernard Spies, "Woher kommen die Geschichten her?—Wirklichkeitserfahrung, gesellschaftliche Zielvorstellungen und die Ästhetik des Erzählens bei Anna Seghers," *Argonautenschiff* 10 (2001): 133.

96. Ibid., 132.

97. Ibid.

98. Bertolt Brecht, "Short Description of a New Technique of Acting," in *Brecht on Theatre*, 137.

99. Friedrich Albrecht, "Zur Gliederung des epischen Raums bei Anna Seghers," *Bemühungen*, 323, 328.

100. Peter Brooks, *Reading for the Plot: Design and Intention in Narrative* (Cambridge, MA: Harvard University Press, 1984), 91.

101. Ibid.

102. Ibid., 92.

103. "Repetition in all its literary manifestations," Brooks explains, "may in fact work as a 'binding,' a binding of textual energies that allows them to be mastered by putting them into serviceable form, usable 'bundles,' within the energetic economy of the narrative" (ibid., 102).

104. Jameson, *Valences*, 531.

105. Brooks, *Reading for the Plot*, 96.

106. Jameson, "The Experiments of Time," 119.

107. Ibid., 106.

108. Ibid., 106–7.

109. Pinneberg is the titular little man in Hans Fallada's *Kleiner Mann—was nun?* (Berlin: Aufbau-Verlag, 1984), originally published in 1932.

110. Jameson, *Valences*, 505.

111. This passage is not in Galston's translation.

112. Walter Benjamin, "On the Mimetic Facility," in *Selected Writings*, vol. 2, part 2, 721.

113. Engelmann, *Poetik des Exils*, 79–87.

114. Among the sources for Seghers's composition of the novel, referred to here, were Hans Beimler's report *Im Mordlager Dachau* [Murder Camp

Dachau 1934] and Gerhart Heinrich Seger's *Oranienburg: Erster Bericht eines aus dem Konzentrationslager Geflüchteten* [Oranienburg: First Report from One Who Has Escaped from the Concentration Camp 1934]. On Beimler, a KPD Reichstag deputy who would later fall in the Spanish Civil War, see Seghers's eulogy "Hans Beimler," in *Aufsätze, Ansprachen, Essays 1927–1953*. Like Heisler, Seghers describes Beimler as a man who understood that "one must toss one's life away in order to save it" (51).

115. See Fehervary's treatment of this essay in relation to Seghers (*Anna Seghers*, 123–24).

116. Ibid., 157. Benjamin juxtaposes the fairy tale to myth in a way very similar to that of Ernst Bloch, whom Benjamin quotes in his essay and who writes of the fairy tale as "the revolt of the little man against the mythical powers" (HT 153).

117. Salvation is understood here as a political, not a theological, concept. See Löwy, *Fire Alarm*, 33–34.

118. Löwy, *Fire Alarm*, 35.

119. Writing of this "fullness of the past," which Benjamin describes as Judgment Day in his third thesis, Löwy writes, "as remembrance of forgotten battles and the rescue of endeavors against the grain, the apokatastasis of the 'lost' utopian moments of socialism is . . . in the service of the revolutionary thought and practice of the present, here and now—*jetzt*!" (*Fire Alarm*, 36).

120. Translation slightly altered.

CHAPTER 5

1. *Lexikon sozialistischer Literatur*, 102–3. See also Claudius's 1968 autobiography, *Ruhelose Jahre; Erinnerungen* (Halle: Mitteldeutscher Verlag, 1968).

2. Bredel mentions Claudius, under his then pseudonym Brendt, as one of the young talents coming into themselves while fighting in Spain in his piece "Junge Schriftsteller in Spaniens Schützengräben," in *Zur Tradition*, 2:219.

3. Claudius, *Ruhelose Jahre*, 129.

4. Horst Haase, "Befragung einer Autobiographie: Zu einigen Motiven im Leben und Werk von Eduard Claudius," *Weimarer Beiträge* 22.7 (1976): 116–17.

5. Horst Haase, "Variationen eines Grossen Themas: Zu zwei Erzählungen von Eduard Claudius," *Sinn und Form* 20.3 (1968): 666.

6. Ibid., 666–67.

7. Erika Pick, "Nachbemerkungen," in Eduard Claudius, *Grüne Oliven und nackte Berge* (Halle: Mitteldeutscher-Verlag, 1976), 28, 75. The novel was originally published in 1944 by the Steinberg-Verlag in Zurich.

8. Wolfgang Engler, *Die Ostdeutschen: Kunde von einem verlorenen Land* (Berlin: Aufbau-Verlag, 1999), 118.

9. Ibid., 320.

10. Anson Rabinbach, "Legacies of Antifascism," *New German Critique* 67 (Winter 1996): 6, 8.

11. Bertolt Brecht, "Deutsche Schriftsteller auf dem II: Internationalen Schriftstellerkongre zur Verteidigung der Kultur," in *Zur Tradition*, 2:174.

Brecht did not actually attend the congress in Valencia and Madrid, sending Ruth Berlau in his stead. Stephan, *Die deutsche Exilliteratur*, 137.

12. Hans ***, "Deutsche Schriftsteller auf dem II: Internationalen Schriftstellerkongre zur Verteidigung der Kultur," in *Zur Tradition*, 2:181.

13. Anna Seghers, "Zum Schriftstellerkongre in Madrid: Deutsche Schriftsteller auf dem II: Internationalen Schriftstellerkongre zur Verteidigung der Kultur," in *Zur Tradition*, 2:214–15.

14. "Der Spanienkrieg 1936–1939: Bewährungsfeld des Antifascismus. Die Volksfront wird zur 'Front' gesäubert. Diskussion mit Walther Bernecker, Silvia Schlenstedt, Ursula Langkau-Alex," in *Die Nacht hat zwölf Stunden, dann kommt der Tag: Antifaschismus, Geschichte und Neubewertung*, ed. Claudia Keller (Berlin: Aufbau-Verlag, 1996).

15. Ibid., 125, 127. The contradiction between winning the war and facilitating the social revolution is also central to Pierre Broué and Emile Temime's account, *The Revolution and Civil War in Spain* (Chicago: Haymarket Books, 2007). See also Birgit Schmidt's account of the martial discipline of the German International Brigades as the founding myth of what would later be East German antifascism in *Wenn die Partei das Volk entdeckt*, 101–44.

16. "Der Spanienkrieg 1936–1939," 137. Also Eley, *Forging Democracy*, 273.

17. Eley, *Forging Democracy*, 274.

18. "Der Spanienkrieg 1936–1939," 135.

19. Michael Rohrwasser, *Stalinismus und die Renegaten: Die Literatur der Exkommunisten* (Stuttgart: Metzler, 1992). The polarization of the left was of course also related to the violence of and internecine struggles within the Spanish left itself, which were exploited and exacerbated during the course of the war as the Soviets exported the terror to the Spanish Republic. At the same time, Payne points out that the violence was much greater in the nationalist zones. *The Spanish Civil War*, 110.

20. Klaus Theweleit points out that for the fascist, psychic drives and desires are integrated into the body armor. *Male Fantasies*, 1:159, 162.

21. Theweleit, *Male Fantasies*, 1:215.

22. It is symptomatic of the kind of structure of feeling that Claudius is negotiating that the Communist partisan figure in this novel is overwhelmingly gendered male.

23. Bredel, *Die Prüfung*, 70.

24. Ibid., 39–40.

25. Petersen, *Unsere Straße*, 184.

26. Bredel, *Die Prüfung*, 43.

27. Ibid., 288.

28. Petersen, *Unsere Straße*, 186.

29. Bredel, *Die Prüfung*, 97, 112, 152.

30. Ibid., 94.

31. Marchwitza, *Sturm auf Essen*, 73.

32. Charity Scribner, *Requiem for Communism* (Cambridge, MA: MIT Press, 2003), 20.

33. On Lethen's notion of the code of conduct, see Chapter 2.

34. Ludwig Turek, *Ein Prolet Erzählt: Lebensschilderung eines deutschen Arbeiters* (Munich: Damnitz Verlag, 1980), 268–69. Turek's memoir was originally published by Wieland Herzfelde's Malik Verlag in 1929.

35. Schöberl, *Kontinuität im Bruch*, 276. In missing this insight, Rohrwasser seems to imply an essential longing of the working class for military discipline.

36. Ibid., 281.

37. Negt and Kluge, *Public Sphere and Experience*, 206.

38. Ibid., 206–7.

39. Ibid., 207.

40. Bertolt Brecht, "The Measures Taken," trans. Carl R. Mueller, in *The Measures Taken and Other Lehrstücke*, ed. John Willet and Ralph Mannheim (New York: Arcade Publishing, 2001), 13.

41. Bredel, *Die Prüfung*, 167.

42. Johannes R. Becher, "Wiedergeburt," in *Zur Tradition der deutschen sozialistischen Literatur: Eine Auswahl von Dokumenten, 1941–1949*, ed. Irmfried Hiebel (Berlin: Aufbau-Verlag, 1979), 36, 37.

43. Theweleit, *Male Fantasies*, 1:432.

44. V. I. Lenin, *"Left-Wing" Communism, an Infantile Disorder: A Popular Essay on Strategy and Tactics* (New York: International Publishers, 1940), 46, 50, 52–54.

45. On the sublime Communist, see Slavoj Žižek, *For They Know Not What They Do: Enjoyment as a Political Factor* (New York: Verso, 1991), 256–60.

46. Theweleit notes that fascist language "constantly employs the postures mentioned above (e.g. 'narration,' 'argumentation'), but merely as empty shells." *Male Fantasies*, 1:215.

47. Jameson, *Brecht and Method*, 53.

48. Badiou, *The Century*, 119.

49. Ibid., 120.

50. Ibid., 122. In practice, however, the intense experiences of Communist solidarity not only during the Spanish Civil War but also during the Soviet Purges of the 1930s, and in illegality or captivity in Germany, tended to produce a more inflexible and ossified Communist discipline that held sway long after the founding of the German Democratic Republic. Catherine Epstein writes of the KPD during the fascist period as a survival community, noting that particularly in the German camps, the party organizations often directly facilitated the survival of party cadres, while being relatively parsimonious in their assistance to those outside the party. Party discipline and loyalty were therefore often prerequisites for survival, leading to a reinforcement of "radical Stalinist values among German Communists." Catherine Epstein, *The Last Revolutionaries: German Communists and Their Century* (Cambridge, MA: Harvard University Press, 2003), 59, 81. See also the protocol of the session in which the German section of the Soviet Writers Union was purged in 1936. Johannes R. Becher, Georg Lukács, Friedrich Wolf, et al., *Die Säuberung. Moscow 1936: Stenogramm einer geschlossenen Parteiversammlung*, ed. Reinhard Müller (Hamburg: Rowohlt, 1991).

51. As Catherine Epstein points out, the German emigration in the Soviet Union was heavily affected by the purges unleashed after the murder of Sergei Kirov in 1934, with over 70 percent of German Communists in the USSR being arrested at some point in the 1930s, most of whom did not survive (*The Last Revolutionaries*, 54). See also Pike, *Deutsche Schriftsteller im sowjetischen Exil*, 417–83.

52. Nordahl Grieg's Paris Commune drama *The Defeat* was adapted by Brecht into his *Tage der Kommune* [Days of the Commune] in 1949, which Brecht intended as a contribution to the cultural revolution in what was then the SBZ. In the event, the play was not performed until after Brecht's death in 1956 . Mittenzwei, *Das Leben des Bertolt Brecht*, 340–52.

53. Rohrwasser, *Stalinismus und die Renegaten*, 64.

54. Ibid., 65, 69.

55. Ibid., 176.

56. Slavoj Žižek, *Did Somebody Say "Totalitarianism"?: Five Interventions in the (Mis)Use of a Notion* (New York: Verso, 2002), 96.

57. Ibid., 97.

58. Ibid., 111.

59. Ibid., 112.

60. Ibid., 114.

61. Palmier, *Weimar in Exile*, 350.

62. This reconciliation between Germany and the USSR caused particular difficulties for German Communist émigrés in France and the USSR. The Hitler-Stalin Pact gave the French government an excuse to ban the Communist Party of France (PCF) and to intern German Communist émigrés as enemy aliens. Male German émigrés were of course being interned as enemy aliens at this point regardless of party affiliation. Lion Feuchtwanger's memoir of his own internment and escape from the Les Milles camp was published as *Unholdes Frankreich* in 1942. Among the interned was Seghers's husband, László Radványi. See Schiller et al., *Exil in Frankreich*, 380ff and Palmier, *Weimar in Exile*, 437ff.

63. Stefan Heym, *Die Architekten* (Munich: btb, 2002), 16–17.

64. Clark, *Moscow*, 251, 254.

65. Kluge associates the Spanish partisans of these years as figures of a particularly conservative mode of *Eigensinn* in their dogged resistance to their own putative social emancipation through Napoleon from clergy and nobility. This is a historical form of *Eigensinn* that Kluge then sees as "represented in Prussia by rebels like Heinrich von Kleist." *History and Obstinacy*, 406.

66. Carl Schmitt, *Theory of the Partisan: Intermediate Commentary on the Concept of the Political*, trans. G. L. Ulmen (New York: Telos Press, 2007), 22.

67. Ibid., 31.

68. Ibid., 55. Schmitt, like many other commentators and historians, notes the relative absence of partisan action in the strict sense during the Spanish Civil War (*Theory of the Partisan*, 56).

69. Ibid., 117.

70. Schmidt, *Wenn die Partei das Volk entdeckt*, 132.

71. Slavoj Žižek, *On Violence* (New York: Picador, 2008), 2.

72. Benjamin, "On the Concept of History," 4:394.

73. Jameson, "Monument to Radical Instants," xxx.

CHAPTER 6

1. Brecht left Denmark for Sweden in 1939 and then spent time in Finland while waiting for U.S. visas for himself and his family. They arrived in the United States in June 1941. On Brecht's Scandinavian exile, see Mittenzwei, *Das Leben des Bertolt Brecht*, 1:457–743.

2. Bertolt Brecht, "Thoughts on the Duration of Exile," in *Poems, 1913–1956*, 301–2.

3. See Robert Leach, "*Mother Courage and Her Children*," in *The Cambridge Companion to Brecht*, ed. Peter Thomson and Glendyr Sacks (Cambridge: Cambridge University Press, 1994), 132–35.

4. On the composition of *Mother Courage and Her Children*, see Jan Knopf, *Brecht-Handbuch. Theater. Eine Ästhetik der Widersprüche* (Stuttgart: J. B. Metzler, 1980), 181 and Werner Hecht, *Brecht Chronik, 1898–1956* (Frankfurt: Suhrkamp Verlag, 1997), 251.

5. Fore, *Realism After Modernism*, 165.

6. Ibid., 166.

7. Brecht, "On Gestic Music," in *Brecht on Theatre*, 104.

8. Fore, *Realism After Modernism*, 167.

9. Ibid. The *Messingkauf Dialogues* were written between 1937 and 1951 and not published in their entirety until after Brecht's death.

10. Ibid., 181.

11. Ibid., 183.

12. Bertolt Brecht, *Flüchtlingsgespräche* (Frankfurt: Suhrkamp Verlag, 2000), 113; Klaus-Detlef Müller, *Die Funktion der Geschichte im Werk Bertolt Brechts: Studien zum Verhältnis von Marxismus und Ästhetik* (Tübingen: Max Niemeyer Verlag, 1972), 93.

13. Brecht, *Flüchtlingsgespräche*, 113.

14. Jameson, *Brecht and Method*, 14.

15. Bertolt Brecht, *Journals, 1934–1955*, trans. Hugh Rorrison (New York: Routledge, 1996), 144.

16. W. H. Auden, "September 1, 1939," in *Selected Poems*, ed. Edward Mendelson (New York: Vintage, 2007), 95.

17. Mittenzwei, *Das Leben des Bertolt Brecht*, 1:652ff.

18. Walter Benjamin, "Diary Entries," in *Selected Writings*, 3:339.

19. Ibid., 3:340.

20. Brecht, *Journals*, 35.

21. Mittenzwei, *Das Leben des Bertolt Brechts*, 1:341.

22. Astrid Oesmann, *Staging History: Brecht's Social Concepts of Ideology* (Albany: SUNY Press, 2005), 153.

23. Mittenzwei, *Das Leben des Bertolt Brechts*, 1:672.

24. Bertolt Brecht, "Mutter Courage in zweifacher Art dargestellt," in *Materialien zu Brechts "Mutter Courage und ihre Kinder,"* ed. Werner Hecht (Frankfurt: Suhrkamp Verlag, 1964), 122.

25. Brecht, "Das Modellbuch: Anmerkungen zur Aufführung 1949," in *Materialien*, 17. The January 11, 1949, premiere of *Mother Courage* at Berlin's Deutsches Theater marked Brecht's return to the Berlin stage.

26. Ibid., 18.

27. Brecht, "Mutter Courage in zweifacher Art," 123.

28. Darko Suvin, "Emotion, Brecht, Empathy v. Sympathy," in *Gestus-Musik-Text*, Brecht Yearbook 33, ed. Freidmann J. Weidauer (Madison: University of Wisconsin Press, 2008), 63.

29. Brecht, "Das Modellbuch," 18–19.

30. Bertolt Brecht, "Anmerkungen zur 'Courage,'" in *Materialien*, 91–92.

31. Brecht, *Journals*, 404.

32. Bertolt Brecht, *The Messingkauf Dialogues*, trans. John Willett (London: Methuen, 1965), 32–34.

33. Bertolt Brecht, "Die Fabel," in *Materialien*, 7.

34. Bertolt Brecht, *Mother Courage and Her Children: A Chronicle of the Thirty Years' War*, trans. John Willett (New York: Penguin, 1997), 25. The standard German edition of the play is Bertolt Brecht, *Mutter Courage und ihre Kinder: Eine Chronik aus dem Dreißigjährigen Krieg* in *Große kommentierte Berliner und Frankfurter Ausgabe, Stücke* 6, ed. Werner Hecht, Jan Knopf, Werner Mittenzwei, and Klaus-Detlev Müller (Berlin: Aufbau-Verlag, 1989).

35. Brecht, "Die Fabel," 7.

36. Franz Norbert Mennemeier, "Die Courage der armen Leute," in *Materialien*, 139.

37. Mayer, "Die plebejische Tradition," 311.

38. Brecht, "On Gestic Music," 104.

39. Oesmann, *Staging History*, 196.

40. Ibid., 153.

41. Sarah Bryant-Bertail, "Women, Space, and Ideology in *Mother Courage and Her Children*," in *Brecht, Women, and Politics*, ed. John Fuegi and Gisela Bahr (Detroit: Wayne State University Press, 1985), 48.

42. Ibid.

43. Walter Benjamin, "What Is Epic Theater? (II)," in *Selected Writings*, 4:305.

44. Mennemeier, "Die Courage der armen Leute," 138.

45. Ibid., 139.

46. Brecht, "Das Modellbuch," 37.

47. Ibid., 44.

48. Mayer, "Die plebejische Tradition," 319–20.

49. Ibid.

50. Hans Mayer, "Anmerkungen zu einer Szene aus *Mutter Courage*," *Brecht*, 376.

51. Mayer, "Die plebejische Tradition," 320–21.

52. Ibid., 320.

53. Bertolt Brecht, "Me-ti/Buch der Wendungen," *Gesammelte Werke: Prosa* 2 (Frankfurt: Suhrkamp Verlag, 1967), 478. This was a series of aphoristic texts that Brecht wrote from the early 1930s on and was not published until after his death.

54. Brecht, *Messingkauf Dialogues*, 35.
55. Ibid.
56. Ibid., 36.
57. Ibid., 37.
58. Brecht, "Short Description of a New Technique of Acting," 137.
59. Brecht, *Messingkauf Dialogues*, 37.
60. Darko Suvin points out the fundamental distinction in Brecht's work between "illusionistic, sentimental, uncritical, pseudo-compassionate empathy . . . and a possibly intense but always reasonable sympathy," which is also a mobilization of emotion and affect but in a mode of critically distanced understanding. Thus Brecht's theatrical pedagogy is not mobilized against emotion or affect but rather is concerned with rendering emotion into a tool of understanding. Suvin, "Emotion, Brecht, Empathy v. Sympathy," 61.
61. On the East German debate around *Mother Courage* in 1949, see Mittenzwei, *Das Leben des Bertolt Brechts*, 2:326–38. Brecht's defenders included his critical champion from the Weimar Republic, Herbert Ihring, the literary critic Paul Rilla, and the philosopher Wolfgang Harich.
62. Bertolt Brecht, "Formal Problems Arising from the Theater's New Content," in *Brecht on Theatre*, 228–29.
63. Fritz Erpenbeck, "Einige Bemerkungen zu Brechts 'Mutter Courage,'" *Die Weltbühne* 2 (1949): 101, cited in Mittenzwei, *Das Leben des Bertolt Brecht*, 2:331. Erpenbeck is careful to insist that Brecht is a great playwright despite his techniques and warns of the consequences of the epic theater in the hands of epigones.
64. Susanne Alterman, "Wo beginnt die Dekadenz? Bemerkungen zur Polemik um Brechts 'Mutter Courage,'" *Tägliche Rundschau*, December 3, 1949, p. 2, cited in Mittenzwei, *Das Leben des Bertolt Brecht*, 2:336.
65. Alterman, "Wo beginnt die Dekadenz?" cited in Mittenzwei, *Das Leben des Bertolt Brecht*, 2:337.
66. Brecht, "Formal Problems," 229.
67. Bertolt Brecht, "Notes on the Realistic Mode of Writing," in *Brecht on Art and Politics*, 257.
68. Italo Michele Battafarano, "Brechts Maternisierung von Grimmelshausens Courasche," *Simpliciana: Schriften der Grimmelshausen-Gesellschaft* 23 (2001): 127–58.
69. Ernest Schonfield, "Brecht and the Modern Picaresque," *Amsterdamer Beiträge zur neueren Germanistik* 66.1 (2008): 58.
70. Claudio Guillén, "Toward a Definition of the Picaresque," *Literature as System: Essays Toward the Theory of Literary History* (Princeton: Princeton University Press, 1971), 80.
71. Schonfield, "Brecht and the Modern Picaresque," 58.
72. Guillén, "Toward a Definition of the Picaresque," 77.
73. Ibid., 83.
74. Brecht, *Journals*, 123.
75. Fredric Jameson, *The Antinomies of Realism* (New York: Verso, 2013), 245.
76. Bertolt Brecht, "A Necessary Observation on the Struggle Against Barbarism," in *Brecht on Art and Politics*, 161.

77. Bertolt Brecht, "Die Courage lernt nichts," in *Materialien*, 93.

78. Friedrich Engels, *The Peasant War in Germany* (New York: International Publishers, 1966), 15. Engels expounds in the amputation of this utopian horizon of Münzer's ideology by the time of the Thirty Years War on pages 15–21 and 79.

79. Brecht, *Journals*, 36.

80. Ibid., 41.

81. Ibid., 37.

82. Ibid., 144.

83. Frank Thomsen, Hans-Harald Müller, and Tom Kindt, *Ungeheuer Brecht: Eine Biographie seines Werks* (Göttingen: Vandenhoeck und Ruprecht, 2006), 214.

84. Schonfield, "Brecht and the Modern Picaresque," 71.

85. Thomsen, Müller, and Kindt, *Ungeheuer Brecht*, 241.

86. Ibid., 244.

87. Ibid., 64–65.

88. Brecht, *Journals*, 136.

89. David Bathrick, *The Powers of Speech: The Politics of Culture in the GDR* (Lincoln: University of Nebraska Press, 1995), 95.

90. Ibid.

91. On wearing down as a motif in *Mother Courage*, see Sean Carney, *Brecht and Critical Theory: Dialectics and Contemporary Aesthetics* (New York: Routledge, 2005), 85–86 and Claire Gleitman, "All in the Family: *Mother Courage* and the Ideology in the 'Gestus,'" *Comparative Drama* 25.2 (Summer 1991): 164.

92. Brecht, "Das Modellbuch," 77.

93. Thomsen, Müller, and Kindt, *Ungeheuer Brecht*, 265.

94. Brecht, "Das Modellbuch," 84.

95. Carney, *Brecht and Critical Theory*, 19.

96. Brecht, "Das Modellbuch," 70.

97. Ibid.

98. Jameson, *Brecht and Method*, 137.

99. Ibid., 138.

100. Ibid., 151.

101. Ibid., 137.

102. Ibid., 139.

103. Ibid., 140.

104. Ibid., 162.

105. Benjamin, "What Is Epic Theater? (II)," 305.

106. Hans Mayer, "Brecht und die Tradition," *Brecht*, 230.

107. Bertolt Brecht, "Alienation Effects in Chinese Acting," in *Brecht on Theatre*, 91.

108. Ibid., 97.

109. Brecht, "Alienation Effects in the Narrative Pictures of the Elder Breughel," in *Brecht on Theatre*, 157.

110. Brecht, "Notes on the Folk Play," in *Brecht on Theatre*, 155.

111. Cited in Mayer, "Die plebejische Tradition," 303.

112. Jameson, *Brecht and Method*, 100.

113. Göran Therborn, "Class in the 21st Century," *New Left Review* 78 (November–December 2012): 15.

114. Ibid., 11.

115. Lauren Berlant, "Cruel Optimism," *Differences: A Journal of Feminist Cultural Studies* 17.3 (2006): 23. On the rising "precariat," see Guy Standing, *The Precariat: The New Dangerous Class* (London: Bloomsbury Academic, 2011).

EPILOGUE

Nicholas Brown and Imre Szemán, "Twenty-five Theses on Philosophy in the Age of Finance Capital," in *A Leftist Ontology: Beyond Relativism and Identity Politics*, ed. Carsten Strathausen (Minneapolis: University of Minnesota Press, 2009), 35.

1. Bertolt Brecht, "Gespräch mit einem jungen Zuschauer," in *Materialien*, 92.

2. Theodor W. Adorno, "Commitment," in *Aesthetics and Politics*, 186. Raimondo Montecuccoli was an imperial general, commanding forces in the Thirty Years War and the Northern Wars.

3. Ibid., 187.

4. Alberto Toscano, "Politics in a Tragic Key," *Radical Philosophy* 180 (July/August 2013): 27. For a discussion of the German Peasant Wars as the template for a Marxist view of tragedy read through the accounts of Engels and Ernst Bloch in his *Thomas Müntzer als Theologe der Revolution* [Thomas Müntzer as Theologian of Revolution 1921], see Alberto Toscano, *Fanaticism: On the Uses of an Idea* (New York: Verso, 2010), 68–92.

5. Cited in Toscano, "Politics in a Tragic Key," 31.

6. Ibid., 29.

7. Marx, "Contribution to the Critique," 60.

8. Toscano, "Politics in a Tragic Key," 30.

9. Ibid., 31.

10. Engels, *The Peasant War in Germany*, 11.

11. Ibid., 15.

12. Ibid., 16.

13. On Münzer, Engels writes: "Münzer's political doctrine . . . overstepped the directly prevailing social and political conditions in much the same way as his theology overstepped the conceptions current in his time. As Münzer's religious philosophy approached atheism, so his political program approached communism, and even on the eve of the February Revolution [of 1848] more than one present-day communist sect lacked as comprehensive a theoretical arsenal as was 'Münzer's' in the sixteenth century. . . . By the kingdom of God Münzer meant a society with no class differences, no private property and no state authority independent of, and foreign to, the members of society" (*The Peasant War in Germany*, 23).

14. Engels, *The Peasant War in Germany*, 16.

15. Toscano, "Politics in a Tragic Key," 27.

16. Engels, *The Peasant War in Germany*, 70–71.

17. Brecht, "Die Courage lernt nichts," 93.

18. Heiner Müller, "I Want to Be a German," in *Germania*, ed. Sylvere Lotringer (New York: Semiotext[e], 1980), 97.

19. From the 1970s onward, Müller self-consciously positions himself as the representative of this discourse.

20. Heiner Müller, "Dem Terrorismus die Utopie entreißen: Alternative DDR," *Zur Lage der Nation* (Berlin: Rotbuch Verlag, 1990), 13.

21. Lucas, *Vom Scheitern der deutschen Arbeiterbewegung*, 163.

22. Jameson, *Valences*, 571.

23. Epstein, *The Last Revolutionaries*, 29. On the social marginalization of the KPD as a result of state violence, mass unemployment, and the party's own strategic and tactical vicissitudes, see Weitz, *Creating German Communism*.

24. Jameson, *Brecht and Method*, 139.

25. Toscano, "Politics in a Tragic Key," 32.

26. Ibid.

27. Therborn, "Class in the 21st Century," 5.

28. Ibid., 11.

29. Indeed, one could argue that the entire massive paratextual apparatus that Brecht arranged around this play, from model books and performance notes to repeated commentary on its reception, was a way of disavowing this type of reading.

30. Hobsbawm, *The Age of Extremes*, 166.

31. Ibid., 82, 176.

32. Eley, *Forging Democracy*, 297.

33. On the 1960s, see Christopher Leigh Connery, "The World Sixties," in *The Worlding Project: Doing Cultural Studies in the Era of Globalization*, ed. Rob Wilson and Christopher Leigh Connery (Santa Cruz: New Pacific Press, 2009). On the notion of the multitude, Michael Hardt and Antonio Negri's books *Empire* and *Multitude* have obviously been very influential, but a more nuanced grasp of this term can be found in Paolo Virno's work, particularly *A Grammar of the Multitude: For an Analysis of Contemporary Forms of Life*, trans. Isabella Bertoletti, James Cascaito, and Andrea Cassen (New York: Semiotext[e], 2004).

34. Marx, "Contribution to the Critique," 64.

35. See Hunter Bivens, "Specters of Work: Literature and Labor in Post-Socialist Germany," in *After the Wall: Germany and Beyond*, ed. Katharina Gerstenberger and Jana Braziel (New York: Palgrave Macmillan, 2011).

36. See, for example, Stefan Hermlin's 1950 *Mansfelder Oratorium*, which narrates the 750-year history of the Mansfeld copper and shale pits as a teleological progression from feudal oppression to socialism. In addition to being a key region in the Reformation and the German Peasant Wars, this part of Germany was also the territory of the March Action of 1921, repeatedly evoked in Braun's text.

37. On the Treuhand and the economics of primitive accumulation in the "new states," see chapter 2 of Paul Smith, *Millennial Dreams: Culture and Capital in the North* (New York: Verso, 1997). Smith writes of the Treuhand,

a public organization set up to liquidate the people's property of the GDR, "the *Treuhand*'s mission was to impose upon the former GDR a system of value production and economic organization of which it had no practical experience and very little historical memory. . . . The *Treuhand* would, in other words, sweep away the value system of a defeated nation. It would appropriate the real estate and the economic infrastructure as if they were natural assets which had just been discovered, and then privatize in the name of making these assets more productive; at the same time as devaluing the physical infrastructure, it would regard the labor power of East Germany as an ongoing productive asset. This is a process which is reminiscent of nothing so much as the history of primitive accumulation that Marx describes in the long coda to the first volume of *Capital*" (75). See also Olaf Baale, *Abbau Ost: Lügen, Vorurteile und sozialistischen Schulden* (Munich: dtv, 2008) and Wolfgang Engler, *Die Ostdeutschen als Avantgarde* (Berlin: Aufbau-Verlag, 2004).

38. Volker Braun, *Die hellen Haufen* (Frankfurt am Main: Suhrkamp Verlag, 2011).

39. Ibid., 23.

40. Ibid., 38.

41. Ibid., 60.

42. Engels, *The Peasant War in Germany*, 52.

43. Braun, *Die hellen Haufen*, 69–70.

44. Ibid., 39.

45. "The 'leading role' of the working class seems to have gone in entirely different directions from those ideologically plotted—more social and colloquial rather than political and organized." Engler, *Die Ostdeutschen*, 190. On the moral economy versus the market economy, see Thompson, *The Making of the English Working Class*, 66.

46. Braun, *Die hellen Haufen*, 96.

47. Benjamin, "On the Concept of History," 4:390.

48. Braun, *Die hellen Haufen*, 70.

49. Ibid., 97.

Index

FLASHPOINTS

1. *On Pain of Speech: Fantasies of the First Order and the Literary Rant,* Dina Al-Kassim
2. *Moses and Multiculturalism,* Barbara Johnson, with a foreword by Barbara Rietveld
3. *The Cosmic Time of Empire: Modern Britain and World Literature,* Adam Barrows
4. *Poetry in Pieces: César Vallejo and Lyric Modernity,* Michelle Clayton
5. *Disarming Words: Empire and the Seductions of Translation in Egypt,* Shaden M. Tageldin
6. *Wings for Our Courage: Gender, Erudition, and Republican Thought,* Stephanie H. Jed
7. *The Cultural Return,* Susan Hegeman
8. *English Heart, Hindi Heartland: The Political Life of Literature in India,* Rashmi Sadana
9. *The Cylinder: Kinematics of the Nineteenth Century,* Helmut Müller-Sievers
10. *Polymorphous Domesticities: Pets, Bodies, and Desire in Four Modern Writers,* Juliana Schiesari
11. *Flesh and Fish Blood: Postcolonialism, Translation, and the Vernacular,* S. Shankar
12. *The Fear of French Negroes: Transcolonial Collaboration in the Revolutionary Americas,* Sara E. Johnson
13. *Figurative Inquisitions: Conversion, Torture, and Truth in the Luso-Hispanic Atlantic,* Erin Graff Zivin
14. *Cosmopolitan Desires: Global Modernity and World Literature in Latin America,* Mariano Siskind
15. *Fiction Beyond Secularism,* Justin Neuman
16. *Periodizing Jameson: Dialectics, the University, and the Desire for Narrative,* Phillip E. Wegner
17. *The Practical Past,* Hayden White
18. *The Powers of the False: Reading, Writing, Thinking Beyond Truth and Fiction,* Doro Wiese
19. *The Object of the Atlantic: Concrete Aesthetics in Cuba, Brazil, and Spain, 1868–1968,* Rachel Price
20. *Epic and Exile: Novels of the German Popular Front, 1933–1945,* Hunter Bivens
21. *An Innocent Abroad: Lectures in China,* J. Hillis Miller